BEGINNING
ANDROID™ 4 APPLICATION DEVELOPMENT

BEGINNING

Android™ 4 Application Development

BEGINNING

Android™ 4 Application Development

Wei-Meng Lee

John Wiley & Sons, Inc.

Beginning Android™ 4 Application Development

Published by
John Wiley & Sons, Inc.
10475 Crosspoint Boulevard
Indianapolis, IN 46256
www.wiley.com

Copyright © 2012 by John Wiley & Sons, Inc., Indianapolis, Indiana

Published simultaneously in Canada

ISBN: 978-1-118-19954-1
ISBN: 978-1-118-22824-1 (ebk)
ISBN: 978-1-118-24067-0 (ebk)
ISBN: 978-1-118-26538-3 (ebk)

Manufactured in the United States of America

10 9 8 7 6 5 4 3 2 1

For general information on our other products and services please contact our Customer Care Department within the United States at (877) 762-2974, outside the United States at (317) 572-3993 or fax (317) 572-4002.

Wiley publishes in a variety of print and electronic formats and by print-on-demand. Some material included with standard print versions of this book may not be included in e-books or in print-on-demand. If this book refers to media such as a CD or DVD that is not included in the version you purchased, you may download this material at http://booksupport.wiley.com. For more information about Wiley products, visit www.wiley.com.

Library of Congress Control Number: 2011945560

To my family:

Thanks for the understanding and support while I worked on getting this book ready. I love you all!

ABOUT THE AUTHOR

WEI-MENG LEE is a technologist and founder of Developer Learning Solutions (www.learn2develop .net), a technology company specializing in hands-on training on the latest mobile technologies. Wei-Meng has many years of training experience and his training courses place special emphasis on the learning-by-doing approach. This hands-on approach to learning programming makes understanding the subject much easier than reading books, tutorials, and other documentation.

Wei-Meng is also the author of Beginning iOS 5 Application Development (Wrox, 2010) and Beginning Android Application Development (Wrox, 2011). Contact Wei-Meng at weimenglee@ learn2develop.net.

ABOUT THE TECHNICAL EDITOR

CHAIM KRAUSE is a Simulation Specialist at the US Army's Command and General Staff College where he develops various software products on a multitude of platforms, from iOS and Android devices to Windows desktops and Linux servers, among other duties. Python is his preferred language, but he is multilingual and also codes in Java and JavaScript/HTML5/CSS, and others. He was fortunate to begin his professional career in the software field at Borland where he was a Senior Developer Support Engineer for Delphi. Outside of computer geek stuff, Chaim enjoys techno and dubstep music and scootering with his two sled dogs, Dasher and Minnie.

CREDITS

ACKNOWLEDGMENTS

WRITING THIS BOOK HAS been a roller-coaster ride. Working with just-released software is always a huge challenge. When I first started working on this book, the Android 4 SDK had just been released; and wading through the documentation was like finding a needle in a haystack. To add to the challenge, the Android emulator for the tablet is extremely slow and unstable, making the development process very laborious.

Now that the book is done, I hope your journey will not be as eventful as mine. Like any good guide, my duty is to make your foray into Android tablet development an enjoyable and fruitful experience. The book you are now holding is the result of the collaborative efforts of many people, and I wish to take this opportunity to acknowledge them here.

First, my personal gratitude to Bob Elliott, executive editor at Wrox. Bob is always ready to lend a listening ear and to offer help when it's needed. It is a great pleasure to work with Bob, as he is one of the most responsive persons I have ever worked with! Thank you, Bob, for the help and guidance!

Of course, I cannot forget Ami Sullivan, my editor (and friend!), who is always a pleasure to work with. After working together on four books, we now know each other so well that we know the content of incoming e-mail messages even before we open them! Thank you, Ami!

Nor can I forget the heroes behind the scenes: copyeditor Luann Rouff and technical editor Chaim Krause. They have been eagle-eye editing the book, making sure that every sentence makes sense — both grammatically and technically. Thanks, Luann and Chaim!

Last, but not least, I want to thank my parents and my wife, Sze Wa, for all the support they have given me. They have selflessly adjusted their schedules to accommodate my busy schedule when I was working on this book. My wife, as always, has stayed up with me on numerous nights as I was furiously working to meet the deadlines, and for this I would like to say to her and my parents, "I love you all!" Finally, to our lovely dog, Ookii, thanks for staying by our side.

CONTENTS

INTRODUCTION

I FIRST STARTED PLAYING WITH THE ANDROID SDK before it was officially released as version 1.0. Back then, the tools were unpolished, the APIs in the SDK were unstable, and the documentation was sparse. Fast-forward three and a half years, Android is now a formidable mobile operating system, with a following no less impressive than the iPhone. Having gone through all the growing pains of Android, I think now is the best time to start learning about Android programming — the APIs have stabilized, and the tools have improved. One challenge remains, however: Getting started is still an elusive goal for many. What's more, Google has recently released their latest version of the Android SDK — 4.0, a unified mobile OS for both smartphones and tablets. The Android 4.0 SDK includes several new features for tablet developers, and understanding all these new features requires some effort on the part of beginners.

It was with this challenge in mind that I was motivated to write this book, one that could benefit beginning Android programmers and enable them to write progressively more sophisticated applications.

As a book written to help jump-start beginning Android developers, it covers the necessary topics in a linear manner so that you can build on your knowledge without being overwhelmed by the details. I adopt the philosophy that the best way to learn is by doing — hence, the numerous Try It Out sections in each chapter, which first show you how to build something and then explain how everything works. I have also taken this opportunity to further improve the previous edition of this book, addressing feedback from readers and adding additional topics that are important to beginning Android developers.

Although Android programming is a huge topic, my aim for this book is threefold: to get you started with the fundamentals, to help you understand the underlying architecture of the SDK, and to appreciate why things are done in certain ways. It is beyond the scope of any book to cover everything under the sun related to Android programming, but I am confident that after reading this book (and doing the exercises), you will be well equipped to tackle your next Android programming challenge.

WHO THIS BOOK IS FOR

This book is targeted for the beginning Android developer who wants to start developing applications using Google's Android SDK. To truly benefit from this book, you should have some background in programming and at least be familiar with object-oriented programming concepts. If you are totally new to Java — the language used for Android development — you might want to take a programming course in Java programming first, or grab one of many good books on Java programming. In my experience, if you already know C# or VB.NET, learning Java is not too much of an effort; you should be comfortable just following along with the Try It Outs.

For those totally new to programming, I know the lure of developing mobile apps and making some money is tempting. However, before attempting to try out the examples in this book, I think a better starting point would be to learn the basics of programming first.

NOTE *All the examples discussed in this book were written and tested using version 4.0 of the Android SDK. While every effort is made to ensure that all the tools used in this book are the latest, it is always possible that by the time you read this book, a newer version of the tools may be available. If so, some of the instructions and/or screenshots may differ slightly. However, any variations should be manageable.*

WHAT THIS BOOK COVERS

This book covers the fundamentals of Android programming using the Android SDK. It is divided into 12 chapters and three appendixes.

Chapter 1: Getting Started with Android Programming covers the basics of the Android OS and its current state. You will learn about the features of Android devices, as well as some of the popular devices on the market. You will also learn how to download and install all the required tools to develop Android applications and then test them on the Android emulator.

Chapter 2: Activities, Fragments, and Intents gets you acquainted with these three fundamental concepts in Android programming. Activities and fragments are the building blocks of an Android application. You will learn how to link activities together to form a complete Android application using intents, one of the unique characteristics of the Android OS.

Chapter 3: Getting to Know the Android User Interface covers the various components that make up the UI of an Android application. You will learn about the various layouts you can use to build the UI of your application, and the numerous events that are associated with the UI when users interact with the application.

Chapter 4: Designing Your User Interface with Views walks you through the various basic views you can use to build your Android UI. You will learn three main groups of views: basic views, picker views, and list views. You will also learn about the specialized fragments available in Android 3.0 and 4.0.

Chapter 5: Displaying Pictures and Menus with Views continues the exploration of views. Here, you will learn how to display images using the various image views, as well as display options and context menus in your application. This chapter ends with some additional cool views that you can use to spice up your application.

Chapter 6: Data Persistence shows you how to save, or store, data in your Android application. In addition to learning the various techniques to store user data, you will also learn file manipulation and how to save files onto internal and external storage (SD card). In addition, you will learn how to create and use a SQLite database in your Android application.

Chapter 7: Content Providers discusses how data can be shared among different applications on an Android device. You will learn how to use a content provider and then build one yourself.

Chapter 8: Messaging explores two of the most interesting topics in mobile programming — sending SMS messages and e-mail. You will learn how to programmatically send and receive SMS and e-mail messages, and how to intercept incoming SMS messages so that the built-in Messaging application will not be able to receive any messages.

Chapter 9: Location-Based Services demonstrates how to build a location-based service application using Google Maps. You will also learn how to obtain geographical location data and then display the location on the map.

Chapter 10: Networking explores how to connect to web servers to download data. You will see how XML and JSON web services can be consumed in an Android application. This chapter also explains sockets programming, and you will learn how to build a chat client in Android.

Chapter 11: Developing Android Services demonstrates how you can write applications using services. Services are background applications that run without a UI. You will learn how to run your services asynchronously on a separate thread, and how your activities can communicate with them.

Chapter 12: Publishing Android Applications discusses the various ways you can publish your Android applications when you are ready. You will also learn about the necessary steps to publishing and selling your applications on the Android Market.

Appendix A: Using Eclipse for Android Development provides a brief overview of the many features in Eclipse.

Appendix B: Using the Android Emulator provides some tips and tricks on using the Android emulator for testing your applications.

Appendix C: Answers to Exercises contains the solutions to the end-of-chapter exercises found in every chapter.

HOW THIS BOOK IS STRUCTURED

This book breaks down the task of learning Android programming into several smaller chunks, enabling you to digest each topic before delving into a more advanced one.

If you are a total beginner to Android programming, start with Chapter 1 first. Once you have familiarized yourself with the basics, head over to the appendixes to read more about Eclipse and the Android emulator. When you are ready, continue with Chapter 2 and gradually move into more advanced topics.

A feature of this book is that all the code samples in each chapter are independent of those discussed in previous chapters. This gives you the flexibility to dive into the topics that interest you and start working on the Try It Out projects.

WHAT YOU NEED TO USE THIS BOOK

All the examples in this book run on the Android emulator (which is included as part of the Android SDK). However, to get the most out of this book, having a real Android device would be useful (though not absolutely necessary).

CONVENTIONS

To help you get the most from the text and keep track of what's happening, a number of conventions are used throughout the book.

TRY IT OUT | These Are Exercises or Examples for You to Follow

The Try It Out sections appear once or more per chapter. These are exercises to work through as you follow the related discussion in the text.

1. They consist of a set of numbered steps.

2. Follow the steps with your copy of the project files.

How It Works

After each Try It Out, the code you've typed is explained in detail.

As for other conventions in the text:

➤ New terms and important words are *highlighted* in italics when first introduced.

➤ Keyboard combinations are treated like this: Ctrl+R.

➤ Filenames, URLs, and code within the text are treated like so: `persistence.properties`.

➤ Code is presented in two different ways:

```
We use a monofont type with no highlighting for most code examples.
```

```
We use bolding to emphasize code that is of particular importance in the
present context.
```

 NOTE *Notes, tips, hints, tricks, and asides to the current discussion look like this.*

SOURCE CODE

As you work through the examples in this book, you may choose either to type in all the code manually or to use the source code files that accompany the book. All the source code used in this book is available for download at www.wrox.com. When at the site, simply locate the book's title (use the Search box or one of the title lists) and click the Download Code link on the book's detail page to obtain all the source code for the book.

You'll find the filename of the project you need in a CodeNote such as this at the beginning of the Try it Out features:

code snippet filename

After you download the code, just decompress it with your favorite compression tool. Alternatively, go to the main Wrox code download page at www.wrox.com/dynamic/books/download.aspx to see the code available for this book and for all other Wrox books.

> **NOTE** *Because many books have similar titles, you may find it easiest to search by ISBN; this book's ISBN is 978-1-118-19954-1.*

ERRATA

We make every effort to ensure that there are no errors in the text or in the code. However, no one is perfect, and mistakes do occur. If you find an error in one of our books, such as a spelling mistake or faulty piece of code, we would be very grateful for your feedback. By sending in errata, you may save another reader hours of frustration and at the same time help us provide even higher-quality information.

To find the errata page for this book, go to www.wrox.com and locate the title using the Search box or one of the title lists. Then, on the book details page, click the Book Errata link. On this page, you can view all errata that has been submitted for this book and posted by Wrox editors.

> **NOTE** *A complete book list, including links to each book's errata, is also available at* www.wrox.com/misc-pages/booklist.shtml.

If you don't spot "your" error on the Book Errata page, go to www.wrox.com/contact/techsupport.shtml and complete the form there to send us the error you have found. We'll check the information and, if appropriate, post a message to the book's errata page and fix the problem in subsequent editions of the book.

P2P.WROX.COM

For author and peer discussion, join the P2P forums at p2p.wrox.com. The forums are a web-based system for you to post messages relating to Wrox books and related technologies and to interact with other readers and technology users. The forums offer a subscription feature to e-mail you topics of interest of your choosing when new posts are made to the forums. Wrox authors, editors, other industry experts, and your fellow readers are present on these forums.

At p2p.wrox.com, you will find a number of different forums that will help you not only as you read this book but also as you develop your own applications. To join the forums, just follow these steps:

1. Go to p2p.wrox.com and click the Register link.

2. Read the terms of use and click Agree.

3. Complete the required information to join as well as any optional information you want to provide and click Submit.

4. You will receive an e-mail with information describing how to verify your account and complete the joining process.

 NOTE You can read messages in the forums without joining P2P, but in order to post your own messages, you must join.

After you join, you can post new messages and respond to messages that other users post. You can read messages at any time on the web. If you want to have new messages from a particular forum e-mailed to you, click the Subscribe to This Forum icon by the forum name in the forum listing.

For more information about how to use the Wrox P2P, be sure to read the P2P FAQs for answers to questions about how the forum software works, as well as many common questions specific to P2P and Wrox books. To read the FAQs, click the FAQ link on any P2P page.

1

Getting Started with Android Programming

WHAT YOU WILL LEARN IN THIS CHAPTER

- ➤ What is Android?
- ➤ Android versions and its feature set
- ➤ The Android architecture
- ➤ The various Android devices on the market
- ➤ The Android Market application store
- ➤ How to obtain the tools and SDK for developing Android applications
- ➤ How to develop your first Android application

Welcome to the world of Android! When I was writing my first book on Android (which was just less than a year ago), I stated that Android was ranked second in the U.S. smartphone market, second to Research In Motion's (RIM) BlackBerry, and overtaking Apple's iPhone. Shortly after the book went to press, comScore (a global leader in measuring the digital world and the preferred source of digital marketing intelligence) reported that Android has overtaken BlackBerry as the most popular smartphone platform in the U.S.

A few months later, Google released Android 3.0, code named *Honeycomb*. With Android 3.0, Google's focus in the new Software Development Kit was the introduction of several new features

designed for widescreen devices, specifically tablets. If you are writing apps for Android smartphones, Android 3.0 is not really useful, as the new features are not supported on smartphones. At the same time that Android 3.0 was released, Google began working on the next version of Android, which can be
used on both smartphones and tablets. In October 2011, Google released Android 4.0, code named *Ice Cream Sandwich*, and that is the focus of this book.

In this chapter you will learn what Android is, and what makes it so compelling to both developers and device manufacturers alike. You will also get started with developing your first Android application, and learn how to obtain all the necessary tools and set them up so that you can test your application on an Android 4.0 emulator. By the end of this chapter, you will be equipped with the basic knowledge you need to explore more sophisticated techniques and tricks for developing your next killer Android application.

WHAT IS ANDROID?

Android is a mobile operating system that is based on a modified version of Linux. It was originally developed by a startup of the same name, Android, Inc. In 2005, as part of its strategy to enter the mobile space, Google purchased Android and took over its development work (as well as its development team).

Google wanted Android to be open and free; hence, most of the Android code was released under the open source Apache License, which means that anyone who wants to use Android can do so by downloading the full Android source code. Moreover, vendors (typically hardware manufacturers) can add their own proprietary extensions to Android and customize Android to differentiate their products from others. This simple development model makes Android very attractive and has thus piqued the interest of many vendors. This has been especially true for companies affected by the phenomenon of Apple's iPhone, a hugely successful product that revolutionized the smartphone industry. Such companies include Motorola and Sony Ericsson, which for many years have been developing their own mobile operating systems. When the iPhone was launched, many of these manufacturers had to scramble to find new ways of revitalizing their products. These manufacturers see Android as a solution — they will continue to design their own hardware and use Android as the operating system that powers it.

The main advantage of adopting Android is that it offers a unified approach to application development. Developers need only develop for Android, and their applications should be able to run on numerous different devices, as long as the devices are powered using Android. In the world of smartphones, applications are the most important part of the success chain. Device manufacturers therefore see Android as their best hope to challenge the onslaught of the iPhone, which already commands a large base of applications.

Android Versions

Android has gone through quite a number of updates since its first release. Table 1-1 shows the various versions of Android and their codenames.

TABLE 1-1: A Brief History of Android Versions

ANDROID VERSION	RELEASE DATE	CODENAME
1.1	9 February 2009	
1.5	30 April 2009	Cupcake
1.6	15 September 2009	Donut
2.0/2.1	26 October 2009	Eclair
2.2	20 May 2010	Froyo
2.3	6 December 2010	Gingerbread
3.0/3.1/3.2	22 February 2011	Honeycomb
4.0	19 October 2011	Ice Cream Sandwich

In February 2011, Google released Android 3.0, a tablet-only release supporting widescreen devices. The key changes in Android 3.0 are as follows.

➤ New user interface optimized for tablets

➤ 3D desktop with new widgets

➤ Refined multi-tasking

➤ New web browser features, such as tabbed browsing, form auto-fill, bookmark synchronization, and private browsing

➤ Support for multi-core processors

Applications written for versions of Android prior to 3.0 are compatible with Android 3.0 devices, and they run without modifications. Android 3.0 tablet applications that make use of the newer features available in 3.0, however, will not be able to run on older devices. To ensure that an Android tablet application can run on all versions of devices, you must programmatically ensure that you only make use of features that are supported in specific versions of Android.

In October 2011, Google released Android 4.0, a version that brought all the features introduced in Android 3.0 to smartphones, along with some new features such as facial recognition unlock, data usage monitoring and control, Near Field Communication (NFC), and more.

Features of Android

Because Android is open source and freely available to manufacturers for customization, there are no fixed hardware or software configurations. However, Android itself supports the following features:

➤ **Storage** — Uses SQLite, a lightweight relational database, for data storage. Chapter 6 discusses data storage in more detail.

➤ **Connectivity** — Supports GSM/EDGE, IDEN, CDMA, EV-DO, UMTS, Bluetooth (includes A2DP and AVRCP), Wi-Fi, LTE, and WiMAX. Chapter 8 discusses networking in more detail.

➤ **Messaging** — Supports both SMS and MMS. Chapter 8 discusses messaging in more detail.

➤ **Web browser** — Based on the open source WebKit, together with Chrome's V8 JavaScript engine

➤ **Media support** — Includes support for the following media: H.263, H.264 (in 3GP or MP4 container), MPEG-4 SP, AMR, AMR-WB (in 3GP container), AAC, HE-AAC (in MP4 or 3GP container), MP3, MIDI, Ogg Vorbis, WAV, JPEG, PNG, GIF, and BMP

➤ **Hardware support** — Accelerometer Sensor, Camera, Digital Compass, Proximity Sensor, and GPS

➤ **Multi-touch** — Supports multi-touch screens

➤ **Multi-tasking** — Supports multi-tasking applications

➤ **Flash support** — Android 2.3 supports Flash 10.1.

➤ **Tethering** — Supports sharing of Internet connections as a wired/wireless hotspot

Architecture of Android

In order to understand how Android works, take a look at Figure 1-1, which shows the various layers that make up the Android operating system (OS).

The Android OS is roughly divided into five sections in four main layers:

➤ **Linux kernel** — This is the kernel on which Android is based. This layer contains all the low-level device drivers for the various hardware components of an Android device.

➤ **Libraries** — These contain all the code that provides the main features of an Android OS. For example, the SQLite library provides database support so that an application can use it for data storage. The WebKit library provides functionalities for web browsing.

➤ **Android runtime** — At the same layer as the libraries, the Android runtime provides a set of core libraries that enable developers to write Android apps using the Java programming language. The Android runtime also includes the Dalvik virtual machine, which enables every Android application to run in its own process, with its own instance of the Dalvik virtual machine (Android applications are compiled into Dalvik executables). Dalvik is a specialized virtual machine designed specifically for Android and optimized for battery-powered mobile devices with limited memory and CPU.

➤ **Application framework** — Exposes the various capabilities of the Android OS to application developers so that they can make use of them in their applications.

➤ **Applications** — At this top layer, you will find applications that ship with the Android device (such as Phone, Contacts, Browser, etc.), as well as applications that you download and install from the Android Market. Any applications that you write are located at this layer.

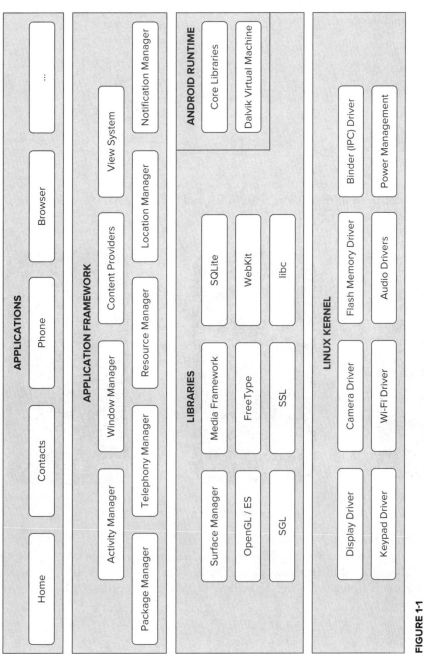

APPLICATIONS

| Home | Contacts | Phone | Browser | ... |

APPLICATION FRAMEWORK

| Activity Manager | Window Manager | Content Providers | View System |
| Package Manager | Telephony Manager | Resource Manager | Location Manager | Notification Manager |

ANDROID RUNTIME

| Core Libraries |
| Dalvik Virtual Machine |

LIBRARIES

Surface Manager	Media Framework	SQLite
OpenGL / ES	FreeType	WebKit
SGL	SSL	libc

LINUX KERNEL

| Display Driver | Camera Driver | Flash Memory Driver | Binder (IPC) Driver |
| Keypad Driver | Wi-Fi Driver | Audio Drivers | Power Management |

FIGURE 1-1

Android Devices in the Market

Android devices come in all shapes and sizes. As of late November 2011, the Android OS powers the following types of devices:

➤ Smartphones

➤ Tablets

➤ E-reader devices

➤ Netbooks

➤ MP4 players

➤ Internet TVs

Chances are good that you own at least one of the preceding devices. Figure 1-2 shows (left to right) the Samsung Galaxy S II, the Motorola Atrix 4G, and the HTC EVO 4G smartphones.

FIGURE 1-2

Another popular category of devices that manufacturers are rushing out is the *tablet*. Tablets typically come in two sizes: seven inches and ten inches, measured diagonally. Figure 1-3 shows the Samsung Galaxy Tab 10.1 (left) and the Asus Eee Pad Transformer TF101 (right), both 10.1-inch tablets. Both the Samsung Galaxy 10.1 and the Asus Eee Pad Transfer TF101 run on Android 3.

FIGURE 1-3

Besides smartphones and tablets, Android is also beginning to appear in dedicated devices, such as e-book readers. Figure 1-4 shows the Barnes and Noble's NOOK Color (left) and Amazon's Kindle Fire (right), both of which are color e-Book readers running the Android OS.

FIGURE 1-4

In addition to these popular mobile devices, Android is also slowly finding its way into your living room. People of Lava, a Swedish company, has developed an Android-based TV, called the Scandinavia Android TV (see Figure 1-5).

Google has also ventured into a proprietary smart TV platform based on Android and codeveloped with companies such as Intel, Sony, and Logitech. Figure 1-6 shows Sony's Google TV.

FIGURE 1-5

FIGURE 1-6

At the time of writing, the Samsung Galaxy Nexus (see Figure 1-7) is the only device running on Android 4.0. However, Google has promised that existing devices (such as the Nexus S) will be able to upgrade to Android 4.0. By the time you are reading this, there should be a plethora of devices running Android 4.0.

FIGURE 1-7

The Android Market

As mentioned earlier, one of the main factors determining the success of a smartphone platform is the applications that support it. It is clear from the success of the iPhone that applications play a very vital role in determining whether a new platform swims or sinks. In addition, making these applications accessible to the general user is extremely important.

As such, in August 2008, Google announced Android Market, an online application store for Android devices, and made it available to users in October 2008. Using the Market application that is preinstalled on their Android device, users can simply download third-party applications directly onto their devices. Both paid and free applications are supported on the Android Market, though paid applications are available only to users in certain countries due to legal issues.

Similarly, in some countries, users can buy paid applications from the Android Market, but developers cannot sell in that country. As an example, at the time of writing, users in India can buy apps from the Android Market, but developers in India cannot sell apps on the Android Market. The reverse may also be true; for example, users in South Korea cannot buy apps, but developers in South Korea can sell apps on the Android Market.

 NOTE *Chapter 12 discusses more about the Android Market and how you can sell your own applications in it.*

The Android Developer Community

With Android in its fourth version, there is a large developer community all over the world. It is now much easier to get solutions to problems, and find like-minded developers to share app ideas and exchange experiences.

Here are some developer communities/sites that you can turn to for help if you run into problems while working with Android:

➤ **Stack Overflow** (www.stackoverflow.com) — Stack Overflow is a collaboratively edited question and answer site for developers. If you have a question about Android, chances are someone at Stack Overflow is probably already discussing the same question and someone else had already provided the answer. Best of all, other developers can vote for the best answer so that you can know which are the answers that are trustworthy.

➤ **Google Android Training** (http://developer.android.com/training/index .html) — Google has launched the Android Training site that contains a number of useful classes grouped by topics. At the time of writing, the classes mostly contain useful code snippets that are very useful to Android developers once they have started with the basics. Once you have learned the basics in this book, I strongly suggest you take a look at the classes.

➤ **Android Discuss** (http://groups.google.com/group/android-discuss) — Android Discuss is a discussion group hosted by Google using the Google Groups service. Here, you will be able to discuss the various aspects of Android programming. This group is monitored closely by the Android team at Google, and so this is good place to clarify your doubts and learn new tips and tricks.

OBTAINING THE REQUIRED TOOLS

Now that you know what Android is and what its feature set contains, you are probably anxious to get your hands dirty and start writing some applications! Before you write your first app, however, you need to download the required tools and SDKs.

For Android development, you can use a Mac, a Windows PC, or a Linux machine. All the tools needed are free and can be downloaded from the Web. Most of the examples provided in this book should work fine with the Android emulator, with the exception of a few examples that require access to the hardware. For this book, I am using a Windows 7 computer to demonstrate all the code samples. If you are using a Mac or Linux computer, the screenshots should look similar; some minor differences may be present, but you should be able to follow along without problems.

Let the fun begin!

JAVA JDK

The Android SDK makes use of the Java SE Development Kit (JDK). If your computer does not have the JDK installed, you should start by downloading it from `www.oracle.com/technetwork/java/javase/downloads/index.html` and installing it prior to moving to the next section.

Android SDK

The first and most important piece of software you need to download is, of course, the Android SDK. The Android SDK contains a debugger, libraries, an emulator, documentation, sample code, and tutorials.

You can download the Android SDK from `http://developer.android.com/sdk/index.html` (see Figure 1-8).

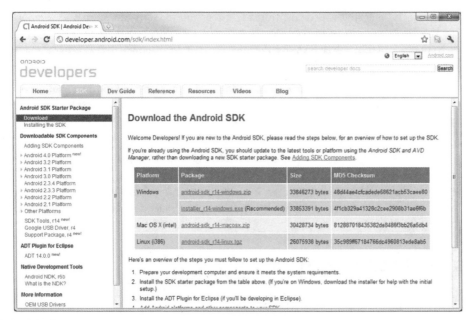

FIGURE 1-8

The Android SDK is packaged in a zip file. You can download it and unzip its content (the `android-sdk-windows` folder) into a folder, say `C:\Android 4.0\`. For Windows user, Google recommends that you download the `installer_r15-windows.exe` file instead and use it to set up the tools for you automatically. The following steps walk you through the installation process using this approach.

Installing the Android SDK Tools

When you have downloaded the `installer_r15-windows.exe` file, double-click it to start the installation of the Android tools. In the welcome screen of the Setup Wizard, click Next to continue.

If your computer does not have Java installed, you will see the error dialog shown in Figure 1-9. However, even if you have Java installed, you may still see this error. If this is the case, click the Report error button and then click Next.

FIGURE 1-9

You will be asked to provide a destination folder to install the Android SDK tools. Enter a destination path (see Figure 1-10) and click Next.

When you are asked to choose a Start Menu folder to create the program's shortcut, take the default "Android SDK Tools" and click Install. When the setup is done, check the "Start SDK Manager (to download system images, etc.)" option and click Finish (see Figure 1-11). This will start the SDK Manager.

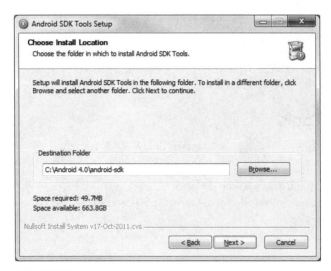

FIGURE 1-10

FIGURE 1-11

Configuring the Android SDK Manager

The Android SDK Manager manages the various versions of the Android SDK currently installed on your computer. When it is launched, you will see a list of items and whether or not they are currently installed on your computer (see Figure 1-12).

Check the relevant tools, documentation, and platforms you need for your project. Once you have selected the items you want, click the Install button to download them. Because it takes a while to download from Google's server, it is a good idea to download only what you need immediately, and download the rest when you have more time. For now, you may want to check the items shown in the figure.

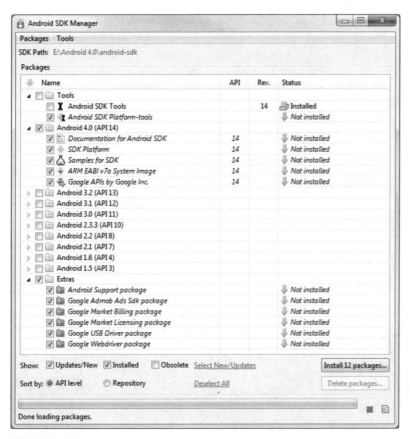

FIGURE 1-12

 NOTE *For a start, you should at least select the latest Android 4.0 SDK platform and the Extras. At the time of writing, the latest SDK platform is SDK Platform Android 4.0, API 14.*

Each version of the Android OS is identified by an API level number. For example, Android 2.3.3 is level 10 (API 10), while Android 3.0 is level 11 (API 11), and so on. For each level, two platforms are available. For example, level 14 offers the following:

➤ SDK Platform

➤ Google APIs by Google Inc.

The key difference between the two is that the Google APIs platform contains additional APIs provided by Google (such as the Google Maps library). Therefore, if the application you are writing requires Google Maps, you need to create an AVD using the Google APIs platform (more on this is provided in Chapter 9, "Location-Based Services."

You will be asked to choose the packages to install (see Figure 1-13). Check the Accept All option and click Install.

FIGURE 1-13

The SDK Manager will proceed to download the packages that you have selected. The installation takes some time, so be patient. When all the packages are installed, you will be asked to restart the ADB (Android Debug Bridge). Click Yes.

Eclipse

The next step is to obtain the integrated development environment (IDE) for developing your Android applications. In the case of Android, the recommended IDE is Eclipse, a multi-language software development environment featuring an extensible plug-in system. It can be used to develop various types of applications, using languages such as Java, Ada, C, C++, COBOL, Python, and others.

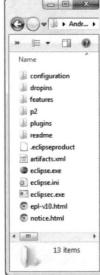

For Android development, you should download the Eclipse IDE for Java EE Developers (`www.eclipse.org/downloads/`). Six editions are available: Windows (32- and 64-bit), Mac OS X (Cocoa 32- and 64), and Linux (32- and 64-bit). Simply select the relevant one for your operating system. All the examples in this book were tested using the 32-bit version of Eclipse for Windows.

Once the Eclipse IDE is downloaded, unzip its content (the `eclipse` folder) into a folder, say `C:\Android 4.0\`. Figure 1-14 shows the content of the `eclipse` folder.

FIGURE 1-14

To launch Eclipse, double-click on the `eclipse.exe` file. You are first asked to specify your workspace. In Eclipse, a workspace is a folder where you store all your projects. Take the default suggested (or you can specify your own folder as the workspace) and click OK.

Android Development Tools (ADT)

When Eclipse is launched, select Help ➪ Install New Software (see Figure 1-15) to install the Android Development Tools (ADT) plug-in for Eclipse.

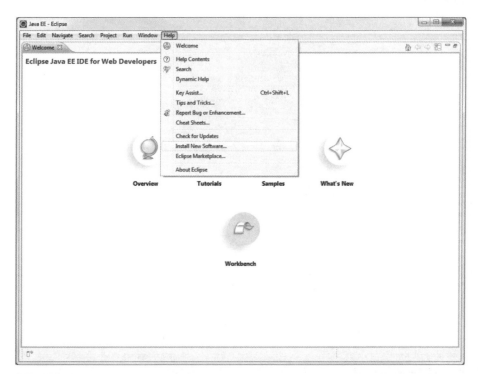

FIGURE 1-15

The ADT is an extension to the Eclipse IDE that supports the creation and debugging of Android applications. Using the ADT, you will be able to do the following in Eclipse:

➤ Create new Android application projects.

➤ Access the tools for accessing your Android emulators and devices.

➤ Compile and debug Android applications.

➤ Export Android applications into Android Packages (APKs).

➤ Create digital certificates for code-signing your APK.

In the Install dialog that appears, specify `https://dl-ssl.google.com/android/eclipse/` and press Enter. After a while, you will see the Developer Tools item appear in the middle of the window (see Figure 1-16). Expand it to reveal its content: Android DDMS, Android Development Tools, Android Hierarchy Viewer, and Android Traceview. Check all of them and click Next twice.

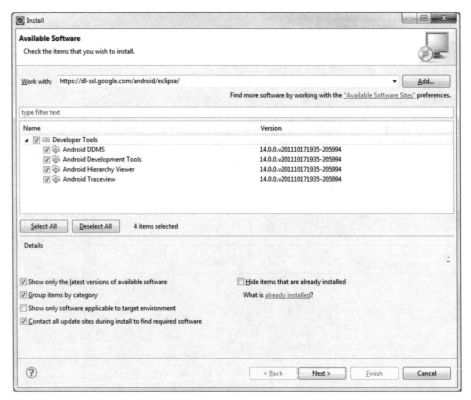

FIGURE 1-16

 NOTE *If you have any problems downloading the ADT, check out Google's help at* `http://developer.android.com/sdk/eclipse-adt.html#installing.`

You will be asked to review and accept the licenses. Check the "I accept the terms of the license agreements" option and click Finish. Once the installation is completed, you will be asked to restart Eclipse. Go ahead and restart Eclipse now.

When Eclipse is restarted, you are asked to configure your Android SDK (see Figure 1-17). As the Android SDK has already been downloaded earlier in the previous section, check the "Use existing SDKs" option and specify the directory where you have installed the Android SDK. Click Next.

After this step, you are asked to send your usage statistics to Google. Once you have selected your choice, click Finish.

FIGURE 1-17

NOTE *As each new version of the SDK is released, the installation steps tend to differ slightly. If you do not experience the same steps as described here, don't worry — just follow the instructions on screen.*

Creating Android Virtual Devices (AVDs)

The next step is to create an Android Virtual Device (AVD) to be used for testing your Android applications. An AVD is an emulator instance that enables you to model an actual device. Each AVD consists of a hardware profile; a mapping to a system image; as well as emulated storage, such as a secure digital (SD) card.

You can create as many AVDs as you want in order to test your applications with several different configurations. This testing is important to confirm the behavior of your application when it is run on different devices with varying capabilities.

 NOTE *Appendix B discusses some of the capabilities of the Android emulator.*

To create an AVD, select Window ⇨ AVD Manager (see Figure 1-18).

FIGURE 1-18

In the Android Virtual Device Manager dialog (see Figure 1-19), click the New... button to create a new AVD.

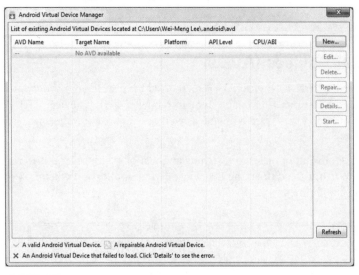

FIGURE 1-19

In the Create new Android Virtual Device (AVD) dialog, enter the items as shown in Figure 1-20. Click the Create AVD button when you are done.

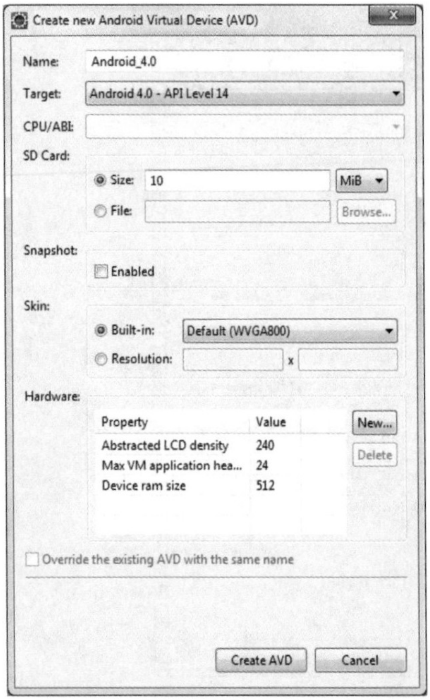

FIGURE 1-20

In this case, you have created an AVD (put simply, an Android emulator) that emulates an Android device running version 4.0 of the OS with a built-in 10-MB SD card. In addition to what you have created, you also have the option to emulate the device with different screen densities and resolutions.

 NOTE *Appendix B explains how to emulate the different types of Android devices.*

It is preferable to create a few AVDs with different API levels and hardware configurations so that your application can be tested on different versions of the Android OS.

Once your ADV has been created, it is time to test it. Select the AVD that you want to test and click the Start... button. The Launch Options dialog will appear (see Figure 1-21). If you have a small monitor, it is recommended that you check the "Scale display to real size" option so that you can set the emulator to a smaller size. Click the Launch button to start the emulator.

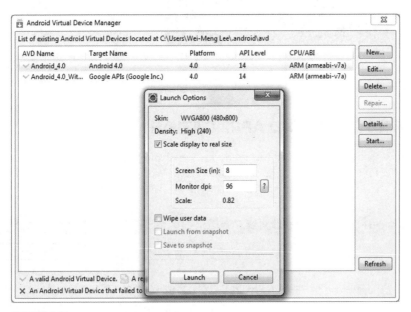

FIGURE 1-21

The Android emulator will start, and after a while it will be ready for use (see Figure 1-22). Go ahead and try out the emulator. It will behave just like a real Android device. After that, in the next section you will learn how to write your first Android application!

FIGURE 1-22

CREATING YOUR FIRST ANDROID APPLICATION

With all the tools and the SDK downloaded and installed, it is now time to start your engine. As in all programming books, the first example uses the ubiquitous Hello World application. This will give you a detailed look at the various components that make up an Android project.

TRY IT OUT Creating Your First Android Application

codefile HelloWorld.zip available for download at Wrox.com

1. Using Eclipse, create a new project by selecting File ⇨ New ⇨ Project . . . (see Figure 1-23).

FIGURE 1-23

 NOTE *After you have created your first Android application, subsequent Android projects can be created by selecting File ⇨ New ⇨ Android Project.*

2. Expand the Android folder and select Android Project (see Figure 1-24). Click Next.

3. Name the Android project **HelloWorld**, as shown in Figure 1-25, and then click Next.

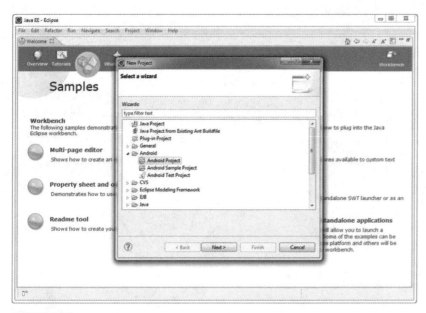

FIGURE 1-24

Eclipse project name (handwritten)

FIGURE 1-25

4. Select the Android 4.0 target and click Next.

5. Fill in the Application Info details as shown in Figure 1-26. Click Finish.

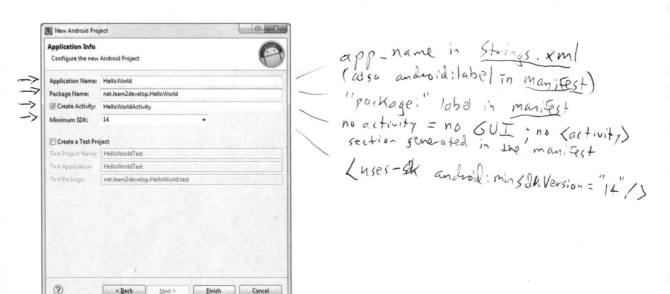

app-name in Strings.xml (handwritten)
(also android:label in manifest)
"package:" label in manifest
no activity = no GUI ; no ⟨activity⟩ section generated in the manifest
⟨uses-sdk android:minSdkVersion="14"/⟩

FIGURE 1-26

NOTE *You need to have at least a period (.) in the package name. The recommended convention for the package name is to use your domain name in reverse order, followed by the project name. For example, my company's domain name is* `learn2develop.net`; *hence, my package name would be* `net.learn2develop.HelloWorld`.

6. The Eclipse IDE should now look like Figure 1-27.

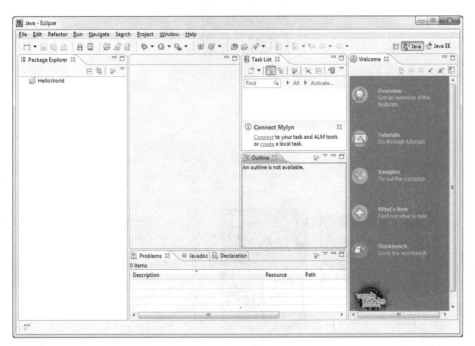

FIGURE 1-27

7. In the Package Explorer (located on the left of the Eclipse IDE), expand the HelloWorld project by clicking on the various arrows displayed to the left of each item in the project (see Figure 1-28). In the `res/layout` folder, double-click the `main.xml` file.

8. The `main.xml` file defines the user interface (UI) of your application. The default view is the Layout view, which lays out the activity graphically. To modify the UI by hand, click the `main.xml` tab located at the bottom (see Figure 1-29).

FIGURE 1-28

FIGURE 1-29

9. Add the following code in bold to the `main.xml` file:

```
<?xml version="1.0" encoding="utf-8"?>
<LinearLayout xmlns:android="http://schemas.android.com/apk/res/
android"
    android:layout_width="fill_parent"
```

```
        android:layout_height="fill_parent"
        android:orientation="vertical" >

    <TextView
        android:layout_width="fill_parent"
        android:layout_height="wrap_content"
        android:text="@string/hello" />

    <TextView
        android:layout_width="fill_parent"
        android:layout_height="wrap_content"
        android:text="This is my first Android Application!" />

    <Button
        android:layout_width="fill_parent"
        android:layout_height="wrap_content"
        android:text="And this is a clickable button!" />

    </LinearLayout>
```

10. To save the changes made to your project, press Ctrl+S.

11. You are now ready to test your application on the Android emulator. Right-click the project name in Eclipse and select Run As ➪ Android Application (see Figure 1-30).

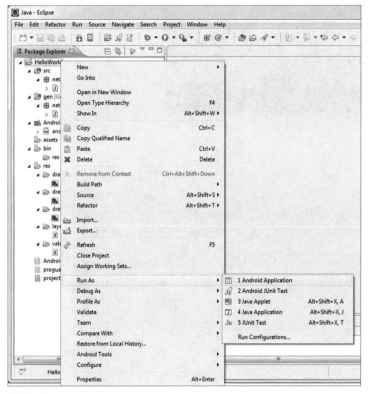

FIGURE 1-30

12. If you have not made any mistakes in the project, you should now be able to see the application installed and running on the Android emulator (see Figure 1-31).

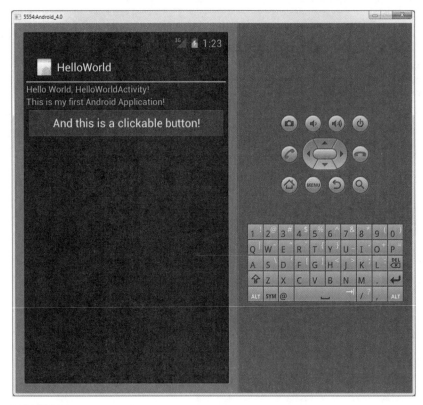

FIGURE 1-31

13. Click the Home button (the house icon in the lower-left corner above the keyboard) so that it now shows the Home screen (see Figure 1-32).

14. Click the application launcher icon to display the list of applications installed on the device. Note that the HelloWorld application is now installed in the application launcher (see Figure 1-33).

FIGURE 1-32

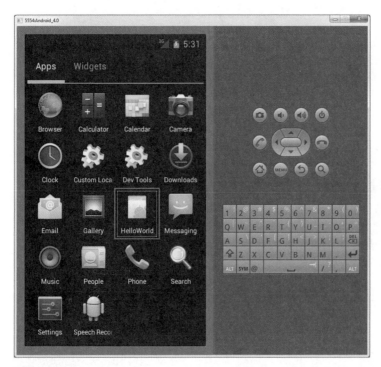

FIGURE 1-33

WHICH AVD WILL BE USED TO TEST YOUR APPLICATION?

Recall that earlier you created a few AVDs using the AVD Manager. So which one will be launched by Eclipse when you run an Android application? Eclipse checks the target that you specified (when you created a new project), comparing it against the list of AVDs that you have created. The first one that matches will be launched to run your application.

If you have more than one suitable AVD running prior to debugging the application, Eclipse will display the Android Device Chooser dialog, which enables you to select the desired emulator/device to debug the application (see Figure 1-34).

FIGURE 1-34

How It Works

To create an Android project using Eclipse, you need to supply the information shown in Table 1-2.

TABLE 1-2: Project Files Created by Default

PROPERTIES	DESCRIPTION
Project name	The name of the project
Application name	A user-friendly name for your application
Package name	The name of the package. You should use a reverse domain name for this.
Create Activity	The name of the first activity in your application
Min SDK Version	The minimum version of the SDK that your project is targeting

In Android, an *activity* is a window that contains the user interface of your applications. An application can have zero or more activities; in this example, the application contains one activity: `HelloWorldActivity`. This `HelloWorldActivity` is the entry point of the application, which is displayed when the application is started. Chapter 2 discusses activities in more detail.

In this simple example, you modified the `main.xml` file to display the string "This is my first Android Application!" and a button. The `main.xml` file contains the user interface of the activity, which is displayed when `HelloWorldActivity` is loaded.

When you debug the application on the Android emulator, the application is automatically installed on the emulator. And that's it — you have developed your first Android application!

The next section unravels how all the various files in your Android project work together to make your application come alive.

ANATOMY OF AN ANDROID APPLICATION

Now that you have created your first Hello World Android application, it is time to dissect the innards of the Android project and examine all the parts that make everything work.

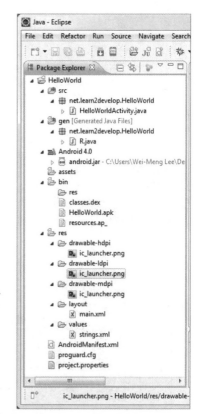

FIGURE 1-35

First, note the various files that make up an Android project in the Package Explorer in Eclipse (see Figure 1-35).

The various folders and their files are as follows:

➤ `src` — Contains the .java source files for your project. In this example, there is one file, `HelloWorldActivity` `.java`. The `HelloWorldActivity.java` file is the source file for your activity. You write the code for your application in this file. The Java file is listed under the package name for your project, which in this case is `net` `.learn2develop.HelloWorld`.

➤ `gen` — Contains the `R.java` file, a compiler-generated file that references all the resources found in your project. You should not modify this file. All the resources in your project are automatically compiled into this class so that you can refer to them using the class.

➤ `Android 4.0` library — This item contains one file, `android.jar`, which contains all the class libraries needed for an Android application.

➤ `assets` — This folder contains all the assets used by your application, such as HTML, text files, databases, etc.

➤ `bin` — This folder contains the files built by the ADT during the build process. In particular, it generates the .apk file (Android Package). An .apk file is the application binary of an Android application. It contains everything needed to run an Android application.

➤ res — This folder contains all the resources used in your application. It also contains a few other subfolders: drawable-<*resolution*>, layout, and values. Chapter 3 talks more about how you can support devices with different screen resolutions and densities.

➤ AndroidManifest.xml — This is the manifest file for your Android application. Here you specify the permissions needed by your application, as well as other features (such as intent-filters, receivers, etc.). Chapter 2 discusses the use of the AndroidManifest.xml file in more detail.

The main.xml file defines the user interface for your activity. Observe the following in bold:

```
<TextView
    android:layout_width="fill_parent"
    android:layout_height="wrap_content"
    android:text="@string/hello" />
```

The @string in this case refers to the strings.xml file located in the res/values folder. Hence, @string/hello refers to the hello string defined in the strings.xml file, which is "Hello World, HelloWorldActivity!":

```
<?xml version="1.0" encoding="utf-8"?>
<resources>

    <string name="hello">Hello World, HelloWorldActivity!</string>
    <string name="app_name">HelloWorld</string>

</resources>
```

It is recommended that you store all the string constants in your application in this strings.xml file and reference these strings using the @string identifier. That way, if you ever need to localize your application to another language, all you need to do is make a copy of the entire values folder and modify the values of strings.xml to contain the string in the language that you want to display. Figure 1-36 shows that I have another folder named values-fr with the strings.xml file containing the same hello string in French.

FIGURE 1-36

If the user loads the same application on a phone configured to display French as the default language, your application will automatically display the `hello` string in French.

The next important file in an Android project is the manifest file. Note the content of the `AndroidManifest.xml` file:

```xml
<?xml version="1.0" encoding="utf-8"?>
<manifest xmlns:android="http://schemas.android.com/apk/res/android"
    package="net.learn2develop.HelloWorld"
    android:versionCode="1"
    android:versionName="1.0" >

    <uses-sdk android:minSdkVersion="14" />

    <application
        android:icon="@drawable/ic_launcher"
        android:label="@string/app_name" >
        <activity
            android:label="@string/app_name"
            android:name=".HelloWorldActivity" >
            <intent-filter >
                <action android:name="android.intent.action.MAIN" />

                <category android:name="android.intent.category.LAUNCHER" />
            </intent-filter>
        </activity>
    </application>

</manifest>
```

The `AndroidManifest.xml` file contains detailed information about the application:

➤ It defines the package name of the application as `net.learn2develop.HelloWorld`.

➤ The version code of the application is 1 (set via the `android:versionCode` attribute). This value is used to identify the version number of your application. It can be used to programmatically determine whether an application needs to be upgraded.

➤ The version name of the application is 1.0 (set via the `android:versionName` attribute). This string value is mainly used for display to the user. You should use the format *<major>.<minor>.<point>* for this value.

➤ The `android:minSdkVersion` attribute of the `<uses-sdk>` element specifies the minimum version of the OS on which the application will run.

➤ The application uses the image named `ic_launcher.png` located in the `drawable` folders.

➤ The name of this application is the string named `app_name` defined in the `strings.xml` file.

➤ There is one activity in the application represented by the `HelloWorldActivity.java` file. The label displayed for this activity is the same as the application name.

*still
don't fully
understand
purpose of
intent Filters
(need to see
more examples)*

➤ Within the definition for this activity, there is an element named `<intent-filter>`:

➤ The action for the intent filter is named `android.intent.action.MAIN` to indicate that this activity serves as the entry point for the application.

➤ The category for the intent-filter is named `android.intent.category.LAUNCHER` to indicate that the application can be launched from the device's launcher icon. Chapter 2 discusses intents in more detail.

As you add more files and folders to your project, Eclipse will automatically generate the content of `R.java`, which currently contains the following:

```
/* AUTO-GENERATED FILE.  DO NOT MODIFY.
 *
 * This class was automatically generated by the
 * aapt tool from the resource data it found.  It
 * should not be modified by hand.
 */

package net.learn2develop.HelloWorld;

public final class R {
    public static final class attr {
    }
    public static final class drawable {
        public static final int ic_launcher=0x7f020000;
    }
    public static final class layout {
        public static final int main=0x7f030000;
    }
    public static final class string {
        public static final int app_name=0x7f040001;
        public static final int hello=0x7f040000;
    }
}
```

*are
these
defining
memory
locations
(they look
HEX)*

You are not supposed to modify the content of the `R.java` file; Eclipse automatically generates the content for you when you modify your project.

> **NOTE** *If you delete* `R.java` *manually, Eclipse will regenerate it for you immediately. Note that in order for Eclipse to generate the* `R.java` *file for you, the project must not contain any errors. If you realize that Eclipse has not regenerated* `R.java` *after you have deleted it, check your project again. The code may contain syntax errors, or your XML files (such as* `AndroidManifest .xml, main.xml,` *etc.) may not be well-formed.*

Finally, the code that connects the activity to the UI (main.xml) is the setContentView() method, which is in the HelloWorldActivity.java file:

```
package net.learn2develop.HelloWorld;

import android.app.Activity;
import android.os.Bundle;

public class HelloWorldActivity extends Activity {
    /** Called when the activity is first created. */
    @Override
    public void onCreate(Bundle savedInstanceState) {
        super.onCreate(savedInstanceState);
        setContentView(R.layout.main);
    }
}
```

[?] — what "super" mean again? [?]

— what is bundled?
— and why does onCreate() take a bundle (what's the purpose?)

Here, R.layout.main refers to the main.xml file located in the res/layout folder. As you add additional XML files to the res/layout folder, the filenames will automatically be generated in the R.java file. The onCreate() method is one of many methods that are fired when an activity is loaded. Chapter 2 discusses the life cycle of an activity in more detail.

SUMMARY

This chapter has provided a brief overview of Android, and highlighted some of its capabilities. If you have followed the sections on downloading the tools and the Android SDK, you should now have a working system — one that is capable of developing more interesting Android applications other than the Hello World application. In the next chapter, you will learn about the concepts of activities and intents, and the very important roles they play in Android.

EXERCISES

1. What is an AVD?

2. What is the difference between the android:versionCode and android:versionName attributes in the AndroidManifest.xml file?

3. What is the use of the strings.xml file?

Answers to the exercises can be found in Appendix C.

▶ WHAT YOU LEARNED IN THIS CHAPTER

TOPIC	KEY CONCEPTS
Android OS	Android is an open source mobile operating system based on the Linux operating system. It is available to anyone who wants to adapt it to run on their own devices.
Languages used for Android application development	You use the Java programming language to develop Android applications. Written applications are compiled into Dalvik executables, which are then run on top of the Dalvik virtual machine.
Android Market	The Android Market hosts all the various Android applications written by third-party developers.
Tools for Android application development	Eclipse IDE, Android SDK, and the ADT
Activities	An activity is represented by a screen in your Android application. Each application can have zero or more activities.
The Android manifest file	The `AndroidManifest.xml` file contains detailed configuration information for your application. As your example application becomes more sophisticated, you will modify this file, and you will see the different information you can add to it as you progress through the chapters.

Activities, Fragments, and Intents

WHAT YOU WILL LEARN IN THIS CHAPTER

- ➤ The life cycles of an activity
- ➤ Using fragments to customize your UI
- ➤ Applying styles and themes to activities
- ➤ How to display activities as dialog windows
- ➤ Understanding the concept of intents
- ➤ Using the Intent object to link activities
- ➤ How intent filters help you selectively connect to other activities
- ➤ Displaying alerts to the user using notifications

In Chapter 1, you learned that an activity is a window that contains the user interface of your application. An application can have zero or more activities. Typically, applications have one or more activities; and the main purpose of an activity is to interact with the user. From the moment an activity appears on the screen to the moment it is hidden, it goes through a number of stages, known as an activity's *life cycle*. Understanding the life cycle of an activity is vital to ensuring that your application works correctly. In addition to activities, Android 4.0 also supports a feature that was introduced in Android 3.0 (for tablets): fragments. Think of fragments as "miniature" activities that can be grouped to form an activity. In this chapter, you will learn about how activities and fragments work together.

Apart from activities, another unique concept in Android is that of an *intent*. An intent is basically the "glue" that enables different activities from different applications to work together seamlessly, ensuring that tasks can be performed as though they all belong to one single application. Later in this chapter, you will learn more about this very important concept and how you can use it to call built-in applications such as the Browser, Phone, Maps, and more.

UNDERSTANDING ACTIVITIES

This chapter begins by looking at how to create an activity. To create an activity, you create a Java class that extends the Activity base class:

```
package net.learn2develop.Activity101;

import android.app.Activity;
import android.os.Bundle;

public class Activity101Activity extends Activity {
    /** Called when the activity is first created. */
    @Override
    public void onCreate(Bundle savedInstanceState) {
        super.onCreate(savedInstanceState);
        setContentView(R.layout.main);
    }
}
```

Your activity class loads its UI component using the XML file defined in your res/layout folder. In this example, you would load the UI from the main.xml file:

```
setContentView(R.layout.main);
```

Every activity you have in your application must be declared in your AndroidManifest.xml file, like this:

```
<?xml version="1.0" encoding="utf-8"?>
<manifest xmlns:android="http://schemas.android.com/apk/res/android"
    package="net.learn2develop.Activity101"
    android:versionCode="1"
    android:versionName="1.0" >

    <uses-sdk android:minSdkVersion="14" />

    <application
        android:icon="@drawable/ic_launcher"
        android:label="@string/app_name" >
        <activity
            android:label="@string/app_name"
            android:name=".Activity101Activity" >
            <intent-filter >
                <action android:name="android.intent.action.MAIN" />

                <category android:name="android.intent.category.LAUNCHER" />
            </intent-filter>
        </activity>
    </application>

</manifest>
```

The Activity base class defines a series of events that govern the life cycle of an activity. The Activity class defines the following events:

➤   onCreate() — Called when the activity is first created

➤   onStart() — Called when the activity becomes visible to the user

➤   onResume() — Called when the activity starts interacting with the user

➤ `onPause()` — Called when the current activity is being paused and the previous activity is being resumed

➤ `onStop()` — Called when the activity is no longer visible to the user

➤ `onDestroy()` — Called before the activity is destroyed by the system (either manually or by the system to conserve memory)

➤ `onRestart()` — Called when the activity has been stopped and is restarting again

By default, the activity created for you contains the `onCreate()` event. Within this event handler is the code that helps to display the UI elements of your screen.

Figure 2-1 shows the life cycle of an activity and the various stages it goes through — from when the activity is started until it ends.

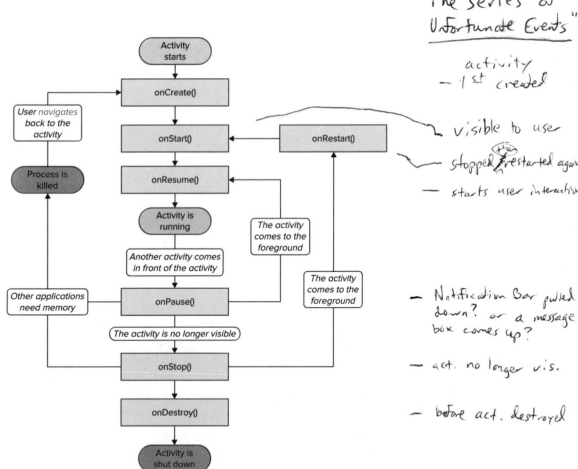

IMAGE REPRODUCED FROM WORK CREATED AND SHARED BY THE ANDROID OPEN
SOURCE PROJECT AND USED ACCORDING TO TERMS DESCRIBED IN THE CREATIVE
COMMONS 2.5 ATTRIBUTION LICENSE. SEE http://developer.android
.com/reference/android/app/Activity.html

FIGURE 2-1

The best way to understand the various stages of an activity is to create a new project, implement the various events, and then subject the activity to various user interactions.

TRY IT OUT **Understanding the Life Cycle of an Activity**

codefile Activity101.zip available for download at Wrox.com

1. Using Eclipse, create a new Android project and name it **Activity101**.

2. In the `Activity101Activity.java` file, add the following statements in bold:

```java
package net.learn2develop.Activity101;

import android.app.Activity;
import android.os.Bundle;
import android.util.Log;

public class Activity101Activity extends Activity {
    String tag = "Lifecycle";

    /** Called when the activity is first created. */
    @Override
    public void onCreate(Bundle savedInstanceState) {
        super.onCreate(savedInstanceState);
        setContentView(R.layout.main);
        Log.d(tag, "In the onCreate() event");
    }

    public void onStart()
    {
        super.onStart();
        Log.d(tag, "In the onStart() event");
    }

    public void onRestart()
    {
        super.onRestart();
        Log.d(tag, "In the onRestart() event");
    }

    public void onResume()
    {
        super.onResume();
        Log.d(tag, "In the onResume() event");
    }

    public void onPause()
    {
        super.onPause();
        Log.d(tag, "In the onPause() event");
    }

    public void onStop()
```

```
    {
        super.onStop();
        Log.d(tag, "In the onStop() event");
    }

    public void onDestroy()
    {
        super.onDestroy();
        Log.d(tag, "In the onDestroy() event");
    }
}
```

3. Press F11 to debug the application on the Android emulator.

4. When the activity is first loaded, you should see something very similar to the following in the LogCat window (click the Debug perspective; see also Figure 2-2):

```
11-16 06:25:59.396: D/Lifecycle(559): In the onCreate() event
11-16 06:25:59.396: D/Lifecycle(559): In the onStart() event
11-16 06:25:59.396: D/Lifecycle(559): In the onResume() event
```

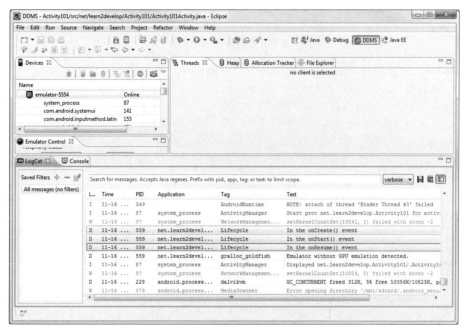

FIGURE 2-2

5. If you click the Back button on the Android emulator, the following is printed:

```
11-16 06:29:26.665: D/Lifecycle(559): In the onPause() event
11-16 06:29:28.465: D/Lifecycle(559): In the onStop() event
11-16 06:29:28.465: D/Lifecycle(559): In the onDestroy() event
```

6. Click the Home button and hold it there. Click the `Activities` icon and observe the following:

```
11-16 06:31:08.905: D/Lifecycle(559): In the onCreate() event
11-16 06:31:08.905: D/Lifecycle(559): In the onStart() event
11-16 06:31:08.925: D/Lifecycle(559): In the onResume() event
```

7. Click the Phone button on the Android emulator so that the activity is pushed to the background. Observe the output in the LogCat window:

```
11-16 06:32:00.585: D/Lifecycle(559): In the onPause() event
11-16 06:32:05.015: D/Lifecycle(559): In the onStop() event
```

8. Notice that the `onDestroy()` event is not called, indicating that the activity is still in memory. Exit the phone dialer by clicking the Back button. The activity is now visible again. Observe the output in the LogCat window:

```
11-16 06:32:50.515: D/Lifecycle(559): In the onRestart() event
11-16 06:32:50.515: D/Lifecycle(559): In the onStart() event
11-16 06:32:50.515: D/Lifecycle(559): In the onResume() event
```

The `onRestart()` event is now fired, followed by the `onStart()` and `onResume()` methods.

How It Works

As you can see from this simple example, an activity is destroyed when you click the Back button. This is crucial to know, as whatever state the activity is currently in will be lost; hence, you need to write additional code in your activity to preserve its state when it is destroyed (Chapter 3 shows you how). At this point, note that the `onPause()` method is called in both scenarios — when an activity is sent to the background, as well as when it is killed when the user presses the Back button.

When an activity is started, the `onStart()` and `onResume()` methods are always called, regardless of whether the activity is restored from the background or newly created. When an activity is created for the first time, the `onCreate()` method is called.

From the preceding example, you can derive the following guidelines:

➤ Use the `onCreate()` method to create and instantiate the objects that you will be using in your application.

➤ Use the `onResume()` method to start any services or code that needs to run while your activity is in the foreground.

➤ Use the `onPause()` method to stop any services or code that does not need to run when your activity is not in the foreground.

➤ Use the `onDestroy()` method to free up resources before your activity is destroyed.

 NOTE *Even if an application has only one activity and the activity is killed, the application will still be running in memory.*

Applying Styles and Themes to an Activity

By default, an activity occupies the entire screen. However, you can apply a dialog theme to an activity so that it is displayed as a floating dialog. For example, you might want to customize your activity to display as a pop-up, warning users about some actions that they are going to perform. In this case, displaying the activity as a dialog is a good way to get their attention.

To apply a dialog theme to an activity, simply modify the `<Activity>` element in the `AndroidManifest.xml` file by adding the `android:theme` attribute:

```xml
<?xml version="1.0" encoding="utf-8"?>
<manifest xmlns:android="http://schemas.android.com/apk/res/android"
    package="net.learn2develop.Activity101"
    android:versionCode="1"
    android:versionName="1.0" >

    <uses-sdk android:minSdkVersion="14" />

    <application
        android:icon="@drawable/ic_launcher"
        android:label="@string/app_name"
        android:theme="@android:style/Theme.Dialog">
        <activity
            android:label="@string/app_name"
            android:name=".Activity101Activity" >
            <intent-filter >
                <action android:name="android.intent.action.MAIN" />

                <category android:name="android.intent.category.LAUNCHER" />
            </intent-filter>
        </activity>
    </application>

</manifest>
```

This will make the activity appear as a dialog, as shown in Figure 2-3.

Hiding the Activity Title

You can also hide the title of an activity if desired (such as when you just want to display a status update to the user). To do so, use the `requestWindowFeature()` method and pass it the `Window.FEATURE_NO_TITLE` constant, like this:

```java
import android.app.Activity;
import android.os.Bundle;
import android.util.Log;
import android.view.Window;

public class Activity101Activity extends Activity {
```

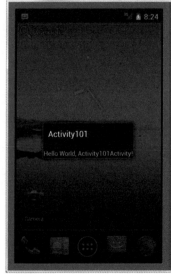

FIGURE 2-3

```
    String tag = "Lifecycle";

    /** Called when the activity is first created. */
    @Override
    public void onCreate(Bundle savedInstanceState) {
        super.onCreate(savedInstanceState);
        //---hides the title bar---
        requestWindowFeature(Window.FEATURE_NO_TITLE);

        setContentView(R.layout.main);
        Log.d(tag, "In the onCreate() event");
    }
}
```

This will hide the title bar, as shown in Figure 2-4.

Displaying a Dialog Window

There are times when you need to display a dialog window to get a confirmation from the user. In this case, you can override the `onCreateDialog()` protected method defined in the `Activity` base class to display a dialog window. The following Try It Out shows you how.

FIGURE 2-4

TRY IT OUT Displaying a Dialog Window Using an Activity

codefile Dialog.zip available for download at Wrox.com

1. Using Eclipse, create a new Android project and name it **Dialog**.

2. Add the following statements in bold to the `main.xml` file:

```xml
<?xml version="1.0" encoding="utf-8"?>
<LinearLayout xmlns:android="http://schemas.android.com/apk/res/android"
    android:layout_width="fill_parent"
    android:layout_height="fill_parent"
    android:orientation="vertical" >

<Button
    android:id="@+id/btn_dialog"
    android:layout_width="fill_parent"
    android:layout_height="wrap_content"
    android:text="Click to display a dialog"
    android:onClick="onClick" />

</LinearLayout>
```

3. Add the following statements in bold to the `DialogActivity.java` file:

```java
package net.learn2develop.Dialog;

import android.app.Activity;
```

```java
import android.app.AlertDialog;
import android.app.Dialog;
import android.content.DialogInterface;
import android.os.Bundle;
import android.view.View;
import android.widget.Toast;

public class DialogActivity extends Activity {
    CharSequence[] items = { "Google", "Apple", "Microsoft" };
    boolean[] itemsChecked = new boolean [items.length];

    /** Called when the activity is first created. */
    @Override
    public void onCreate(Bundle savedInstanceState) {
        super.onCreate(savedInstanceState);
        setContentView(R.layout.main);
    }

    public void onClick(View v) {
        showDialog(0);
    }

    @Override
    protected Dialog onCreateDialog(int id) {
        switch (id) {
        case 0:
            return new AlertDialog.Builder(this)
            .setIcon(R.drawable.ic_launcher)
            .setTitle("This is a dialog with some simple text...")
            .setPositiveButton("OK",
                new DialogInterface.OnClickListener() {
                    public void onClick(DialogInterface dialog, int whichButton)
                    {
                        Toast.makeText(getBaseContext(),
                            "OK clicked!", Toast.LENGTH_SHORT).show();
                    }
                }
            )
            .setNegativeButton("Cancel",
                new DialogInterface.OnClickListener() {
                    public void onClick(DialogInterface dialog, int whichButton)
                    {
                        Toast.makeText(getBaseContext(),
                            "Cancel clicked!", Toast.LENGTH_SHORT).show();
                    }
                }
            )
            .setMultiChoiceItems(items, itemsChecked,
                new DialogInterface.OnMultiChoiceClickListener() {
                    public void onClick(DialogInterface dialog,
                    int which, boolean isChecked) {
                        Toast.makeText(getBaseContext(),
                            items[which] + (isChecked ? " checked!":" unchecked!"),
                            Toast.LENGTH_SHORT).show();
```

```
                }
            }
        ).create();


    }
    return null;
}


}
```

4.   Press F11 to debug the application on the Android emulator.
Click the button to display the dialog (see Figure 2-5).
Checking the various checkboxes will cause the `Toast` class
to display the text of the item checked/unchecked. To dismiss
the dialog, click the OK or Cancel button.

FIGURE 2-5

How It Works

To display a dialog, you first implement the `onCreateDialog()`
method in the `Activity` class:

```
@Override
protected Dialog onCreateDialog(int id) {
    //...
}
```

This method is called when you call the `showDialog()` method:

```
public void onClick(View v) {
    showDialog(0);
}
```

The `onCreateDialog()` method is a callback for creating dialogs that are managed by the activity. When
you call the `showDialog()` method, this callback will be invoked. The `showDialog()` method accepts
an integer argument identifying a particular dialog to display. In this case, we used a `switch` statement
to identify the different types of dialogs to create, although the current example creates only one type of
dialog. Subsequent Try It Out exercises will extend this example to create different types of dialogs.

To create a dialog, you use the `AlertDialog` class's `Builder` constructor. You set the various
properties, such as icon, title, and buttons, as well as checkboxes:

```
@Override
protected Dialog onCreateDialog(int id) {
    switch (id) {
    case 0:
        return new AlertDialog.Builder(this)
        .setIcon(R.drawable.ic_launcher)
        .setTitle("This is a dialog with some simple text...")
        .setPositiveButton("OK",
            new DialogInterface.OnClickListener() {
                public void onClick(DialogInterface dialog, int whichButton)
```

```
                    {
                        Toast.makeText(getBaseContext(),
                            "OK clicked!", Toast.LENGTH_SHORT).show();
                    }
                }
            )
            .setNegativeButton("Cancel",
                new DialogInterface.OnClickListener() {
                    public void onClick(DialogInterface dialog, int whichButton)
                    {
                        Toast.makeText(getBaseContext(),
                            "Cancel clicked!", Toast.LENGTH_SHORT).show();
                    }
                }
            )
            .setMultiChoiceItems(items, itemsChecked,
                new DialogInterface.OnMultiChoiceClickListener() {
                    public void onClick(DialogInterface dialog,
                    int which, boolean isChecked) {
                        Toast.makeText(getBaseContext(),
                            items[which] + (isChecked ? " checked!":" unchecked!"),
                            Toast.LENGTH_SHORT).show();
                    }
                }
            ).create();


        }
        return null;
    }
```

The preceding code sets two buttons, OK and Cancel, using the `setPositiveButton()` and `setNegativeButton()` methods, respectively. You also set a list of checkboxes for users to choose via the `setMultiChoiceItems()` method. For the `setMultiChoiceItems()` method, you passed in two arrays: one for the list of items to display and another to contain the value of each item, to indicate if they are checked. When each item is checked, you use the `Toast` class to display a message indicating the item that was checked.

The preceding code for creating the dialog looks complicated, but it could easily be rewritten as follows:

```
package net.learn2develop.Dialog;

import android.app.Activity;
import android.app.AlertDialog;
import android.app.AlertDialog.Builder;
import android.app.Dialog;
import android.content.DialogInterface;
import android.os.Bundle;
import android.view.View;
import android.widget.Toast;

public class DialogActivity extends Activity {
```

```java
CharSequence[] items = { "Google", "Apple", "Microsoft" };
boolean[] itemsChecked = new boolean [items.length];

/** Called when the activity is first created. */
@Override
public void onCreate(Bundle savedInstanceState) {
    super.onCreate(savedInstanceState);
    setContentView(R.layout.main);
}

public void onClick(View v) {
    showDialog(0);
}

@Override
protected Dialog onCreateDialog(int id) {
    switch (id) {
    case 0:
        Builder builder = new AlertDialog.Builder(this);
        builder.setIcon(R.drawable.ic_launcher);
        builder.setTitle("This is a dialog with some simple text...");
        builder.setPositiveButton("OK",
            new DialogInterface.OnClickListener() {
                public void onClick(DialogInterface dialog,    int whichButton) {
                    Toast.makeText(getBaseContext(),
                            "OK clicked!", Toast.LENGTH_SHORT).show();
                }
            }
        );

        builder.setNegativeButton("Cancel",
            new DialogInterface.OnClickListener() {
                public void onClick(DialogInterface dialog, int whichButton) {
                    Toast.makeText(getBaseContext(),
                        "Cancel clicked!", Toast.LENGTH_SHORT).show();
                }
            }
        );

        builder.setMultiChoiceItems(items, itemsChecked,
            new DialogInterface.OnMultiChoiceClickListener() {
                public void onClick(DialogInterface dialog,
                int which, boolean isChecked) {
                    Toast.makeText(getBaseContext(),
                        items[which] + (isChecked ? " checked!":" unchecked!"),
                        Toast.LENGTH_SHORT).show();
                }
            }
        );
        return builder.create();
    }
    return null;
}
}
```

THE CONTEXT OBJECT

In Android, you often encounter the `Context` class and its instances. Instances of the `Context` class are often used to provide references to your application. For example, in the following code snippet, the first parameter of the `Toast` class takes in a `Context` object:

```
.setPositiveButton("OK",
    new DialogInterface.OnClickListener() {
        public void onClick(DialogInterface dialog, int whichButton)
        {
            Toast.makeText(getBaseContext(),
                    "OK clicked!", Toast.LENGTH_SHORT).show();
        }
    }
```

However, because the `Toast()` class is not used directly in the activity (it is used within the `AlertDialog` class), you need to return an instance of the `Context` class by using the `getBaseContext()` method.

You also encounter the `Context` class when creating a view dynamically in an activity. For example, you may want to dynamically create a `TextView` from code. To do so, you instantiate the `TextView` class, like this:

```
TextView tv = new TextView(this);
```

The constructor for the `TextView` class takes a `Context` object; and because the `Activity` class is a subclass of `Context`, you can use the `this` keyword to represent the `Context` object.

Displaying a Progress Dialog

One common UI feature in an Android device is the "Please wait" dialog that you typically see when an application is performing a long-running task. For example, the application may be logging in to a server before the user is allowed to use it, or it may be doing a calculation before displaying the result to the user. In such cases, it is helpful to display a dialog, known as a *progress dialog*, so that the user is kept in the loop.

The following Try It Out demonstrates how to display such a dialog.

TRY IT OUT Displaying a Progress (Please Wait) Dialog

1. Using the same project created in the previous section, add the following statements in bold to the `main.xml` file:

```
<?xml version="1.0" encoding="utf-8"?>
<LinearLayout xmlns:android="http://schemas.android.com/apk/res/android"
```

```
        android:layout_width="fill_parent"
        android:layout_height="fill_parent"
        android:orientation="vertical" >

    <Button
        android:id="@+id/btn_dialog"
        android:layout_width="fill_parent"
        android:layout_height="wrap_content"
        android:text="Click to display a dialog"
        android:onClick="onClick" />

    <Button
        android:id="@+id/btn_dialog2"
        android:layout_width="fill_parent"
        android:layout_height="wrap_content"
        android:text="Click to display a progress dialog"
        android:onClick="onClick2" />

</LinearLayout>
```

2. Add the following statements in bold to the `DialogActivity.java` file:

```java
package net.learn2develop.Dialog;

import android.app.Activity;
import android.app.AlertDialog;
import android.app.AlertDialog.Builder;
import android.app.Dialog;
import android.app.ProgressDialog;
import android.content.DialogInterface;
import android.os.Bundle;
import android.view.View;
import android.widget.Toast;

public class DialogActivity extends Activity {
    CharSequence[] items = { "Google", "Apple", "Microsoft" };
    boolean[] itemsChecked = new boolean [items.length];

    /** Called when the activity is first created. */
    @Override
    public void onCreate(Bundle savedInstanceState) {
        super.onCreate(savedInstanceState);
        setContentView(R.layout.main);
    }

    public void onClick(View v) {
        showDialog(0);
    }

    public void onClick2(View v) {
        //---show the dialog---
        final ProgressDialog dialog = ProgressDialog.show(
            this, "Doing something", "Please wait...", true);
        new Thread(new Runnable(){
```

```
        public void run(){
            try {
                //---simulate doing something lengthy---
                Thread.sleep(5000);
                //---dismiss the dialog---
                dialog.dismiss();
            } catch (InterruptedException e) {
                e.printStackTrace();
            }
        }
    }).start();
}

@Override
protected Dialog onCreateDialog(int id) { ... }

}
```

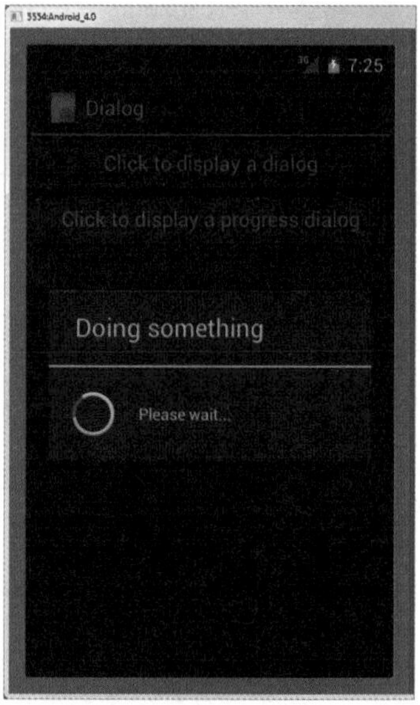

3. Press F11 to debug the application on the Android emulator. Clicking the second button will display the progress dialog, as shown in Figure 2-6. It will go away after five seconds.

How It Works

Basically, to create a progress dialog, you created an instance of the ProgressDialog class and called its show() method:

FIGURE 2-6

```
//---show the dialog---
final ProgressDialog dialog = ProgressDialog.show(
    this, "Doing something", "Please wait...", true);
```

This displays the progress dialog that you have just seen. Because this is a modal dialog, it will block the UI until it is dismissed. To perform a long-running task in the background, you created a Thread using a Runnable block (you will learn more about threading in Chapter 11). The code that you placed inside the run() method will be executed in a separate thread, and in this case you simulated it performing something for five seconds by inserting a delay using the sleep() method:

```
new Thread(new Runnable(){
    public void run(){
        try {
            //---simulate doing something lengthy---
            Thread.sleep(5000);
            //---dismiss the dialog---
            dialog.dismiss();
        } catch (InterruptedException e) {
            e.printStackTrace();
        }
    }
}).start();
```

After the five seconds elapse, you dismiss the dialog by calling the dismss() method.

Displaying a More Sophisticated Progress Dialog

Besides the generic "please wait" dialog that you created in the previous section, you can also create a dialog that displays the progress of an operation, such as the status of a download.

The following Try It Out shows you how to display a specialized progress dialog.

TRY IT OUT Displaying the Progress of an Operation

1. Using the same project created in the previous section, add the following lines in bold to the main.xml file:

```xml
<?xml version="1.0" encoding="utf-8"?>
<LinearLayout xmlns:android="http://schemas.android.com/apk/res/android"
    android:layout_width="fill_parent"
    android:layout_height="fill_parent"
    android:orientation="vertical" >

<Button
    android:id="@+id/btn_dialog"
    android:layout_width="fill_parent"
    android:layout_height="wrap_content"
    android:text="Click to display a dialog"
    android:onClick="onClick" />

<Button
    android:id="@+id/btn_dialog2"
    android:layout_width="fill_parent"
    android:layout_height="wrap_content"
    android:text="Click to display a progress dialog"
    android:onClick="onClick2" />

<Button
    android:id="@+id/btn_dialog3"
    android:layout_width="fill_parent"
    android:layout_height="wrap_content"
    android:text="Click to display a detailed progress dialog"
    android:onClick="onClick3" />

</LinearLayout>
```

2. Add the following statements in bold to the DialogActivity.java file:

```java
package net.learn2develop.Dialog;

import android.app.Activity;
import android.app.AlertDialog;
import android.app.AlertDialog.Builder;
import android.app.Dialog;
import android.app.ProgressDialog;
import android.content.DialogInterface;
import android.os.Bundle;
import android.view.View;
```

```java
import android.widget.Toast;

public class DialogActivity extends Activity {
    CharSequence[] items = { "Google", "Apple", "Microsoft" };
    boolean[] itemsChecked = new boolean [items.length];

    ProgressDialog progressDialog;

    /** Called when the activity is first created. */
    @Override
    public void onCreate(Bundle savedInstanceState) { ... }

    public void onClick(View v) { ... }

    public void onClick2(View v) { ... }

    public void onClick3(View v) {
        showDialog(1);
        progressDialog.setProgress(0);

        new Thread(new Runnable(){
            public void run(){
                for (int i=1; i<=15; i++) {
                    try {
                        //---simulate doing something lengthy---
                        Thread.sleep(1000);
                        //---update the dialog---
                        progressDialog.incrementProgressBy((int)(100/15));
                    } catch (InterruptedException e) {
                        e.printStackTrace();
                    }
                }
                progressDialog.dismiss();
            }
        }).start();
    }

    @Override
    protected Dialog onCreateDialog(int id) {
        switch (id) {
        case 0:
            return new AlertDialog.Builder(this)
                //...
            ).create();

        case 1:
            progressDialog = new ProgressDialog(this);
            progressDialog.setIcon(R.drawable.ic_launcher);
            progressDialog.setTitle("Downloading files...");
            progressDialog.setProgressStyle(ProgressDialog.STYLE_HORIZONTAL);
            progressDialog.setButton(DialogInterface.BUTTON_POSITIVE, "OK",
                new DialogInterface.OnClickListener() {
                    public void onClick(DialogInterface dialog,
                    int whichButton)
```

```
                    {
                        Toast.makeText(getBaseContext(),
                                "OK clicked!", Toast.LENGTH_SHORT).show();
                    }
                });
                progressDialog.setButton(DialogInterface.BUTTON_NEGATIVE, "Cancel",
                    new DialogInterface.OnClickListener() {
                        public void onClick(DialogInterface dialog,
                            int whichButton)
                        {
                            Toast.makeText(getBaseContext(),
                                    "Cancel clicked!", Toast.LENGTH_SHORT).show();
                        }
                });
                return progressDialog;
            }

            return null;
        }
    }
```

3. Press F11 to debug the application on the Android emulator. Click the third button to display the progress dialog (see Figure 2-7). Note that the progress bar will count up to 100%.

FIGURE 2-7

How It Works

To create a dialog that shows the progress of an operation, you first create an instance of the ProgressDialog class and set its various properties, such as icon, title, and style:

```
progressDialog = new ProgressDialog(this);
progressDialog.setIcon(R.drawable.ic_launcher);
progressDialog.setTitle("Downloading files...");
progressDialog.setProgressStyle(ProgressDialog.STYLE_HORIZONTAL);
```

You then set the two buttons that you want to display inside the progress dialog:

```
progressDialog.setButton(DialogInterface.BUTTON_POSITIVE, "OK",
    new DialogInterface.OnClickListener() {
        public void onClick(DialogInterface dialog,
        int whichButton)
        {
            Toast.makeText(getBaseContext(),
                    "OK clicked!", Toast.LENGTH_SHORT).show();
        }
});
progressDialog.setButton(DialogInterface.BUTTON_NEGATIVE, "Cancel",
    new DialogInterface.OnClickListener() {
```

```
                    public void onClick(DialogInterface dialog,
                        int whichButton)
                    {
                        Toast.makeText(getBaseContext(),
                            "Cancel clicked!", Toast.LENGTH_SHORT).show();
                    }
                });
                return progressDialog;
```

The preceding code causes a progress dialog to appear (see Figure 2-8).

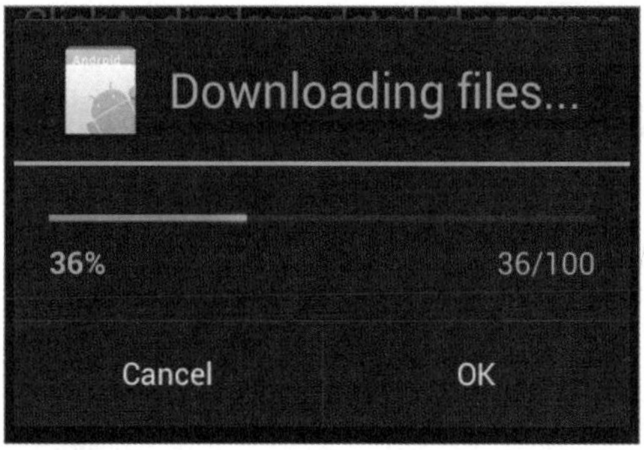

To display the progress status in the progress dialog, you can use a `Thread` object to run a `Runnable` block of code:

```
        progressDialog.setProgress(0);

    new Thread(new Runnable(){
        public void run(){
            for (int i=1; i<=15; i++) {
                try {
                    //---simulate doing something lengthy---
                    Thread.sleep(1000);
                    //---update the dialog---
                    progressDialog.incrementProgressBy((int)(100/15));
                } catch (InterruptedException e) {
                    e.printStackTrace();
                }
            }
            progressDialog.dismiss();
        }
    }).start();
```

FIGURE 2-8

In this case, you want to count from 1 to 15, with a delay of one second between each number. The `incrementProgressBy()` method increments the counter in the progress dialog. When the progress dialog reaches 100%, it is dismissed.

LINKING ACTIVITIES USING INTENTS

An Android application can contain zero or more activities. When your application has more than one activity, you often need to navigate from one to another. In Android, you navigate between activities through what is known as an *intent*.

The best way to understand this very important but somewhat abstract concept in Android is to experience it firsthand and see what it helps you to achieve. The following Try It Out shows how to add another activity to an existing project and then navigate between the two activities.

TRY IT OUT Linking Activities with Intents

codefile UsingIntent.zip available for download at Wrox.com

1. Using Eclipse, create a new Android project and name it **UsingIntent**.

2. Right-click on the package name under the `src` folder and select New ⇨ Class (see Figure 2-9).

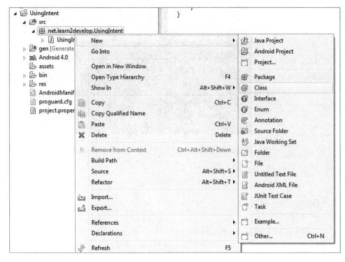

FIGURE 2-9

3. Name the new class **SecondActivity** and click Finish.

4. Add the following statements in bold to the `AndroidManifest.xml` file:

```xml
<?xml version="1.0" encoding="utf-8"?>
<manifest xmlns:android="http://schemas.android.com/apk/res/android"
    package="net.learn2develop.UsingIntent"
    android:versionCode="1"
    android:versionName="1.0" >

    <uses-sdk android:minSdkVersion="14" />

    <application
        android:icon="@drawable/ic_launcher"
        android:label="@string/app_name" >
        <activity
            android:label="@string/app_name"
            android:name=".UsingIntentActivity" >
            <intent-filter >
                <action android:name="android.intent.action.MAIN" />
                <category android:name="android.intent.category.LAUNCHER" />
            </intent-filter>
        </activity>
        <activity
            android:label="Second Activity"
            android:name=".SecondActivity" >
```

```
    <intent-filter >
        <action android:name="net.learn2develop.SecondActivity" />
        <category android:name="android.intent.category.DEFAULT" />
    </intent-filter>
    </activity>
</application>

</manifest>
```

5. Make a copy of the `main.xml` file (in the `res/layout` folder) by right-clicking on it and selecting `Copy`. Then, right-click on the `res/layout` folder and select `Paste`. Name the file `secondactivity.xml`. The `res/layout` folder will now contain the `secondactivity.xml` file (see Figure 2-10).

6. Modify the `secondactivity.xml` file as follows:

FIGURE 2-10

```xml
<?xml version="1.0" encoding="utf-8"?>
<LinearLayout xmlns:android="http://schemas.android.com/apk/res/android"
    android:layout_width="fill_parent"
    android:layout_height="fill_parent"
    android:orientation="vertical" >

    <TextView
        android:layout_width="fill_parent"
        android:layout_height="wrap_content"
        android:text="This is the Second Activity!" />

</LinearLayout>
```

7. In the `SecondActivity.java` file, add the following statements in bold:

```java
package net.learn2develop.UsingIntent;

import android.app.Activity;
import android.os.Bundle;

public class SecondActivity extends Activity{
    @Override
    public void onCreate(Bundle savedInstanceState) {
        super.onCreate(savedInstanceState);
        setContentView(R.layout.secondactivity);
    }
}
```

8. Add the following lines in bold to the `main.xml` file:

```xml
<?xml version="1.0" encoding="utf-8"?>
<LinearLayout xmlns:android="http://schemas.android.com/apk/res/android"
    android:layout_width="fill_parent"
    android:layout_height="fill_parent"
    android:orientation="vertical" >

<Button
```

```
    android:layout_width="fill_parent"
    android:layout_height="wrap_content"
    android:text="Display second activity"
    android:onClick="onClick"/>

</LinearLayout>
```

9. Modify the `UsingIntentActivity.java` file as shown in bold:

```
package net.learn2develop.UsingIntent;

import android.app.Activity;
import android.content.Intent;
import android.os.Bundle;
import android.view.View;

public class UsingIntentActivity extends Activity {
    /** Called when the activity is first created. */
    @Override
    public void onCreate(Bundle savedInstanceState) {
        super.onCreate(savedInstanceState);
        setContentView(R.layout.main);
    }

    public void onClick(View view) {
        startActivity(new Intent("net.learn2develop.SecondActivity"));
    }
}
```

10. Press F11 to debug the application on the Android emulator. When the first activity is loaded, click the button and the second activity will now be loaded (see Figure 2-11).

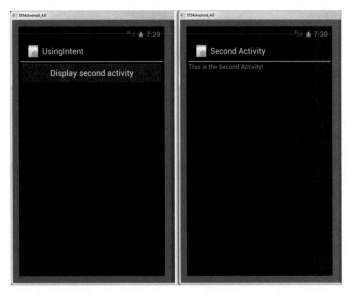

FIGURE 2-11

How It Works

As you have learned, an activity is made up of a UI component (for example, `main.xml`) and a class component (for example, `UsingIntentActivity.java`). Hence, if you want to add another activity to a project, you need to create these two components.

In the `AndroidManifest.xml` file, specifically you have added the following:

```
<activity
    android:label=" Second Activity"
    android:name=".SecondActivity" >
    <intent-filter >
        <action android:name="net.learn2develop.SecondActivity" />
        <category android:name="android.intent.category.DEFAULT" />
    </intent-filter>
</activity>
```

Here, you have added a new activity to the application. Note the following:

➤ The name (class) of the new activity added is `SecondActivity`.

➤ The label for the new activity is named `Second Activity`.

➤ The intent filter name for the new activity is `net.learn2develop.SecondActivity`. Other activities that wish to call this activity will invoke it via this name. Ideally, you should use the reverse domain name of your company as the intent filter name in order to reduce the chances of another application having the same intent filter name. (The next section discusses what happens when two or more activities have the same intent filter.)

➤ The category for the intent filter is `android.intent.category.DEFAULT`. You need to add this to the intent filter so that this activity can be started by another activity using the `startActivity()` method (more on this shortly).

When the button is clicked, you use the `startActivity()` method to display `SecondActivity` by creating an instance of the `Intent` class and passing it the intent filter name of `SecondActivity` (which is `net.learn2develop.SecondActivity`):

```
public void onClick(View view) {
    startActivity(new Intent("net.learn2develop.SecondActivity"));
}
```

Activities in Android can be invoked by any application running on the device. For example, you can create a new Android project and then display `SecondActivity` by using its `net.learn2develop.SecondActivity` intent filter. This is one of the fundamental concepts in Android that enables an application to invoke another easily.

If the activity that you want to invoke is defined within the same project, you can rewrite the preceding statement like this:

```
startActivity(new Intent(this, SecondActivity.class));
```

However, this approach is applicable only when the activity you want to display is within the same project as the current activity.

Resolving Intent Filter Collision

In the previous section, you learned that the `<intent-filter>` element defines how your activity can be invoked by another activity. What happens if another activity (in either the same or a separate application) has the same filter name? For example, suppose your application has another activity named `Activity3`, with the following entry in the `AndroidManifest.xml` file:

```xml
<?xml version="1.0" encoding="utf-8"?>
<manifest xmlns:android="http://schemas.android.com/apk/res/android"
    package="net.learn2develop.UsingIntent"
    android:versionCode="1"
    android:versionName="1.0" >

    <uses-sdk android:minSdkVersion="14" />

    <application
        android:icon="@drawable/ic_launcher"
        android:label="@string/app_name" >
        <activity
            android:label="@string/app_name"
            android:name=".UsingIntentActivity" >
            <intent-filter >
                <action android:name="android.intent.action.MAIN" />
                <category android:name="android.intent.category.LAUNCHER" />
            </intent-filter>
        </activity>
        <activity
            android:label="Second Activity"
            android:name=".SecondActivity" >
            <intent-filter >
                <action android:name="net.learn2develop.SecondActivity" />
                <category android:name="android.intent.category.DEFAULT" />
            </intent-filter>
        </activity>

        <activity
            android:label="Third Activity"
            android:name=".ThirdActivity" >
            <intent-filter >
                <action android:name="net.learn2develop.SecondActivity" />
                <category android:name="android.intent.category.DEFAULT" />
            </intent-filter>
        </activity>

    </application>

</manifest>
```

If you call the `startActivity()` method with the following intent, then the Android OS will display a selection of activities, as shown in Figure 2-12:

```java
startActivity(new Intent("net.learn2develop.SecondActivity"));
```

If you check the "Use by default for this action" item and then select an activity, then the next time the intent "net.learn2develop.SecondActivity" is called again, it will launch the previous activity that you have selected.

To clear this default, go to the Settings application in Android and select Apps ➪ Manage applications, and then select the application name (see Figure 2-13). When the details of the application are shown, scroll down to the bottom and click the Clear defaults button.

FIGURE 2-12

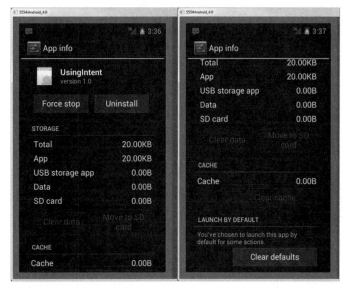

FIGURE 2-13

Returning Results from an Intent

The startActivity() method invokes another activity but does not return a result to the current activity. For example, you may have an activity that prompts the user for user name and password. The information entered by the user in that activity needs to be passed back to the calling activity for further processing. If you need to pass data back from an activity, you should instead use the startActivityForResult() method. The following Try It Out demonstrates this.

TRY IT OUT   Obtaining a Result from an Activity

1. Using the same project from the previous section, add the following statements in bold to the secondactivity.xml file:

```
<?xml version="1.0" encoding="utf-8"?>
<LinearLayout xmlns:android="http://schemas.android.com/apk/res/android"
    android:layout_width="fill_parent"
    android:layout_height="fill_parent"
```

```
            android:orientation="vertical" >

    <TextView
        android:layout_width="fill_parent"
        android:layout_height="wrap_content"
        android:text="This is the Second Activity!" />

    <TextView
        android:layout_width="fill_parent"
        android:layout_height="wrap_content"
        android:text="Please enter your name" />

    <EditText
        android:id="@+id/txt_username"
        android:layout_width="fill_parent"
        android:layout_height="wrap_content" />

    <Button
        android:id="@+id/btn_OK"
        android:layout_width="fill_parent"
        android:layout_height="wrap_content"
        android:text="OK"
        android:onClick="onClick"/>

</LinearLayout>
```

2. Add the following statements in bold to SecondActivity.java:

```
package net.learn2develop.UsingIntent;

import android.app.Activity;
import android.content.Intent;
import android.net.Uri;
import android.os.Bundle;
import android.view.View;
import android.widget.EditText;

public class SecondActivity extends Activity{
    @Override
    public void onCreate(Bundle savedInstanceState) {
        super.onCreate(savedInstanceState);
        setContentView(R.layout.secondactivity);
    }

    public void onClick(View view) {
        Intent data = new Intent();

        //---get the EditText view---
        EditText txt_username =
            (EditText) findViewById(R.id.txt_username);

        //---set the data to pass back---
        data.setData(Uri.parse(
```

```
                    txt_username.getText().toString()));
            setResult(RESULT_OK, data);

            //---closes the activity---
            finish();
        }
    }
```

3. Add the following statements in bold to the `UsingIntentActivity.java` file:

```
package net.learn2develop.UsingIntent;

import android.app.Activity;
import android.content.Intent;
import android.os.Bundle;
import android.view.View;
import android.widget.Toast;

public class UsingIntentActivity extends Activity {
    int request_Code = 1;

    /** Called when the activity is first created. */
    @Override
    public void onCreate(Bundle savedInstanceState) {
        super.onCreate(savedInstanceState);
        setContentView(R.layout.main);
    }

    public void onClick(View view) {
        //startActivity(new Intent("net.learn2develop.SecondActivity"));
        //or
        //startActivity(new Intent(this, SecondActivity.class));
        startActivityForResult(new Intent(
            "net.learn2develop.SecondActivity"),
            request_Code);
    }

    public void onActivityResult(int requestCode, int resultCode, Intent data)
    {
        if (requestCode == request_Code) {
            if (resultCode == RESULT_OK) {
                Toast.makeText(this,data.getData().toString(),
                    Toast.LENGTH_SHORT).show();
            }
        }
    }
}
```

4. Press F11 to debug the application on the Android emulator. When the first activity is loaded, click the button. `SecondActivity` will now be loaded. Enter your name (see Figure 2-14) and click the OK button. The first activity will display the name you have entered using the `Toast` class.

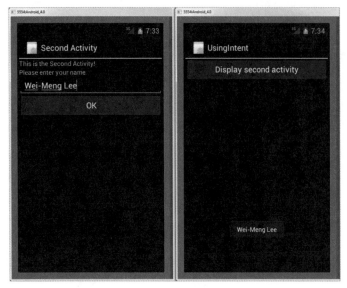

FIGURE 2-14

How It Works

To call an activity and wait for a result to be returned from it, you need to use the
`startActivityForResult()` method, like this:

```
startActivityForResult(new Intent(
    "net.learn2develop.SecondActivity"),
    request_Code);
```

In addition to passing in an `Intent` object, you need to pass in a request code as well. The request code is
simply an integer value that identifies an activity you are calling. This is needed because when an activity
returns a value, you must have a way to identify it. For example, you may be calling multiple activities at the
same time, and some activities may not return immediately (for example, waiting for a reply from a server).
When an activity returns, you need this request code to determine which activity is actually returned.

 NOTE *If the request code is set to -1, then calling it using the*
`startActivityForResult()` *method is equivalent to calling it using*
the `startActivity()` *method. That is, no result will be returned.*

In order for an activity to return a value to the calling activity, you use an `Intent` object to send data
back via the `setData()` method:

```
Intent data = new Intent();

//---get the EditText view---
```

```
EditText txt_username =
    (EditText) findViewById(R.id.txt_username);

//---set the data to pass back---
data.setData(Uri.parse(
    txt_username.getText().toString()));
setResult(RESULT_OK, data);

//---closes the activity---
finish();
```

The setResult() method sets a result code (either RESULT_OK or RESULT_CANCELLED) and the data (an Intent object) to be returned back to the calling activity. The finish() method closes the activity and returns control back to the calling activity.

In the calling activity, you need to implement the onActivityResult() method, which is called whenever an activity returns:

```
public void onActivityResult(int requestCode, int resultCode,
Intent data)
{
    if (requestCode == request_Code) {
        if (resultCode == RESULT_OK) {
            Toast.makeText(this,data.getData().toString(),
                Toast.LENGTH_SHORT).show();
        }
    }
}
```

Here, you check for the appropriate request and result codes and display the result that is returned. The returned result is passed in via the data argument; and you obtain its details through the getData() method.

Passing Data Using an Intent Object

Besides returning data from an activity, it is also common to pass data to an activity. For example, in the previous example you may want to set some default text in the EditText view before the activity is displayed. In this case, you can use the Intent object to pass the data to the target activity.

The following Try It Out shows you the various ways in which you can pass data between activities.

TRY IT OUT   Passing Data to the Target Activity

1.   Using Eclipse, create a new Android project and name it **PassingData**.

2.   Add the following statements in bold to the main.xml file:

```
<?xml version="1.0" encoding="utf-8"?>
<LinearLayout xmlns:android="http://schemas.android.com/apk/res/android"
    android:layout_width="fill_parent"
    android:layout_height="fill_parent"
```

```
            android:orientation="vertical" >

    <Button
        android:id="@+id/btn_SecondActivity"
        android:layout_width="fill_parent"
        android:layout_height="wrap_content"
        android:text="Click to go to Second Activity"
        android:onClick="onClick"/>

</LinearLayout>
```

3. Add a new XML file to the res/layout folder and name it secondactivity.xml. Populate it as follows:

```xml
<?xml version="1.0" encoding="utf-8"?>
<LinearLayout xmlns:android="http://schemas.android.com/apk/res/android"
    android:layout_width="fill_parent"
    android:layout_height="fill_parent"
    android:orientation="vertical" >

<TextView
    android:layout_width="fill_parent"
    android:layout_height="wrap_content"
    android:text="Welcome to Second Activity" />

<Button
    android:id="@+id/btn_MainActivity"
    android:layout_width="fill_parent"
    android:layout_height="wrap_content"
    android:text="Click to return to main activity"
    android:onClick="onClick"/>

</LinearLayout>
```

4. Add a new Class file to the package and name it SecondActivity. Populate the SecondActivity.java file as follows:

```java
package net.learn2develop.PassingData;

import android.app.Activity;
import android.content.Intent;
import android.net.Uri;
import android.os.Bundle;
import android.view.View;
import android.widget.Toast;

public class SecondActivity extends Activity {
    @Override
    public void onCreate(Bundle savedInstanceState) {
        super.onCreate(savedInstanceState);
        setContentView(R.layout.secondactivity);

        //---get the data passed in using getStringExtra()---
        Toast.makeText(this,getIntent().getStringExtra("str1"),
                Toast.LENGTH_SHORT).show();

        //---get the data passed in using getIntExtra()---
```

```
      Toast.makeText(this,Integer.toString(
            getIntent().getIntExtra("age1", 0)),
            Toast.LENGTH_SHORT).show();

      //---get the Bundle object passed in---
      Bundle bundle = getIntent().getExtras();

      //---get the data using the getString()---
      Toast.makeText(this, bundle.getString("str2"),
            Toast.LENGTH_SHORT).show();

      //---get the data using the getInt() method---
      Toast.makeText(this,Integer.toString(bundle.getInt("age2")),
            Toast.LENGTH_SHORT).show();
   }

   public void onClick(View view) {
      //---use an Intent object to return data---
      Intent i = new Intent();

      //---use the putExtra() method to return some
      // value---
      i.putExtra("age3", 45);

      //---use the setData() method to return some value---
      i.setData(Uri.parse(
            "Something passed back to main activity"));

      //---set the result with OK and the Intent object---
      setResult(RESULT_OK, i);

      //---destroy the current activity---
      finish();
   }
}
```

5. Add the following statements in bold to the `AndroidManifest.xml` file:

```xml
<?xml version="1.0" encoding="utf-8"?>
<manifest xmlns:android="http://schemas.android.com/apk/res/android"
    package="net.learn2develop.PassingData"
    android:versionCode="1"
    android:versionName="1.0" >

    <uses-sdk android:minSdkVersion="14" />

    <application
        android:icon="@drawable/ic_launcher"
        android:label="@string/app_name" >
        <activity
            android:label="@string/app_name"
            android:name=".PassingDataActivity" >
            <intent-filter >
                <action android:name="android.intent.action.MAIN" />
                <category android:name="android.intent.category.LAUNCHER" />
            </intent-filter>
        </activity>
```

```
                <activity
                    android:label="Second Activity"
                    android:name=".SecondActivity" >
                    <intent-filter >
                        <action android:name="net.learn2develop.PassingDataSecondActivity" />
                        <category android:name="android.intent.category.DEFAULT" />
                    </intent-filter>
                </activity>
        </application>

    </manifest>
```

6. Add the following statements in bold to the PassingDataActivity.java file:

```java
package net.learn2develop.PassingData;

import android.app.Activity;
import android.content.Intent;
import android.os.Bundle;
import android.view.View;
import android.widget.Toast;

public class PassingDataActivity extends Activity {
    /** Called when the activity is first created. */
    @Override
    public void onCreate(Bundle savedInstanceState) {
        super.onCreate(savedInstanceState);
        setContentView(R.layout.main);
    }

    public void onClick(View view) {
        Intent i = new
                Intent("net.learn2develop.PassingDataSecondActivity");
        //---use putExtra() to add new name/value pairs---
        i.putExtra("str1", "This is a string");
        i.putExtra("age1", 25);

        //---use a Bundle object to add new name/values
        // pairs---
        Bundle extras = new Bundle();
        extras.putString("str2", "This is another string");
        extras.putInt("age2", 35);

        //---attach the Bundle object to the Intent object---
        i.putExtras(extras);

        //---start the activity to get a result back---
        startActivityForResult(i, 1);
    }

    public void onActivityResult(int requestCode,
    int resultCode, Intent data)
    {
        //---check if the request code is 1---
        if (requestCode == 1) {

            //---if the result is OK---
```

```
            if (resultCode == RESULT_OK) {

                //---get the result using getIntExtra()---
                Toast.makeText(this, Integer.toString(
                    data.getIntExtra("age3", 0)),
                    Toast.LENGTH_SHORT).show();

                //---get the result using getData()---
                Toast.makeText(this, data.getData().toString(),
                    Toast.LENGTH_SHORT).show();
            }
        }
    }

}
```

7. Press F11 to debug the application on the Android emulator. Click the button on each activity and observe the values displayed.

How It Works

While this application is not visually exciting, it does illustrate some important ways to pass data between activities.

First, you can use the putExtra() method of an Intent object to add a name/value pair:

```
//---use putExtra() to add new name/value pairs---
i.putExtra("str1", "This is a string");
i.putExtra("age1", 25);
```

The preceding statements add two name/value pairs to the Intent object: one of type string and one of type integer.

Besides using the putExtra() method, you can also create a Bundle object and then attach it using the putExtras() method. Think of a Bundle object as a dictionary object — it contains a set of name/value pairs. The following statements create a Bundle object and then add two name/value pairs to it. It is then attached to the Intent object:

```
//---use a Bundle object to add new name/values pairs---
Bundle extras = new Bundle();
extras.putString("str2", "This is another string");
extras.putInt("age2", 35);

//---attach the Bundle object to the Intent object---
i.putExtras(extras);
```

On the second activity, to obtain the data sent using the Intent object, you first obtain the Intent object using the getIntent() method. Then, call its getStringExtra() method to get the string value set using the putExtra() method:

```
//---get the data passed in using getStringExtra()---
Toast.makeText(this, getIntent().getStringExtra("str1"),
    Toast.LENGTH_SHORT).show();
```

In this case, you have to call the appropriate method to extract the name/value pair based on the type of data set. For the integer value, use the `getIntExtra()` method (the second argument is the default value in case no value is stored in the specified name):

```
//---get the data passed in using getIntExtra()---
Toast.makeText(this,Integer.toString(
        getIntent().getIntExtra("age1", 0)),
        Toast.LENGTH_SHORT).show();
```

To retrieve the `Bundle` object, use the `getExtras()` method:

```
//---get the Bundle object passed in---
Bundle bundle = getIntent().getExtras();
```

To get the individual name/value pairs, use the appropriate method. For the string value, use the `getString()` method:

```
//---get the data using the getString()---
Toast.makeText(this, bundle.getString("str2"),
        Toast.LENGTH_SHORT).show();
```

Likewise, use the `getInt()` method to retrieve an integer value:

```
//---get the data using the getInt() method---
Toast.makeText(this,Integer.toString(bundle.getInt("age2")),
        Toast.LENGTH_SHORT).show();
```

Another way to pass data to an activity is to use the `setData()` method (as used in the previous section), like this:

```
//---use the setData() method to return some value---
i.setData(Uri.parse(
        "Something passed back to main activity"));
```

Usually, you use the `setData()` method to set the data on which an `Intent` object is going to operate (such as passing a URL to an `Intent` object so that it can invoke a web browser to view a web page; see the section "Calling Built-In Applications Using Intents" later in this chapter for more examples).

To retrieve the data set using the `setData()` method, use the `getData()` method (in this example `data` is an `Intent` object):

```
//---get the result using getData()---
Toast.makeText(this, data.getData().toString(),
        Toast.LENGTH_SHORT).show();
```

FRAGMENTS

In the previous section you learned what an activity is and how to use it. In a small-screen device (such as a smartphone), an activity typically fills the entire screen, displaying the various views that make up the user interface of an application. The activity is essentially a container for views. However, when an activity is displayed in a large-screen device, such as on a tablet, it is somewhat out of place. Because the screen is much bigger, all the views in an activity must be arranged to make full use of the increased space, resulting in complex changes to the view hierarchy. A better approach is to have "mini-activities," each containing its own set of views. During runtime, an activity can contain one or more of these mini-activities, depending on the screen orientation in which the device is held. In Android 3.0 and later, these mini-activities are known as *fragments*.

Think of a fragment as another form of activity. You create fragments to contain views, just like activities. Fragments are always embedded in an activity. For example, Figure 2-15 shows two fragments. Fragment 1 might contain a `ListView` showing a list of book titles. Fragment 2 might contain some `TextViews` and `ImageViews` showing some text and images.

Now imagine the application is running on an Android tablet in portrait mode (or on an Android smartphone). In this case, Fragment 1 may be embedded in one activity, while Fragment 2 may be embedded in another activity (see Figure 2-16). When users select an item in the list in Fragment 1, Activity 2 will be started.

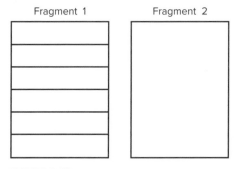

FIGURE 2-15

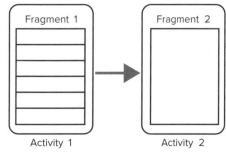

FIGURE 2-16

If the application is now displayed in a tablet in landscape mode, both fragments can be embedded within a single activity, as shown in Figure 2-17.

From this discussion, it becomes apparent that fragments present a versatile way in which you can create the user interface of an Android application. Fragments form the atomic unit of your user interface, and they can be dynamically added (or removed) to activities in order to create the best user experience possible for the target device.

The following Try It Out shows you the basics of working with fragments.

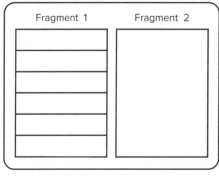

FIGURE 2-17

TRY IT OUT   Using Fragments

codefile Fragments.zip available for download at Wrox.com

1.   Using Eclipse, create a new Android project and name it **Fragments**.

2.   In the `res/layout` folder, add a new file and name it `fragment1.xml`. Populate it with the following:

```xml
<?xml version="1.0" encoding="utf-8"?>
<LinearLayout
    xmlns:android="http://schemas.android.com/apk/res/android"
    android:orientation="vertical"
    android:layout_width="fill_parent"
    android:layout_height="fill_parent"
    android:background="#00FF00"
    >
<TextView
    android:layout_width="fill_parent"
    android:layout_height="wrap_content"
    android:text="This is fragment #1"
    android:textColor="#000000"
    android:textSize="25sp" />
</LinearLayout>
```

3.   Also in the `res/layout` folder, add another new file and name it `fragment2.xml`. Populate it as follows:

```xml
<?xml version="1.0" encoding="utf-8"?>
<LinearLayout
    xmlns:android="http://schemas.android.com/apk/res/android"
    android:orientation="vertical"
    android:layout_width="fill_parent"
    android:layout_height="fill_parent"
    android:background="#FFFE00"
    >
<TextView
    android:layout_width="fill_parent"
    android:layout_height="wrap_content"
    android:text="This is fragment #2"
    android:textColor="#000000"
    android:textSize="25sp" />
</LinearLayout>
```

4.   In `main.xml`, add the following code in bold:

```xml
<?xml version="1.0" encoding="utf-8"?>
<LinearLayout xmlns:android="http://schemas.android.com/apk/res/android"
    android:layout_width="fill_parent"
    android:layout_height="fill_parent"
    android:orientation="horizontal" >

    <fragment
        android:name="net.learn2develop.Fragments.Fragment1"
        android:id="@+id/fragment1"
```

```
        android:layout_weight="1"
        android:layout_width="0px"
        android:layout_height="match_parent" />
    <fragment
        android:name="net.learn2develop.Fragments.Fragment2"
        android:id="@+id/fragment2"
        android:layout_weight="1"
        android:layout_width="0px"
        android:layout_height="match_parent" />

</LinearLayout>
```

5. Under the net.learn2develop.Fragments package name, add two
   Java class files and name them Fragment1.java and Fragment2
   .java (see Figure 2-18).

6. Add the following code to Fragment1.java:

```java
package net.learn2develop.Fragments;

import android.app.Fragment;
import android.os.Bundle;
import android.view.LayoutInflater;
import android.view.View;
import android.view.ViewGroup;

public class Fragment1 extends Fragment {
    @Override
    public View onCreateView(LayoutInflater inflater,
    ViewGroup container, Bundle savedInstanceState) {
        //---Inflate the layout for this fragment---
        return inflater.inflate(
            R.layout.fragment1, container, false);
    }
}
```

7. Add the following code to Fragment2.java:

```java
package net.learn2develop.Fragments;

import android.app.Fragment;
import android.os.Bundle;
import android.view.LayoutInflater;
import android.view.View;
import android.view.ViewGroup;

public class Fragment2 extends Fragment {
    @Override
    public View onCreateView(LayoutInflater inflater,
    ViewGroup container, Bundle savedInstanceState) {
        //---Inflate the layout for this fragment---
        return inflater.inflate(
            R.layout.fragment2, container, false);
    }
}
```

FIGURE 2-18

8. Press F11 to debug the application on the Android emulator. Figure 2-19 shows the two fragments contained within the activity.

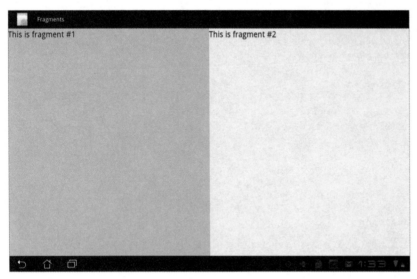

This is fragment #1

This is fragment #2

FIGURE 2-19

How It Works

A fragment behaves very much like an activity — it has a Java class and it loads its UI from an XML file. The XML file contains all the usual UI elements that you expect from an activity: `TextView`, `EditText`, `Button`, and so on. The Java class for a fragment needs to extend the `Fragment` base class:

```
public class Fragment1 extends Fragment {
}
```

> **NOTE** Besides the Fragment base class, a fragment can also extend a few other subclasses of the `Fragment` class, such as `DialogFragment`, `ListFragment`, and `PreferenceFragment`. Chapter 4 discusses these types of fragments in more detail.

To draw the UI for a fragment, you override the `onCreateView()` method. This method needs to return a `View` object, like this:

```
public View onCreateView(LayoutInflater inflater,
ViewGroup container, Bundle savedInstanceState) {
    //---Inflate the layout for this fragment---
    return inflater.inflate(
```

```
                R.layout.fragment1, container, false);
    }
```

Here, you use a `LayoutInflater` object to inflate the UI from the specified XML file (`R.layout`
`.fragment1` in this case). The `container` argument refers to the parent `ViewGroup`, which is the
activity in which you are trying to embed the fragment. The `savedInstanceState` argument enables
you to restore the fragment to its previously saved state.

To add a fragment to an activity, you use the `<fragment>` element:

```xml
<?xml version="1.0" encoding="utf-8"?>
<LinearLayout xmlns:android="http://schemas.android.com/apk/res/android"
    android:layout_width="fill_parent"
    android:layout_height="fill_parent"
    android:orientation="horizontal" >

    <fragment
        android:name="net.learn2develop.Fragments.Fragment1"
        android:id="@+id/fragment1"
        android:layout_weight="1"
        android:layout_width="0px"
        android:layout_height="match_parent" />
    <fragment
        android:name="net.learn2develop.Fragments.Fragment2"
        android:id="@+id/fragment2"
        android:layout_weight="1"
        android:layout_width="0px"
        android:layout_height="match_parent" />

</LinearLayout>
```

Note that each fragment needs a unique identifier. You can assign one via the `android:id` or
`android:tag` attribute.

Adding Fragments Dynamically

While fragments enable you to compartmentalize your UI into various configurable parts,
the real power of fragments is realized when you add them dynamically to activities during
runtime. In the previous section, you saw how you can add fragments to an activity by modifying
the XML file during design time. In reality, it is much more useful if you create fragments and
add them to activities during runtime. This enables you to create a customizable user interface
for your application. For example, if the application is running on a smartphone, you might fill
an activity with a single fragment; if the application is running on a tablet, you might then fill the
activity with two or more fragments, as the tablet has much more screen real estate compared to a
smartphone.

The following Try It Out shows how fragments can be added programmatically to an activity during
runtime.

TRY IT OUT   Adding Fragments during Runtime

1. Using the same project created in the previous section, modify the main.xml file by commenting out the two <fragment> elements:

```xml
<?xml version="1.0" encoding="utf-8"?>
<LinearLayout xmlns:android="http://schemas.android.com/apk/res/android"
    android:layout_width="fill_parent"
    android:layout_height="fill_parent"
    android:orientation="horizontal" >

    <!--
    <fragment
        android:name="net.learn2develop.Fragments.Fragment1"
        android:id="@+id/fragment1"
        android:layout_weight="1"
        android:layout_width="0px"
        android:layout_height="match_parent" />
    <fragment
        android:name="net.learn2develop.Fragments.Fragment2"
        android:id="@+id/fragment2"
        android:layout_weight="1"
        android:layout_width="0px"
        android:layout_height="match_parent" />
    -->
</LinearLayout>
```

2. Add the following code in bold to the FragmentsActivity.java file:

```java
package net.learn2develop.Fragments;

import android.app.Activity;
import android.app.FragmentManager;
import android.app.FragmentTransaction;
import android.os.Bundle;
import android.view.Display;
import android.view.WindowManager;

public class FragmentsActivity extends Activity {
    /** Called when the activity is first created. */
    @Override
    public void onCreate(Bundle savedInstanceState) {
        super.onCreate(savedInstanceState);

        FragmentManager fragmentManager = getFragmentManager();
        FragmentTransaction fragmentTransaction =
                fragmentManager.beginTransaction();

        //---get the current display info---
        WindowManager wm = getWindowManager();
        Display d = wm.getDefaultDisplay();
        if (d.getWidth() > d.getHeight())
        {
            //---landscape mode---
```

```
        Fragment1 fragment1 = new Fragment1();
        // android.R.id.content refers to the content
        // view of the activity
        fragmentTransaction.replace(
                android.R.id.content, fragment1);
    }
    else
    {
        //---portrait mode---
        Fragment2 fragment2 = new Fragment2();
        fragmentTransaction.replace(
                android.R.id.content, fragment2);
    }
    fragmentTransaction.commit();
    }
}
```

3. Press F11 to run the application on the Android emulator. Observe that when the emulator is in portrait mode, fragment 2 (yellow) is displayed (see Figure 2-20). If you press Ctrl+F11 to change the orientation of the emulator to landscape, fragment 1 (green) is shown instead (see Figure 2-21).

FIGURE 2-20   **FIGURE 2-21**

How It Works

To add fragments to an activity, you use the FragmentManager class by first obtaining an instance of it:

```
FragmentManager fragmentManager = getFragmentManager();
```

You also need to use the `FragmentTransaction` class to perform fragment transactions in your activity (such as add, remove or replace):

```
FragmentTransaction fragmentTransaction =
        fragmentManager.beginTransaction();
```

In this example, you used the `WindowManager` to determine whether the device is currently in portrait mode or landscape mode. Once that is determined, you add the appropriate fragment to the activity by creating the fragment and then calling the `replace()` method of the `FragmentTransaction` object to add the fragment to the specified view container (in this case, `android.R.id.content` refers to the content view of the activity):

```
//---landscape mode---
Fragment1 fragment1 = new Fragment1();
// android.R.id.content refers to the content
// view of the activity
fragmentTransaction.replace(
        android.R.id.content, fragment1);
```

Using the `replace()` method is essentially the same as calling the `remove()` method followed by the `add()` method of the `FragmentTransaction` object. To ensure that the changes take effect, you need to call the `commit()` method:

```
fragmentTransaction.commit();
```

Life Cycle of a Fragment

Like activities, fragments have their own life cycle. Understanding the life cycle of a fragment enables you to properly save an instance of the fragment when it is destroyed, and restore it to its previous state when it is recreated.

The following Try It Out examines the various states experienced by a fragment.

TRY IT OUT   Understanding the Life Cycle of a Fragment

codefile Fragments.zip available for download at Wrox.com

1.   Using the same project created in the previous section, add the following code in bold to the `Fragment1.java` file:

```
package net.learn2develop.Fragments;

import android.app.Activity;
import android.app.Fragment;
import android.os.Bundle;
import android.util.Log;
import android.view.LayoutInflater;
import android.view.View;
```

```java
import android.view.ViewGroup;

public class Fragment1 extends Fragment {
    @Override
    public View onCreateView(LayoutInflater inflater,
    ViewGroup container, Bundle savedInstanceState) {

        Log.d("Fragment 1", "onCreateView");

        //---Inflate the layout for this fragment---
        return inflater.inflate(
            R.layout.fragment1, container, false);
    }

    @Override
    public void onAttach(Activity activity) {
        super.onAttach(activity);
        Log.d("Fragment 1", "onAttach");
    }

    @Override
    public void onCreate(Bundle savedInstanceState) {
        super.onCreate(savedInstanceState);
        Log.d("Fragment 1", "onCreate");
    }

    @Override
    public void onActivityCreated(Bundle savedInstanceState) {
        super.onActivityCreated(savedInstanceState);
        Log.d("Fragment 1", "onActivityCreated");
    }

    @Override
    public void onStart() {
        super.onStart();
        Log.d("Fragment 1", "onStart");
    }

    @Override
    public void onResume() {
        super.onResume();
        Log.d("Fragment 1", "onResume");
    }

    @Override
    public void onPause() {
        super.onPause();
        Log.d("Fragment 1", "onPause");
    }

    @Override
    public void onStop() {
        super.onStop();
        Log.d("Fragment 1", "onStop");
```

```
    }

    @Override
    public void onDestroyView() {
        super.onDestroyView();
        Log.d("Fragment 1", "onDestroyView");
    }

    @Override
    public void onDestroy() {
        super.onDestroy();
        Log.d("Fragment 1", "onDestroy");
    }

    @Override
    public void onDetach() {
        super.onDetach();
        Log.d("Fragment 1", "onDetach");
    }

}
```

2. Switch the Android emulator to landscape mode by pressing Ctrl+F11.

3. Press F11 in Eclipse to debug the application on the Android emulator.

4. When the application is loaded on the emulator, the following is displayed in the LogCat window (Windows ⇨ Show View ⇨ LogCat):

```
12-09 04:17:43.436: D/Fragment 1(2995): onAttach
12-09 04:17:43.466: D/Fragment 1(2995): onCreate
12-09 04:17:43.476: D/Fragment 1(2995): onCreateView
12-09 04:17:43.506: D/Fragment 1(2995): onActivityCreated
12-09 04:17:43.506: D/Fragment 1(2995): onStart
12-09 04:17:43.537: D/Fragment 1(2995): onResume
```

5. Click the Home button on the emulator. The following output will be displayed in the LogCat window:

```
12-09 04:18:47.696: D/Fragment 1(2995): onPause
12-09 04:18:50.346: D/Fragment 1(2995): onStop
```

6. On the emulator, click the Home button and hold it. Launch the application again. This time, the following is displayed:

```
12-09 04:20:08.726: D/Fragment 1(2995): onStart
12-09 04:20:08.766: D/Fragment 1(2995): onResume
```

7. Finally, click the Back button on the emulator. Now you should see the following output:

```
12-09 04:21:01.426: D/Fragment 1(2995): onPause
12-09 04:21:02.346: D/Fragment 1(2995): onStop
12-09 04:21:02.346: D/Fragment 1(2995): onDestroyView
```

```
12-09 04:21:02.346: D/Fragment 1(2995): onDestroy
12-09 04:21:02.346: D/Fragment 1(2995): onDetach
```

How It Works

Like activities, fragments in Android also have their own life cycle. As you have seen, when a fragment is being created, it goes through the following states:

➤ onAttach()

➤ onCreate()

➤ onCreateView()

➤ onActivityCreated()

When the fragment becomes visible, it goes through these states:

➤ onStart()

➤ onResume()

When the fragment goes into the background mode, it goes through these states:

➤ onPause()

➤ onStop()

When the fragment is destroyed (when the activity it is currently hosted in is destroyed), it goes through the following states:

➤ onPause()

➤ onStop()

➤ onDestroyView()

➤ onDestroy()

➤ onDetach()

Like activities, you can restore an instance of a fragment using a Bundle object, in the following states:

➤ onCreate()

➤ onCreateView()

➤ onActivityCreated()

 NOTE *You can save a fragment's state in the* onSaveInstanceState() *method. Chapter 3 discusses this topic in more detail.*

Most of the states experienced by a fragment are similar to those of activities. However, a few new states are specific to fragments:

➤ onAttached() — Called when the fragment has been associated with the activity

➤ onCreateView() — Called to create the view for the fragment

➤ onActivityCreated() — Called when the activity's onCreate() method has been returned

➤ onDestroyView() — Called when the fragment's view is being removed

➤ onDetach() — Called when the fragment is detached from the activity

Note one of the main differences between activities and fragments: When an activity goes into the background, the activity is placed in the back stack. This allows the activity to be resumed when the user presses the Back button. In the case of fragments, however, they are not automatically placed in the back stack when they go into the background. Rather, to place a fragment into the back stack, you need to explicitly call the addToBackStack() method during a fragment transaction, like this:

```
//---get the current display info---
WindowManager wm = getWindowManager();
Display d = wm.getDefaultDisplay();
if (d.getWidth() > d.getHeight())
{
    //---landscape mode---
    Fragment1 fragment1 = new Fragment1();
    // android.R.id.content refers to the content
    // view of the activity
    fragmentTransaction.replace(
            android.R.id.content, fragment1);
}
else
{
    //---portrait mode---
    Fragment2 fragment2 = new Fragment2();
    fragmentTransaction.replace(
            android.R.id.content, fragment2);
}
//---add to the back stack---
fragmentTransaction.addToBackStack(null);
fragmentTransaction.commit();
```

The preceding code ensures that after the fragment has been added to the activity, the user can click the Back button to remove it.

Interactions between Fragments

Very often, an activity may contain one or more fragments working together to present a coherent UI to the user. In this case, it is very important for fragments to communicate with one another and exchange data. For example, one fragment might contain a list of items (such as postings from an RSS feed) and when the user taps on an item in that fragment, details about the selected item may be displayed in another fragment.

The following Try It Out shows how one fragment can access the views contained within another fragment.

TRY IT OUT Communication between Fragments

1. Using the same project created in the previous section, add the following statement in bold to the
Fragment1.xml file:

```xml
<?xml version="1.0" encoding="utf-8"?>
<LinearLayout
    xmlns:android="http://schemas.android.com/apk/res/android"
    android:orientation="vertical"
    android:layout_width="fill_parent"
    android:layout_height="fill_parent"
    android:background="#00FF00" >
<TextView
    android:id="@+id/lblFragment1"
    android:layout_width="fill_parent"
    android:layout_height="wrap_content"
    android:text="This is fragment #1"
    android:textColor="#000000"
    android:textSize="25sp" />
</LinearLayout>
```

2. Add the following lines in bold to fragment2.xml:

```xml
<?xml version="1.0" encoding="utf-8"?>
<LinearLayout
    xmlns:android="http://schemas.android.com/apk/res/android"
    android:orientation="vertical"
    android:layout_width="fill_parent"
    android:layout_height="fill_parent"
    android:background="#FFFE00" >
<TextView
    android:layout_width="fill_parent"
    android:layout_height="wrap_content"
    android:text="This is fragment #2"
    android:textColor="#000000"
    android:textSize="25sp" />

<Button
    android:id="@+id/btnGetText"
    android:layout_width="wrap_content"
    android:layout_height="wrap_content"
    android:text="Get text in Fragment #1"
    android:textColor="#000000"
    android:onClick="onClick" />

</LinearLayout>
```

3. Put back the two fragments in main.xml:

```xml
<?xml version="1.0" encoding="utf-8"?>
<LinearLayout xmlns:android="http://schemas.android.com/apk/res/android"
```

```
      android:layout_width="fill_parent"
      android:layout_height="fill_parent"
      android:orientation="horizontal" >

  <fragment
      android:name="net.learn2develop.Fragments.Fragment1"
      android:id="@+id/fragment1"
      android:layout_weight="1"
      android:layout_width="0px"
      android:layout_height="match_parent" />
  <fragment
      android:name="net.learn2develop.Fragments.Fragment2"
      android:id="@+id/fragment2"
      android:layout_weight="1"
      android:layout_width="0px"
      android:layout_height="match_parent" />

</LinearLayout>
```

4. Modify the `FragmentsActivity.java` file by commenting out the code that you added in the earlier sections. It should look like this after modification:

```java
public class FragmentsActivity extends Activity {
    /** Called when the activity is first created. */
    @Override
    public void onCreate(Bundle savedInstanceState) {
        super.onCreate(savedInstanceState);
        setContentView(R.layout.main);
        /*
        FragmentManager fragmentManager = getFragmentManager();
        FragmentTransaction fragmentTransaction =
                fragmentManager.beginTransaction();

        //---get the current display info---
        WindowManager wm = getWindowManager();
        Display d = wm.getDefaultDisplay();
        if (d.getWidth() > d.getHeight())
        {
            //---landscape mode---
            Fragment1 fragment1 = new Fragment1();
            // android.R.id.content refers to the content
            // view of the activity
            fragmentTransaction.replace(
                    android.R.id.content, fragment1);
        }
        else
        {
            //---portrait mode---
            Fragment2 fragment2 = new Fragment2();
            fragmentTransaction.replace(
                    android.R.id.content, fragment2);
        }
```

```
                    //---add to the back stack---
                    fragmentTransaction.addToBackStack(null);
                    fragmentTransaction.commit();
                    */
            }
      }
```

5. Add the following statements in bold to the `Fragment2.java` file:

```
package net.learn2develop.Fragments;

import android.app.Fragment;
import android.os.Bundle;
import android.view.LayoutInflater;
import android.view.View;
import android.view.ViewGroup;
import android.widget.Button;
import android.widget.TextView;
import android.widget.Toast;

public class Fragment2 extends Fragment {
    @Override
    public View onCreateView(LayoutInflater inflater,
    ViewGroup container, Bundle savedInstanceState) {
        //---Inflate the layout for this fragment---
        return inflater.inflate(
            R.layout.fragment2, container, false);
    }

    @Override
    public void onStart() {
        super.onStart();
        //---Button view---
        Button btnGetText = (Button)
            getActivity().findViewById(R.id.btnGetText);
        btnGetText.setOnClickListener(new View.OnClickListener() {
            public void onClick(View v) {
                TextView lbl = (TextView)
                    getActivity().findViewById(R.id.lblFragment1);
                Toast.makeText(getActivity(), lbl.getText(),
                    Toast.LENGTH_SHORT).show();
            }
        });
    }

}
```

6. Press F11 to debug the application on the Android emulator. In the second fragment on the right, click the button. You should see the `Toast` class displaying the text "This is fragment #1" (see Figure 2-22).

FIGURE 2-22

How It Works

Because fragments are embedded within activities, you can obtain the activity in which a fragment is currently embedded by first using the getActivity() method and then using the findViewById() method to locate the view(s) contained within the fragment:

```
TextView lbl = (TextView)
    getActivity().findViewById(R.id.lblFragment1);
Toast.makeText(getActivity(), lbl.getText(),
    Toast.LENGTH_SHORT).show();
```

The getActivity() method returns the activity with which the current fragment is currently associated.

Alternatively, you can also add the following method to the FragmentsActivity.java file:

```
public void onClick(View v) {
    TextView lbl = (TextView)
        findViewById(R.id.lblFragment1);
    Toast.makeText(this, lbl.getText(),
        Toast.LENGTH_SHORT).show();
}
```

CALLING BUILT-IN APPLICATIONS USING INTENTS

Until this point, you have seen how to call activities within your own application. One of the key aspects of Android programming is using the intent to call activities from other applications. In particular, your application can call the many built-in applications that are included with an Android device. For example, if your application needs to load a web page, you can use the `Intent` object to invoke the built-in web browser to display the web page, instead of building your own web browser for this purpose.

The following Try It Out demonstrates how to call some of the built-in applications commonly found on an Android device.

TRY IT OUT Calling Built-In Applications Using Intents

codefile Intents.zip available for download at Wrox.com

1. Using Eclipse, create a new Android project and name it **Intents**.

2. Add the following statements in bold to the `main.xml` file:

```xml
<?xml version="1.0" encoding="utf-8"?>
<LinearLayout xmlns:android="http://schemas.android.com/apk/res/android"
    android:layout_width="fill_parent"
    android:layout_height="fill_parent"
    android:orientation="vertical" >

<Button
    android:id="@+id/btn_webbrowser"
    android:layout_width="fill_parent"
    android:layout_height="wrap_content"
    android:text="Web Browser"
    android:onClick="onClickWebBrowser" />

<Button
    android:id="@+id/btn_makecalls"
    android:layout_width="fill_parent"
    android:layout_height="wrap_content"
    android:text="Make Calls"
    android:onClick="onClickMakeCalls" />

<Button
    android:id="@+id/btn_showMap"
    android:layout_width="fill_parent"
    android:layout_height="wrap_content"
    android:text="Show Map"
    android:onClick="onClickShowMap" />

</LinearLayout>
```

3. Add the following statements in bold to the `IntentsActivity.java` file:

```java
package net.learn2develop.Intents;

import android.app.Activity;
import android.content.Intent;
import android.net.Uri;
import android.os.Bundle;
import android.view.View;

public class IntentsActivity extends Activity {

    int request_Code = 1;

    /** Called when the activity is first created. */
    @Override
    public void onCreate(Bundle savedInstanceState) {
        super.onCreate(savedInstanceState);
        setContentView(R.layout.main);
    }

    public void onClickWebBrowser(View view) {
        Intent i = new
                Intent(android.content.Intent.ACTION_VIEW,
                        Uri.parse("http://www.amazon.com"));
        startActivity(i);
    }

    public void onClickMakeCalls(View view) {
        Intent i = new
                Intent(android.content.Intent.ACTION_DIAL,
                        Uri.parse("tel:+651234567"));
        startActivity(i);
    }

    public void onClickShowMap(View view) {
        Intent i = new
                Intent(android.content.Intent.ACTION_VIEW,
                        Uri.parse("geo:37.827500,-122.481670"));
        startActivity(i);
    }
}
```

4. Press F11 to debug the application on the Android emulator.

5. Click the Web Browser button to load the Browser application on the emulator. Figure 2-23 shows the built-in Browser application displaying the site www.amazon.com.

6. Click the Make Calls button and the Phone application, as shown in Figure 2-24, will load.

FIGURE 2-23

FIGURE 2-24

7. Similarly, to load the Maps application, shown in Figure 2-25, click the Show Map button.

> **NOTE** *In order to display the Maps application, you need to run the application on an AVD that supports the Google APIs.*

How It Works

In this example, you saw how you can use the Intent class to invoke some of the built-in applications in Android (such as Maps, Phone, Contacts, and Browser).

In Android, intents usually come in pairs: *action* and *data*. The *action* describes what is to be performed, such as editing an item, viewing the content of an item, and so on. The *data* specifies what is affected, such as a person in the Contacts database. The data is specified as an Uri object.

Some examples of action are as follows:

➤ ACTION_VIEW

➤ ACTION_DIAL

➤ ACTION_PICK

FIGURE 2-25

Some examples of data include the following:

➤ www.google.com

➤ tel:+651234567

➤ geo:37.827500,-122.481670

➤ content://contacts

 NOTE *The section "Using Intent Filters" explains the type of data you can define for use in an activity.*

Collectively, the action and data pair describes the operation to be performed. For example, to dial a phone number, you would use the pair ACTION_DIAL/tel:+651234567. To display a list of contacts stored in your phone, you use the pair ACTION_VIEW/content://contacts. To pick a contact from the list of contacts, you use the pair ACTION_PICK/content://contacts.

In the first button, you create an Intent object and then pass two arguments to its constructor, the action and the data:

```
Intent i = new
        Intent(android.content.Intent.ACTION_VIEW,
            Uri.parse("http://www.amazon.com"));
startActivity(i);
```

The action here is represented by the android.content.Intent.ACTION_VIEW constant. You use the parse() method of the Uri class to convert a URL string into a Uri object.

The android.content.Intent.ACTION_VIEW constant actually refers to the "android.intent .action.VIEW" action, so the preceding could be rewritten as follows:

```
Intent i = new
        Intent("android.intent.action.VIEW",
            Uri.parse("http://www.amazon.com"));
startActivity(i);
```

The preceding code snippet can also be rewritten like this:

```
Intent i = new
        Intent("android.intent.action.VIEW");
i.setData(Uri.parse("http://www.amazon.com"));
startActivity(i);
```

Here, you set the data separately using the setData() method.

For the second button, you dial a specific number by passing in the telephone number in the data portion:

```
Intent i = new
        Intent(android.content.Intent.ACTION_DIAL,
            Uri.parse("tel:+651234567"));
startActivity(i);
```

In this case, the dialer will display the number to be called. The user must still press the dial button to dial the number. If you want to directly call the number without user intervention, change the action as follows:

```
Intent i = new
          Intent(android.content.Intent.ACTION_CALL,
                Uri.parse("tel:+651234567"));
startActivity(i);
```

 NOTE *If you want your application to directly call the specified number, you need to add the* android.permission.CALL_PHONE *permission to your application.*

To display the dialer without specifying any number, simply omit the data portion, like this:

```
Intent i = new
          Intent(android.content.Intent.ACTION_DIAL);
startActivity(i);
```

The third button displays a map using the ACTION_VIEW constant:

```
Intent i = new
          Intent(android.content.Intent.ACTION_VIEW,
                Uri.parse("geo:37.827500,-122.481670"));
startActivity(i);
```

Here, instead of using "http" you use the "geo" scheme.

Understanding the Intent Object

So far, you have seen the use of the Intent object to call other activities. This is a good time to recap and gain a more detailed understanding of how the Intent object performs its magic.

First, you learned that you can call another activity by passing its action to the constructor of an Intent object:

```
startActivity(new Intent("net.learn2develop.SecondActivity"));
```

The action (in this example "net.learn2develop.SecondActivity") is also known as the *component name*. This is used to identify the target activity/application that you want to invoke. You can also rewrite the component name by specifying the class name of the activity if it resides in your project, like this:

```
startActivity(new Intent(this, SecondActivity.class));
```

You can also create an `Intent` object by passing in an action constant and data, such as the following:

```
Intent i = new
        Intent(android.content.Intent.ACTION_VIEW,
                Uri.parse("http://www.amazon.com"));
startActivity(i);
```

The action portion defines what you want to do, while the data portion contains the data for the target activity to act upon. You can also pass the data to the `Intent` object using the `setData()` method:

```
Intent i = new
        Intent("android.intent.action.VIEW");
i.setData(Uri.parse("http://www.amazon.com"));
```

In this example, you indicate that you want to view a web page with the specified URL. The Android OS will look for all activities that are able to satisfy your request. This process is known as *intent resolution*. The next section discusses in more detail how your activities can be the target of other activities.

For some intents, there is no need to specify the data. For example, to select a contact from the Contacts application, you specify the action and then indicate the MIME type using the `setType()` method:

```
Intent i = new
        Intent(android.content.Intent.ACTION_PICK);
i.setType(ContactsContract.Contacts.CONTENT_TYPE);
```

 NOTE *Chapter 7 discusses how to use the Contacts application from within your application.*

The `setType()` method explicitly specifies the MIME data type to indicate the type of data to return. The MIME type for `ContactsContract.Contacts.CONTENT_TYPE` is `"vnd.android .cursor.dir/contact"`.

Besides specifying the action, the data, and the type, an `Intent` object can also specify a category. A category groups activities into logical units so that Android can use it for further filtering. The next section discusses categories in more detail.

To summarize, an `Intent` object can contain the following information:

➤ Action

➤ Data

➤ Type

➤ Category

Using Intent Filters

Earlier, you saw how an activity can invoke another activity using the Intent object. In order for other activities to invoke your activity, you need to specify the action and category within the <intent-filter> element in the AndroidManifest.xml file, like this:

```
<intent-filter >
    <action android:name="net.learn2develop.SecondActivity" />
    <category android:name="android.intent.category.DEFAULT" />
</intent-filter>
```

This is a very simple example in which one activity calls another using the "net.learn2develop .SecondActivity" action. The following Try It Out shows you a more sophisticated example.

TRY IT OUT Specifying Intent Filters in More Detail

1. Using the Intents project created earlier, add a new class to the project and name it MyBrowserActivity. Also add a new XML file to the res/layout folder and name it **browser.xml.**

2. Add the following statements in bold to the AndroidManifest.xml file:

```
<?xml version="1.0" encoding="utf-8"?>
<manifest xmlns:android="http://schemas.android.com/apk/res/android"
    package="net.learn2develop.Intents"
    android:versionCode="1"
    android:versionName="1.0" >

    <uses-sdk android:minSdkVersion="14" />
    <uses-permission android:name="android.permission.CALL_PHONE"/>
    <uses-permission android:name="android.permission.INTERNET"/>
    <application
        android:icon="@drawable/ic_launcher"
        android:label="@string/app_name" >
        <activity
            android:label="@string/app_name"
            android:name=".IntentsActivity" >
            <intent-filter >
                <action android:name="android.intent.action.MAIN" />
                <category android:name="android.intent.category.LAUNCHER" />
            </intent-filter>
        </activity>
        <activity android:name=".MyBrowserActivity"
                android:label="@string/app_name">
            <intent-filter>
                <action android:name="android.intent.action.VIEW" />
                <action android:name="net.learn2develop.MyBrowser" />
                <category android:name="android.intent.category.DEFAULT" />
                <data android:scheme="http" />
            </intent-filter>
        </activity>

    </application>

</manifest>
```

3. Add the following statements in bold to the main.xml file:

```xml
<?xml version="1.0" encoding="utf-8"?>
<LinearLayout xmlns:android="http://schemas.android.com/apk/res/android"
    android:layout_width="fill_parent"
    android:layout_height="fill_parent"
    android:orientation="vertical" >

<Button
    android:id="@+id/btn_webbrowser"
    android:layout_width="fill_parent"
    android:layout_height="wrap_content"
    android:text="Web Browser"
    android:onClick="onClickWebBrowser" />

<Button
    android:id="@+id/btn_makecalls"
    android:layout_width="fill_parent"
    android:layout_height="wrap_content"
    android:text="Make Calls"
    android:onClick="onClickMakeCalls"  />

<Button
    android:id="@+id/btn_showMap"
    android:layout_width="fill_parent"
    android:layout_height="wrap_content"
    android:text="Show Map"
    android:onClick="onClickShowMap" />

<Button
    android:id="@+id/btn_launchMyBrowser"
    android:layout_width="fill_parent"
    android:layout_height="wrap_content"
    android:text="Launch My Browser"
    android:onClick="onClickLaunchMyBrowser" />

</LinearLayout>
```

4. Add the following statements in bold to the IntentsActivity.java file:

```java
package net.learn2develop.Intents;

import android.app.Activity;
import android.content.Intent;
import android.net.Uri;
import android.os.Bundle;
import android.view.View;

public class IntentsActivity extends Activity {

    int request_Code = 1;

    /** Called when the activity is first created. */
```

```java
    @Override
    public void onCreate(Bundle savedInstanceState) { … }

    public void onClickWebBrowser(View view) { … }

    public void onClickMakeCalls(View view) { ... }

    public void onClickShowMap(View view) { ... }

    public void onClickLaunchMyBrowser(View view) {
        Intent i = new
                Intent("net.learn2develop.MyBrowser");
        i.setData(Uri.parse("http://www.amazon.com"));
        startActivity(i);
    }

}
```

5. Add the following statements in bold to the browser.xml file:

```xml
<?xml version="1.0" encoding="utf-8"?>
<LinearLayout xmlns:android="http://schemas.android.com/apk/res/android"
    android:orientation="vertical"
    android:layout_width="fill_parent"
    android:layout_height="fill_parent" >
<WebView
    android:id="@+id/WebView01"
    android:layout_width="wrap_content"
    android:layout_height="wrap_content" />
</LinearLayout>
```

6. Add the following statements in bold to the MyBrowserActivity.java file:

```java
package net.learn2develop.Intents;

import android.app.Activity;
import android.net.Uri;
import android.os.Bundle;
import android.webkit.WebView;
import android.webkit.WebViewClient;

public class MyBrowserActivity extends Activity {
    @Override
    public void onCreate(Bundle savedInstanceState) {
        super.onCreate(savedInstanceState);
        setContentView(R.layout.browser);

        Uri url = getIntent().getData();
        WebView webView = (WebView) findViewById(R.id.WebView01);
        webView.setWebViewClient(new Callback());
```

```
        webView.loadUrl(url.toString());
}

private class Callback extends WebViewClient {
    @Override
    public boolean shouldOverrideUrlLoading
    (WebView view, String url) {
        return(false);
    }
}
}
```

7. Press F11 to debug the application on the Android emulator.

8. Click the Launch my Browser button and you should see the new activity displaying the Amazon.com web page (see Figure 2-26).

How It Works

In this example, you created a new activity named MyBrowserActivity. You first needed to declare it in the AndroidManifest.xml file:

FIGURE 2-26

```xml
<activity android:name=".MyBrowserActivity"
        android:label="@string/app_name">
    <intent-filter>
        <action android:name="android.intent.action.VIEW" />
        <action android:name="net.learn2develop.MyBrowser" />
        <category android:name="android.intent.category.DEFAULT" />
        <data android:scheme="http" />
    </intent-filter>
</activity>
```

In the <intent-filter> element, you declared it to have two actions, one category, and one data. This means that all other activities can invoke this activity using either the "android.intent.action .VIEW" or the "net.learn2develop.MyBrowser" action. For all activities that you want others to call using the startActivity() or startActivityForResult() methods, they need to have the "android.intent.category.DEFAULT" category. If not, your activity will not be callable by others. The <data> element specifies the type of data expected by the activity. In this case, it expects the data to start with the "http://" prefix.

The preceding intent filter could also be rewritten as follows:

```xml
<activity android:name=".MyBrowserActivity"
        android:label="@string/app_name">
    <intent-filter>
        <action android:name="android.intent.action.VIEW" />
        <category android:name="android.intent.category.DEFAULT" />
        <data android:scheme="http" />
    </intent-filter>
    <intent-filter>
        <action android:name="net.learn2develop.MyBrowser" />
        <category android:name="android.intent.category.DEFAULT" />
```

```
                    <data android:scheme="http" />
                </intent-filter>
            </activity>
```

Writing the intent filter this way makes it much more readable, and it logically groups the action, category, and data within an intent filter.

If you now use the ACTION_VIEW action with the data shown here, Android will display a selection (as shown in Figure 2-27):

```
Intent i = new
        Intent(android.content.Intent.ACTION_VIEW,
            Uri.parse("http://www.amazon.com"));
```

You can choose between using the Browser application or the Intents application that you are currently building.

FIGURE 2-27

Notice that when multiple activities match your Intent object, the dialog titled "Complete action using" appears. You can customize this by using the createChooser() method from the Intent class, like this:

```
Intent i = new
        Intent(android.content.Intent.ACTION_VIEW,
            Uri.parse("http://www.amazon.com"));
startActivity(Intent.createChooser(i, "Open URL using..."));
```

The preceding will change the dialog title to "Open URL using...," as shown in Figure 2-28. Note that the "Use by default for this action" option is now not available.

The added benefit of using the createChooser() method is that in the event that no activity matches your Intent object, your application will not crash. Instead, it will display the message shown in Figure 2-29.

FIGURE 2-28

FIGURE 2-29

Adding Categories

You can group your activities into categories by using the `<category>` element in the intent filter. Suppose you have added the following `<category>` element to the `AndroidManifest.xml` file:

```xml
<?xml version="1.0" encoding="utf-8"?>
<manifest xmlns:android="http://schemas.android.com/apk/res/android"
    package="net.learn2develop.Intents"
    android:versionCode="1"
    android:versionName="1.0" >

    <uses-sdk android:minSdkVersion="14" />
    <uses-permission android:name="android.permission.CALL_PHONE"/>
    <uses-permission android:name="android.permission.INTERNET"/>
    <application
        android:icon="@drawable/ic_launcher"
        android:label="@string/app_name" >
        <activity
            android:label="@string/app_name"
            android:name=".IntentsActivity" >
            <intent-filter >
                <action android:name="android.intent.action.MAIN" />
                <category android:name="android.intent.category.LAUNCHER" />
            </intent-filter>
        </activity>

        <activity android:name=".MyBrowserActivity"
                android:label="@string/app_name">
            <intent-filter>
                <action android:name="android.intent.action.VIEW" />
                <action android:name="net.learn2develop.MyBrowser" />
                <category android:name="android.intent.category.DEFAULT" />
                <category android:name="net.learn2develop.Apps" />
                <data android:scheme="http" />
            </intent-filter>
        </activity>

    </application>

</manifest>
```

In this case, the following code will directly invoke the `MyBrowerActivity` activity:

```java
Intent i = new
        Intent(android.content.Intent.ACTION_VIEW,
            Uri.parse("http://www.amazon.com"));
i.addCategory("net.learn2develop.Apps");
startActivity(Intent.createChooser(i, "Open URL using..."));
```

You add the category to the `Intent` object using the `addCategory()` method. If you omit the `addCategory()` statement, the preceding code will still invoke the `MyBrowerActivity` activity because it will still match the default category `android.intent.category.DEFAULT`.

However, if you specify a category that does not match the category defined in the intent filter, it will not work (no activity will be launched):

```
Intent i = new
        Intent(android.content.Intent.ACTION_VIEW,
            Uri.parse("http://www.amazon.com"));
//i.addCategory("net.learn2develop.Apps");
//---this category does not match any in the intent-filter---
i.addCategory("net.learn2develop.OtherApps");
startActivity(Intent.createChooser(i, "Open URL using..."));
```

The preceding category (net.learn2develop.OtherApps) does not match any category in the intent filter, so a run-time exception will be raised (if you don't use the createChoose() method of the Intent class).

If you add the following category in the intent filter of MyBrowerActivity, then the preceding code will work:

```
<activity android:name=".MyBrowserActivity"
        android:label="@string/app_name">
    <intent-filter>
        <action android:name="android.intent.action.VIEW" />
        <action android:name="net.learn2develop.MyBrowser" />
        <category android:name="android.intent.category.DEFAULT" />
        <category android:name="net.learn2develop.Apps" />
        <category android:name="net.learn2develop.OtherApps" />
        <data android:scheme="http" />
    </intent-filter>
</activity>
```

You can add multiple categories to an Intent object; for example, the following statements add the net.learn2develop.SomeOtherApps category to the Intent object:

```
Intent i = new
        Intent(android.content.Intent.ACTION_VIEW,
            Uri.parse("http://www.amazon.com"));
//i.addCategory("net.learn2develop.Apps");
//---this category does not match any in the intent-filter---
i.addCategory("net.learn2develop.OtherApps");
i.addCategory("net.learn2develop.SomeOtherApps");
startActivity(Intent.createChooser(i, "Open URL using..."));
```

Because the intent filter does not define the net.learn2develop.SomeOtherApps category, the preceding code will not be able to invoke the MyBrowerActivity activity. To fix this, you need to add the net.learn2develop.SomeOtherApps category to the intent filter again.

From this example, it is evident that when using an Intent object with categories, all categories added to the Intent object must fully match those defined in the intent filter before an activity can be invoked.

DISPLAYING NOTIFICATIONS

So far, you have been using the Toast class to display messages to the user. While the Toast class is a handy way to show users alerts, it is not persistent. It flashes on the screen for a few seconds and then disappears. If it contains important information, users may easily miss it if they are not looking at the screen.

For messages that are important, you should use a more persistent method. In this case, you should use the NotificationManager to display a persistent message at the top of the device, commonly known as the *status bar* (sometimes also referred to as the *notification bar*). The following Try It Out demonstrates how.

TRY IT OUT Displaying Notifications on the Status Bar

codefile Notifications.zip available for download at Wrox.com

1. Using Eclipse, create a new Android project and name it **Notifications**.

2. Add a new class file named NotificationView to the package. In addition, add a new notification.xml file to the res/layout folder.

3. Populate the notification.xml file as follows:

```xml
<?xml version="1.0" encoding="utf-8"?>
<LinearLayout xmlns:android="http://schemas.android.com/apk/res/android"
    android:orientation="vertical"
    android:layout_width="fill_parent"
    android:layout_height="fill_parent" >
<TextView
    android:layout_width="fill_parent"
    android:layout_height="wrap_content"
    android:text="Here are the details for the notification..." />
</LinearLayout>
```

4. Populate the NotificationView.java file as follows:

```java
package net.learn2develop.Notifications;

import android.app.Activity;
import android.app.NotificationManager;
import android.os.Bundle;

public class NotificationView extends Activity
{
    @Override
    public void onCreate(Bundle savedInstanceState)
    {
        super.onCreate(savedInstanceState);
        setContentView(R.layout.notification);

        //---look up the notification manager service---
        NotificationManager nm = (NotificationManager)
```

```
                getSystemService(NOTIFICATION_SERVICE);

        //---cancel the notification that we started---
        nm.cancel(getIntent().getExtras().getInt("notificationID"));
    }
}
```

5. Add the following statements in bold to the AndroidManifest.xml file:

```xml
<?xml version="1.0" encoding="utf-8"?>
<manifest xmlns:android="http://schemas.android.com/apk/res/android"
    package="net.learn2develop.Notifications"
    android:versionCode="1"
    android:versionName="1.0" >

    <uses-sdk android:minSdkVersion="14" />
    <uses-permission android:name="android.permission.VIBRATE"/>

    <application
        android:icon="@drawable/ic_launcher"
        android:label="@string/app_name" >
        <activity
            android:label="@string/app_name"
            android:name=".NotificationsActivity" >
            <intent-filter >
                <action android:name="android.intent.action.MAIN" />

                <category android:name="android.intent.category.LAUNCHER" />
            </intent-filter>
        </activity>
        <activity android:name=".NotificationView"
            android:label="Details of notification">
            <intent-filter>
                <action android:name="android.intent.action.MAIN" />
                <category android:name="android.intent.category.DEFAULT" />
            </intent-filter>
        </activity>
    </application>

</manifest>
```

6. Add the following statements in bold to the main.xml file:

```xml
<?xml version="1.0" encoding="utf-8"?>
<LinearLayout xmlns:android="http://schemas.android.com/apk/res/android"
    android:layout_width="fill_parent"
    android:layout_height="fill_parent"
    android:orientation="vertical" >

<Button
    android:id="@+id/btn_displaynotif"
    android:layout_width="fill_parent"
    android:layout_height="wrap_content"
    android:text="Display Notification"
    android:onClick="onClick"/>

</LinearLayout>
```

7. Finally, add the following statements in bold to the `NotificationsActivity.java` file:

```java
package net.learn2develop.Notifications;

import android.app.Activity;
import android.app.Notification;
import android.app.NotificationManager;
import android.app.PendingIntent;
import android.content.Intent;
import android.os.Bundle;
import android.view.View;

public class NotificationsActivity extends Activity {
    int notificationID = 1;

    /** Called when the activity is first created. */
    @Override
    public void onCreate(Bundle savedInstanceState) {
        super.onCreate(savedInstanceState);
        setContentView(R.layout.main);
    }

    public void onClick(View view) {
        displayNotification();
    }

    protected void displayNotification()
    {
        //---PendingIntent to launch activity if the user selects
        // this notification---
        Intent i = new Intent(this, NotificationView.class);
        i.putExtra("notificationID", notificationID);

        PendingIntent pendingIntent =
            PendingIntent.getActivity(this, 0, i, 0);

        NotificationManager nm = (NotificationManager)
            getSystemService(NOTIFICATION_SERVICE);

        Notification notif = new Notification(
            R.drawable.ic_launcher,
            "Reminder: Meeting starts in 5 minutes",
            System.currentTimeMillis());

        CharSequence from = "System Alarm";
        CharSequence message = "Meeting with customer at 3pm...";

        notif.setLatestEventInfo(this, from, message, pendingIntent);

        //---100ms delay, vibrate for 250ms, pause for 100 ms and
        // then vibrate for 500ms---
        notif.vibrate = new long[] { 100, 250, 100, 500};
        nm.notify(notificationID, notif);
    }

}
```

8. Press F11 to debug the application on the Android emulator.

9. Click the Display Notification button and a notification ticker text (set in the constructor of the `Notification` object) will appear on the status bar (see Figure 2-30).

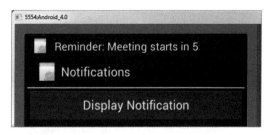

10. Clicking and dragging the status bar down will reveal the notification details set using the

FIGURE 2-30

`setLatestEventInfo()` method of the `Notification` object (see Figure 2-31).

11. Clicking on the notification will reveal the `NotificationView` activity (see Figure 2-32). This also causes the notification to be dismissed from the status bar.

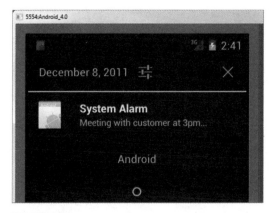

FIGURE 2-31

FIGURE 2-32

How It Works

To display a notification, you first created an `Intent` object to point to the `NotificationView` class:

```
Intent i = new Intent(this, NotificationView.class);
i.putExtra("notificationID", notificationID);
```

This intent is used to launch another activity when the user selects a notification from the list of notifications. In this example, you added a name/value pair to the `Intent` object so that you can tag the notification ID, identifying the notification to the target activity. This ID will be used to dismiss the notification later.

You also need to create a `PendingIntent` object. A `PendingIntent` object helps you to perform an action on your application's behalf, often at a later time, regardless of whether your application is running or not. In this case, you initialized it as follows:

```
PendingIntent pendingIntent =
    PendingIntent.getActivity(this, 0, i, 0);
```

The getActivity() method retrieves a PendingIntent object and you set it using the following arguments:

➤ **context** — Application context

➤ **request code** — Request code for the intent

➤ **intent** — The intent for launching the target activity

➤ **flags** — The flags in which the activity is to be launched

You then obtain an instance of the NotificationManager class and create an instance of the Notification class:

```
NotificationManager nm = (NotificationManager)
    getSystemService(NOTIFICATION_SERVICE);

Notification notif = new Notification(
    R.drawable.ic_launcher,
    "Reminder: Meeting starts in 5 minutes",
    System.currentTimeMillis());
```

The Notification class enables you to specify the notification's main information when the notification first appears on the status bar. The second argument to the Notification constructor sets the "ticker text" on the status bar (see Figure 2-33).

FIGURE 2-33

Next, you set the details of the notification using the setLatestEventInfo() method:

```
CharSequence from = "System Alarm";
CharSequence message = "Meeting with customer at 3pm...";

notif.setLatestEventInfo(this, from, message, pendingIntent);

//---100ms delay, vibrate for 250ms, pause for 100 ms and
// then vibrate for 500ms---
notif.vibrate = new long[] { 100, 250, 100, 500};
```

The preceding also sets the notification to vibrate the phone. Finally, to display the notification you use the notify() method:

```
nm.notify(notificationID, notif);
```

When the user clicks on the notification, the NotificationView activity is launched. Here, you dismiss the notification by using the cancel() method of the NotificationManager object and passing it the ID of the notification (passed in via the Intent object):

```
//---look up the notification manager service---
NotificationManager nm = (NotificationManager)
    getSystemService(NOTIFICATION_SERVICE);

//---cancel the notification that we started---
nm.cancel(getIntent().getExtras().getInt("notificationID"));
```

SUMMARY

This chapter first provided a detailed look at how activities and fragments work and the various forms in which you can display them. You also learned how to display dialog windows using activities.

The second part of this chapter demonstrated a very important concept in Android — the intent. The intent is the "glue" that enables different activities to be connected, and it is a vital concept to understand when developing for the Android platform.

EXERCISES

1. What will happen if you have two or more activities with the same intent filter action name?

2. Write the code to invoke the built-in Browser application.

3. Which components can you specify in an intent filter?

4. What is the difference between the Toast class and the NotificationManager class?

5. Name the two ways to add fragments to an activity.

6. Name one key difference between a fragment and an activity.

Answers to the exercises can be found in Appendix C.

▶ WHAT YOU LEARNED IN THIS CHAPTER

TOPIC	KEY CONCEPTS
Creating an activity	All activities must be declared in the `AndroidManifest.xml` file.
Key life cycle of an activity	When an activity is started, the `onStart()` and `onResume()` events are always called.
	When an activity is killed or sent to the background, the `onPause()` event is always called.
Displaying an activity as a dialog	Use the `showDialog()` method and implement the `onCreateDialog()` method.
Fragments	Fragments are "mini-activities" that can be added or removed from activities.
Manipulating fragments programmatically	You need to use the `FragmentManager` and `FragmentTransaction` classes when adding, removing, or replacing fragments during runtime.
Life cycle of a fragment	Similar to that of an activity — you save the state of a fragment in the `onPause()` event, and restore its state in one of the following events: `onCreate()`, `onCreateView()`, or `onActivityCreated()`.
Intent	The "glue" that connects different activities
Intent filter	The "filter" that enables you to specify how your activities should be called
Calling an activity	Use the `startActivity()` or `startActivityForResult()` method.
Passing data to an activity	Use the `Bundle` object.
Components in an `Intent` object	An `Intent` object can contain the following: action, data, type, and category.
Displaying notifications	Use the `NotificationManager` class.
`PendingIntent` object	A `PendingIntent` object helps you to perform an action on your application's behalf, often at a later time, regardless of whether or not your application is running.

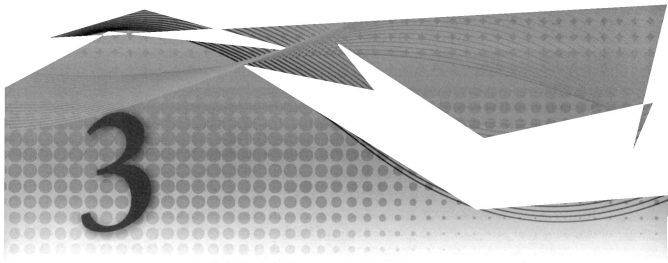

Getting to Know the Android User Interface

➤ The various ViewGroups you can use to lay out your views

➤ How to adapt and manage changes in screen orientation

➤ How to create the UI programmatically

➤ How to listen for UI notifications

In Chapter 2, you learned about the Activity class and its life cycle. You learned that an activity is a means by which users interact with the application. However, an activity by itself does not have a presence on the screen. Instead, it has to draw the screen using *Views* and *ViewGroups*. In this chapter, you will learn the details about creating user interfaces in Android, and how users interact with them. In addition, you will learn how to handle changes in screen orientation on your Android devices.

UNDERSTANDING THE COMPONENTS OF A SCREEN

In Chapter 2, you learned that the basic unit of an Android application is an *activity*. An *activity* displays the user interface of your application, which may contain widgets such as buttons, labels, textboxes, and so on. Typically, you define your UI using an XML file (e.g., the main.xml file located in the res/layout folder of your project), which looks similar to the following:

```xml
<?xml version="1.0" encoding="utf-8"?>
<LinearLayout xmlns:android="http://schemas.android.com/apk/res/android"
    android:layout_width="fill_parent"
    android:layout_height="fill_parent"
```

```
    android:orientation="vertical" >

    <TextView
        android:layout_width="fill_parent"
        android:layout_height="wrap_content"
        android:text="@string/hello" />

</LinearLayout>
```

During runtime, you load the XML UI in the `onCreate()` method handler in your `Activity` class, using the `setContentView()` method of the `Activity` class:

```
@Override
public void onCreate(Bundle savedInstanceState) {
    super.onCreate(savedInstanceState);
    setContentView(R.layout.main);
}
```

During compilation, each element in the XML file is compiled into its equivalent Android GUI class, with attributes represented by methods. The Android system then creates the UI of the activity when it is loaded.

 NOTE *Although it is always easier to build your UI using an XML file, sometimes you need to build your UI dynamically during runtime (for example, when writing games). Hence, it is also possible to create your UI entirely using code. Later in this chapter you will see an example showing how this can be done.*

Views and ViewGroups

An activity contains *views* and *ViewGroups*. A view is a widget that has an appearance on screen. Examples of views are buttons, labels, and textboxes. A view derives from the base class `android .view.View`.

 NOTE *Chapters 4 and 5 discuss the various common views in Android.*

One or more views can be grouped together into a ViewGroup. A ViewGroup (which is itself a special type of view) provides the layout in which you can order the appearance and sequence of views. Examples of ViewGroups include `LinearLayout` and `FrameLayout`. A ViewGroup derives from the base class `android.view.ViewGroup`.

Android supports the following ViewGroups:

➤ `LinearLayout`

➤ `AbsoluteLayout`

➤   TableLayout

➤   RelativeLayout

➤   FrameLayout

➤   ScrollView

The following sections describe each of these ViewGroups in more detail. Note that in practice it is common to combine different types of layouts to create the UI you want.

LinearLayout

The LinearLayout arranges views in a single column or a single row. Child views can be arranged either vertically or horizontally. To see how LinearLayout works, consider the following elements typically contained in the main.xml file:

```xml
<?xml version="1.0" encoding="utf-8"?>
<LinearLayout xmlns:android="http://schemas.android.com/apk/res/android"
    android:layout_width="fill_parent"
    android:layout_height="fill_parent"
    android:orientation="vertical" >

    <TextView
        android:layout_width="fill_parent"
        android:layout_height="wrap_content"
        android:text="@string/hello" />
</LinearLayout>
```

In the main.xml file, observe that the root element is <LinearLayout> and it has a <TextView> element contained within it. The <LinearLayout> element controls the order in which the views contained within it appear.

Each View and ViewGroup has a set of common attributes, some of which are described in Table 3-1.

TABLE 3-1: Common Attributes Used in Views and ViewGroups

ATTRIBUTE	DESCRIPTION
layout_width	Specifies the width of the View or ViewGroup
layout_height	Specifies the height of the View or ViewGroup
layout_marginTop	Specifies extra space on the top side of the View or ViewGroup
layout_marginBottom	Specifies extra space on the bottom side of the View or ViewGroup
layout_marginLeft	Specifies extra space on the left side of the View or ViewGroup
layout_marginRight	Specifies extra space on the right side of the View or ViewGroup

continues

TABLE 3-1 *(continued)*

ATTRIBUTE	DESCRIPTION
layout_gravity	Specifies how child Views are positioned
layout_weight	Specifies how much of the extra space in the layout should be allocated to the View
layout_x	Specifies the x-coordinate of the View or ViewGroup
layout_y	Specifies the y-coordinate of the View or ViewGroup

 NOTE *Some of these attributes are applicable only when a View is in a specific ViewGroup. For example, the* layout_weight *and* layout_gravity *attributes are applicable only when a View is in either a* LinearLayout *or a* TableLayout.

For example, the width of the <TextView> element fills the entire width of its parent (which is the screen in this case) using the fill_parent constant. Its height is indicated by the wrap_content constant, which means that its height is the height of its content (in this case, the text contained within it). If you don't want the <TextView> view to occupy the entire row, you can set its layout_width attribute to wrap_content, like this:

```
<TextView
    android:layout_width="wrap_content"
    android:layout_height="wrap_content"
    android:text="@string/hello" />
```

The preceding code will set the width of the view to be equal to the width of the text contained within it.

Consider the following layout:

```
<?xml version="1.0" encoding="utf-8"?>
<LinearLayout xmlns:android="http://schemas.android.com/apk/res/android"
    android:layout_width="fill_parent"
    android:layout_height="fill_parent"
    android:orientation="vertical" >

<TextView
    android:layout_width="100dp"
    android:layout_height="wrap_content"
    android:text="@string/hello" />

<Button
    android:layout_width="160dp"
    android:layout_height="wrap_content"
    android:text="Button"
    android:onClick="onClick" />

</LinearLayout>
```

UNITS OF MEASUREMENT

When specifying the size of an element on an Android UI, you should be aware of the following units of measurement:

dp — Density-independent pixel. 1 dp is equivalent to one pixel on a 160 dpi screen. This is the recommended unit of measurement when specifying the dimension of views in your layout. The 160 dpi screen is the baseline density assumed by Android. You can specify either "dp" or "dip" when referring to a density-independent pixel.

sp — Scale-independent pixel. This is similar to dp and is recommended for specifying font sizes.

pt — Point. A point is defined to be 1/72 of an inch, based on the physical screen size.

px — Pixel. Corresponds to actual pixels on the screen. Using this unit is not recommended, as your UI may not render correctly on devices with a different screen resolution.

Here, you set the width of both the TextView and Button views to an absolute value. In this case, the width for the TextView is set to 100 density-independent pixels wide, and the Button to 160 density-independent pixels wide. Before you see how the views will look like on different screens with different pixel density, it is important to understand how Android recognizes screens of varying sizes and density.

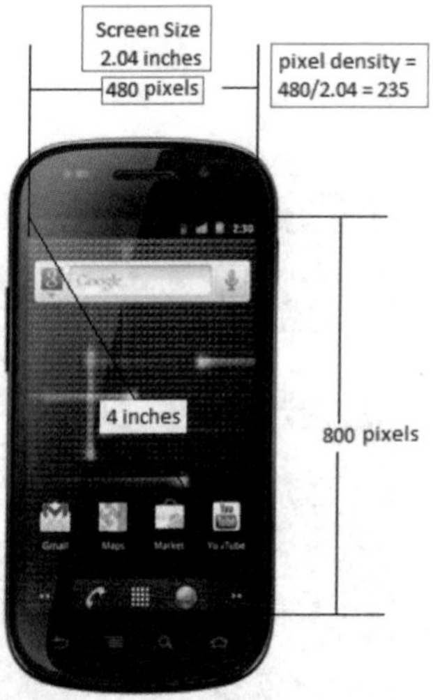

Figure 3-1 shows the screen of the Nexus S. It has a 4-inch screen (diagonally), with a screen width of 2.04 inches. Its resolution is 480 (width) × 800 (height) pixels. With 480 pixels spread across a width of 2.04 inches, the result is a pixel density of about 235 dots per inch (dpi).

As you can see from the figure, the pixel density of a screen varies according to screen size and resolution.

Android defines and recognizes four screen densities:

➤ Low density (*ldpi*) — 120 dpi

➤ Medium density (*mdpi*) — 160 dpi

➤ High density (*hdpi*) — 240 dpi

➤ Extra High density (*xhdpi*) — 320 dpi

FIGURE 3-1

Your device will fall into one of the densities defined in the preceding list. For example, the Nexus S is regarded as a *hdpi* device, as its pixel density is closest to 240 dpi. The HTC Hero, however, has a

3.2-inch (diagonal) screen size and a resolution of 320 × 480. Its pixel density works out to be about 180 dpi. Therefore, it would be considered an *mdpi* device, as its pixel density is closest to 160 dpi.

To test how the views defined in the XML file will look when displayed on screens of different densities, create two AVDs with different screen resolutions and abstracted LCD densities. Figure 3-2 shows an AVD with 480 × 800 resolution and LCD density of 235, emulating the Nexus S.

Figure 3-3 shows another AVD with 320 × 480 resolution and LCD density of 180, emulating the HTC Hero.

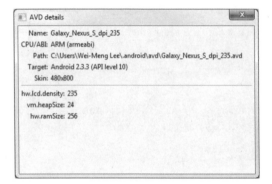

FIGURE 3-2

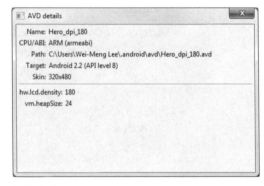

FIGURE 3-3

Figure 3-4 shows what the views look like when viewed on the emulator with a screen density of 235 dpi.

Figure 3-5 shows what the views look like when viewed on the emulator with a screen density of 180 dpi.

FIGURE 3-4

FIGURE 3-5

Using the *dp* unit ensures that your views are always displayed in the right proportion regardless of the screen density — Android automatically scales the size of the view depending on the density of the screen. Using the Button as an example, if it is displayed on a 180 dpi screen (a 180 dpi screen is treated just like a 160 dpi screen), its width would be 160 pixels. However, if it is displayed on a 235 dpi screen (which is treated as a 240 dpi screen), then its width would be 240 pixels.

HOW TO CONVERT DP TO PX

The formula for converting dp to px (pixels) is as follows:

Actual pixels = dp * (dpi / 160), where dpi is either 120, 160, 240, or 320.

Therefore, in the case of the Button on a 235 dpi screen, its actual width is 160 * (240/160) = 240 px. When run on the 180 dpi emulator (regarded as a 160 dpi device), its actual pixel is now 160 * (160/160) = 160 px. In this case, one dp is equivalent to one px.

To prove that this is indeed correct, you can use the getWidth() method of a View object to get its width in pixels:

```java
public void onClick(View view) {
    Toast.makeText(this,
        String.valueOf(view.getWidth()),
        Toast.LENGTH_LONG).show();
}
```

What if instead of using dp you now specify the size using pixels (px)?

```xml
<TextView
    android:layout_width="100px"
    android:layout_height="wrap_content"
    android:text="@string/hello" />
<Button
    android:layout_width="160px"
    android:layout_height="wrap_content"
    android:text="Button"
    android:onClick="onClick"/>
```

Figure 3-6 shows what the Label and Button look like on a 235 dpi screen. Figure 3-7 shows the same views on a 180 dpi screen. In this case, Android does not perform any conversion, as all the sizes are specified in pixels. In general (with screen sizes being equal), if you use pixels for view sizes, the views will appear smaller on a device with a high dpi screen, compared to one with a lower dpi.

FIGURE 3-6

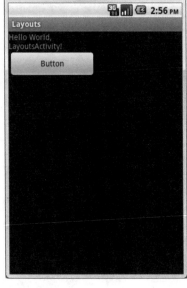

FIGURE 3-7

The preceding example also specifies that the orientation of the layout is vertical:

```
<LinearLayout xmlns:android="http://schemas.android.com/apk/res/android"
    android:layout_width="fill_parent"
    android:layout_height="fill_parent"
    android:orientation="vertical" >
```

The default orientation layout is horizontal, so if you omit the `android:orientation` attribute, the views will appear as shown in Figure 3-8.

FIGURE 3-8

In `LinearLayout`, you can apply the `layout_weight` and `layout_gravity` attributes to views contained within it, as the following modifications to `main.xml` show:

```
<LinearLayout xmlns:android="http://schemas.android.com/apk/res/android"
    android:layout_width="fill_parent"
    android:layout_height="fill_parent"
    android:orientation="vertical" >

<Button
    android:layout_width="160dp"
    android:layout_height="wrap_content"
    android:text="Button"
    android:layout_gravity="left"
    android:layout_weight="1" />

<Button
    android:layout_width="160dp"
    android:layout_height="wrap_content"
    android:text="Button"
```

```
        android:layout_gravity="center"
        android:layout_weight="2" />

<Button
    android:layout_width="160dp"
    android:layout_height="wrap_content"
    android:text="Button"
    android:layout_gravity="right"
    android:layout_weight="3" />

</LinearLayout>
```

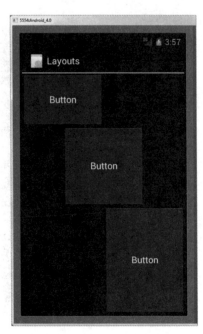

Figure 3-9 shows the positioning of the views as well as their heights. The `layout_gravity` attribute indicates the positions the views should gravitate towards, while the `layout_weight` attribute specifies the distribution of available space. In the preceding example, the three buttons occupy about 16.6% (1/(1+2+3) * 100), 33.3% (2/(1+2+3) * 100), and 50% (3/(1+2+3) * 100) of the available height, respectively.

If you change the orientation of the `LinearLayout` to horizontal, you need to change the width of each view to 0 dp, and the views will be displayed as shown in Figure 3-10:

FIGURE 3-9

```
<LinearLayout xmlns:android="http://schemas.android.com/apk/res/android"
    android:layout_width="fill_parent"
    android:layout_height="fill_parent"
    android:orientation="horizontal" >

<Button
    android:layout_width="0dp"
    android:layout_height="wrap_content"
    android:text="Button"
    android:layout_gravity="left"
    android:layout_weight="1" />

<Button
    android:layout_width="0dp"
    android:layout_height="wrap_content"
    android:text="Button"
    android:layout_gravity="center_horizontal"
    android:layout_weight="2" />

<Button
    android:layout_width="0dp"
    android:layout_height="wrap_content"
    android:text="Button"
    android:layout_gravity="right"
    android:layout_weight="3" />

</LinearLayout>
```

FIGURE 3-10

AbsoluteLayout

The `AbsoluteLayout` enables you to specify the exact location of its children. Consider the following UI defined in `main.xml`:

```xml
<AbsoluteLayout
    android:layout_width="fill_parent"
    android:layout_height="fill_parent"
    xmlns:android="http://schemas.android.com/apk/res/android" >
<Button
    android:layout_width="188dp"
    android:layout_height="wrap_content"
    android:text="Button"
    android:layout_x="126px"
    android:layout_y="361px" />
<Button
    android:layout_width="113dp"
    android:layout_height="wrap_content"
    android:text="Button"
    android:layout_x="12px"
    android:layout_y="361px" />
</AbsoluteLayout>
```

Figure 3-11 shows the two `Button` views (tested on a 180 dpi AVD) located at their specified positions using the `android_layout_x` and `android_layout_y` attributes.

However, there is a problem with the `AbsoluteLayout` when the activity is viewed on a high-resolution screen (see Figure 3-12). For this reason, the `AbsoluteLayout` has been deprecated since Android 1.5 (although it is still supported in the current version). You should avoid using the `AbsoluteLayout` in your UI, as it is not guaranteed to be supported in future versions of Android. You should instead use the other layouts described in this chapter.

FIGURE 3-11

FIGURE 3-12

TableLayout

The TableLayout groups views into rows and columns. You use the <TableRow> element to designate a row in the table. Each row can contain one or more views. Each view you place within a row forms a cell. The width of each column is determined by the largest width of each cell in that column.

Consider the content of main.xml shown here:

```xml
<TableLayout
    xmlns:android="http://schemas.android.com/apk/res/android"
    android:layout_height="fill_parent"
    android:layout_width="fill_parent" >
    <TableRow>
        <TextView
            android:text="User Name:"
            android:width ="120dp"
            />
        <EditText
            android:id="@+id/txtUserName"
            android:width="200dp" />
    </TableRow>
    <TableRow>
        <TextView
            android:text="Password:"
            />
        <EditText
            android:id="@+id/txtPassword"
            android:password="true"
            />
    </TableRow>
    <TableRow>
        <TextView />
        <CheckBox android:id="@+id/chkRememberPassword"
            android:layout_width="fill_parent"
            android:layout_height="wrap_content"
            android:text="Remember Password"
            />
    </TableRow>
    <TableRow>
        <Button
            android:id="@+id/buttonSignIn"
            android:text="Log In" />
    </TableRow>
</TableLayout>
```

Figure 3-13 shows what the preceding looks like when rendered on the Android emulator.

Note that in the preceding example, there are two columns and four rows in the `TableLayout`. The cell directly under the Password `TextView` is populated with a `<TextView/>` empty element. If you don't do this, the Remember Password checkbox will appear under the Password `TextView`, as shown in Figure 3-14.

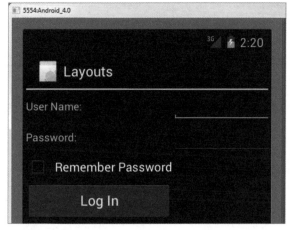

FIGURE 3-13   **FIGURE 3-14**

RelativeLayout

The `RelativeLayout` enables you to specify how child views are positioned relative to each other. Consider the following `main.xml` file:

```xml
<?xml version="1.0" encoding="utf-8"?>
<RelativeLayout
    android:id="@+id/RLayout"
    android:layout_width="fill_parent"
    android:layout_height="fill_parent"
    xmlns:android="http://schemas.android.com/apk/res/android" >

    <TextView
        android:id="@+id/lblComments"
        android:layout_width="wrap_content"
        android:layout_height="wrap_content"
        android:text="Comments"
        android:layout_alignParentTop="true"
        android:layout_alignParentLeft="true" />

    <EditText
        android:id="@+id/txtComments"
```

```
        android:layout_width="fill_parent"
        android:layout_height="170px"
        android:textSize="18sp"
        android:layout_alignLeft="@+id/lblComments"
        android:layout_below="@+id/lblComments"
        android:layout_centerHorizontal="true" />

    <Button
        android:id="@+id/btnSave"
        android:layout_width="125px"
        android:layout_height="wrap_content"
        android:text="Save"
        android:layout_below="@+id/txtComments"
        android:layout_alignRight="@+id/txtComments" />

    <Button
        android:id="@+id/btnCancel"
        android:layout_width="124px"
        android:layout_height="wrap_content"
        android:text="Cancel"
        android:layout_below="@+id/txtComments"
        android:layout_alignLeft="@+id/txtComments" />
</RelativeLayout>
```

Notice that each view embedded within the `RelativeLayout` has attributes that enable it to align with another view. These attributes are as follows:

➤ `layout_alignParentTop`

➤ `layout_alignParentLeft`

➤ `layout_alignLeft`

➤ `layout_alignRight`

➤ `layout_below`

➤ `layout_centerHorizontal`

The value for each of these attributes is the ID for the view that you are referencing. The preceding XML UI creates the screen shown in Figure 3-15.

FrameLayout

The `FrameLayout` is a placeholder on screen that you can use to display a single view. Views that you add to a `FrameLayout` are always anchored to the top left of the layout. Consider the following content in `main.xml`:

```
<?xml version="1.0" encoding="utf-8"?>
<RelativeLayout
    android:id="@+id/RLayout"
```

FIGURE 3-15

```
        android:layout_width="fill_parent"
        android:layout_height="fill_parent"
        xmlns:android="http://schemas.android.com/apk/res/android" >

    <TextView
        android:id="@+id/lblComments"
        android:layout_width="wrap_content"
        android:layout_height="wrap_content"
        android:text="Hello, Android!"
        android:layout_alignParentTop="true"
        android:layout_alignParentLeft="true" />

    <FrameLayout
        android:layout_width="wrap_content"
        android:layout_height="wrap_content"
        android:layout_alignLeft="@+id/lblComments"
        android:layout_below="@+id/lblComments"
        android:layout_centerHorizontal="true" >

        <ImageView
            android:src = "@drawable/droid"
            android:layout_width="wrap_content"
            android:layout_height="wrap_content" />

    </FrameLayout>
</RelativeLayout>
```

Here, you have a `FrameLayout` within a `RelativeLayout`. Within the `FrameLayout`, you embed an `ImageView`. The UI is shown in Figure 3-16.

FIGURE 3-16

NOTE *This example assumes that the* `res/drawable-mdpi` *folder has an image named* `droid.png`*.*

If you add another view (such as a `Button` view) within the `FrameLayout`, the view will overlap the previous view (see Figure 3-17):

```xml
<?xml version="1.0" encoding="utf-8"?>
<RelativeLayout
    android:id="@+id/RLayout"
    android:layout_width="fill_parent"
    android:layout_height="fill_parent"
    xmlns:android="http://schemas.android.com/apk/res/android"
    >
    <TextView
        android:id="@+id/lblComments"
        android:layout_width="wrap_content"
        android:layout_height="wrap_content"
        android:text="Hello, Android!"
        android:layout_alignParentTop="true"
        android:layout_alignParentLeft="true"
        />
    <FrameLayout
        android:layout_width="wrap_content"
        android:layout_height="wrap_content"
        android:layout_alignLeft="@+id/lblComments"
        android:layout_below="@+id/lblComments"
        android:layout_centerHorizontal="true" >
        <ImageView
            android:src = "@drawable/droid"
            android:layout_width="wrap_content"
            android:layout_height="wrap_content" />

        <Button
            android:layout_width="124dp"
            android:layout_height="wrap_content"
            android:text="Print Picture" />

    </FrameLayout>
</RelativeLayout>
```

FIGURE 3-17

 NOTE *You can add multiple views to a* FrameLayout, *but each will be stacked on top of the previous one. This is when you want to animate a series of images, with only one visible at a time.*

ScrollView

A ScrollView is a special type of FrameLayout in that it enables users to scroll through a list of views that occupy more space than the physical display. The ScrollView can contain only one child view or ViewGroup, which normally is a LinearLayout.

 NOTE *Do not use a* ListView *(discussed in Chapter 4) together with the* ScrollView. *The* ListView *is designed for showing a list of related information and is optimized for dealing with large lists.*

The following main.xml content shows a ScrollView containing a LinearLayout, which in turn contains some Button and EditText views:

```
<ScrollView
    android:layout_width="fill_parent"
    android:layout_height="fill_parent"
    xmlns:android="http://schemas.android.com/apk/res/android" >

    <LinearLayout
        android:layout_width="fill_parent"
        android:layout_height="wrap_content"
        android:orientation="vertical" >
        <Button
            android:id="@+id/button1"
```

```
            android:layout_width="fill_parent"
            android:layout_height="wrap_content"
            android:text="Button 1" />
        <Button
            android:id="@+id/button2"
            android:layout_width="fill_parent"
            android:layout_height="wrap_content"
            android:text="Button 2" />
        <Button
            android:id="@+id/button3"
            android:layout_width="fill_parent"
            android:layout_height="wrap_content"
            android:text="Button 3" />
        <EditText
            android:id="@+id/txt"
            android:layout_width="fill_parent"
            android:layout_height="600dp" />
        <Button
            android:id="@+id/button4"
            android:layout_width="fill_parent"
            android:layout_height="wrap_content"
            android:text="Button 4" />
        <Button
            android:id="@+id/button5"
            android:layout_width="fill_parent"
            android:layout_height="wrap_content"
            android:text="Button 5" />
    </LinearLayout>
</ScrollView>
```

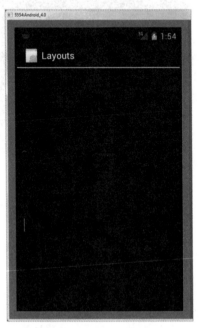

If you load the preceding code on the Android emulator, you will see something like Figure 3-18.

FIGURE 3-18

Because the EditText automatically gets the focus, it fills up the entire activity (as the height was set to 600dp). To prevent it from getting the focus, add the following two attributes to the <LinearLayout> element:

```
    <LinearLayout
        android:layout_width="fill_parent"
        android:layout_height="wrap_content"
        android:orientation="vertical"
        android:focusable="true"
        android:focusableInTouchMode="true" >
```

You will now be able to view the buttons and scroll through the list of views (see Figure 3-19).

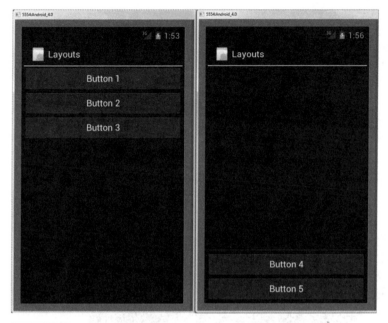

FIGURE 3-19

Sometimes you may want the `EditText` to automatically get the focus, but you do not want the soft input panel (keyboard) to appear automatically (which happens on a real device). To prevent the keyboard from appearing, add the following attribute to the `<activity>` element in the `AndroidManifest.xml` file:

```
<activity
    android:label="@string/app_name"
    android:name=".LayoutsActivity"
    android:windowSoftInputMode="stateHidden" >
    <intent-filter >
        <action android:name="android.intent.action.MAIN" />
        <category android:name="android.intent.category.LAUNCHER" />
    </intent-filter>
</activity>
```

ADAPTING TO DISPLAY ORIENTATION

One of the key features of modern smartphones is their ability to switch screen orientation, and Android is no exception. Android supports two screen orientations: *portrait* and *landscape.* By default, when you change the display orientation of your Android device, the current activity that is displayed automatically redraws its content in the new orientation. This is because the `onCreate()` method of the activity is fired whenever there is a change in display orientation.

NOTE *When you change the orientation of your Android device, your current activity is actually destroyed and then recreated.*

However, when the views are redrawn, they may be drawn in their original locations (depending on the layout selected). Figure 3-20 shows one of the examples illustrated earlier displayed in both portrait and landscape mode.

Note that in landscape mode, a lot of empty space on the right of the screen could be used. Furthermore, any additional views at the bottom of the screen would be hidden when the screen orientation is set to landscape.

FIGURE 3-20

In general, you can employ two techniques to handle changes in screen orientation:

➤ **Anchoring** — The easiest way is to "anchor" your views to the four edges of the screen. When the screen orientation changes, the views can anchor neatly to the edges.

➤ **Resizing and repositioning** — Whereas anchoring and centralizing are simple techniques to ensure that views can handle changes in screen orientation, the ultimate technique is resizing each and every view according to the current screen orientation.

Anchoring Views

Anchoring can be easily achieved by using `RelativeLayout`. Consider the following `main.xml` file, which contains five `Button` views embedded within the `<RelativeLayout>` element:

```xml
<RelativeLayout
    android:layout_width="fill_parent"
    android:layout_height="fill_parent"
    xmlns:android="http://schemas.android.com/apk/res/android">
    <Button
        android:id="@+id/button1"
        android:layout_width="wrap_content"
        android:layout_height="wrap_content"
        android:text="Top Left"
        android:layout_alignParentLeft="true"
        android:layout_alignParentTop="true" />
    <Button
        android:id="@+id/button2"
        android:layout_width="wrap_content"
        android:layout_height="wrap_content"
        android:text="Top Right"
        android:layout_alignParentTop="true"
        android:layout_alignParentRight="true" />
    <Button
        android:id="@+id/button3"
        android:layout_width="wrap_content"
        android:layout_height="wrap_content"
        android:text="Bottom Left"
        android:layout_alignParentLeft="true"
        android:layout_alignParentBottom="true" />
    <Button
        android:id="@+id/button4"
        android:layout_width="wrap_content"
        android:layout_height="wrap_content"
        android:text="Bottom Right"
        android:layout_alignParentRight="true"
        android:layout_alignParentBottom="true" />
    <Button
        android:id="@+id/button5"
        android:layout_width="fill_parent"
        android:layout_height="wrap_content"
        android:text="Middle"
        android:layout_centerVertical="true"
        android:layout_centerHorizontal="true" />
</RelativeLayout>
```

Note the following attributes found in the various `Button` views:

➤ `layout_alignParentLeft` — Aligns the view to the left of the parent view

➤ `layout_alignParentRight` — Aligns the view to the right of the parent view

➤ `layout_alignParentTop` — Aligns the view to the top of the parent view

➤ `layout_alignParentBottom` — Aligns the view to the bottom of the parent view

➤ `layout_centerVertical` — Centers the view vertically within its parent view

➤ `layout_centerHorizontal` — Centers the view horizontally within its parent view

Figure 3-21 shows the activity when viewed in portrait mode.

When the screen orientation changes to landscape mode, the four buttons are aligned to the four edges of the screen, and the center button is centered in the middle of the screen with its width fully stretched (see Figure 3-22).

FIGURE 3-21

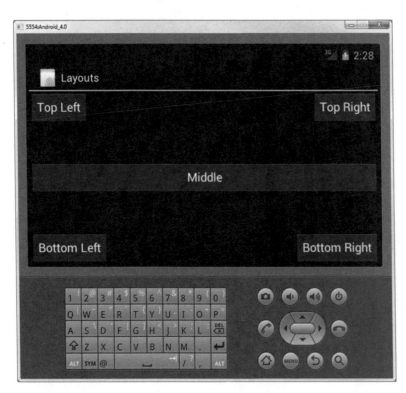

FIGURE 3-22

Resizing and Repositioning

Apart from anchoring your views to the four edges of the screen, an easier way to customize the UI based on screen orientation is to create a separate res/layout folder containing the XML files for the UI of each orientation. To support landscape mode, you can create a new folder in the res folder and name it as layout-land (representing landscape). Figure 3-23 shows the new folder containing the file main.xml.

Basically, the main.xml file contained within the layout folder defines the UI for the activity in portrait mode, whereas the main.xml file in the layout-land folder defines the UI in landscape mode.

The following code shows the content of main.xml under the layout folder:

FIGURE 3-23

```xml
<?xml version="1.0" encoding="utf-8"?>
<RelativeLayout
    android:layout_width="fill_parent"
    android:layout_height="fill_parent"
    xmlns:android="http://schemas.android.com/apk/res/android">
    <Button
        android:id="@+id/button1"
        android:layout_width="wrap_content"
        android:layout_height="wrap_content"
        android:text="Top Left"
        android:layout_alignParentLeft="true"
        android:layout_alignParentTop="true" />
    <Button
        android:id="@+id/button2"
        android:layout_width="wrap_content"
        android:layout_height="wrap_content"
        android:text="Top Right"
        android:layout_alignParentTop="true"
        android:layout_alignParentRight="true" />
    <Button
        android:id="@+id/button3"
        android:layout_width="wrap_content"
        android:layout_height="wrap_content"
        android:text="Bottom Left"
        android:layout_alignParentLeft="true"
        android:layout_alignParentBottom="true" />
    <Button
        android:id="@+id/button4"
        android:layout_width="wrap_content"
        android:layout_height="wrap_content"
        android:text="Bottom Right"
        android:layout_alignParentRight="true"
        android:layout_alignParentBottom="true" />
    <Button
        android:id="@+id/button5"
        android:layout_width="fill_parent"
```

```
        android:layout_height="wrap_content"
        android:text="Middle"
        android:layout_centerVertical="true"
        android:layout_centerHorizontal="true" />
</RelativeLayout>
```

The following shows the content of main.xml under the layout-land folder (the statements in bold
are the additional views to display in landscape mode):

```
<?xml version="1.0" encoding="utf-8"?>
<RelativeLayout
    android:layout_width="fill_parent"
    android:layout_height="fill_parent"
    xmlns:android="http://schemas.android.com/apk/res/android">
    <Button
        android:id="@+id/button1"
        android:layout_width="wrap_content"
        android:layout_height="wrap_content"
        android:text="Top Left"
        android:layout_alignParentLeft="true"
        android:layout_alignParentTop="true" />
    <Button
        android:id="@+id/button2"
        android:layout_width="wrap_content"
        android:layout_height="wrap_content"
        android:text="Top Right"
        android:layout_alignParentTop="true"
        android:layout_alignParentRight="true" />
    <Button
        android:id="@+id/button3"
        android:layout_width="wrap_content"
        android:layout_height="wrap_content"
        android:text="Bottom Left"
        android:layout_alignParentLeft="true"
        android:layout_alignParentBottom="true" />
    <Button
        android:id="@+id/button4"
        android:layout_width="wrap_content"
        android:layout_height="wrap_content"
        android:text="Bottom Right"
        android:layout_alignParentRight="true"
        android:layout_alignParentBottom="true" />
    <Button
        android:id="@+id/button5"
        android:layout_width="fill_parent"
        android:layout_height="wrap_content"
        android:text="Middle"
        android:layout_centerVertical="true"
        android:layout_centerHorizontal="true" />
    <Button
        android:id="@+id/button6"
        android:layout_width="180px"
```

```
            android:layout_height="wrap_content"
            android:text="Top Middle"
            android:layout_centerVertical="true"
            android:layout_centerHorizontal="true"
            android:layout_alignParentTop="true" />
        <Button
            android:id="@+id/button7"
            android:layout_width="180px"
            android:layout_height="wrap_content"
            android:text="Bottom Middle"
            android:layout_centerVertical="true"
            android:layout_centerHorizontal="true"
            android:layout_alignParentBottom="true" />
    </RelativeLayout>
```

When the activity is loaded in portrait mode, it will display five buttons, as shown in Figure 3-24.

When the activity is loaded in landscape mode, seven buttons are displayed (see Figure 3-25), demonstrating that different XML files are loaded when the device is in different orientations.

FIGURE 3-24

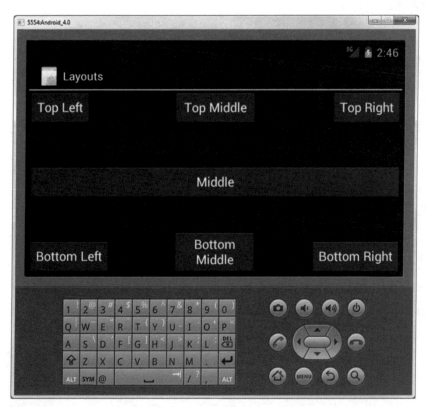

FIGURE 3-25

Using this method, when the orientation of the device changes, Android automatically loads the appropriate XML file for your activity depending on the current screen orientation.

MANAGING CHANGES TO SCREEN ORIENTATION

Now that you have looked at how to implement the two techniques for adapting to screen orientation changes, let's explore what happens to an activity's state when the device changes orientation.

The following Try It Out demonstrates the behavior of an activity when the device changes orientation.

TRY IT OUT Understanding Activity Behavior When Orientation Changes

codefile Orientations.zip available for download at Wrox.com

1. Using Eclipse, create a new Android project and name it **Orientations**.

2. Add the following statements in bold to the `main.xml` file:

```xml
<?xml version="1.0" encoding="utf-8"?>
<LinearLayout xmlns:android="http://schemas.android.com/apk/res/android"
    android:layout_width="fill_parent"
    android:layout_height="fill_parent"
    android:orientation="vertical" >

<EditText
    android:id="@+id/txtField1"
    android:layout_width="fill_parent"
    android:layout_height="wrap_content" />

<EditText
    android:layout_width="fill_parent"
    android:layout_height="wrap_content" />
</LinearLayout>
```

3. Add the following statements in bold to the `OrientationsActivity.java` file:

```java
package net.learn2develop.Orientations;

import android.app.Activity;
import android.os.Bundle;
import android.util.Log;

public class OrientationsActivity extends Activity {
    /** Called when the activity is first created. */
    @Override
```

```java
public void onCreate(Bundle savedInstanceState) {
    super.onCreate(savedInstanceState);
    setContentView(R.layout.main);
    Log.d("StateInfo", "onCreate");
}

@Override
public void onStart() {
    Log.d("StateInfo", "onStart");
    super.onStart();
}

@Override
public void onResume() {
    Log.d("StateInfo", "onResume");
    super.onResume();
}

@Override
public void onPause() {
    Log.d("StateInfo", "onPause");
    super.onPause();
}

@Override
public void onStop() {
    Log.d("StateInfo", "onStop");
    super.onStop();
}

@Override
public void onDestroy() {
    Log.d("StateInfo", "onDestroy");
    super.onDestroy();
}

@Override
public void onRestart() {
    Log.d("StateInfo", "onRestart");
    super.onRestart();
}
```

4. Press F11 to debug the application on the Android emulator.

5. Enter some text into the two EditText views (see Figure 3-26).

FIGURE 3-26

6.   Change the orientation of the Android emulator by pressing Ctrl+F11. Figure 3-27 shows the emulator in landscape mode. Note that the text in the first `EditText` view is still visible, while the second `EditText` view is now empty.

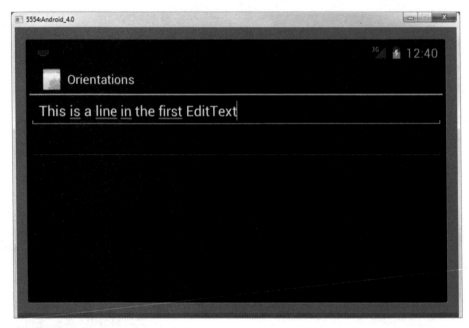

FIGURE 3-27

7.   Observe the output in the LogCat window (you need to switch to the Debug perspective in Eclipse). You should see something like this:

```
12-15 12:27:20.747: D/StateInfo(557): onCreate
12-15 12:27:20.747: D/StateInfo(557): onStart
12-15 12:27:20.747: D/StateInfo(557): onResume
...
12-15 12:39:37.846: D/StateInfo(557): onPause
12-15 12:39:37.846: D/StateInfo(557): onStop
12-15 12:39:37.866: D/StateInfo(557): onDestroy
12-15 12:39:38.206: D/StateInfo(557): onCreate
12-15 12:39:38.216: D/StateInfo(557): onStart
12-15 12:39:38.257: D/StateInfo(557): onResume
```

How It Works

From the output shown in the LogCat window, it is apparent that when the device changes orientation, the activity is destroyed:

```
12-15 12:39:37.846: D/StateInfo(557): onPause
12-15 12:39:37.846: D/StateInfo(557): onStop
12-15 12:39:37.866: D/StateInfo(557): onDestroy
```

It is then recreated:

```
12-15 12:39:38.206: D/StateInfo(557): onCreate
12-15 12:39:38.216: D/StateInfo(557): onStart
12-15 12:39:38.257: D/StateInfo(557): onResume
```

It is important to understand this behavior because you need to ensure that you take the necessary steps to preserve the state of your activity before it changes orientation. For example, your activity may have variables that contain values needed for some calculations in the activity. For any activity, you should save whatever state you need to save in the onPause() method, which is fired every time the activity changes orientation. The following section demonstrates the different ways to save this state information.

Another important behavior to understand is that only views that are named (via the android:id attribute) in an activity will have their state persisted when the activity they are contained in is destroyed. For example, the user may change orientation while entering some text into an EditText view. When this happens, any text inside the EditText view will be persisted and restored automatically when the activity is recreated. Conversely, if you do not name the EditText view using the android:id attribute, the activity will not be able to persist the text currently contained within it.

Persisting State Information during Changes in Configuration

So far, you have learned that changing screen orientation destroys an activity and recreates it. Keep in mind that when an activity is recreated, its current state may be lost. When an activity is killed, it will fire one or both of the following two methods:

➤ onPause() — This method is always fired whenever an activity is killed or pushed into the background.

➤ onSaveInstanceState() — This method is also fired whenever an activity is about to be killed or put into the background (just like the onPause() method). However, unlike the onPause() method, the onSaveInstanceState() method is not fired when an activity is being unloaded from the stack (such as when the user pressed the back button), because there is no need to restore its state later.

In short, to preserve the state of an activity, you could always implement the onPause() method, and then use your own ways to preserve the state of your activity, such as using a database, internal or external file storage, and so on.

If you simply want to preserve the state of an activity so that it can be restored later when the activity is recreated (such as when the device changes orientation), a much simpler way is to implement the onSaveInstanceState() method, as it provides a Bundle object as an argument so that you can use it to save your activity's state. The following code shows that you can save the string ID into the Bundle object during the onSaveInstanceState() method:

```java
@Override
public void onSaveInstanceState(Bundle outState) {
    //---save whatever you need to persist---
    outState.putString("ID", "1234567890");
    super.onSaveInstanceState(outState);
}
```

When an activity is recreated, the onCreate() method is first fired, followed by the onRestoreInstanceState() method, which enables you to retrieve the state that you saved previously in the onSaveInstanceState() method through the Bundle object in its argument:

```
@Override
public void onRestoreInstanceState(Bundle savedInstanceState) {
    super.onRestoreInstanceState(savedInstanceState);
    //---retrieve the information persisted earlier---
    String ID = savedInstanceState.getString("ID");
}
```

Although you can use the onSaveInstanceState() method to save state information, note the limitation that you can only save your state information in a Bundle object. If you need to save more complex data structures, then this is not an adequate solution.

Another method that you can use is the onRetainNonConfigurationInstance() method. This method is fired when an activity is about to be destroyed due to a *configuration change* (such as a change in screen orientation, keyboard availability, etc.). You can save your current data by returning it in this method, like this:

```
@Override
public Object onRetainNonConfigurationInstance() {
    //---save whatever you want here; it takes in an Object type--
    return("Some text to preserve");
}
```

> **NOTE** When screen orientation changes, this change is part of what is known as a configuration change. A configuration change will cause your current activity to be destroyed.

Note that this method returns an Object type, which allows you to return nearly any data type. To extract the saved data, you can extract it in the onCreate() method, using the getLastNonConfigurationInstance() method:

```
@Override
public void onCreate(Bundle savedInstanceState) {
    super.onCreate(savedInstanceState);
    setContentView(R.layout.main);
    Log.d("StateInfo", "onCreate");
    String str = (String) getLastNonConfigurationInstance();
}
```

A good use for using the onRetainNonConfigurationInstance() and getLastNonConfigurationInstance() methods is when you need to persist some data momentarily, such as when you have downloaded data from a web service and the user changes the screen orientation. In this scenario, saving the data using the preceding two methods is much more efficient than downloading the data again.

Detecting Orientation Changes

Sometimes you need to know the device's current orientation during runtime. To determine that, you can use the `WindowManager` class. The following code snippet demonstrates how you can programmatically detect the current orientation of your activity:

```java
import android.view.Display;
import android.view.WindowManager;

    @Override
    public void onCreate(Bundle savedInstanceState) {
        super.onCreate(savedInstanceState);
        setContentView(R.layout.main);

        //---get the current display info---
        WindowManager wm = getWindowManager();
        Display d = wm.getDefaultDisplay();

        if (d.getWidth() > d.getHeight()) {
            //---landscape mode---
            Log.d("Orientation", "Landscape mode");
        }
        else {
            //---portrait mode---
            Log.d("Orientation", "Portrait mode");
        }
    }
```

The `getDefaultDisplay()` method returns a `Display` object representing the screen of the device. You can then get its width and height and deduce the current orientation.

Controlling the Orientation of the Activity

Occasionally, you might want to ensure that your application is displayed in only a certain orientation. For example, you may be writing a game that should be viewed only in landscape mode. In this case, you can programmatically force a change in orientation using the `setRequestOrientation()` method of the `Activity` class:

```java
import android.content.pm.ActivityInfo;
    @Override
    public void onCreate(Bundle savedInstanceState) {
        super.onCreate(savedInstanceState);
        setContentView(R.layout.main);

        //---change to landscape mode---
        setRequestedOrientation(ActivityInfo.SCREEN_ORIENTATION_LANDSCAPE);
    }
```

To change to portrait mode, use the `ActivityInfo.SCREEN_ORIENTATION_PORTRAIT` constant.

Besides using the `setRequestOrientation()` method, you can also use the `android:screenOrientation` attribute on the `<activity>` element in `AndroidManifest.xml` as follows to constrain the activity to a certain orientation:

```xml
<?xml version="1.0" encoding="utf-8"?>
<manifest xmlns:android="http://schemas.android.com/apk/res/android"
    package="net.learn2develop.Orientations"
    android:versionCode="1"
    android:versionName="1.0" >

    <uses-sdk android:minSdkVersion="14" />

    <application
        android:icon="@drawable/ic_launcher"
        android:label="@string/app_name" >
        <activity
            android:label="@string/app_name"
            android:name=".OrientationsActivity"
            android:screenOrientation="landscape" >
            <intent-filter >
                <action android:name="android.intent.action.MAIN" />
                <category android:name="android.intent.category.LAUNCHER" />
            </intent-filter>
        </activity>
    </application>

</manifest>
```

The preceding example constrains the activity to a certain orientation (landscape in this case) and prevents the activity from being destroyed; that is, the activity will not be destroyed and the `onCreate()` method will not be fired again when the orientation of the device changes.

Following are two other values that you can specify in the `android:screenOrientation` attribute:

➤ `portrait` — Portrait mode

➤ `sensor` — Based on the accelerometer (default)

UTILIZING THE ACTION BAR

Besides fragments, another newer feature introduced in Android 3 and 4 is the Action Bar. In place of the traditional title bar located at the top of the device's screen, the Action Bar displays the application icon together with the activity title. Optionally, on the right side of the Action Bar are *action items*. Figure 3-28 shows the built-in Email application displaying the application icon, the activity title, and some action items in the Action Bar. The next section discusses action items in more detail.

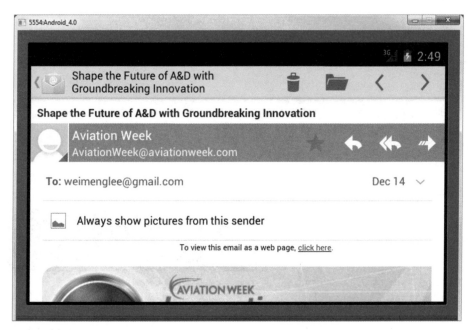

FIGURE 3-28

The following Try It Out shows how you can programmatically hide or display the Action Bar.

TRY IT OUT Showing and Hiding the Action Bar

1. Using Eclipse, create a new Android project and name it **MyActionBar**.

2. Press F11 to debug the application on the Android emulator. You should see the application and its Action Bar located at the top of the screen (containing the application icon and the application name "MyActionBar"; see Figure 3-29).

FIGURE 3-29

3. To hide the Action Bar, add the following line in bold to the AndroidManifest .xml file:

```xml
<?xml version="1.0" encoding="utf-8"?>
<manifest xmlns:android="http://schemas.android.com/apk/res/android"
    package="net.learn2develop.MyActionBar"
    android:versionCode="1"
    android:versionName="1.0" >

    <uses-sdk android:minSdkVersion="14" />

    <application
        android:icon="@drawable/ic_launcher"
        android:label="@string/app_name" >
```

```
<activity
    android:label="@string/app_name"
    android:name=".MyActionBarActivity"
    android:theme="@android:style/Theme.Holo.NoActionBar" >
    <intent-filter >
        <action android:name="android.intent.action.MAIN" />
        <category android:name="android.intent.category.LAUNCHER" />
    </intent-filter>
</activity>
</application>

</manifest>
```

4. Select the project name in Eclipse and then press F11 to debug the application on the Android emulator again. This time, the Action Bar is not displayed (see Figure 3-30).

> 5554:Android_4.0
>
> 3G 🔋 2:56
> Hello World, MyActionBarActivity!

FIGURE 3-30

5. You can also programmatically remove the Action Bar using the `ActionBar` class. To do so, you first need to remove the `android:theme` attribute you added in the previous step. This is important, otherwise the next step will cause the application to raise an exception.

6. Modify the `MyActionBarActivity.java` file as follows:

```
package net.learn2develop.MyActionBar;

import android.app.ActionBar;
import android.app.Activity;
import android.os.Bundle;

public class MyActionBarActivity extends Activity {
    /** Called when the activity is first created. */
    @Override
    public void onCreate(Bundle savedInstanceState) {
        super.onCreate(savedInstanceState);
        setContentView(R.layout.main);

        ActionBar actionBar = getActionBar();
        actionBar.hide();
        //actionBar.show(); //---show it again---
    }
}
```

7. Press F11 to debug the application on the emulator again. The Action Bar remains hidden.

How It Works

The `android:theme` attribute enables you to turn off the display of the Action Bar for your activity. Setting this attribute to "@android:style/Theme.Holo.NoActionBar" hides the Action Bar. Alternatively, you can programmatically get a reference to the Action Bar during runtime by using the `getActionBar()` method. Calling the `hide()` method hides the Action Bar, and calling the `show()` method displays it.

Note that if you use the `android:theme` attribute to turn off the Action Bar, calling the `getActionBar()` method returns a `null` during runtime. Hence, it is always better to turn the Action Bar on/off programmatically using the `ActionBar` class.

Adding Action Items to the Action Bar

Besides displaying the application icon and the activity title on the left of the Action Bar, you can also display additional items on the Action Bar. These additional items are called *action items*. Action items are shortcuts to some of the commonly performed operations in your application. For example, you might be building an RSS reader application, in which case some of the action items might be "Refresh feed," "Delete feed" and "Add new feed."

The following Try It Out shows how you can add action items to the Action Bar.

TRY IT OUT Adding Action Items

1. Using the MyActionBar project created in the previous section, add the following code in bold to the `MyActionBarActivity.java` file:

```
package net.learn2develop.MyActionBar;

import android.app.Activity;
import android.os.Bundle;
import android.view.Menu;
import android.view.MenuItem;
import android.widget.Toast;

public class MyActionBarActivity extends Activity {
    /** Called when the activity is first created. */
    @Override
    public void onCreate(Bundle savedInstanceState) {
        super.onCreate(savedInstanceState);
        setContentView(R.layout.main);

        //ActionBar actionBar = getActionBar();
        //actionBar.hide();
        //actionBar.show(); //---show it again---
    }

    @Override
    public boolean onCreateOptionsMenu(Menu menu) {
        super.onCreateOptionsMenu(menu);
        CreateMenu(menu);
        return true;
    }

    @Override
    public boolean onOptionsItemSelected(MenuItem item)
    {
        return MenuChoice(item);
```

```java
    }

    private void CreateMenu(Menu menu)
    {
        MenuItem mnu1 = menu.add(0, 0, 0, "Item 1");
        {
            mnu1.setIcon(R.drawable.ic_launcher);
            mnu1.setShowAsAction(MenuItem.SHOW_AS_ACTION_IF_ROOM);
        }
        MenuItem mnu2 = menu.add(0, 1, 1, "Item 2");
        {
            mnu2.setIcon(R.drawable.ic_launcher);
            mnu2.setShowAsAction(MenuItem.SHOW_AS_ACTION_IF_ROOM);
        }
        MenuItem mnu3 = menu.add(0, 2, 2, "Item 3");
        {
            mnu3.setIcon(R.drawable.ic_launcher);
            mnu3.setShowAsAction(MenuItem.SHOW_AS_ACTION_IF_ROOM);
        }
        MenuItem mnu4 = menu.add(0, 3, 3, "Item 4");
        {
            mnu4.setShowAsAction(MenuItem.SHOW_AS_ACTION_IF_ROOM);
        }
        MenuItem mnu5 = menu.add(0, 4, 4, "Item 5");
        {
            mnu5.setShowAsAction(MenuItem.SHOW_AS_ACTION_IF_ROOM);
        }
    }

    private boolean MenuChoice(MenuItem item)
    {
        switch (item.getItemId()) {
        case 0:
            Toast.makeText(this, "You clicked on Item 1",
                Toast.LENGTH_LONG).show();
            return true;
        case 1:
            Toast.makeText(this, "You clicked on Item 2",
                Toast.LENGTH_LONG).show();
            return true;
        case 2:
            Toast.makeText(this, "You clicked on Item 3",
                Toast.LENGTH_LONG).show();
            return true;
        case 3:
            Toast.makeText(this, "You clicked on Item 4",
                Toast.LENGTH_LONG).show();
            return true;
        case 4:
            Toast.makeText(this, "You clicked on Item 5",
                Toast.LENGTH_LONG).show();
            return true;
        }
        return false;
    }
}
```

2. Press F11 to debug the application on the Android emulator. Observe the icons on the right side of the Action Bar (see Figure 3-31). If you click the MENU button on the emulator, you will see the rest of the menu items (see Figure 3-32). This is known as the *overflow menu*. On devices that do not have the MENU button, an overflow menu is represented by an icon with an arrow. Figure 3-33 shows the same application running on the Asus Eee Pad Transformer (Android 3.2.1). Clicking the overflow menu displays the rest of the menu items.

3. Clicking each menu item will cause the Toast class to display the name of the menu item selected (see Figure 3-34).

FIGURE 3-31

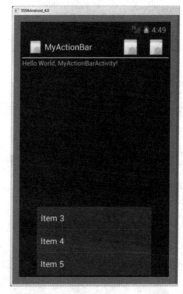

FIGURE 3-32

FIGURE 3-33

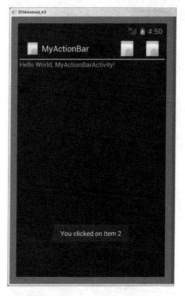

FIGURE 3-34

4. Press Control-F11 to change the display orientation of the emulator to landscape mode. You will now see four action items on the Action Bar, as shown in Figure 3-35, three with icons and one with text.

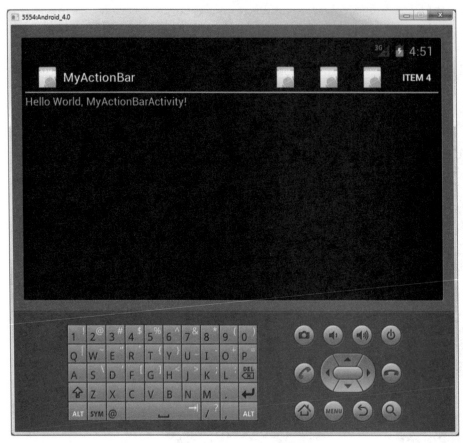

FIGURE 3-35

How It Works

The Action Bar populates its action items by calling the onCreateOptionsMenu() method of an activity:

```
@Override
public boolean onCreateOptionsMenu(Menu menu) {
    super.onCreateOptionsMenu(menu);
    CreateMenu(menu);
    return true;
}
```

In the preceding example, you called the CreateMenu() method to display a list of menu items:

```
private void CreateMenu(Menu menu)
{
    MenuItem mnu1 = menu.add(0, 0, 0, "Item 1");
```

```
        {
            mnu1.setIcon(R.drawable.ic_launcher);
            mnu1.setShowAsAction(MenuItem.SHOW_AS_ACTION_IF_ROOM);
        }
        MenuItem mnu2 = menu.add(0, 1, 1, "Item 2");
        {
            mnu2.setIcon(R.drawable.ic_launcher);
            mnu2.setShowAsAction(MenuItem.SHOW_AS_ACTION_IF_ROOM);
        }
        MenuItem mnu3 = menu.add(0, 2, 2, "Item 3");
        {
            mnu3.setIcon(R.drawable.ic_launcher);
            mnu3.setShowAsAction(MenuItem.SHOW_AS_ACTION_IF_ROOM);
        }
        MenuItem mnu4 = menu.add(0, 3, 3, "Item 4");
        {
            mnu4.setShowAsAction(MenuItem.SHOW_AS_ACTION_IF_ROOM);
        }
        MenuItem mnu5 = menu.add(0, 4, 4, "Item 5");
        {
            mnu5.setShowAsAction(MenuItem.SHOW_AS_ACTION_IF_ROOM);
        }
    }
```

To make the menu item appear as an action item, you call its setShowAsAction() method using the SHOW_AS_ACTION_IF_ROOM constant. This tells the Android device to display the menu item as an action item if there is room for it.

When a menu item is selected by the user, the onOptionsItemSelected() method is called:

```
@Override
public boolean onOptionsItemSelected(MenuItem item)
{
        return MenuChoice(item);
}
```

Here, you called the self-defined MenuChoice() method to check which menu item was clicked, and then printed out a message:

```
private boolean MenuChoice(MenuItem item)
{
    switch (item.getItemId()) {
    case 0:
        Toast.makeText(this, "You clicked on Item 1",
            Toast.LENGTH_LONG).show();
        return true;
    case 1:
        Toast.makeText(this, "You clicked on Item 2",
            Toast.LENGTH_LONG).show();
        return true;
    case 2:
        Toast.makeText(this, "You clicked on Item 3",
            Toast.LENGTH_LONG).show();
        return true;
```

```
        case 3:
            Toast.makeText(this, "You clicked on Item 4",
               · Toast.LENGTH_LONG).show();
            return true;
        case 4:
            Toast.makeText(this, "You clicked on Item 5",
                Toast.LENGTH_LONG).show();
            return true;
        }
        return false;
    }
```

Customizing the Action Items and Application Icon

In the previous example, the menu items are displayed without the text. If you want to display the text for the action item together with the icon, you could use the "|" operator together with the MenuItem.SHOW_AS_ACTION_WITH_TEXT constant:

```
        MenuItem mnu1 = menu.add(0, 0, 0, "Item 1");
        {
            mnu1.setIcon(R.drawable.ic_launcher);
            mnu1.setShowAsAction(
                MenuItem.SHOW_AS_ACTION_IF_ROOM |
                MenuItem.SHOW_AS_ACTION_WITH_TEXT);
        }
```

This causes the icon to be displayed together with the text of the menu item (see Figure 3-36).

FIGURE 3-36

Besides clicking the action items, users can also click the application icon on the Action Bar. When the application icon is clicked, the onOptionsItemSelected() method is called. To identify the application icon being called, you check the item ID against the android.R.id.home constant:

```
        private boolean MenuChoice(MenuItem item)
        {
            switch (item.getItemId()) {
            case android.R.id.home:
                Toast.makeText(this,
                    "You clicked on the Application icon",
                    Toast.LENGTH_LONG).show();
```

```
            return true;

    case 0:
        Toast.makeText(this, "You clicked on Item 1",
            Toast.LENGTH_LONG).show();
        return true;
    case 1:
        //...
    }
    return false;
}
```

To make the application icon clickable, you need to call the setDisplayHomeAsUpEnabled() method:

```
@Override
public void onCreate(Bundle savedInstanceState) {
    super.onCreate(savedInstanceState);
    setContentView(R.layout.main);

    ActionBar actionBar = getActionBar();
    actionBar.setDisplayHomeAsUpEnabled(true);
    //actionBar.hide();
    //actionBar.show(); //---show it again---
}
```

Figure 3-37 shows the arrow button displayed next to the application icon.

FIGURE 3-37

The application icon is often used by applications to enable them to return to the main activity of the application. For example, your application may have several activities, and you can use the application icon as a shortcut for users to return directly to the main activity of your application. To do this, it is always a good practice to create an `Intent` object and set it using the `Intent.FLAG_ACTIVITY_CLEAR_TOP` flag:

```
case android.R.id.home:
    Toast.makeText(this,
        "You clicked on the Application icon",
        Toast.LENGTH_LONG).show();

    Intent i = new Intent(this, MyActionBarActivity.class);
    i.addFlags(Intent.FLAG_ACTIVITY_CLEAR_TOP);
    startActivity(i);

    return true;
```

The `Intent.FLAG_ACTIVITY_CLEAR_TOP` flag ensures that the series of activities in the back stack is cleared when the user clicks the application icon on the Action Bar. This way, if the user clicks the back button, the other activities in the application do not appear again.

CREATING THE USER INTERFACE PROGRAMMATICALLY

So far, all the UIs you have seen in this chapter are created using XML. As mentioned earlier, besides using XML you can also create the UI using code. This approach is useful if your UI needs to be dynamically generated during runtime. For example, suppose you are building a cinema ticket reservation system and your application will display the seats of each cinema using buttons. In this case, you would need to dynamically generate the UI based on the cinema selected by the user.

The following Try It Out demonstrates the code needed to dynamically build the UI in your activity.

TRY IT OUT Creating the UI via Code

codefile UICode.zip available for download at Wrox.com

1. Using Eclipse, create a new Android project and name it **UICode**.

2. In the `UICodeActivity.java` file, add the following statements in bold:

```
package net.learn2develop.UICode;

import android.app.Activity;
import android.os.Bundle;
import android.view.ViewGroup.LayoutParams;
import android.widget.Button;
import android.widget.LinearLayout;
import android.widget.TextView;

public class UICodeActivity extends Activity {
    /** Called when the activity is first created. */
    @Override
```

```java
public void onCreate(Bundle savedInstanceState) {
    super.onCreate(savedInstanceState);
    //setContentView(R.layout.main);
    //---param for views---
    LayoutParams params =
        new LinearLayout.LayoutParams(
            LayoutParams.FILL_PARENT,
            LayoutParams.WRAP_CONTENT);

    //---create a layout---
    LinearLayout layout = new LinearLayout(this);
    layout.setOrientation(LinearLayout.VERTICAL);

    //---create a textview---
    TextView tv = new TextView(this);
    tv.setText("This is a TextView");
    tv.setLayoutParams(params);

    //---create a button---
    Button btn = new Button(this);
    btn.setText("This is a Button");
    btn.setLayoutParams(params);

    //---adds the textview---
    layout.addView(tv);

    //---adds the button---
    layout.addView(btn);

    //---create a layout param for the layout---
    LinearLayout.LayoutParams layoutParam =
        new LinearLayout.LayoutParams(
            LayoutParams.FILL_PARENT,
            LayoutParams.WRAP_CONTENT );

    this.addContentView(layout, layoutParam);
    }
}
```

3. Press F11 to debug the application on the Android emulator.
Figure 3-38 shows the activity created.

FIGURE 3-38

How It Works

In this example, you first commented out the setContentView() statement so that it does not load the
UI from the main.xml file.

You then created a LayoutParams object to specify the layout parameter that can be used by other
views (which you will create next):

```java
//---param for views---
LayoutParams params =
    new LinearLayout.LayoutParams(
        LayoutParams.FILL_PARENT,
        LayoutParams.WRAP_CONTENT);
```

You also created a `LinearLayout` object to contain all the views in your activity:

```
//---create a layout---
LinearLayout layout = new LinearLayout(this);
layout.setOrientation(LinearLayout.VERTICAL);
```

Next, you created a `TextView` and a `Button` view:

```
//---create a textview---
TextView tv = new TextView(this);
tv.setText("This is a TextView");
tv.setLayoutParams(params);

//---create a button---
Button btn = new Button(this);
btn.setText("This is a Button");
btn.setLayoutParams(params);
```

You then added them to the `LinearLayout` object:

```
//---adds the textview---
layout.addView(tv);

//---adds the button---
layout.addView(btn);
```

You also created a `LayoutParams` object to be used by the `LinearLayout` object:

```
//---create a layout param for the layout---
LinearLayout.LayoutParams layoutParam =
    new LinearLayout.LayoutParams(
        LayoutParams.FILL_PARENT,
        LayoutParams.WRAP_CONTENT );
```

Finally, you added the `LinearLayout` object to the activity:

```
this.addContentView(layout, layoutParam);
```

As you can see, using code to create the UI is quite a laborious affair. Hence, dynamically generate your UI using code only when necessary.

LISTENING FOR UI NOTIFICATIONS

Users interact with your UI at two levels: the activity level and the view level. At the activity level, the `Activity` class exposes methods that you can override. Some common methods that you can override in your activities include the following:

➤ `onKeyDown` — Called when a key was pressed and not handled by any of the views contained within the activity

➤ onKeyUp — Called when a key was released and not handled by any of the views contained within the activity

➤ onMenuItemSelected — Called when a panel's menu item has been selected by the user (covered in Chapter 5)

➤ onMenuOpened — Called when a panel's menu is opened by the user (covered in Chapter 5)

Overriding Methods Defined in an Activity

To demonstrate how activities interact with the user, the following example overrides some of the methods defined in the activity's base class.

TRY IT OUT Overriding Activity Methods

codefile UIActivity.zip available for download at Wrox.com

1. Using Eclipse, create a new Android project and name it **UIActivity**.

2. Add the following statements in bold to `main.xml` (replacing the `TextView`):

```xml
<?xml version="1.0" encoding="utf-8"?>
<LinearLayout xmlns:android="http://schemas.android.com/apk/res/android"
    android:layout_width="fill_parent"
    android:layout_height="fill_parent"
    android:orientation="vertical" >

    <TextView
        android:layout_width="214dp"
        android:layout_height="wrap_content"
        android:text="Your Name" />
    <EditText
        android:id="@+id/txt1"
        android:layout_width="214dp"
        android:layout_height="wrap_content" />
    <Button
        android:id="@+id/btn1"
        android:layout_width="106dp"
        android:layout_height="wrap_content"
        android:text="OK" />
    <Button
        android:id="@+id/btn2"
        android:layout_width="106dp"
        android:layout_height="wrap_content"
        android:text="Cancel" />

</LinearLayout>
```

3. Add the following statements in bold to the `UIActivityActivity.java` file:

```java
package net.learn2develop.UIActivity;

import android.app.Activity;
import android.os.Bundle;
```

```
import android.view.KeyEvent;
import android.widget.Toast;

public class UIActivityActivity extends Activity {
    /** Called when the activity is first created. */
    @Override
    public void onCreate(Bundle savedInstanceState) {
        super.onCreate(savedInstanceState);
        setContentView(R.layout.main);
    }

    @Override
    public boolean onKeyDown(int keyCode, KeyEvent event)
    {
        switch (keyCode)
        {
            case KeyEvent.KEYCODE_DPAD_CENTER:
                Toast.makeText(getBaseContext(),
                        "Center was clicked",
                        Toast.LENGTH_LONG).show();
                break;
            case KeyEvent.KEYCODE_DPAD_LEFT:
                Toast.makeText(getBaseContext(),
                        "Left arrow was clicked",
                        Toast.LENGTH_LONG).show();
                break;
            case KeyEvent.KEYCODE_DPAD_RIGHT:
                Toast.makeText(getBaseContext(),
                        "Right arrow was clicked",
                        Toast.LENGTH_LONG).show();
                break;
            case KeyEvent.KEYCODE_DPAD_UP:
                Toast.makeText(getBaseContext(),
                        "Up arrow was clicked",
                        Toast.LENGTH_LONG).show();

                break;
            case KeyEvent.KEYCODE_DPAD_DOWN:
                Toast.makeText(getBaseContext(),
                        "Down arrow was clicked",
                        Toast.LENGTH_LONG).show();
                break;
        }
        return false;
    }
}
```

FIGURE 3-39

4. Press F11 to debug the application on the Android emulator.

5. When the activity is loaded, type some text into the EditText. Next, click the down arrow key on the directional pad. Observe the message shown on the screen, as shown in Figure 3-39.

How It Works

When the activity is loaded, the cursor will be blinking in the EditText view, as it has the focus.

In the MainActivitiy class, you override the onKeyDown() method of the base Activity class:

```
@Override
public boolean onKeyDown(int keyCode, KeyEvent event)
{
    switch (keyCode)
    {
        case KeyEvent.KEYCODE_DPAD_CENTER:
            //...
            break;
        case KeyEvent.KEYCODE_DPAD_LEFT:
            //...
            break;
        case KeyEvent.KEYCODE_DPAD_RIGHT:
            //...
            break;
        case KeyEvent.KEYCODE_DPAD_UP:
            //...
            break;
        case KeyEvent.KEYCODE_DPAD_DOWN:
            //...
            break;
    }
    return false;
}
```

In Android, whenever you press any keys on your device, the view that currently has the focus will try to handle the event generated. In this case, when the EditText has the focus and you press a key, the EditText view handles the event and displays the character you have just pressed in the view. However, if you press the up or down directional arrow key, the EditText view does not handle this, and instead passes the event to the activity. In this case, the onKeyDown() method is called. In this example, you checked the key that was pressed and displayed a message indicating the key pressed. Observe that the focus is now also transferred to the next view, which is the OK button.

Interestingly, if the EditText view already has some text in it and the cursor is at the end of the text, then clicking the left arrow key does not fire the onKeyDown() method; it simply moves the cursor one character to the left. This is because the EditText view has already handled the event. If you press the right arrow key instead (when the cursor is at the end of the text), then the onKeyDown() method will be called (because now the EditText view will not be handling the event). The same applies when the cursor is at the beginning of the EditText view. Clicking the left arrow will fire the onKeyDown() method, whereas clicking the right arrow will simply move the cursor one character to the right.

With the OK button in focus, press the center button in the directional pad. Note that the message "Center was clicked" is not displayed. This is because the Button view itself is handling the click event. Hence, the event is not caught by the onKeyDown() method.

Note also that the onKeyDown() method returns a boolean result. You should return true when you want to tell the system that you are done with the event and that the system should not proceed further with it. For example, consider the case when you return true after each key has been matched:

```
@Override
public boolean onKeyDown(int keyCode, KeyEvent event)
{
    switch (keyCode)
    {
        case KeyEvent.KEYCODE_DPAD_CENTER:
            Toast.makeText(getBaseContext(),
                    "Center was clicked",
                    Toast.LENGTH_LONG).show();
            //break;
            return true;
        case KeyEvent.KEYCODE_DPAD_LEFT:
            Toast.makeText(getBaseContext(),
                    "Left arrow was clicked",
                    Toast.LENGTH_LONG).show();
            //break;
            return true;
        case KeyEvent.KEYCODE_DPAD_RIGHT:
            Toast.makeText(getBaseContext(),
                    "Right arrow was clicked",
                    Toast.LENGTH_LONG).show();
            //break;
            return true;
        case KeyEvent.KEYCODE_DPAD_UP:
            Toast.makeText(getBaseContext(),
                    "Up arrow was clicked",
                    Toast.LENGTH_LONG).show();

            //break;
            return true;
        case KeyEvent.KEYCODE_DPAD_DOWN:
            Toast.makeText(getBaseContext(),
                    "Down arrow was clicked",
                    Toast.LENGTH_LONG).show();
            //break;
            return true;
    }
    return false;
}
```

If you test this, you will see that now you cannot navigate between the views using the arrow keys.

Registering Events for Views

Views can fire events when users interact with them. For example, when a user touches a Button view, you need to service the event so that the appropriate action can be performed. To do so, you need to explicitly register events for views.

Using the same example discussed in the previous section, recall that the activity has two Button views; therefore, you can register the button click events using an anonymous class, as shown here:

```
package net.learn2develop.UIActivity;

import android.app.Activity;
import android.os.Bundle;
import android.view.KeyEvent;
import android.view.View;
import android.view.View.OnClickListener;
import android.widget.Button;
import android.widget.Toast;

public class UIActivityActivity extends Activity {
    /** Called when the activity is first created. */
    @Override
    public void onCreate(Bundle savedInstanceState) {
        super.onCreate(savedInstanceState);
        setContentView(R.layout.main);

        //---the two buttons are wired to the same event handler---
        Button btn1 = (Button)findViewById(R.id.btn1);
        btn1.setOnClickListener(btnListener);

        Button btn2 = (Button)findViewById(R.id.btn2);
        btn2.setOnClickListener(btnListener);
    }

    //---create an anonymous class to act as a button click listener---
    private OnClickListener btnListener = new OnClickListener()
    {
        public void onClick(View v)
        {
            Toast.makeText(getBaseContext(),
                    ((Button) v).getText() + " was clicked",
                    Toast.LENGTH_LONG).show();
        }
    };

    @Override
    public boolean onKeyDown(int keyCode, KeyEvent event)
    {
        //...
    }
}
```

If you now click either the OK button or the Cancel button, the appropriate message will be displayed (see Figure 3-40), proving that the event is wired up properly.

FIGURE 3-40

Besides defining an anonymous class for the event handler, you can also define an anonymous inner class to handle an event. The following example shows how you can handle the onFocusChange() method for the EditText view:

```
import android.widget.EditText;

    @Override
    public void onCreate(Bundle savedInstanceState) {
        super.onCreate(savedInstanceState);
        setContentView(R.layout.main);

        //---the two buttons are wired to the same event handler---
        Button btn1 = (Button)findViewById(R.id.btn1);
        btn1.setOnClickListener(btnListener);

        Button btn2 = (Button)findViewById(R.id.btn2);
        btn2.setOnClickListener(btnListener);

        //---create an anonymous inner class to act as an onfocus listener---
        EditText txt1 = (EditText)findViewById(R.id.txt1);
        txt1.setOnFocusChangeListener(new View.OnFocusChangeListener()
        {
            @Override
            public void onFocusChange(View v, boolean hasFocus) {
                Toast.makeText(getBaseContext(),
```

```
                          ((EditText) v).getId() + " has focus - " + hasFocus,
                          Toast.LENGTH_LONG).show();
              }
          });
      }
```

 NOTE *For this example, you should ensure that the* `onKeyDown()` *method returns a* `false`, *instead of* `true` *as you have tried in the previous section.*

As shown in Figure 3-41, when the `EditText` view receives the focus, a message is printed on the screen.

FIGURE 3-41

Using the anonymous inner class, the click event handler for the two `Buttons` can also be rewritten as follows:

```
//---the two buttons are wired to the same event handler---
Button btn1 = (Button)findViewById(R.id.btn1);
//btn1.setOnClickListener(btnListener);
btn1.setOnClickListener(new View.OnClickListener() {
    public void onClick(View v) {
        //---do something---
    }
});

Button btn2 = (Button)findViewById(R.id.btn2);
```

```
//btn2.setOnClickListener(btnListener);
btn2.setOnClickListener(new View.OnClickListener() {
    public void onClick(View v) {
        //---do something---
    }
});
```

Which method should you use to handle events? An anonymous class is useful if you have multiple views handled by one event handler. The anonymous inner class method (the latter method described) is useful if you have an event handler for a single view.

SUMMARY

In this chapter, you have learned how user interfaces are created in Android. You have also learned about the different layouts that you can use to position the views in your Android UI. Because Android devices support more than one screen orientation, you need to take special care to ensure that your UI can adapt to changes in screen orientation.

EXERCISES

1. What is the difference between the dp unit and the px unit? Which one should you use to specify the dimension of a view?

2. Why is the AbsoluteLayout not recommended for use?

3. What is the difference between the onPause() method and the onSaveInstanceState() method?

4. Name the three methods you can override to save an activity's state. In what instances should you use the various methods?

5. How do you add action items to the Action Bar?

Answers to the exercises can be found in Appendix C.

▶ WHAT YOU LEARNED IN THIS CHAPTER

TOPIC	KEY CONCEPTS
`LinearLayout`	Arranges views in a single column or single row
`AbsoluteLayout`	Enables you to specify the exact location of its children
`TableLayout`	Groups views into rows and columns
`RelativeLayout`	Enables you to specify how child views are positioned relative to each other
`FrameLayout`	A placeholder on screen that you can use to display a single view
`ScrollView`	A special type of `FrameLayout` in that it enables users to scroll through a list of views that occupy more space than the physical display allows
Unit of Measure	Use `dp` for specifying the dimension of views and `sp` for font size.
Two ways to adapt to changes in orientation	Anchoring, and resizing and repositioning
Using different XML files for different orientations	Use the `layout` folder for portrait UI, and `layout-land` for landscape UI.
Three ways to persist activity state	Use the `onPause()` method. Use the `onSaveInstanceState()` method. Use the `onRetainNonConfigurationInstance()` method.
Getting the dimension of the current device	Use the `WindowManager` class's `getDefaultDisplay()` method.
Constraining the activity's orientation	Use the `setRequestOrientation()` method, or the `android:screenOrientation` attribute in the `AndroidManifest.xml` file.
Action Bar	Replaces the traditional title bar for older versions of Android
Action items	Action items are displayed on the right of the Action Bar. They are created just like options menus.
Application icon	Usually used to return to the "home" activity of an application. It is advisable to use the `Intent` object with the `Intent.FLAG_ACTIVITY_CLEAR_TOP` flag.

Designing Your User Interface With Views

WHAT YOU WILL LEARN IN THIS CHAPTER

➤ How to use the basic views in Android to design your user interface

➤ How to use the picker views to display lists of items

➤ How to use the list views to display lists of items

➤ How to use specialized fragments

In the previous chapter, you learned about the various layouts that you can use to position your views in an activity. You also learned about the techniques you can use to adapt to different screen resolutions and sizes. In this chapter, you will take a look at the various views that you can use to design the user interface for your applications.

In particular, you will learn about the following ViewGroups:

➤ **Basic views** — Commonly used views such as the `TextView`, `EditText`, and `Button` views

➤ **Picker views** — Views that enable users to select from a list, such as the `TimePicker` and `DatePicker` views

➤ **List views** — Views that display a long list of items, such as the `ListView` and the `SpinnerView` views

➤ **Specialized fragments** — Special fragments that perform specific functions

Subsequent chapters cover the other views not covered in this chapter, such as the analog and digital clock views and other views for displaying graphics, and so on.

USING BASIC VIEWS

To get started, this section explores some of the basic views that you can use to design the UI of your Android applications:

➤   TextView

➤   EditText

➤   Button

➤   ImageButton

➤   CheckBox

➤   ToggleButton

➤   RadioButton

➤   RadioGroup

These basic views enable you to display text information, as well as perform some basic selection. The following sections explore all these views in more detail.

TextView View

When you create a new Android project, Eclipse always creates the `main.xml` file (located in the `res/layout` folder), which contains a `<TextView>` element:

```xml
<?xml version="1.0" encoding="utf-8"?>
<LinearLayout xmlns:android="http://schemas.android.com/apk/res/android"
    android:layout_width="fill_parent"
    android:layout_height="fill_parent"
    android:orientation="vertical" >

    <TextView
        android:layout_width="fill_parent"
        android:layout_height="wrap_content"
        android:text="@string/hello" />

</LinearLayout>
```

The `TextView` view is used to display text to the user. This is the most basic view and one that you will frequently use when you develop Android applications. If you need to allow users to edit the text displayed, you should use the subclass of `TextView`, `EditText`, which is discussed in the next section.

NOTE *In some other platforms, the* `TextView` *is commonly known as the* label *view. Its sole purpose is to display text on the screen.*

Button, ImageButton, EditText, CheckBox, ToggleButton, RadioButton, and RadioGroup Views

Besides the `TextView` view, which you will likely use the most often, there are some other basic views that you will find yourself frequently using:

➤   `Button` — Represents a push-button widget

➤   `ImageButton` — Similar to the `Button` view, except that it also displays an image

➤   `EditText` — A subclass of the `TextView` view that allows users to edit its text content

➤   `CheckBox` — A special type of button that has two states: checked or unchecked

➤   `RadioGroup` and `RadioButton` — The `RadioButton` has two states: either checked or unchecked.. A `RadioGroup` is used to group together one or more `RadioButton` views, thereby allowing only one `RadioButton` to be checked within the `RadioGroup`.

➤   `ToggleButton` — Displays checked/unchecked states using a light indicator

The following Try It Out provides details about how these views work.

TRY IT OUT   **Using the Basic Views**

codefile BasicViews1.zip available for download at Wrox.com

1.   Using Eclipse, create an Android project and name it **BasicViews1**.

2.   Modify the `main.xml` file located in the `res/layout` folder by adding the following elements shown in bold:

```xml
<?xml version="1.0" encoding="utf-8"?>
<LinearLayout xmlns:android="http://schemas.android.com/apk/res/android"
    android:layout_width="fill_parent"
    android:layout_height="fill_parent"
    android:orientation="vertical" >

<Button android:id="@+id/btnSave"
    android:layout_width="fill_parent"
    android:layout_height="wrap_content"
    android:text="save" />

<Button android:id="@+id/btnOpen"
    android:layout_width="wrap_content"
    android:layout_height="wrap_content"
    android:text="Open" />

<ImageButton android:id="@+id/btnImg1"
    android:layout_width="fill_parent"
    android:layout_height="wrap_content"
    android:src="@drawable/ic_launcher" />

<EditText android:id="@+id/txtName"
    android:layout_width="fill_parent"
```

```
        android:layout_height="wrap_content" />

<CheckBox android:id="@+id/chkAutosave"
    android:layout_width="fill_parent"
    android:layout_height="wrap_content"
    android:text="Autosave" />

<CheckBox android:id="@+id/star"
    style="?android:attr/starStyle"
    android:layout_width="wrap_content"
    android:layout_height="wrap_content" />

<RadioGroup android:id="@+id/rdbGp1"
    android:layout_width="fill_parent"
    android:layout_height="wrap_content"
    android:orientation="vertical" >

    <RadioButton android:id="@+id/rdb1"
        android:layout_width="fill_parent"
        android:layout_height="wrap_content"
        android:text="Option 1" />

    <RadioButton android:id="@+id/rdb2"
        android:layout_width="fill_parent"
        android:layout_height="wrap_content"
        android:text="Option 2" />

</RadioGroup>

<ToggleButton android:id="@+id/toggle1"
    android:layout_width="wrap_content"
    android:layout_height="wrap_content" />

</LinearLayout>
```

3. To see the views in action, debug the project in Eclipse by selecting the project name and pressing F11. Figure 4-1 shows the various views displayed in the Android emulator.

4. Click the various views and note how they vary in their look and feel. Figure 4-2 shows the following changes to the view:

➤   The first CheckBox view (Autosave) is checked.

➤   The second CheckBox View (star) is selected.

➤   The second RadioButton (Option 2) is selected.

➤   The ToggleButton is turned on.

FIGURE 4-1

FIGURE 4-2

How It Works

So far, all the views are relatively straightforward — they are listed using the `<LinearLayout>` element, so they are stacked on top of each other when they are displayed in the activity.

For the first `Button`, the `layout_width` attribute is set to `fill_parent` so that its width occupies the entire width of the screen:

```
<Button android:id="@+id/btnSave"
    android:layout_width="fill_parent"
    android:layout_height="wrap_content"
    android:text="save" />
```

For the second Button, the `layout_width` attribute is set to `wrap_content` so that its width will be the width of its content — specifically, the text that it is displaying (i.e.,"Open"):

```
<Button android:id="@+id/btnOpen"
    android:layout_width="wrap_content"
    android:layout_height="wrap_content"
    android:text="Open" />
```

The `ImageButton` displays a button with an image. The image is set through the `src` attribute. In this case, you simply used the image for the application icon:

```
<ImageButton android:id="@+id/btnImg1"
    android:layout_width="fill_parent"
    android:layout_height="wrap_content"
    android:src="@drawable/ic_launcher" />
```

The EditText view displays a rectangular region where the user can enter some text. You set the layout_height to wrap_content so that if the user enters a long string of text, its height will automatically be adjusted to fit the content (see Figure 4-3).

```
<EditText android:id="@+id/txtName"
    android:layout_width="fill_parent"
    android:layout_height="wrap_content" />
```

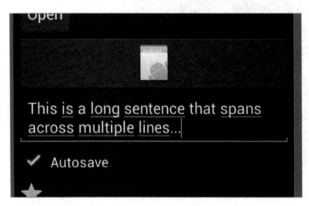

FIGURE 4-3

The CheckBox displays a checkbox that users can tap to check or uncheck:

```
<CheckBox android:id="@+id/chkAutosave"
    android:layout_width="fill_parent"
      android:layout_height="wrap_content"
      android:text="Autosave" />
```

If you do not like the default look of the CheckBox, you can apply a style attribute to it to display it as another image, such as a star:

```
<CheckBox android:id="@+id/star"
    style="?android:attr/starStyle"
    android:layout_width="wrap_content"
    android:layout_height="wrap_content" />
```

The format for the value of the style attribute is as follows:

```
?[package:][type:]name
```

The RadioGroup encloses two RadioButtons. This is important because radio buttons are usually used to present multiple options to the user for selection. When a RadioButton in a RadioGroup is selected, all other RadioButtons are automatically unselected:

```
<RadioGroup android:id="@+id/rdbGp1"
    android:layout_width="fill_parent"
    android:layout_height="wrap_content"
```

```
    android:orientation="vertical" >

    <RadioButton android:id="@+id/rdb1"
        android:layout_width="fill_parent"
        android:layout_height="wrap_content"
        android:text="Option 1" />

    <RadioButton android:id="@+id/rdb2"
        android:layout_width="fill_parent"
        android:layout_height="wrap_content"
        android:text="Option 2" />

</RadioGroup>
```

Notice that the `RadioButtons` are listed vertically, one on top of another. If you want to list them horizontally, you need to change the `orientation` attribute to `horizontal`. You would also need to ensure that the `layout_width` attribute of the `RadioButtons` are set to `wrap_content`:

```
<RadioGroup android:id="@+id/rdbGp1"
    android:layout_width="fill_parent"
    android:layout_height="wrap_content"
    android:orientation="horizontal" >
    <RadioButton android:id="@+id/rdb1"
        android:layout_width="wrap_content"
        android:layout_height="wrap_content"
        android:text="Option 1" />
    <RadioButton android:id="@+id/rdb2"
        android:layout_width="wrap_content"
        android:layout_height="wrap_content"
        android:text="Option 2" />
</RadioGroup>
```

Figure 4-4 shows the `RadioButtons` displayed horizontally.

FIGURE 4-4

The `ToogleButton` displays a rectangular button that users can toggle on and off by clicking:

```
<ToggleButton android:id="@+id/toggle1"
    android:layout_width="wrap_content"
    android:layout_height="wrap_content" />
```

One thing that has been consistent throughout this example is that each view has the `id` attribute set to a particular value, such as in the case of the `Button`:

```
<Button android:id="@+id/btnSave"
    android:layout_width="fill_parent"
    android:layout_height="wrap_content"
    android:text="@string/save" />
```

The `id` attribute is an identifier for a view so that it may later be retrieved using the `View.findViewById()` or `Activity.findViewById()` methods.

The various views that you have just seen were tested on an Android emulator emulating an Android 4.0 smartphone. What will they look like when run on older versions of Android devices? What about Android tablets?

Figure 4-5 shows what your activity will look like if you change the `android:minSdkVersion` attribute in the `AndroidManifest.xml` file to 10 and run it on the Google Nexus S running Android 2.3.6:

```
<uses-sdk android:minSdkVersion="10" />
```

Figure 4-6 shows what your activity will look like if you change the `android:minSdkVersion` attribute in the `AndroidManifest.xml` file to 13 and run it on the Asus Eee Pad Transformer running Android 3.2.1.

FIGURE 4-5

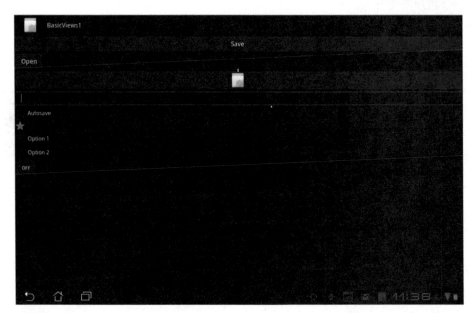

FIGURE 4-6

If you now run it on the Asus Eee Pad Transformer running Android 3.2.1 with the `android:minSdkVersion` attribute set to 8 or smaller, you will see the additional button that appears in Figure 4-7.

FIGURE 4-7

Tapping on the button will reveal the option to stretch the activity to fill the entire screen (default) or zoom the activity to fill the screen (see Figure 4-8).

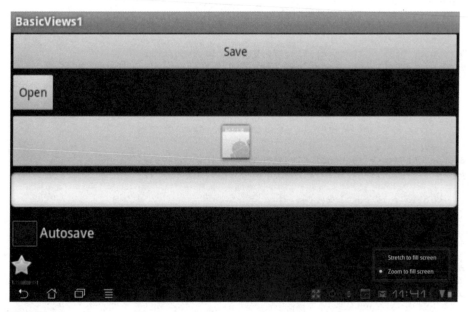

FIGURE 4-8

In short, applications with the minimum SDK version set to 8 or lower can be displayed at the screen ratios with which they were originally designed, or they can automatically stretch to fill the screen (default behavior).

Now that you have seen what the various views for an activity look like, the following Try It Out demonstrates how you can programmatically control them.

TRY IT OUT Handling View Events

1. Using the BasicViews1 project created in the previous Try It Out, modify the BasicViews1Activity .java file by adding the following statements in bold:

```java
package net.learn2develop.BasicViews1;

import android.app.Activity;
import android.os.Bundle;
import android.view.View;
import android.widget.Button;
import android.widget.CheckBox;
import android.widget.RadioButton;
import android.widget.RadioGroup;
import android.widget.RadioGroup.OnCheckedChangeListener;
import android.widget.Toast;
import android.widget.ToggleButton;

public class BasicViews1Activity extends Activity {
    /** Called when the activity is first created. */
    @Override
    public void onCreate(Bundle savedInstanceState) {
        super.onCreate(savedInstanceState);
        setContentView(R.layout.main);

        //---Button view---
        Button btnOpen = (Button) findViewById(R.id.btnOpen);
        btnOpen.setOnClickListener(new View.OnClickListener() {
            public void onClick(View v) {
                DisplayToast("You have clicked the Open button");
            }
        });

        //---Button view---
        Button btnSave = (Button) findViewById(R.id.btnSave);
        btnSave.setOnClickListener(new View.OnClickListener()
        {
            public void onClick(View v) {
                DisplayToast("You have clicked the Save button");
            }
        });

        //---CheckBox---
        CheckBox checkBox = (CheckBox) findViewById(R.id.chkAutosave);
        checkBox.setOnClickListener(new View.OnClickListener()
        {
            public void onClick(View v) {
```

```
                    if (((CheckBox)v).isChecked())
                        DisplayToast("CheckBox is checked");
                    else
                        DisplayToast("CheckBox is unchecked");
                }
            });

            //---RadioButton---
            RadioGroup radioGroup = (RadioGroup) findViewById(R.id.rdbGp1);
            radioGroup.setOnCheckedChangeListener(new OnCheckedChangeListener()
            {
                public void onCheckedChanged(RadioGroup group, int checkedId) {
                    RadioButton rb1 = (RadioButton) findViewById(R.id.rdb1);
                    if (rb1.isChecked()) {
                        DisplayToast("Option 1 checked!");
                    } else {
                        DisplayToast("Option 2 checked!");
                    }
                }
            });

            //---ToggleButton---
            ToggleButton toggleButton =
                    (ToggleButton) findViewById(R.id.toggle1);
            toggleButton.setOnClickListener(new View.OnClickListener()
            {
                public void onClick(View v) {
                    if (((ToggleButton)v).isChecked())
                        DisplayToast("Toggle button is On");
                    else
                        DisplayToast("Toggle button is Off");
                }
            });
        }

        private void DisplayToast(String msg)
        {
            Toast.makeText(getBaseContext(), msg,
                    Toast.LENGTH_SHORT).show();
        }

    }
```

2.   Press F11 to debug the project on the Android emulator.

3.   Click on the various views and observe the message displayed in the Toast window.

How It Works

To handle the events fired by each view, you first have to programmatically locate the view that you created during the onCreate() event. You do so using the findViewById() method (belonging to the Activity base class), supplying it with the ID of the view:

```
                //---Button view---
                Button btnOpen = (Button) findViewById(R.id.btnOpen);
```

The setOnClickListener() method registers a callback to be invoked later when the view is clicked:

```
btnOpen.setOnClickListener(new View.OnClickListener() {
    public void onClick(View v) {
        DisplayToast("You have clicked the Open button");
    }
});
```

The onClick() method is called when the view is clicked.

To determine the state of the CheckBox, you have to typecast the argument of the onClick() method to a CheckBox and then check its isChecked() method to see if it is checked:

```
CheckBox checkBox = (CheckBox) findViewById(R.id.chkAutosave);
checkBox.setOnClickListener(new View.OnClickListener()
{
    public void onClick(View v) {
        if (((CheckBox)v).isChecked())
            DisplayToast("CheckBox is checked");
        else
            DisplayToast("CheckBox is unchecked");
    }
});
```

For the RadioButton, you need to use the setOnCheckedChangeListener() method on the RadioGroup to register a callback to be invoked when the checked RadioButton changes in this group:

```
//---RadioButton---
RadioGroup radioGroup = (RadioGroup) findViewById(R.id.rdbGp1);
radioGroup.setOnCheckedChangeListener(new OnCheckedChangeListener()
{
    public void onCheckedChanged(RadioGroup group, int checkedId) {
        RadioButton rb1 = (RadioButton) findViewById(R.id.rdb1);
        if (rb1.isChecked()) {
            DisplayToast("Option 1 checked!");
        } else {
            DisplayToast("Option 2 checked!");
        }
    }
});
```

When a RadioButton is selected, the onCheckedChanged() method is fired. Within it, you locate individual RadioButtons and then call their isChecked() method to determine which RadioButton is selected. Alternatively, the onCheckedChanged() method contains a second argument that contains a unique identifier of the RadioButton selected.

The ToggleButton works just like the CheckBox.

So far, to handle the events on the views, you first had to get a reference to the view and then register a callback to handle the event. There is another way to handle view events. Using the Button as an example, you can add an attribute called onClick to it:

```
<Button android:id="@+id/btnSave"
    android:layout_width="fill_parent"
    android:layout_height="wrap_content"
    android:text="@string/save"
    android:onClick="btnSaved_clicked"/>
```

The onClick attribute specifies the click event of the button. The value of this attribute is the name of the event handler. Therefore, to handle the click event of the button, you simply need to create a method called btnSaved_clicked, as shown in the following example (note that the method must have a single parameter of type View):

```
public class BasicViews1Activity extends Activity {

    public void btnSaved_clicked (View view) {
        DisplayToast("You have clicked the Save button1");
    }

    /** Called when the activity is first created. */
    @Override
    public void onCreate(Bundle savedInstanceState) {
        super.onCreate(savedInstanceState);
        setContentView(R.layout.main);

        //...
    }

    private void DisplayToast(String msg)
    {
        Toast.makeText(getBaseContext(), msg,
                Toast.LENGTH_SHORT).show();
    }

}
```

If you compare this approach to the earlier ones used, this is much simpler. Which method you use is really up to you, but this book mostly uses the latter approach.

ProgressBar View

The ProgressBar view provides visual feedback about some ongoing tasks, such as when you are performing a task in the background. For example, you might be downloading some data from the web and need to update the user about the status of the download. In this case, the ProgressBar view is a good choice for this task. The following activity demonstrates how to use this view.

Using the ProgressBar View

codefile BasicViews2.zip available for download at Wrox.com

1. Using Eclipse, create an Android project and name it **BasicViews2**.

2. Modify the main.xml file located in the res/layout folder by adding the following code in bold:

```xml
<?xml version="1.0" encoding="utf-8"?>
<LinearLayout xmlns:android="http://schemas.android.com/apk/res/android"
    android:layout_width="fill_parent"
    android:layout_height="fill_parent"
    android:orientation="vertical" >

<ProgressBar android:id="@+id/progressbar"
    android:layout_width="wrap_content"
    android:layout_height="wrap_content" />

</LinearLayout>
```

3. In the BasicViews2Activity.java file, add the following statements in bold:

```java
package net.learn2develop.BasicViews2;

import android.app.Activity;
import android.os.Bundle;
import android.os.Handler;
import android.view.View;
import android.widget.ProgressBar;

public class BasicViews2Activity extends Activity {
    static int progress;
    ProgressBar progressBar;
    int progressStatus = 0;
    Handler handler = new Handler();

    /** Called when the activity is first created. */
    @Override
    public void onCreate(Bundle savedInstanceState) {
        super.onCreate(savedInstanceState);
        setContentView(R.layout.main);

        progress = 0;
        progressBar = (ProgressBar) findViewById(R.id.progressbar);

        //---do some work in background thread---
        new Thread(new Runnable()
        {
            public void run()
            {
                //---do some work here---
                while (progressStatus < 10)
                {
                    progressStatus = doSomeWork();
                }

                //---hides the progress bar---
```

```
                    handler.post(new Runnable()
                    {
                        public void run()
                        {
                            //---0 - VISIBLE; 4 - INVISIBLE; 8 - GONE---
                            progressBar.setVisibility(View.GONE);
                        }
                    });
                }

                //---do some long running work here---
                private int doSomeWork()
                {
                    try {
                        //---simulate doing some work---
                        Thread.sleep(500);
                    } catch (InterruptedException e)
                    {
                        e.printStackTrace();
                    }
                    return ++progress;
                }
            }).start();
        }
    }
```

4. Press F11 to debug the project on the Android emulator. Figure 4-9 shows the ProgressBar animating. After about five seconds, it will disappear.

FIGURE 4-9

How It Works

The default mode of the ProgressBar view is indeterminate — that is, it shows a cyclic animation. This mode is useful for tasks that do not have specific completion times, such as when you are sending some data to a web service and waiting for the server to respond. If you simply put the <ProgressBar> element in your main.xml file, it will display a spinning icon continuously. It is your responsibility to stop it when your background task has completed.

The code that you have added in the Java file shows how you can spin off a background thread to simulate performing some long-running tasks. To do so, you use the Thread class together with a Runnable object. The run() method starts the execution of the thread, which in this case calls the doSomeWork() method to simulate doing some work. When the simulated work is done (after about five seconds), you use a Handler object to send a message to the thread to dismiss the ProgressBar:

```
            //---do some work in background thread---
            new Thread(new Runnable()
            {
                public void run()
                {
                    //---do some work here---
                    while (progressStatus < 10)
                    {
                        progressStatus = doSomeWork();
```

```
            }

            //---hides the progress bar---
            handler.post(new Runnable()
            {
                public void run()
                {
                    //---0 - VISIBLE; 4 - INVISIBLE; 8 - GONE---
                    progressBar.setVisibility(View.GONE);
                }
            });
        }

        //---do some long running work here---
        private int doSomeWork()
        {
            try {
                //---simulate doing some work---
                Thread.sleep(500);
            } catch (InterruptedException e)
            {
                e.printStackTrace();
            }
            return ++progress;
        }
    }).start();
```

When the task is completed, you hide the ProgressBar by setting its Visibility property to View
.GONE (value 8). The difference between the INVISIBLE and GONE constants is that the INVISIBLE
constant simply hides the ProgressBar (the region occupied by the ProgressBar is still taking up
space in the activity); whereas the GONE constant removes the ProgressBar view from the activity and
does not take up any space on it.

The next Try It Out shows how you can change the look of the ProgressBar.

TRY IT OUT   Customizing the ProgressBar View

1.   Using the BasicViews2 project created in the previous Try It Out, modify the main.xml file
as shown here:

```xml
<?xml version="1.0" encoding="utf-8"?>
<LinearLayout xmlns:android="http://schemas.android.com/apk/res/android"
    android:layout_width="fill_parent"
    android:layout_height="fill_parent"
    android:orientation="vertical" >

<ProgressBar android:id="@+id/progressbar"
    android:layout_width="wrap_content"
    android:layout_height="wrap_content"
    style="@android:style/Widget.ProgressBar.Horizontal" />

</LinearLayout>
```

2. Modify the `BasicViews2Activity.java` file by adding the following statements in bold:

```java
package net.learn2develop.BasicViews2;

import android.app.Activity;
import android.os.Bundle;
import android.os.Handler;
import android.view.View;
import android.widget.ProgressBar;

public class BasicViews2Activity extends Activity {
    static int progress;
    ProgressBar progressBar;
    int progressStatus = 0;
    Handler handler = new Handler();

    /** Called when the activity is first created. */
    @Override
    public void onCreate(Bundle savedInstanceState) {
        super.onCreate(savedInstanceState);
        setContentView(R.layout.main);

        progress = 0;
        progressBar = (ProgressBar) findViewById(R.id.progressbar);
        progressBar.setMax(200);

        //---do some work in background thread---
        new Thread(new Runnable()
        {
            public void run()
            {
                //---do some work here---
                while (progressStatus < 100)
                {
                    progressStatus = doSomeWork();

                    //---Update the progress bar---
                    handler.post(new Runnable()
                    {
                        public void run() {
                            progressBar.setProgress(progressStatus);
                        }
                    });
                }

                //---hides the progress bar---
                handler.post(new Runnable()
                {
                    public void run()
                    {
                        //---0 - VISIBLE; 4 - INVISIBLE; 8 - GONE---
                        progressBar.setVisibility(View.GONE);
                    }
                });
```

```
        }

        //---do some long running work here---
        private int doSomeWork()
        {
            try {
                //---simulate doing some work---
                Thread.sleep(500);
            } catch (InterruptedException e)
            {
                e.printStackTrace();
            }
            return ++progress;
        }
    }).start();
    }
}
```

3. Press F11 to debug the project on the
   Android emulator.

4. Figure 4-10 shows the ProgressBar
   displaying the progress. The
   ProgressBar disappears when the
   progress reaches 50%.

FIGURE 4-10

How It Works

To make the ProgressBar display horizontally, simply set its style attribute to @android:style/
Widget.ProgressBar.Horizontal:

```
<ProgressBar android:id="@+id/progressbar"
    android:layout_width="wrap_content"
    android:layout_height="wrap_content"
    style="@android:style/Widget.ProgressBar.Horizontal" />
```

To display the progress, call its setProgress() method, passing in an integer indicating its progress:

```
//---Update the progress bar---
handler.post(new Runnable()
{
    public void run() {
        progressBar.setProgress(progressStatus);
    }
});
```

In this example, you set the range of the ProgressBar from 0 to 200 (via the setMax() method).
Hence, the ProgressBar will stop and then disappear when it is halfway through (since you only
continue to call the doSomeWork() method as long as the progressStatus is less than 100). To ensure
that the ProgressBar disappears only when the progress reaches 100%, either set the maximum value
to 100 or modify the while loop to stop when the progressStatus reaches 200, like this:

```
//---do some work here---
while (progressStatus < 200)
```

Besides the horizontal style for the `ProgressBar` that you have used for this example, you can also use the following constants:

➤   `Widget.ProgressBar.Horizontal`

➤   `Widget.ProgressBar.Small`

➤   `Widget.ProgressBar.Large`

➤   `Widget.ProgressBar.Inverse`

➤   `Widget.ProgressBar.Small.Inverse`

➤   `Widget.ProgressBar.Large.Inverse`

AutoCompleteTextView View

The `AutoCompleteTextView` is a view that is similar to `EditText` (in fact it is a subclass of `EditText`), except that it shows a list of completion suggestions automatically while the user is typing. The following Try It Out shows how to use the `AutoCompleteTextView` to automatically help users complete the text entry.

TRY IT OUT   Using the AutoCompleteTextView

codefile BasicViews3.zip available for download at Wrox.com

1.   Using Eclipse, create an Android project and name it **BasicViews3**.

2.   Modify the `main.xml` file located in the `res/layout` folder as shown here in bold:

```xml
<?xml version="1.0" encoding="utf-8"?>
<LinearLayout xmlns:android="http://schemas.android.com/apk/res/android"
    android:layout_width="fill_parent"
    android:layout_height="fill_parent"
    android:orientation="vertical" >

<TextView
    android:layout_width="fill_parent"
    android:layout_height="wrap_content"
    android:text="Name of President" />

<AutoCompleteTextView android:id="@+id/txtCountries"
    android:layout_width="fill_parent"
    android:layout_height="wrap_content" />

</LinearLayout>
```

3.   Add the following statements in bold to the `BasicViews3Activity.java` file:

```java
package net.learn2develop.BasicViews3;

import android.app.Activity;
import android.os.Bundle;
```

```
import android.widget.ArrayAdapter;
import android.widget.AutoCompleteTextView;

public class BasicViews3Activity extends Activity {
    String[] presidents = {
            "Dwight D. Eisenhower",
            "John F. Kennedy",
            "Lyndon B. Johnson",
            "Richard Nixon",
            "Gerald Ford",
            "Jimmy Carter",
            "Ronald Reagan",
            "George H. W. Bush",
            "Bill Clinton",
            "George W. Bush",
            "Barack Obama"
        };

    /** Called when the activity is first created. */
    @Override
    public void onCreate(Bundle savedInstanceState) {
        super.onCreate(savedInstanceState);
        setContentView(R.layout.main);

        ArrayAdapter<String> adapter = new ArrayAdapter<String>(this,
            android.R.layout.simple_dropdown_item_1line, presidents);

        AutoCompleteTextView textView = (AutoCompleteTextView)
            findViewById(R.id.txtCountries);

        textView.setThreshold(3);
        textView.setAdapter(adapter);
    }
}
```

4. Press F11 to debug the application on the Android emulator. As shown in Figure 4-11, a list of matching names appears as you type into the AutoCompleteTextView.

How It Works

In the BasicViews3Activity class, you first created a String array containing a list of presidents' names:

```
String[] presidents = {
        "Dwight D. Eisenhower",
        "John F. Kennedy",
        "Lyndon B. Johnson",
        "Richard Nixon",
        "Gerald Ford",
        "Jimmy Carter",
        "Ronald Reagan",
        "George H. W. Bush",
        "Bill Clinton",
```

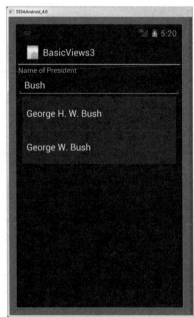

FIGURE 4-11

```
                    "George W. Bush",
                    "Barack Obama"
            };
```

The `ArrayAdapter` object manages the array of strings that will be displayed by the `AutoCompleteTextView`. In the preceding example, you set the `AutoCompleteTextView` to display in the `simple_dropdown_item_1line` mode:

```
            ArrayAdapter<String> adapter = new ArrayAdapter<String>(this,
                    android.R.layout.simple_dropdown_item_1line, presidents);
```

The `setThreshold()` method sets the minimum number of characters the user must type before the suggestions appear as a drop-down menu:

```
            textView.setThreshold(3);
```

The list of suggestions to display for the `AutoCompleteTextView` is obtained from the `ArrayAdapter` object:

```
            textView.setAdapter(adapter);
```

USING PICKER VIEWS

Selecting the date and time is one of the common tasks you need to perform in a mobile application. Android supports this functionality through the `TimePicker` and `DatePicker` views. The following sections demonstrate how to use these views in your activity.

TimePicker View

The `TimePicker` view enables users to select a time of the day, in either 24-hour mode or AM/PM mode. The following Try It Out shows you how to use it.

TRY IT OUT   Using the TimePicker View

codefile BasicViews4.zip available for download at Wrox.com

1.   Using Eclipse, create an Android project and name it **BasicViews4**.

2.   Modify the `main.xml` file located in the `res/layout` folder by adding the following lines in bold:

```
<?xml version="1.0" encoding="utf-8"?>
<LinearLayout xmlns:android="http://schemas.android.com/apk/res/android"
    android:layout_width="fill_parent"
    android:layout_height="fill_parent"
    android:orientation="vertical" >

<TimePicker android:id="@+id/timePicker"
    android:layout_width="wrap_content"
```

```
    android:layout_height="wrap_content" />

<Button android:id="@+id/btnSet"
    android:layout_width="wrap_content"
    android:layout_height="wrap_content"
    android:text="I am all set!"
    android:onClick="onClick" />

</LinearLayout>
```

3. Select the project name in Eclipse and press F11 to debug the application on the Android emulator. Figure 4-12 shows the `TimePicker` in action. Besides clicking the plus (+) and minus (-) buttons, you can use the numeric keypad on the device to change the hour and minute, and click the AM button to toggle between AM and PM.

4. Back in Eclipse, add the following statements in bold to the `BasicViews4Activity.java` file:

FIGURE 4-12

```
package net.learn2develop.BasicViews4;

import android.app.Activity;
import android.os.Bundle;
import android.view.View;
import android.widget.TimePicker;
import android.widget.Toast;

public class BasicViews4Activity extends Activity {
    TimePicker timePicker;

    /** Called when the activity is first created. */
    @Override
    public void onCreate(Bundle savedInstanceState) {
        super.onCreate(savedInstanceState);
        setContentView(R.layout.main);

        timePicker = (TimePicker) findViewById(R.id.timePicker);
        timePicker.setIs24HourView(true);
    }

    public void onClick(View view) {
        Toast.makeText(getBaseContext(),
                "Time selected:" +
                timePicker.getCurrentHour() +
                ":" + timePicker.getCurrentMinute(),
                Toast.LENGTH_SHORT).show();
    }

}
```

5. Press F11 to debug the application on the Android emulator. This time, the `TimePicker` will be displayed in the 24-hour format. Clicking the `Button` will display the time that you have set in the `TimePicker` (see Figure 4-13).

How It Works

The `TimePicker` displays a standard UI to enable users to set a time. By default, it displays the time in the AM/PM format. If you wish to display the time in the 24-hour format, you can use the `setIs24HourView()` method.

To programmatically get the time set by the user, use the `getCurrentHour()` and `getCurrentMinute()` methods:

```
Toast.makeText(getBaseContext(),
    "Time selected:" +
    timePicker.getCurrentHour() +
    ":" + timePicker.getCurrentMinute(),
    Toast.LENGTH_SHORT).show();
```

FIGURE 4-13

 NOTE *The* `getCurrentHour()` *method always returns the hour in 24-hour format (i.e., a value from 0 to 23).*

Although you can display the `TimePicker` in an activity, it's better to display it in a dialog window; that way, once the time is set, it disappears and doesn't take up any space in an activity. The following Try It Out demonstrates how to do just that.

TRY IT OUT   Using a Dialog to Display the TimePicker View

1. Using the BasicViews4 project created in the previous Try It Out, modify the `BasicViews4Activity` `.java` file as shown here:

```
package net.learn2develop.BasicViews4;

import java.text.SimpleDateFormat;
import java.util.Date;

import android.app.Activity;
import android.app.Dialog;
import android.app.TimePickerDialog;
import android.os.Bundle;
import android.view.View;
import android.widget.TimePicker;
```

```java
import android.widget.Toast;

public class BasicViews4Activity extends Activity {
    TimePicker timePicker;

    int hour, minute;
    static final int TIME_DIALOG_ID = 0;

    /** Called when the activity is first created. */
    @Override
    public void onCreate(Bundle savedInstanceState) {
        super.onCreate(savedInstanceState);
        setContentView(R.layout.main);

        timePicker = (TimePicker) findViewById(R.id.timePicker);
        timePicker.setIs24HourView(true);

        showDialog(TIME_DIALOG_ID);
    }

    @Override
    protected Dialog onCreateDialog(int id)
    {
        switch (id) {
        case TIME_DIALOG_ID:
            return new TimePickerDialog(
                    this, mTimeSetListener, hour, minute, false);
        }
        return null;
    }

    private TimePickerDialog.OnTimeSetListener mTimeSetListener =
    new TimePickerDialog.OnTimeSetListener()
    {
        public void onTimeSet(
                TimePicker view, int hourOfDay, int minuteOfHour)
        {
            hour = hourOfDay;
            minute = minuteOfHour;

            SimpleDateFormat timeFormat = new SimpleDateFormat("hh:mm aa");
            Date date = new Date(0,0,0, hour, minute);
            String strDate = timeFormat.format(date);

            Toast.makeText(getBaseContext(),
                    "You have selected " + strDate,
                    Toast.LENGTH_SHORT).show();
        }
    };

    public void onClick(View view) {
        Toast.makeText(getBaseContext(),
                "Time selected:" +
```

```
                          timePicker.getCurrentHour() +
                          ":" + timePicker.getCurrentMinute(),
                          Toast.LENGTH_SHORT).show();
    }

}
```

2. Press F11 to debug the application on the Android emulator. When the activity is loaded, you can see the `TimePicker` displayed in a dialog window (see Figure 4-14). Set a time and then click the Set button. You will see the Toast window displaying the time that you just set.

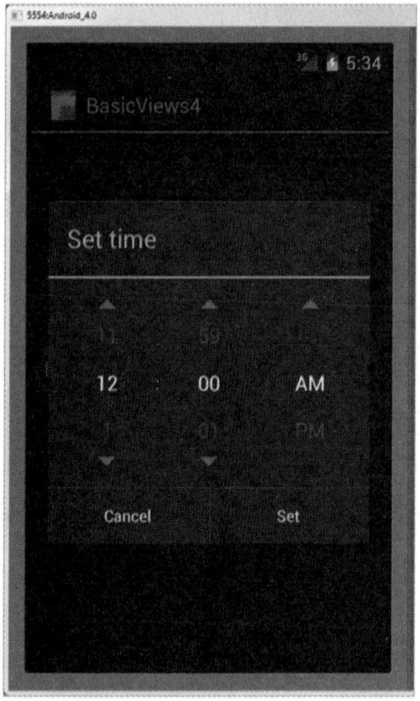

How It Works

To display a dialog window, you use the `showDialog()` method, passing it an ID to identify the source of the dialog:

```
showDialog(TIME_DIALOG_ID);
```

When the `showDialog()` method is called, the `onCreateDialog()` method will be called:

```
@Override
protected Dialog onCreateDialog(int id)
{
    switch (id) {
    case TIME_DIALOG_ID:
        return new TimePickerDialog(
                this, mTimeSetListener, hour, minute, false);
    }
    return null;
}
```

FIGURE 4-14

Here, you create a new instance of the `TimePickerDialog` class, passing it the current context, the callback, the initial hour and minute, as well as whether the `TimePicker` should be displayed in 24-hour format.

When the user clicks the Set button in the `TimePicker` dialog window, the `onTimeSet()` method is called:

```
private TimePickerDialog.OnTimeSetListener mTimeSetListener =
new TimePickerDialog.OnTimeSetListener()
{
    public void onTimeSet(
            TimePicker view, int hourOfDay, int minuteOfHour)
    {
        hour = hourOfDay;
        minute = minuteOfHour;

        SimpleDateFormat timeFormat = new SimpleDateFormat("hh:mm aa");
        Date date = new Date(0,0,0, hour, minute);
```

```
              String strDate = timeFormat.format(date);

              Toast.makeText(getBaseContext(),
                      "You have selected " + strDate,
                      Toast.LENGTH_SHORT).show();
          }
      };
```

Here, the onTimeSet() method contains the hour and minute set by the user via the hourOfDay and minuteOfHour arguments, respectively.

DatePicker View

Another view that is similar to the TimePicker is the DatePicker. Using the DatePicker, you can enable users to select a particular date on the activity. The following Try It Out shows you how to use the DatePicker.

TRY IT OUT   Using the DatePicker View

1.   Using the BasicViews4 project created earlier, modify the main.xml file as shown here:

```xml
<?xml version="1.0" encoding="utf-8"?>
<LinearLayout xmlns:android="http://schemas.android.com/apk/res/android"
    android:layout_width="fill_parent"
    android:layout_height="fill_parent"
    android:orientation="vertical" >

<Button android:id="@+id/btnSet"
    android:layout_width="wrap_content"
    android:layout_height="wrap_content"
    android:text="I am all set!"
    android:onClick="onClick" />

<DatePicker android:id="@+id/datePicker"
    android:layout_width="wrap_content"
    android:layout_height="wrap_content" />

<TimePicker android:id="@+id/timePicker"
    android:layout_width="wrap_content"
    android:layout_height="wrap_content" />

</LinearLayout>
```

2.   Press F11 to debug the application on the Android emulator. Figure 4-15 shows the DatePicker view (you have to change the emulator's orientation to landscape by pressing Ctrl-F11; portrait mode is too narrow to display the DatePicker).

FIGURE 4-15

3. Back in Eclipse, add the following statements in bold to the `BasicViews4Activity.java` file:

```
package net.learn2develop.BasicViews4;

import java.text.SimpleDateFormat;
import java.util.Date;

import android.app.Activity;
import android.app.Dialog;
import android.app.TimePickerDialog;
import android.os.Bundle;
import android.view.View;
import android.widget.DatePicker;
import android.widget.TimePicker;
import android.widget.Toast;

public class BasicViews4Activity extends Activity {
    TimePicker timePicker;
    DatePicker datePicker;

    int hour, minute;
    static final int TIME_DIALOG_ID = 0;

    /** Called when the activity is first created. */
    @Override
    public void onCreate(Bundle savedInstanceState) {
        super.onCreate(savedInstanceState);
```

```
        setContentView(R.layout.main);

        timePicker = (TimePicker) findViewById(R.id.timePicker);
        timePicker.setIs24HourView(true);

        // showDialog(TIME_DIALOG_ID);
        datePicker = (DatePicker) findViewById(R.id.datePicker);
    }

    @Override
    protected Dialog onCreateDialog(int id)
    {
        switch (id) {
        case TIME_DIALOG_ID:
            return new TimePickerDialog(
                    this, mTimeSetListener, hour, minute, false);
        }
        return null;
    }

    private TimePickerDialog.OnTimeSetListener mTimeSetListener =
    new TimePickerDialog.OnTimeSetListener()
    {
        public void onTimeSet(
                TimePicker view, int hourOfDay, int minuteOfHour)
        {
            hour = hourOfDay;
            minute = minuteOfHour;

            SimpleDateFormat timeFormat = new SimpleDateFormat("hh:mm aa");
            Date date = new Date(0,0,0, hour, minute);
            String strDate = timeFormat.format(date);

            Toast.makeText(getBaseContext(),
                    "You have selected " + strDate,
                    Toast.LENGTH_SHORT).show();
        }
    };

    public void onClick(View view) {
        Toast.makeText(getBaseContext(),
                "Date selected:" + (datePicker.getMonth() + 1) +
                "/" + datePicker.getDayOfMonth() +
                "/" + datePicker.getYear() + "\n" +
                "Time selected:" + timePicker.getCurrentHour() +
                ":" + timePicker.getCurrentMinute(),
                Toast.LENGTH_SHORT).show();
    }

}
```

4. Press F11 to debug the application on the Android emulator. Once the date is set, clicking the
    Button will display the date set (see Figure 4-16).

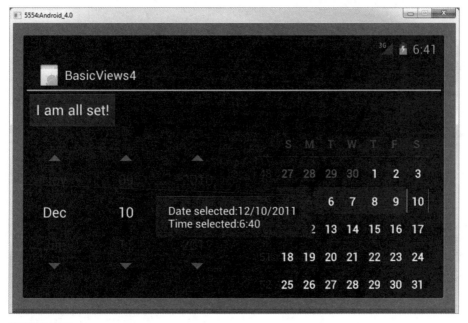

FIGURE 4-16

How It Works

Like the `TimePicker`, you call the `getMonth()`, `getDayOfMonth()`, and `getYear()` methods to get the month, day, and year, respectively:

```
"Date selected:" + (datePicker.getMonth() + 1) +
"/" + datePicker.getDayOfMonth() +
"/" + datePicker.getYear() + "\n" +
```

Note that the `getMonth()` method returns 0 for January, 1 for February, and so on. Hence, you need to increment the result of this method by one to get the corresponding month number.

Like the `TimePicker`, you can also display the `DatePicker` in a dialog window. The following Try It Out shows you how.

TRY IT OUT Using a Dialog to Display the DatePicker View

1. Using the BasicViews4 project created earlier, add the following statements in bold to the `BasicViews4Activity.java` file:

```
package net.learn2develop.BasicViews4;

import java.text.SimpleDateFormat;
import java.util.Calendar;
```

```java
import java.util.Date;

import android.app.Activity;
import android.app.DatePickerDialog;
import android.app.Dialog;
import android.app.TimePickerDialog;
import android.os.Bundle;
import android.view.View;
import android.widget.DatePicker;
import android.widget.TimePicker;
import android.widget.Toast;

public class BasicViews4Activity extends Activity {
    TimePicker timePicker;
    DatePicker datePicker;

    int hour, minute;
    int yr, month, day;

    static final int TIME_DIALOG_ID = 0;
    static final int DATE_DIALOG_ID = 1;

    /** Called when the activity is first created. */
    @Override
    public void onCreate(Bundle savedInstanceState) {
        super.onCreate(savedInstanceState);
        setContentView(R.layout.main);

        timePicker = (TimePicker) findViewById(R.id.timePicker);
        timePicker.setIs24HourView(true);

        // showDialog(TIME_DIALOG_ID);
        datePicker = (DatePicker) findViewById(R.id.datePicker);

        //---get the current date---
        Calendar today = Calendar.getInstance();
        yr = today.get(Calendar.YEAR);
        month = today.get(Calendar.MONTH);
        day = today.get(Calendar.DAY_OF_MONTH);

        showDialog(DATE_DIALOG_ID);
    }

    @Override
    protected Dialog onCreateDialog(int id)
    {
        switch (id) {
        case TIME_DIALOG_ID:
            return new TimePickerDialog(
                    this, mTimeSetListener, hour, minute, false);
        case DATE_DIALOG_ID:
            return new DatePickerDialog(
```

```java
                    this, mDateSetListener, yr, month, day);
        }
        return null;
    }

    private DatePickerDialog.OnDateSetListener mDateSetListener =
    new DatePickerDialog.OnDateSetListener()
    {
        public void onDateSet(
                DatePicker view, int year, int monthOfYear, int dayOfMonth)
        {
            yr = year;
            month = monthOfYear;
            day = dayOfMonth;
            Toast.makeText(getBaseContext(),
                    "You have selected : " + (month + 1) +
                    "/" + day + "/" + year,
                    Toast.LENGTH_SHORT).show();
        }
    };

    private TimePickerDialog.OnTimeSetListener mTimeSetListener =
    new TimePickerDialog.OnTimeSetListener()
    {
        public void onTimeSet(
                TimePicker view, int hourOfDay, int minuteOfHour)
        {
            hour = hourOfDay;
            minute = minuteOfHour;

            SimpleDateFormat timeFormat = new SimpleDateFormat("hh:mm aa");
            Date date = new Date(0,0,0, hour, minute);
            String strDate = timeFormat.format(date);

            Toast.makeText(getBaseContext(),
                    "You have selected " + strDate,
                    Toast.LENGTH_SHORT).show();
        }
    };

    public void onClick(View view) {
        Toast.makeText(getBaseContext(),
                "Date selected:" + (datePicker.getMonth() + 1) +
                "/" + datePicker.getDayOfMonth() +
                "/" + datePicker.getYear() + "\n" +
                "Time selected:" + timePicker.getCurrentHour() +
                ":" + timePicker.getCurrentMinute(),
                Toast.LENGTH_SHORT).show();
    }

}
```

2. Press F11 to debug the application on the Android emulator. When the activity is loaded, you can see the DatePicker displayed in a dialog window (see Figure 4-17). Select a date and then click the Set button. The Toast window will display the date you have just set.

FIGURE 4-17

How It Works

The DatePicker works exactly like the TimePicker. When a date is set, it fires the onDateSet() method, where you can obtain the date set by the user:

```
public void onDateSet(
        DatePicker view, int year, int monthOfYear, int dayOfMonth)
{
    yr = year;
    month = monthOfYear;
    day = dayOfMonth;
    Toast.makeText(getBaseContext(),
            "You have selected : " + (month + 1) +
            "/" + day + "/" + year,
            Toast.LENGTH_SHORT).show();
}
```

Note that you have to initialize the three variables — yr, month, and day — before showing the dialog:

```
//---get the current date---
Calendar today = Calendar.getInstance();
yr = today.get(Calendar.YEAR);
```

```
month = today.get(Calendar.MONTH);
day = today.get(Calendar.DAY_OF_MONTH);

showDialog(DATE_DIALOG_ID);
```

If you don't, you will get an illegal argument exception error
("current should be >= start and <= end") during runtime when you create an instance of the
DatePickerDialog class.

USING LIST VIEWS TO DISPLAY LONG LISTS

List views are views that enable you to display a long list of items. In Android, there are two types
of list views: ListView and SpinnerView. Both are useful for displaying long lists of items. The
following Try It Outs show them in action.

ListView View

The ListView displays a list of items in a vertically scrolling list. The following Try It Out
demonstrates how to display a list of items using the ListView.

TRY IT OUT　**Displaying a Long List of Items Using the ListView**

1. Using Eclipse, create an Android project and name it **BasicViews5**.

codefile BasicViews5.zip available for download at Wrox.com

2. Modify the BasicViews5Activity.java file by inserting the statements shown here in bold:

```
package net.learn2develop.BasicViews5;

import android.app.ListActivity;
import android.os.Bundle;
import android.view.View;
import android.widget.ArrayAdapter;
import android.widget.ListView;
import android.widget.Toast;

public class BasicViews5Activity extends ListActivity {
    String[] presidents = {
            "Dwight D. Eisenhower",
            "John F. Kennedy",
            "Lyndon B. Johnson",
            "Richard Nixon",
            "Gerald Ford",
            "Jimmy Carter",
            "Ronald Reagan",
            "George H. W. Bush",
            "Bill Clinton",
            "George W. Bush",
```

```
        "Barack Obama"
    };

    /** Called when the activity is first created. */
    @Override
    public void onCreate(Bundle savedInstanceState) {
        super.onCreate(savedInstanceState);
        //---no need to call this---
        //setContentView(R.layout.main);

        setListAdapter(new ArrayAdapter<String>(this,
            android.R.layout.simple_list_item_1, presidents));
    }

    public void onListItemClick(
    ListView parent, View v, int position, long id)
    {
        Toast.makeText(this,
            "You have selected " + presidents[position],
            Toast.LENGTH_SHORT).show();
    }

}
```

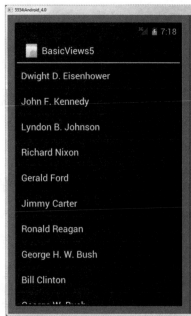

3. Press F11 to debug the application on the Android emulator. Figure 4-18 shows the activity displaying the list of presidents' names.

4. Click on an item. A message containing the item selected will be displayed.

How It Works

The first thing to notice in this example is that the BasicViews5Activity class extends the ListActivity class. The ListActivity class extends the Activity class and it displays a list of items by binding to a data source. Also note that there is no need to modify the main.xml file to include the ListView; the ListActivity class itself contains a ListView. Hence, in the onCreate() method, you don't need to call the setContentView() method to load the UI from the main.xml file:

```
//---no need to call this---
//setContentView(R.layout.main);
```

FIGURE 4-18

In the onCreate() method, you use the setListAdapter() method to programmatically fill the entire screen of the activity with a ListView. The ArrayAdapter object manages the array of strings that will be displayed by the ListView. In the preceding example, you set the ListView to display in the simple_list_item_1 mode:

```
setListAdapter(new ArrayAdapter<String>(this,
    android.R.layout.simple_list_item_1, presidents));
```

The `onListItemClick()` method is fired whenever an item in the `ListView` has been clicked:

```
public void onListItemClick(
ListView parent, View v, int position, long id)
{
    Toast.makeText(this,
        "You have selected " + presidents[position],
        Toast.LENGTH_SHORT).show();
}
```

Here, you simply display the name of the president selected using the `Toast` class.

Customizing the ListView

The `ListView` is a versatile view that you can further customize. The following Try It Out shows how you can allow multiple items in the `ListView` to be selected and how you can enable filtering support.

TRY IT OUT Enabling Filtering and Multi-Item Support in the ListView

1. Using the BasicViews5 project created in the previous section, add the following statements in bold to the `BasicViews5Activity.java` file:

```
/** Called when the activity is first created. */
@Override
public void onCreate(Bundle savedInstanceState) {
    super.onCreate(savedInstanceState);

    //---no need to call this---
    //setContentView(R.layout.main);

    ListView lstView = getListView();
    //lstView.setChoiceMode(ListView.CHOICE_MODE_NONE);
    //lstView.setChoiceMode(ListView.CHOICE_MODE_SINGLE);
    lstView.setChoiceMode(ListView.CHOICE_MODE_MULTIPLE);
    lstView.setTextFilterEnabled(true);

    setListAdapter(new ArrayAdapter<String>(this,
        android.R.layout.simple_list_item_checked, presidents));
}
```

2. Press F11 to debug the application on the Android emulator. You can now click on each item to display the check icon next to it (see Figure 4-19).

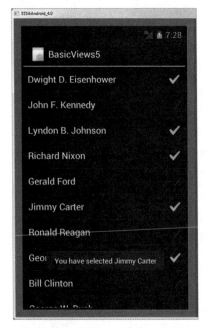

FIGURE 4-19

How It Works

To programmatically get a reference to the `ListView` object, you use the `getListView()` method, which fetches the `ListActivity`'s list view. You need to do this so that you can programmatically modify the behavior of the `ListView`. In this case, you used the `setChoiceMode()` method to specify how the `ListView` should handle a user's click. For this example, you set it to `ListView.CHOICE_MODE_MULTIPLE`, which means that the user can select multiple items:

```
ListView lstView = getListView();
//lstView.setChoiceMode(ListView.CHOICE_MODE_NONE);
//lstView.setChoiceMode(ListView.CHOICE_MODE_SINGLE);
lstView.setChoiceMode(ListView.CHOICE_MODE_MULTIPLE);
```

A very cool feature of the `ListView` is its support for filtering. When you enable filtering through the `setTextFilterEnabled()` method, users will be able to type on the keypad and the `ListView` will automatically filter the items to match what was typed:

```
lstView.setTextFilterEnabled(true);
```

Figure 4-20 shows the list filtering in action. Here, all items in the list that contain the word "john" will appear in the result list.

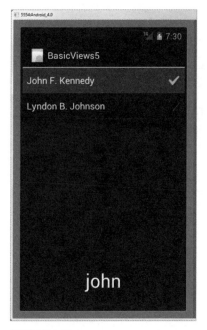

FIGURE 4-20

While the previous example shows that the list of presidents' names is stored in an array, in a real-life application it is recommended that you either retrieve them from a database or at least store them in the `strings.xml` file. The following Try It Out shows you how.

TRY IT OUT Storing Items in the strings.xml File

1. Using the BasicViews5 project created earlier, add the following lines in bold to the `strings.xml` file located in the `res/values` folder:

```xml
<?xml version="1.0" encoding="utf-8"?>
<resources>
    <string name="hello">Hello World, BasicViews5Activity!</string>
    <string name="app_name">BasicViews5</string>
    <string-array name="presidents_array">
        <item>Dwight D. Eisenhower</item>
        <item>John F. Kennedy</item>
        <item>Lyndon B. Johnson</item>
        <item>Richard Nixon</item>
        <item>Gerald Ford</item>
        <item>Jimmy Carter</item>
        <item>Ronald Reagan</item>
        <item>George H. W. Bush</item>
        <item>Bill Clinton</item>
        <item>George W. Bush</item>
```

```
        <item>Barack Obama</item>
    </string-array>
</resources>
```

2. Modify the `BasicViews5Activity.java` file as shown in bold:

```java
public class BasicViews5Activity extends ListActivity  {
    String[] presidents;

    /** Called when the activity is first created. */
    @Override
    public void onCreate(Bundle savedInstanceState) {
        super.onCreate(savedInstanceState);

        //---no need to call this---
        //setContentView(R.layout.main);

        ListView lstView = getListView();
        //lstView.setChoiceMode(ListView.CHOICE_MODE_NONE);
        //lstView.setChoiceMode(ListView.CHOICE_MODE_SINGLE);
        lstView.setChoiceMode(ListView.CHOICE_MODE_MULTIPLE);
        lstView.setTextFilterEnabled(true);

        presidents =
                getResources().getStringArray(R.array.presidents_array);

        setListAdapter(new ArrayAdapter<String>(this,
            android.R.layout.simple_list_item_checked, presidents));
    }

    public void onListItemClick(
    ListView parent, View v, int position, long id)
    {
        Toast.makeText(this,
            "You have selected " + presidents[position],
            Toast.LENGTH_SHORT).show();
    }

}
```

3. Press F11 to debug the application on the Android emulator. You should see the same list of names that appeared in the previous Try It Out.

How It Works

With the names now stored in the `strings.xml` file, you can retrieve it programmatically in the `BasicViews5Activity.java` file using the `getResources()` method:

```java
        presidents =
                getResources().getStringArray(R.array.presidents_array);
```

In general, you can programmatically retrieve resources bundled with your application using the `getResources()` method.

This example demonstrated how to make items in a `ListView` selectable. At the end of the selection process, how do you know which item or items are selected? The following Try It Out shows you how.

TRY IT OUT Checking Which Items Are Selected

1. Using the BasicViews5 project again, add the following lines in bold to the `main.xml` file:

```xml
<?xml version="1.0" encoding="utf-8"?>
<LinearLayout xmlns:android="http://schemas.android.com/apk/res/android"
    android:layout_width="fill_parent"
    android:layout_height="fill_parent"
    android:orientation="vertical" >

<Button
    android:id="@+id/btn"
    android:layout_width="fill_parent"
    android:layout_height="wrap_content"
    android:text="Show selected items"
    android:onClick="onClick"/>

<ListView
    android:id="@+id/android:list"
    android:layout_width="wrap_content"
    android:layout_height="wrap_content" />

</LinearLayout>
```

2. Add the following lines in bold to the `BasicViews5Activity.java` file:

```java
package net.learn2develop.BasicViews5;

import android.app.ListActivity;
import android.os.Bundle;
import android.view.View;
import android.widget.ArrayAdapter;
import android.widget.ListView;
import android.widget.Toast;

public class BasicViews5Activity extends ListActivity {

    String[] presidents;

    /** Called when the activity is first created. */
    @Override
    public void onCreate(Bundle savedInstanceState) {
        super.onCreate(savedInstanceState);

        setContentView(R.layout.main);

        ListView lstView = getListView();
        //lstView.setChoiceMode(ListView.CHOICE_MODE_NONE);
        //lstView.setChoiceMode(ListView.CHOICE_MODE_SINGLE);
        lstView.setChoiceMode(ListView.CHOICE_MODE_MULTIPLE);
        lstView.setTextFilterEnabled(true);

        presidents =
```

```
                getResources().getStringArray(R.array.presidents_array);

        setListAdapter(new ArrayAdapter<String>(this,
            android.R.layout.simple_list_item_checked, presidents));
    }

    public void onListItemClick(
    ListView parent, View v, int position, long id)
    {
        Toast.makeText(this,
            "You have selected " + presidents[position],
            Toast.LENGTH_SHORT).show();
    }

    public void onClick(View view) {
        ListView lstView = getListView();

        String itemsSelected = "Selected items: \n";
        for (int i=0; i<lstView.getCount(); i++) {
            if (lstView.isItemChecked(i)) {
                itemsSelected += lstView.getItemAtPosition(i) + "\n";
            }
        }
        Toast.makeText(this, itemsSelected, Toast.LENGTH_LONG).show();
    }

}
```

3. Press F11 to debug the application on the Android emulator. Click on a few items and then click the Show selected items button (see Figure 4-21). The list of names selected will be displayed.

How It Works

In the previous section's exercise, you saw how to populate a ListView that occupies the entire activity — in that example, there is no need to add a <ListView> element to the main.xml file. In this example, you saw how a ListView can partially fill up an activity. To do that, you needed to add a <ListView> element with the id attribute set to @+id/android:list:

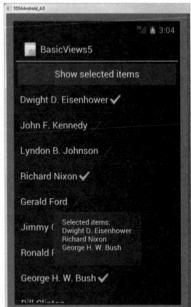

FIGURE 4-21

```
<ListView
    android:id="@+id/android:list"
    android:layout_width="wrap_content"
    android:layout_height="wrap_content" />
```

You then needed to load the content of the activity using the setContentView() method (previously commented out):

```
        setContentView(R.layout.main);
```

To find out which items in the `ListView` have been checked, you use the `isItemChecked()` method:

```
ListView lstView = getListView();
String itemsSelected = "Selected items: \n";
for (int i=0; i<lstView.getCount(); i++) {
    if (lstView.isItemChecked(i)) {
        itemsSelected += lstView.getItemAtPosition(i) + "\n";
    }
}
Toast.makeText(this, itemsSelected, Toast.LENGTH_LONG).show();
```

The `getItemAtPosition()` method returns the name of the item at the specified position.

 NOTE *So far, all the examples show how to use the* `ListView` *inside a* `ListActivity`. *This is not absolutely necessary — you can also use the* `ListView` *inside an* `Activity`. *In this case, to programmatically refer to the* `ListView`, *you use the* `findViewByID()` *method instead of the* `getListView()` *method; and the* id *attribute of the* `<ListView>` *element can use the format of* `@+id/<view_name>`.

Using the Spinner View

The `ListView` displays a long list of items in an activity, but sometimes you may want your user interface to display other views, and hence you do not have the additional space for a full-screen view like the `ListView`. In such cases, you should use the `SpinnerView`. The `SpinnerView` displays one item at a time from a list and enables users to choose among them.

The following Try It Out shows how you can use the `SpinnerView` in your activity.

TRY IT OUT Using the SpinnerView to Display One Item at a Time

codefile BasicViews6.zip available for download at Wrox.com

1. Using Eclipse, create an Android project and name it **BasicViews6**.

2. Modify the `main.xml` file located in the `res/layout` folder as shown here:

```
<?xml version="1.0" encoding="utf-8"?>
<LinearLayout xmlns:android="http://schemas.android.com/apk/res/android"
    android:layout_width="fill_parent"
    android:layout_height="fill_parent"
    android:orientation="vertical" >

<Spinner
    android:id="@+id/spinner1"
    android:layout_width="wrap_content"
```

```
            android:layout_height="wrap_content"
            android:drawSelectorOnTop="true" />

    </LinearLayout>
```

3. Add the following lines in bold to the `strings.xml` file located in the `res/values` folder:

```xml
<?xml version="1.0" encoding="utf-8"?>
<resources>
    <string name="hello">Hello World, BasicViews6Activity!</string>
    <string name="app_name">BasicViews6</string>
    <string-array name="presidents_array">
        <item>Dwight D. Eisenhower</item>
        <item>John F. Kennedy</item>
        <item>Lyndon B. Johnson</item>
        <item>Richard Nixon</item>
        <item>Gerald Ford</item>
        <item>Jimmy Carter</item>
        <item>Ronald Reagan</item>
        <item>George H. W. Bush</item>
        <item>Bill Clinton</item>
        <item>George W. Bush</item>
        <item>Barack Obama</item>
    </string-array>
</resources>
```

4. Add the following statements in bold to the `BasicViews6Activity.java` file:

```java
package net.learn2develop.BasicViews6;

import android.app.Activity;
import android.os.Bundle;
import android.view.View;
import android.widget.AdapterView;
import android.widget.AdapterView.OnItemSelectedListener;
import android.widget.ArrayAdapter;
import android.widget.Spinner;
import android.widget.Toast;

public class BasicViews6Activity extends Activity {
    String[] presidents;

    /** Called when the activity is first created. */
    @Override
    public void onCreate(Bundle savedInstanceState) {
        super.onCreate(savedInstanceState);
        setContentView(R.layout.main);

        presidents =
                getResources().getStringArray(R.array.presidents_array);
```

```
Spinner s1 = (Spinner) findViewById(R.id.spinner1);

ArrayAdapter<String> adapter = new ArrayAdapter<String>(this,
        android.R.layout.simple_spinner_item, presidents);

s1.setAdapter(adapter);
s1.setOnItemSelectedListener(new OnItemSelectedListener()
{
    @Override
    public void onItemSelected(AdapterView<?> arg0,
    View arg1, int arg2, long arg3)
    {
        int index = arg0.getSelectedItemPosition();
        Toast.makeText(getBaseContext(),
                "You have selected item : " + presidents[index],
                Toast.LENGTH_SHORT).show();
    }

    @Override
    public void onNothingSelected(AdapterView<?> arg0) { }
});
    }
}
```

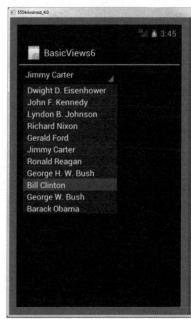

5. Press F11 to debug the application on the Android emulator. Click on the `SpinnerView` and you will see a pop-up displaying the list of presidents' names (see Figure 4-22). Clicking an item will display a message showing you the item selected.

How It Works

The preceding example works very much like the `ListView`. One additional method you need to implement is the `onNothingSelected()` method. This method is fired when the user presses the back button, which dismisses the list of items displayed. In this case, nothing is selected so you do not need to do anything.

Instead of displaying the items in the `ArrayAdapter` as a simple list, you can also display them using radio buttons. To do so, modify the second parameter in the constructor of the `ArrayAdapter` class:

FIGURE 4-22

```
ArrayAdapter<String> adapter = new ArrayAdapter<String>(this,
        android.R.layout.simple_list_item_single_choice, presidents);
```

This causes the items to be displayed as a list of radio buttons (see Figure 4-23).

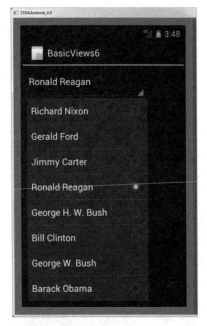

FIGURE 4-23

UNDERSTANDING SPECIALIZED FRAGMENTS

In Chapter 2, you learned about the fragment feature that is available beginning with Android 3. Using fragments, you can customize the user interface of your Android application by dynamically rearranging fragments to fit within an activity. This enables you to build applications that run on devices with different screen sizes.

As you have learned, fragments are really "mini-activities" that have their own life cycles. To create a fragment, you need a class that extends the `Fragment` base class. Besides the `Fragment` base class, you can also extend from some other subclasses of the `Fragment` base class to create more specialized fragments. The following sections discuss the three subclasses of `Fragment`: `ListFragment`, `DialogFragment`, and `PreferenceFragment`.

Using a ListFragment

A list fragment is a fragment that contains a `ListView`, displaying a list of items from a data source such as an array or a `Cursor`. A list fragment is very useful, as you may often have one fragment that contains a list of items (such as a list of RSS postings), and another fragment that displays details about the selected posting. To create a list fragment, you need to extend the ListFragment base class.

The following Try It Out shows you how to get started with a list fragment.

TRY IT OUT Creating and Using a List Fragment

codefile ListFragmentExample.zip available for download at Wrox.com

1. Using Eclipse, create an Android project and name it **ListFragmentExample**.

2. Modify the main.xml file as shown in bold:

```xml
<?xml version="1.0" encoding="utf-8"?>
<LinearLayout xmlns:android="http://schemas.android.com/apk/res/android"
    android:layout_width="fill_parent"
    android:layout_height="fill_parent"
    android:orientation="horizontal" >

<fragment
    android:name="net.learn2develop.ListFragmentExample.Fragment1"
    android:id="@+id/fragment1"
    android:layout_weight="0.5"
    android:layout_width="0dp"
    android:layout_height="200dp" />

<fragment
    android:name="net.learn2develop.ListFragmentExample.Fragment1"
    android:id="@+id/fragment2"
    android:layout_weight="0.5"
    android:layout_width="0dp"
    android:layout_height="300dp" />

</LinearLayout>
```

3. Add an XML file to the res/layout folder and name it fragment1.xml.

4. Populate the fragment1.xml as follows:

```xml
<?xml version="1.0" encoding="utf-8"?>
<LinearLayout xmlns:android="http://schemas.android.com/apk/res/android"
    android:orientation="vertical"
    android:layout_width="fill_parent"
    android:layout_height="fill_parent">
    <ListView
        android:id="@id/android:list"
        android:layout_width="match_parent"
        android:layout_height="match_parent"
        android:layout_weight="1"
        android:drawSelectorOnTop="false"/>
</LinearLayout>
```

5. Add a Java Class file to the package and name it Fragment1.

6. Populate the `Fragment1.java` file as follows:

```java
package net.learn2develop.ListFragmentExample;

import android.app.ListFragment;
import android.os.Bundle;
import android.view.LayoutInflater;
import android.view.View;
import android.view.ViewGroup;
import android.widget.ArrayAdapter;
import android.widget.ListView;
import android.widget.Toast;

public class Fragment1 extends ListFragment {
    String[] presidents = {
        "Dwight D. Eisenhower",
        "John F. Kennedy",
        "Lyndon B. Johnson",
        "Richard Nixon",
        "Gerald Ford",
        "Jimmy Carter",
        "Ronald Reagan",
        "George H. W. Bush",
        "Bill Clinton",
        "George W. Bush",
        "Barack Obama"
    };

    @Override
    public View onCreateView(LayoutInflater inflater,
    ViewGroup container, Bundle savedInstanceState) {
        return inflater.inflate(R.layout.fragment1, container, false);
    }

    @Override
    public void onCreate(Bundle savedInstanceState) {
        super.onCreate(savedInstanceState);
        setListAdapter(new ArrayAdapter<String>(getActivity(),
            android.R.layout.simple_list_item_1, presidents));
    }

    public void onListItemClick(ListView parent, View v,
    int position, long id)
    {
        Toast.makeText(getActivity(),
            "You have selected " + presidents[position],
            Toast.LENGTH_SHORT).show();
    }

}
```

7. Press F11 to debug the application on the Android emulator. Figure 4-24 shows the two list fragments displaying the two lists of presidents' names.

8. Click on any of the items in the two `ListView` views, and a message is displayed (see Figure 4-25).

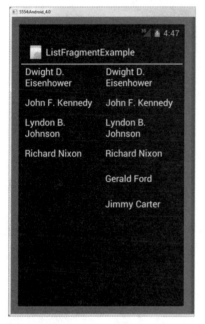

FIGURE 4-24

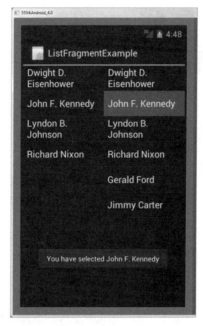

FIGURE 4-25

How It Works

First, you created the XML file for the fragment by adding a `ListView` element to it:

```xml
<?xml version="1.0" encoding="utf-8"?>
<LinearLayout xmlns:android="http://schemas.android.com/apk/res/android"
    android:orientation="vertical"
    android:layout_width="fill_parent"
    android:layout_height="fill_parent">
    <ListView
        android:id="@id/android:list"
        android:layout_width="match_parent"
        android:layout_height="match_parent"
        android:layout_weight="1"
        android:drawSelectorOnTop="false"/>
</LinearLayout>
```

To create a list fragment, the Java class for the fragment must extend the `ListFragment` base class:

```
public class Fragment1 extends ListFragment {
}
```

You then declared an array to contain the list of presidents' names in your activity:

```
String[] presidents = {
    "Dwight D. Eisenhower",
    "John F. Kennedy",
    "Lyndon B. Johnson",
    "Richard Nixon",
    "Gerald Ford",
    "Jimmy Carter",
    "Ronald Reagan",
    "George H. W. Bush",
    "Bill Clinton",
    "George W. Bush",
    "Barack Obama"
};
```

In the `onCreate()` event, you use the `setListAdapter()` method to programmatically fill the `ListView` with the content of the array. The `ArrayAdapter` object manages the array of strings that will be displayed by the `ListView`. In this example, you set the `ListView` to display in the `simple_list_item_1` mode:

```
@Override
public void onCreate(Bundle savedInstanceState) {
    super.onCreate(savedInstanceState);
    setListAdapter(new ArrayAdapter<String>(getActivity(),
        android.R.layout.simple_list_item_1, presidents));
}
```

The `onListItemClick()` method is fired whenever an item in the `ListView` is clicked:

```
public void onListItemClick(ListView parent, View v,
int position, long id)
{
    Toast.makeText(getActivity(),
        "You have selected " + presidents[position],
        Toast.LENGTH_SHORT).show();
}
```

Finally, you added two fragments to the activity. Note the height of each fragment:

```
<?xml version="1.0" encoding="utf-8"?>
<LinearLayout xmlns:android="http://schemas.android.com/apk/res/android"
    android:layout_width="fill_parent"
    android:layout_height="fill_parent"
    android:orientation="horizontal" >

<fragment
    android:name="net.learn2develop.ListFragmentExample.Fragment1"
    android:id="@+id/fragment1"
    android:layout_weight="0.5"
```

```
        android:layout_width="0dp"
        android:layout_height="200dp" />

    <fragment
        android:name="net.learn2develop.ListFragmentExample.Fragment1"
        android:id="@+id/fragment2"
        android:layout_weight="0.5"
        android:layout_width="0dp"
        android:layout_height="300dp" />

</LinearLayout>
```

Using a DialogFragment

Another type of fragment that you can create is a dialog fragment. A dialog fragment floats on top of an activity and is displayed modally. Dialog fragments are useful for cases in which you need to obtain the user's response before continuing with execution. To create a dialog fragment, you need to extend the DialogFragment base class.

The following Try It Out shows how to create a dialog fragment.

TRY IT OUT   Creating and Using a Dialog Fragment

codefile DialogFragmentExample.zip available for download at Wrox.com

1.   Using Eclipse, create an Android project and name it **DialogFragmentExample**.

2.   Add a Java Class file under the package and name it **Fragment1**.

3.   Populate the Fragment1.java file as follows:

```java
package net.learn2develop.DialogFragmentExample;

import android.app.AlertDialog;
import android.app.Dialog;
import android.app.DialogFragment;
import android.content.DialogInterface;
import android.os.Bundle;

public class Fragment1 extends DialogFragment {

    static Fragment1 newInstance(String title) {
        Fragment1 fragment = new Fragment1();
        Bundle args = new Bundle();
        args.putString("title", title);
        fragment.setArguments(args);
        return fragment;
    }

    @Override
    public Dialog onCreateDialog(Bundle savedInstanceState) {
```

```
        String title = getArguments().getString("title");
        return new AlertDialog.Builder(getActivity())
        .setIcon(R.drawable.ic_launcher)
        .setTitle(title)
        .setPositiveButton("OK",
                new DialogInterface.OnClickListener() {
            public void onClick(DialogInterface dialog,
                    int whichButton) {
                ((DialogFragmentExampleActivity)
                        getActivity()).doPositiveClick();
            }
        })
        .setNegativeButton("Cancel",
                new DialogInterface.OnClickListener() {
            public void onClick(DialogInterface dialog,
                    int whichButton) {
                ((DialogFragmentExampleActivity)
                        getActivity()).doNegativeClick();
            }
        }).create();
    }

}
```

4. Populate the `DialogFragmentExampleActivity.java` file as shown here in bold:

```
package net.learn2develop.DialogFragmentExample;

import android.app.Activity;
import android.os.Bundle;
import android.util.Log;

public class DialogFragmentExampleActivity extends Activity {
    /** Called when the activity is first created. */
    @Override
    public void onCreate(Bundle savedInstanceState) {
        super.onCreate(savedInstanceState);
        setContentView(R.layout.main);

        Fragment1 dialogFragment = Fragment1.newInstance(
                "Are you sure you want to do this?");
            dialogFragment.show(getFragmentManager(), "dialog");
    }

    public void doPositiveClick() {
        //---perform steps when user clicks on OK---
        Log.d("DialogFragmentExample", "User clicks on OK");
    }

    public void doNegativeClick() {
        //---perform steps when user clicks on Cancel---
        Log.d("DialogFragmentExample", "User clicks on Cancel");
    }

}
```

5. Press F11 to debug the application on the Android emulator. Figure 4-26 shows the fragment displayed as an alert dialog. Click either the OK button or the Cancel button and observe the message displayed.

How It Works

To create a dialog fragment, first your Java class must extend the `DialogFragment` base class:

```
public class Fragment1 extends DialogFragment {
}
```

In this example, you created an alert dialog, which is a dialog window that displays a message with optional buttons. Within the `Fragment1` class, you defined the `newInstance()` method:

```
static Fragment1 newInstance(String title) {
    Fragment1 fragment = new Fragment1();
    Bundle args = new Bundle();
    args.putString("title", title);
    fragment.setArguments(args);
    return fragment;
}
```

FIGURE 4-26

The `newInstance()` method allows a new instance of the fragment to be created, and at the same time it accepts an argument specifying the string (`title`) to display in the alert dialog. The `title` is then stored in a `Bundle` object for use later.

Next, you defined the `onCreateDialog()` method, which is called after `onCreate()` and before `onCreateView()`:

```
@Override
public Dialog onCreateDialog(Bundle savedInstanceState) {
    String title = getArguments().getString("title");
    return new AlertDialog.Builder(getActivity())
    .setIcon(R.drawable.ic_launcher)
    .setTitle(title)
    .setPositiveButton("OK",
            new DialogInterface.OnClickListener() {
        public void onClick(DialogInterface dialog,
                int whichButton) {
            ((DialogFragmentExampleActivity)
                    getActivity()).doPositiveClick();
        }
    })
    .setNegativeButton("Cancel",
            new DialogInterface.OnClickListener() {
        public void onClick(DialogInterface dialog,
                int whichButton) {
            ((DialogFragmentExampleActivity)
                    getActivity()).doNegativeClick();
```

```
        }
    }).create();
}
```

Here, you created an alert dialog with two buttons: OK and Cancel. The string to be displayed in it is obtained from the `title` argument saved in the `Bundle` object.

To display the dialog fragment, you created an instance of it and then called its `show()` method:

```
Fragment1 dialogFragment = Fragment1.newInstance(
    "Are you sure you want to do this?");
dialogFragment.show(getFragmentManager(), "dialog");
```

You also needed to implement two methods, `doPositiveClick()` and `doNegativeClick()`, to handle the user clicking the OK or Cancel buttons, respectively:

```
public void doPositiveClick() {
    //---perform steps when user clicks on OK---
    Log.d("DialogFragmentExample", "User clicks on OK");
}

public void doNegativeClick() {
    //---perform steps when user clicks on Cancel---
    Log.d("DialogFragmentExample", "User clicks on Cancel");
}
```

Using a PreferenceFragment

Your Android applications will typically provide preferences that allow users to personalize the application for their own use. For example, you may allow users to save the login credentials that they use to access their web resources, or save information such as how often the feeds must be refreshed (such as in an RSS reader application), and so on. In Android, you can use the `PreferenceActivity` base class to display an activity for the user to edit the preferences. In Android 3.0 and later, you can use the `PreferenceFragment` class to do the same thing.

The following Try It Out shows you how to create and use a preference fragment in Android 3 and 4.

TRY IT OUT Creating and Using a Preference Fragment

codefile PreferenceFragmentExample.zip available for download at Wrox.com

1. Using Eclipse, create an Android project and name it **PreferenceFragmentExample**.

2. Create a new `xml` folder under the `res` folder and then add a new Android XML file to it. Name the XML file `preferences.xml` (see Figure 4-27).

FIGURE 4-27

3. Populate the `preferences.xml` file as follows:

```xml
<?xml version="1.0" encoding="utf-8"?>
<PreferenceScreen
    xmlns:android="http://schemas.android.com/apk/res/android">

    <PreferenceCategory android:title="Category 1">
        <CheckBoxPreference
            android:title="Checkbox"
            android:defaultValue="false"
            android:summary="True of False"
            android:key="checkboxPref" />
    </PreferenceCategory>

    <PreferenceCategory android:title="Category 2">
        <EditTextPreference
            android:name="EditText"
            android:summary="Enter a string"
            android:defaultValue="[Enter a string here]"
            android:title="Edit Text"
            android:key="editTextPref" />
        <RingtonePreference
            android:name="Ringtone Preference"
            android:summary="Select a ringtone"
            android:title="Ringtones"
            android:key="ringtonePref" />
        <PreferenceScreen
            android:title="Second Preference Screen"
            android:summary=
                "Click here to go to the second Preference Screen"
            android:key="secondPrefScreenPref">
            <EditTextPreference
                android:name="EditText"
```

```
                    android:summary="Enter a string"
                    android:title="Edit Text (second Screen)"
                    android:key="secondEditTextPref" />
        </PreferenceScreen>
    </PreferenceCategory>

</PreferenceScreen>
```

4. Add a Java Class file to the package and name it `Fragment1`.

5. Populate the `Fragment1.java` file as follows:

```
package net.learn2develop.PreferenceFragmentExample;

import android.os.Bundle;
import android.preference.PreferenceFragment;

public class Fragment1 extends PreferenceFragment {
    @Override
    public void onCreate(Bundle savedInstanceState) {
        super.onCreate(savedInstanceState);

        //---load the preferences from an XML file---
        addPreferencesFromResource(R.xml.preferences);
    }
}
```

6. Modify the `PreferenceFragmentExampleActivity.java` file as shown in bold:

```
package net.learn2develop.PreferenceFragmentExample;

import android.app.Activity;
import android.app.FragmentManager;
import android.app.FragmentTransaction;
import android.os.Bundle;

public class PreferenceFragmentExampleActivity extends Activity {
    /** Called when the activity is first created. */
    @Override
    public void onCreate(Bundle savedInstanceState) {
        super.onCreate(savedInstanceState);
        setContentView(R.layout.main);

        FragmentManager fragmentManager = getFragmentManager();
        FragmentTransaction fragmentTransaction =
            fragmentManager.beginTransaction();
        Fragment1 fragment1 = new Fragment1();
        fragmentTransaction.replace(android.R.id.content, fragment1);
        fragmentTransaction.addToBackStack(null);
        fragmentTransaction.commit();
    }
}
```

7. Press F11 to debug the application on the Android emulator. Figure 4-28 shows the preference fragment displaying the list of preferences that the user can modify.

8. When the Edit Text preference is clicked, a pop-up will be displayed (see Figure 4-29).

9. Clicking the Second Preference Screen item will cause a second preference screen to be displayed (see Figure 4-30).

FIGURE 4-28 **FIGURE 4-29** **FIGURE 4-30**

10. To cause the preference fragment to go away, click the back button on the emulator.

11. If you look at the File Explorer (available in the DDMS perspective), you will be able to locate the preferences file located in the `/data/data/net.learn2develop.PreferenceFragmentExample/shared_prefs/` folder (see Figure 4-31). All changes made by the user are persisted in this file.

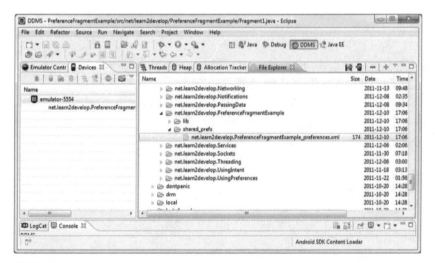

FIGURE 4-31

NOTE *Chapter 6 describes how to retrieve the values saved in a preference file.*

How It Works

To create a list of preferences in your Android application, you first needed to create the `preferences` `.xml` file and populate it with the various XML elements. This XML file defines the various items that you want to persist in your application.

To create the preference fragment, you needed to extend the `PreferenceFragment` base class:

```
public class Fragment1 extends PreferenceFragment {
}
```

To load the preferences file in the preference fragment, you use the `addPreferencesFromResource()` method:

```
@Override
public void onCreate(Bundle savedInstanceState) {
    super.onCreate(savedInstanceState);

    //---load the preferences from an XML file---
    addPreferencesFromResource(R.xml.preferences);
}
```

To display the preference fragment in your activity, you can make use of the `FragmentManager` and the `FragmentTransaction` classes:

```
FragmentManager fragmentManager = getFragmentManager();
FragmentTransaction fragmentTransaction =
    fragmentManager.beginTransaction();
Fragment1 fragment1 = new Fragment1();
fragmentTransaction.replace(android.R.id.content, fragment1);
fragmentTransaction.addToBackStack(null);
fragmentTransaction.commit();
```

You needed to add the preference fragment to the back stack using the `addToBackStack()` method so that the user can dismiss the fragment by clicking the back button.

SUMMARY

This chapter provided a brief look at some of the commonly used views in an Android application. While it is not possible to exhaustively examine each view in detail, the views you learned about here should provide a good foundation for designing your Android application's user interface, regardless of its requirements.

EXERCISES

1. How do you programmatically determine whether a `RadioButton` is checked?

2. How do you access the string resource stored in the `strings.xml` file?

3. Write the code snippet to obtain the current date.

4. Name the three specialized fragments you can use in your Android application and describe their uses.

Answers to the exercises can be found in Appendix C.

▶ **WHAT YOU LEARNED IN THIS CHAPTER**

TOPIC	KEY CONCEPTS

TextView	`<TextView`
	
	`    android:layout_width="fill_parent"`
	
	`    android:layout_height="wrap_content"`
	
	`    android:text="@string/hello"`
	
	`    />`

Button	`<Button android:id="@+id/btnSave"`
	
	`    android:layout_width="fill_parent"`
	
	`    android:layout_height="wrap_content"`
	
	`    android:text="Save" />`

ImageButton	`<ImageButton android:id="@+id/btnImg1"`
	
	`    android:layout_width="fill_parent"`
	
	`    android:layout_height="wrap_content"`
	
	`    android:src="@drawable/icon" />`

EditText	`<EditText android:id="@+id/txtName"`
	
	`    android:layout_width="fill_parent"`
	
	`    android:layout_height="wrap_content" />`

CheckBox	`<CheckBox android:id="@+id/chkAutosave"`
	
	`    android:layout_width="fill_parent"`
	
	`    android:layout_height="wrap_content"`
	
	`    android:text="Autosave" />`

RadioGroup and RadioButton	`<RadioGroup android:id="@+id/rdbGp1"`
	
	`    android:layout_width="fill_parent"`
	
	`    android:layout_height="wrap_content"`
	
	`    android:orientation="vertical" >`
	
	`    <RadioButton android:id="@+id/rdb1"`
	
	`        android:layout_width="fill_parent"`

TOPIC	KEY CONCEPTS
	`android:layout_height="wrap_content"`
	`android:text="Option 1" />`
	`<RadioButton android:id="@+id/rdb2"`
	`android:layout_width="fill_parent"`
	`android:layout_height="wrap_content"`
	`android:text="Option 2" />`
	`</RadioGroup>`
ToggleButton	`<ToggleButton android:id="@+id/toggle1"`
	`android:layout_width="wrap_content"`
ProgressBar	`<ProgressBar android:id="@+id/progressbar"`
	`android:layout_width="wrap_content"`
	`android:layout_height="wrap_content" />`
AutoCompleteTextBox	`<AutoCompleteTextView android:id="@+id/txtCountries"`
	`android:layout_width="fill_parent"`
	`android:layout_height="wrap_content" />`
TimePicker	`<TimePicker android:id="@+id/timePicker"`
	`android:layout_width="wrap_content"`
	`android:layout_height="wrap_content" />`
DatePicker	`<DatePicker android:id="@+id/datePicker"`
	`android:layout_width="wrap_content"`
	`android:layout_height="wrap_content" />`
Spinner	`<Spinner android:id="@+id/spinner1"`
	`android:layout_width="wrap_content"`
	`android:layout_height="wrap_content"`
	`android:drawSelectorOnTop="true" />`
Specialized fragment types	`ListFragment`, `DialogFragment`, and `PreferenceFragment`

Displaying Pictures
and Menus with Views

WHAT YOU WILL LEARN IN THIS CHAPTER

➤ How to use the Gallery, ImageSwitcher, GridView, and ImageView views to display images

➤ How to display options menus and context menus

➤ How to display time using the AnalogClock and DigitalClock views

➤ How to display web content using the WebView view

In the previous chapter, you learned about the various views that you can use to build the user interface of your Android application. In this chapter, you continue your exploration of the other views that you can use to create robust and compelling applications.

In particular, you will learn how to work with views that enable you to display images. In addition, you will learn how to create option and context menus in your Android application. This chapter ends with a discussion of some helpful views that enable users to display the current time and web content.

USING IMAGE VIEWS TO DISPLAY PICTURES

So far, all the views you have seen until this point are used to display text information. For displaying images, you can use the ImageView, Gallery, ImageSwitcher, and GridView views.

The following sections discuss each view in detail.

Gallery and ImageView Views

The Gallery is a view that shows items (such as images) in a center-locked, horizontal scrolling list. Figure 5-1 shows how the Gallery view looks when it is displaying some images.

The following Try It Out shows you how to use the Gallery view to display a set of images.

FIGURE 5-1

TRY IT OUT **Using the Gallery View**

codefile Gallery.zip available for download at Wrox.com

1. Using Eclipse, create a new Android project and name it **Gallery**.

2. Modify the main.xml file as shown in bold:

```xml
<?xml version="1.0" encoding="utf-8"?>
<LinearLayout xmlns:android="http://schemas.android.com/apk/res/android"
    android:layout_width="fill_parent"
    android:layout_height="fill_parent"
    android:orientation="vertical" >

<TextView
    android:layout_width="fill_parent"
    android:layout_height="wrap_content"
    android:text="Images of San Francisco" />

<Gallery
    android:id="@+id/gallery1"
    android:layout_width="fill_parent"
    android:layout_height="wrap_content" />

<ImageView
    android:id="@+id/image1"
    android:layout_width="320dp"
    android:layout_height="250dp"
    android:scaleType="fitXY" />

</LinearLayout>
```

3. Right-click on the res/values folder and select New ➪ File. Name the file **attrs.xml**.

4. Populate the attrs.xml file as follows:

```xml
<?xml version="1.0" encoding="utf-8"?>
<resources>
    <declare-styleable name="Gallery1">
        <attr name="android:galleryItemBackground" />
    </declare-styleable>
</resources>
```

5. Prepare a series of images and name them pic1.png, pic2.png, and so on for each subsequent image (see Figure 5-2).

FIGURE 5-2

 NOTE *You can download the series of images from this book's support website at* www.wrox.com.

6. Drag and drop all the images into the res/drawable-mdpi folder (see Figure 5-3). When a dialog is displayed, check the Copy files option and click OK.

FIGURE 5-3

 NOTE *This example assumes that this project will be tested on an AVD with medium DPI screen resolution. For a real-life project, you need to ensure that each* drawable *folder has a set of images (of different resolutions).*

7. Add the following statements in bold to the `GalleryActivity.java` file:

```java
package net.learn2develop.Gallery;

import android.app.Activity;
import android.content.Context;
import android.content.res.TypedArray;
import android.os.Bundle;
import android.view.View;
import android.view.ViewGroup;
import android.widget.AdapterView;
import android.widget.AdapterView.OnItemClickListener;
import android.widget.BaseAdapter;
import android.widget.Gallery;
import android.widget.ImageView;
import android.widget.Toast;

public class GalleryActivity extends Activity {
    //---the images to display---
    Integer[] imageIDs = {
            R.drawable.pic1,
            R.drawable.pic2,
            R.drawable.pic3,
            R.drawable.pic4,
            R.drawable.pic5,
            R.drawable.pic6,
            R.drawable.pic7
    };

    /** Called when the activity is first created. */
    @Override
    public void onCreate(Bundle savedInstanceState) {
        super.onCreate(savedInstanceState);
        setContentView(R.layout.main);

        Gallery gallery = (Gallery) findViewById(R.id.gallery1);

        gallery.setAdapter(new ImageAdapter(this));
        gallery.setOnItemClickListener(new OnItemClickListener()
        {
            public void onItemClick(AdapterView parent, View v,
            int position, long id)
            {
                Toast.makeText(getBaseContext(),
                        "pic" + (position + 1) + " selected",
                        Toast.LENGTH_SHORT).show();
            }
        });
    }

    public class ImageAdapter extends BaseAdapter
    {
        Context context;
```

```
            int itemBackground;

            public ImageAdapter(Context c)
            {
                context = c;
                //---setting the style---
                TypedArray a = obtainStyledAttributes(
                                    R.styleable.Gallery1);
                itemBackground = a.getResourceId(
                R.styleable.Gallery1_android_galleryItemBackground,
                0);
                a.recycle();
            }

        //---returns the number of images---
        public int getCount() {
            return imageIDs.length;
        }

        //---returns the item---
        public Object getItem(int position) {
            return position;
        }

         //---returns the ID of an item---
        public long getItemId(int position) {
            return position;
        }

        //---returns an ImageView view---
        public View getView(int position, View convertView,
        ViewGroup parent) {
            ImageView imageView;
            if (convertView == null) {
                imageView = new ImageView(context);
                imageView.setImageResource(imageIDs[position]);
                imageView.setScaleType(
                    ImageView.ScaleType.FIT_XY);
                imageView.setLayoutParams(
                    new Gallery.LayoutParams(150, 120));
            } else {
                imageView = (ImageView) convertView;
            }
            imageView.setBackgroundResource(itemBackground);
            return imageView;
        }
    }
}

}
```

8. Press F11 to debug the application on the Android emulator. Figure 5-4 shows the Gallery view displaying the series of images. You can swipe the images to view the entire series. Observe that as you click on an image, the Toast class displays its name.

FIGURE 5-4

9. To display the selected image in the ImageView, add the following statements in bold to the GalleryActivity.java file:

```
@Override
public void onCreate(Bundle savedInstanceState) {
    super.onCreate(savedInstanceState);
    setContentView(R.layout.main);

    Gallery gallery = (Gallery) findViewById(R.id.gallery1);

    gallery.setAdapter(new ImageAdapter(this));
    gallery.setOnItemClickListener(new OnItemClickListener()
    {
        public void onItemClick(AdapterView parent, View v,
        int position, long id)
        {
            Toast.makeText(getBaseContext(),
                    "pic" + (position + 1) + " selected",
                    Toast.LENGTH_SHORT).show();

            //---display the images selected---
            ImageView imageView =
                (ImageView) findViewById(R.id.image1);
            imageView.setImageResource(imageIDs[position]);
        }
    });
}
```

10. Press F11 to debug the application again. This time, the image selected will be displayed in the ImageView (see Figure 5-5).

How It Works

You first added the `Gallery` and `ImageView` views to `main.xml`:

```
<Gallery
    android:id="@+id/gallery1"
    android:layout_width="fill_parent"
    android:layout_height="wrap_content" />

<ImageView
    android:id="@+id/image1"
    android:layout_width="320dp"
    android:layout_height="250dp"
    android:scaleType="fitXY" />
```

As mentioned earlier, the `Gallery` view is used to display a series of images in a horizontal scrolling list. The `ImageView` is used to display the image selected by the user.

The list of images to be displayed is stored in the `imageIDs` array:

```
//---the images to display---
Integer[] imageIDs = {
        R.drawable.pic1,
        R.drawable.pic2,
        R.drawable.pic3,
        R.drawable.pic4,
        R.drawable.pic5,
        R.drawable.pic6,
        R.drawable.pic7
};
```

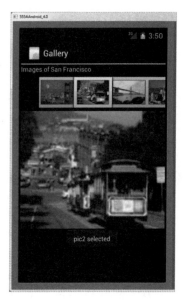

FIGURE 5-5

You create the `ImageAdapter` class (which extends the `BaseAdapter` class) so that it can bind to the `Gallery` view with a series of `ImageView` views. The `BaseAdapter` class acts as a bridge between an `AdapterView` and the data source that feeds data into it. Examples of `AdapterViews` are as follows:

➤ ListView

➤ GridView

➤ Spinner

➤ Gallery

There are several subclasses of the `BaseAdapter` class in Android:

➤ ListAdapter

➤ ArrayAdapter

➤ CursorAdapter

➤ SpinnerAdapter

For the `ImageAdapter` class, you implemented the following methods in bold:

```
public class ImageAdapter extends BaseAdapter {
    public ImageAdapter(Context c) { ... }

    //---returns the number of images---
    public int getCount() { ... }

    //---returns the item---
    public Object getItem(int position) { ... }

    //---returns the ID of an item---
    public long getItemId(int position) { ... }

    //---returns an ImageView view---
    public View getView(int position, View convertView,
    ViewGroup parent) { ... }
}
```

In particular, the `getView()` method returns a `View` at the specified position. In this case, you returned an `ImageView` object.

When an image in the `Gallery` view is selected (i.e., clicked), the selected image's position (0 for the first image, 1 for the second image, and so on) is displayed and the image is displayed in the `ImageView`:

```
Gallery gallery = (Gallery) findViewById(R.id.gallery1);

gallery.setAdapter(new ImageAdapter(this));
gallery.setOnItemClickListener(new OnItemClickListener()
{
    public void onItemClick(AdapterView<?> parent, View v,
    int position, long id)
    {
        Toast.makeText(getBaseContext(),
                "pic" + (position + 1) + " selected",
                Toast.LENGTH_SHORT).show();

        //---display the images selected---
        ImageView imageView =
            (ImageView) findViewById(R.id.image1);
        imageView.setImageResource(imageIDs[position]);
    }
});
```

ImageSwitcher

The previous section demonstrated how to use the `Gallery` view together with an `ImageView` to display a series of thumbnail images so that when one is selected, it is displayed in the `ImageView`. However, sometimes you don't want an image to appear abruptly when the user selects it in the `Gallery` view — you might, for example, want to apply some animation to the image when it transitions from one image to another. In this case, you need to use the ImageSwitcher together with the Gallery view. The following Try It Out shows you how.

TRY IT OUT Using the ImageSwitcher View

codefile ImageSwitcher.zip available for download at Wrox.com

1. Using Eclipse, create a new Android project and name it **ImageSwitcher**.

2. Modify the main.xml file by adding the following statements in bold:

```xml
<?xml version="1.0" encoding="utf-8"?>
<LinearLayout xmlns:android="http://schemas.android.com/apk/res/android"
    android:layout_width="fill_parent"
    android:layout_height="fill_parent"
    android:orientation="vertical" >

<TextView
    android:layout_width="fill_parent"
    android:layout_height="wrap_content"
    android:text="Images of San Francisco" />

<Gallery
    android:id="@+id/gallery1"
    android:layout_width="fill_parent"
    android:layout_height="wrap_content" />

<ImageSwitcher
    android:id="@+id/switcher1"
    android:layout_width="fill_parent"
    android:layout_height="fill_parent"
    android:layout_alignParentLeft="true"
    android:layout_alignParentRight="true"
    android:layout_alignParentBottom="true" />

</LinearLayout>
```

3. Right-click on the res/values folder and select New ⇨ File. Name the file **attrs.xml**.

4. Populate the attrs.xml file as follows:

```xml
<?xml version="1.0" encoding="utf-8"?>
<resources>
    <declare-styleable name="Gallery1">
        <attr name="android:galleryItemBackground" />
    </declare-styleable>
</resources>
```

5. Drag and drop a series of images into the res/drawable-mdpi folder (refer to the previous example for the images). When a dialog is displayed, check the Copy files option and click OK.

6. Add the following bold statements to the `ImageSwitcherActivity.java` file:

```java
package net.learn2develop.ImageSwitcher;

import android.app.Activity;
import android.content.Context;
import android.content.res.TypedArray;
import android.os.Bundle;
import android.view.View;
import android.view.ViewGroup;
import android.view.ViewGroup.LayoutParams;
import android.view.animation.AnimationUtils;
import android.widget.AdapterView;
import android.widget.AdapterView.OnItemClickListener;
import android.widget.BaseAdapter;
import android.widget.Gallery;
import android.widget.ImageSwitcher;
import android.widget.ImageView;
import android.widget.ViewSwitcher.ViewFactory;

public class ImageSwitcherActivity extends Activity implements ViewFactory {
    //---the images to display---
    Integer[] imageIDs = {
            R.drawable.pic1,
            R.drawable.pic2,
            R.drawable.pic3,
            R.drawable.pic4,
            R.drawable.pic5,
            R.drawable.pic6,
            R.drawable.pic7
    };

    private ImageSwitcher imageSwitcher;

    /** Called when the activity is first created. */
    @Override
    public void onCreate(Bundle savedInstanceState) {
        super.onCreate(savedInstanceState);
        setContentView(R.layout.main);

        imageSwitcher = (ImageSwitcher) findViewById(R.id.switcher1);
        imageSwitcher.setFactory(this);
        imageSwitcher.setInAnimation(AnimationUtils.loadAnimation(this,
                android.R.anim.fade_in));
        imageSwitcher.setOutAnimation(AnimationUtils.loadAnimation(this,
                android.R.anim.fade_out));

        Gallery gallery = (Gallery) findViewById(R.id.gallery1);
        gallery.setAdapter(new ImageAdapter(this));
        gallery.setOnItemClickListener(new OnItemClickListener()
        {
            public void onItemClick(AdapterView<?> parent,
            View v, int position, long id)
            {
                imageSwitcher.setImageResource(imageIDs[position]);
```

```
        }
    });
}

public View makeView()
{
    ImageView imageView = new ImageView(this);
    imageView.setBackgroundColor(0xFF000000);
    imageView.setScaleType(ImageView.ScaleType.FIT_CENTER);
    imageView.setLayoutParams(new
            ImageSwitcher.LayoutParams(
                    LayoutParams.FILL_PARENT,
                    LayoutParams.FILL_PARENT));
    return imageView;
}

public class ImageAdapter extends BaseAdapter
{
    private Context context;
    private int itemBackground;

    public ImageAdapter(Context c)
    {
        context = c;

        //---setting the style---
        TypedArray a = obtainStyledAttributes(R.styleable.Gallery1);
        itemBackground = a.getResourceId(
                R.styleable.Gallery1_android_galleryItemBackground, 0);
        a.recycle();
    }

    //---returns the number of images---
    public int getCount()
    {
        return imageIDs.length;
    }

    //---returns the item---
    public Object getItem(int position)
    {
        return position;
    }

    //---returns the ID of an item---
    public long getItemId(int position)
    {
        return position;
    }

    //---returns an ImageView view---
    public View getView(int position, View convertView, ViewGroup parent)
    {
        ImageView imageView = new ImageView(context);

        imageView.setImageResource(imageIDs[position]);
```

```
        imageView.setScaleType(ImageView.ScaleType.FIT_XY);
        imageView.setLayoutParams(new Gallery.LayoutParams(150, 120));
        imageView.setBackgroundResource(itemBackground);

        return imageView;
    }
}
```

```
}
```

7. Press F11 to debug the application on the Android emulator.
Figure 5-6 shows the Gallery and ImageSwitcher views, with
both the collection of images as well as the image selected.

How It Works

The first thing to note in this example is that the
ImageSwitcherActivity not only extends Activity, but also
implements ViewFactory. To use the ImageSwitcher view, you need
to implement the ViewFactory interface, which creates the views for
use with the ImageSwitcher view. For this, you need to implement
the makeView() method:

```
public View makeView()
{
    ImageView imageView = new ImageView(this);
    imageView.setBackgroundColor(0xFF000000);
    imageView.setScaleType(ImageView.ScaleType.FIT_CENTER);
    imageView.setLayoutParams(new
            ImageSwitcher.LayoutParams(
                    LayoutParams.FILL_PARENT,
                    LayoutParams.FILL_PARENT));
    return imageView;
}
```

FIGURE 5-6

This method creates a new View to be added in the ImageSwitcher view, which in this case is an
ImageView.

Like the Gallery example in the previous section, you also implemented an ImageAdapter class so that
it can bind to the Gallery view with a series of ImageView views.

In the onCreate() method, you get a reference to the ImageSwitcher view and set the animation,
specifying how images should "fade" in and out of the view. Finally, when an image is selected from the
Gallery view, the image is displayed in the ImageSwitcher view:

```
@Override
public void onCreate(Bundle savedInstanceState) {
    super.onCreate(savedInstanceState);
    setContentView(R.layout.main);

    imageSwitcher = (ImageSwitcher) findViewById(R.id.switcher1);
    imageSwitcher.setFactory(this);
    imageSwitcher.setInAnimation(AnimationUtils.loadAnimation(this,
```

```
                    android.R.anim.fade_in));
    imageSwitcher.setOutAnimation(AnimationUtils.loadAnimation(this,
                    android.R.anim.fade_out));

    Gallery gallery = (Gallery) findViewById(R.id.gallery1);
    gallery.setAdapter(new ImageAdapter(this));
    gallery.setOnItemClickListener(new OnItemClickListener()
    {
        public void onItemClick(AdapterView<?> parent,
        View v, int position, long id)
        {
            imageSwitcher.setImageResource(imageIDs[position]);
        }
    });
}
```

In this example, when an image is selected in the Gallery view, it appears by "fading" in. When the next image is selected, the current image fades out. If you want the image to slide in from the left and slide out to the right when another image is selected, try the following animation:

```
    imageSwitcher.setInAnimation(AnimationUtils.loadAnimation(this,
            android.R.anim.slide_in_left));
    imageSwitcher.setOutAnimation(AnimationUtils.loadAnimation(this,
            android.R.anim.slide_out_right));
```

GridView

The GridView shows items in a two-dimensional scrolling grid. You can use the GridView together with an ImageView to display a series of images. The following Try It Out demonstrates how.

TRY IT OUT   Using the GridView View

codefile Grid.zip available for download at Wrox.com

1.   Using Eclipse, create a new Android project and name it **Grid**.

2.   Drag and drop a series of images into the res/drawable-mdpi folder (see the previous example for the images). When a dialog is displayed, check the Copy files option and click OK.

3.   Populate the main.xml file with the following content:

```
<?xml version="1.0" encoding="utf-8"?>
<LinearLayout xmlns:android="http://schemas.android.com/apk/res/android"
    android:layout_width="fill_parent"
    android:layout_height="fill_parent"
    android:orientation="vertical" >

<GridView
    android:id="@+id/gridview"
    android:layout_width="fill_parent"
    android:layout_height="fill_parent"
```

```
        android:numColumns="auto_fit"
        android:verticalSpacing="10dp"
        android:horizontalSpacing="10dp"
        android:columnWidth="90dp"
        android:stretchMode="columnWidth"
        android:gravity="center" />

</LinearLayout>
```

4. Add the following statements in bold to the `GridActivity.java` file:

```java
package net.learn2develop.Grid;

import android.app.Activity;
import android.content.Context;
import android.os.Bundle;
import android.view.View;
import android.view.ViewGroup;
import android.widget.AdapterView;
import android.widget.AdapterView.OnItemClickListener;
import android.widget.BaseAdapter;
import android.widget.GridView;
import android.widget.ImageView;
import android.widget.Toast;

public class GridActivity extends Activity {
    //---the images to display---
    Integer[] imageIDs = {
            R.drawable.pic1,
            R.drawable.pic2,
            R.drawable.pic3,
            R.drawable.pic4,
            R.drawable.pic5,
            R.drawable.pic6,
            R.drawable.pic7
    };

    /** Called when the activity is first created. */
    @Override
    public void onCreate(Bundle savedInstanceState) {
        super.onCreate(savedInstanceState);
        setContentView(R.layout.main);

        GridView gridView = (GridView) findViewById(R.id.gridview);
        gridView.setAdapter(new ImageAdapter(this));

        gridView.setOnItemClickListener(new OnItemClickListener()
        {
            public void onItemClick(AdapterView parent,
            View v, int position, long id)
            {
                Toast.makeText(getBaseContext(),
                        "pic" + (position + 1) + " selected",
                        Toast.LENGTH_SHORT).show();
            }
```

```java
            });
    }

    public class ImageAdapter extends BaseAdapter
    {
        private Context context;

        public ImageAdapter(Context c)
        {
            context = c;
        }

        //---returns the number of images---
        public int getCount() {
            return imageIDs.length;
        }

        //---returns the item---
        public Object getItem(int position) {
            return position;
        }

        //---returns the ID of an item---
        public long getItemId(int position) {
            return position;
        }

        //---returns an ImageView view---
        public View getView(int position, View convertView,
        ViewGroup parent)
        {
            ImageView imageView;
            if (convertView == null) {
                imageView = new ImageView(context);
                imageView.setLayoutParams(new
                    GridView.LayoutParams(85, 85));
                imageView.setScaleType(
                    ImageView.ScaleType.CENTER_CROP);
                imageView.setPadding(5, 5, 5, 5);
            } else {
                imageView = (ImageView) convertView;
            }
            imageView.setImageResource(imageIDs[position]);
            return imageView;
        }
    }
}
```

5. Press F11 to debug the application on the Android emulator. Figure 5-7 shows the GridView displaying all the images.

FIGURE 5-7

How It Works

Like the `Gallery` and `ImageSwitcher` example, you implemented the `ImageAdapter` class and then bound it to the `GridView`:

```
GridView gridView = (GridView) findViewById(R.id.gridview);
gridView.setAdapter(new ImageAdapter(this));

gridView.setOnItemClickListener(new OnItemClickListener()
{
    public void onItemClick(AdapterView parent,
    View v, int position, long id)
    {
        Toast.makeText(getBaseContext(),
                "pic" + (position + 1) + " selected",
                Toast.LENGTH_SHORT).show();
    }
});
```

When an image is selected, you display a `Toast` message indicating the selected image.

Within the `getView()` method you can specify the size of the images and how images are spaced in the `GridView` by setting the padding for each image:

```
//---returns an ImageView view---
public View getView(int position, View convertView,
ViewGroup parent)
{
    ImageView imageView;
    if (convertView == null) {
        imageView = new ImageView(context);
        imageView.setLayoutParams(new
            GridView.LayoutParams(85, 85));
        imageView.setScaleType(
            ImageView.ScaleType.CENTER_CROP);
        imageView.setPadding(5, 5, 5, 5);
    } else {
        imageView = (ImageView) convertView;
    }
    imageView.setImageResource(imageIDs[position]);
    return imageView;
}
```

USING MENUS WITH VIEWS

Menus are useful for displaying additional options that are not directly visible on the main UI of an application. There are two main types of menus in Android:

➤ **Options menu** — Displays information related to the current activity. In Android, you activate the options menu by pressing the MENU button.

➤ **Context menu** — Displays information related to a particular view on an activity. In Android, to activate a context menu you tap and hold on to it.

Figure 5-8 shows an example of an options menu in the Browser application. The options menu is displayed whenever the user presses the MENU button. The menu items displayed vary according to the current activity that is running.

Figure 5-9 shows a context menu that is displayed when the user taps and holds on an image displayed on the page. The menu items displayed vary according to the component or view currently selected. In general, to activate the context menu, the user selects an item on the screen and taps and holds it.

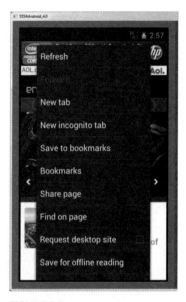

FIGURE 5-8

FIGURE 5-9

Creating the Helper Methods

Before you go ahead and create your options and context menus, you need to create two helper methods. One creates a list of items to show inside a menu, while the other handles the event that is fired when the user selects an item inside the menu.

TRY IT OUT Creating the Menu Helper Methods

codefile Menus.zip available for download at Wrox.com

1. Using Eclipse, create a new Android project and name it **Menus**.

2. In the `MenusActivity.java` file, add the following statements in bold:

```
package net.learn2develop.Menus;

import android.app.Activity;
```

```java
import android.os.Bundle;
import android.view.Menu;
import android.view.MenuItem;
import android.widget.Toast;

public class MenusActivity extends Activity {
    /** Called when the activity is first created. */
    @Override
    public void onCreate(Bundle savedInstanceState) {
        super.onCreate(savedInstanceState);
        setContentView(R.layout.main);
    }

    private void CreateMenu(Menu menu)
    {
        MenuItem mnu1 = menu.add(0, 0, 0, "Item 1");
        {
            mnu1.setAlphabeticShortcut('a');
            mnu1.setIcon(R.drawable.ic_launcher);
        }
        MenuItem mnu2 = menu.add(0, 1, 1, "Item 2");
        {
            mnu2.setAlphabeticShortcut('b');
            mnu2.setIcon(R.drawable.ic_launcher);
        }
        MenuItem mnu3 = menu.add(0, 2, 2, "Item 3");
        {
            mnu3.setAlphabeticShortcut('c');
            mnu3.setIcon(R.drawable.ic_launcher);
        }
        MenuItem mnu4 = menu.add(0, 3, 3, "Item 4");
        {
            mnu4.setAlphabeticShortcut('d');
        }
        menu.add(0, 4, 4, "Item 5");
        menu.add(0, 5, 5, "Item 6");
        menu.add(0, 6, 6, "Item 7");
    }

    private boolean MenuChoice(MenuItem item)
    {
        switch (item.getItemId()) {
        case 0:
            Toast.makeText(this, "You clicked on Item 1",
                Toast.LENGTH_LONG).show();
            return true;
        case 1:
            Toast.makeText(this, "You clicked on Item 2",
                Toast.LENGTH_LONG).show();
            return true;
        case 2:
            Toast.makeText(this, "You clicked on Item 3",
                Toast.LENGTH_LONG).show();
            return true;
        case 3:
```

```
            Toast.makeText(this, "You clicked on Item 4",
                Toast.LENGTH_LONG).show();
            return true;
    case 4:
            Toast.makeText(this, "You clicked on Item 5",
                Toast.LENGTH_LONG).show();
            return true;
    case 5:
            Toast.makeText(this, "You clicked on Item 6",
                Toast.LENGTH_LONG).show();
            return true;
    case 6:
            Toast.makeText(this, "You clicked on Item 7",
                Toast.LENGTH_LONG).show();
            return true;
    }
    return false;
}

}
```

How It Works

The preceding example creates two methods: CreateMenu() and MenuChoice(). The CreateMenu() method takes a Menu argument and adds a series of menu items to it.

To add a menu item to the menu, you create an instance of the MenuItem class and use the add() method of the Menu object:

```
MenuItem mnu1 = menu.add(0, 0, 0, "Item 1");
{
    mnu1.setAlphabeticShortcut('a');
    mnu1.setIcon(R.drawable.ic_launcher);
}
```

The four arguments of the add() method are as follows:

➤ groupId — The group identifier that the menu item should be part of. Use 0 if an item is not in a group.

➤ itemId — A unique item ID

➤ order — The order in which the item should be displayed

➤ title — The text to display for the menu item

You can use the setAlphabeticShortcut() method to assign a shortcut key to the menu item so that users can select an item by pressing a key on the keyboard. The setIcon() method sets an image to be displayed on the menu item.

The MenuChoice() method takes a MenuItem argument and checks its ID to determine the menu item that is selected. It then displays a Toast message to let the user know which menu item was selected.

Options Menu

You are now ready to modify the application to display the options menu when the user presses the MENU key on the Android device.

TRY IT OUT   Displaying an Options Menu

1. Using the same project created in the previous section, add the following statements in bold to the `MenusActivity.java` file:

```java
package net.learn2develop.Menus;

import android.app.Activity;
import android.os.Bundle;
import android.view.Menu;
import android.view.MenuItem;
import android.widget.Toast;

public class MenusActivity extends Activity {
    /** Called when the activity is first created. */
    @Override
    public void onCreate(Bundle savedInstanceState) {
        super.onCreate(savedInstanceState);
        setContentView(R.layout.main);
    }

    @Override
    public boolean onCreateOptionsMenu(Menu menu) {
        super.onCreateOptionsMenu(menu);
        CreateMenu(menu);
        return true;
    }

    @Override
    public boolean onOptionsItemSelected(MenuItem item)
    {
        return MenuChoice(item);
    }

    private void CreateMenu(Menu menu)
    {
        //...
    }

    private boolean MenuChoice(MenuItem item)
    {
        //...
    }
}
```

2. Press F11 to debug the application on the Android emulator. Figure 5-10 shows the options menu that pops up when you click the MENU button. To select a menu item, either click on an individual item or use its shortcut key (A to D; applicable only to the first four items). Note that menu items 1 to 3 did not display the icons even though the code explicitly did so.

3. If you now change the minimum SDK attribute of the `AndroidManifest.xml` file to a value of 10 or less and then rerun the application on the emulator, the icons will be displayed as shown in Figure 5-11. Note that any menu items after the fifth item are encapsulated in the item named More. Clicking on More will reveal the rest of the menu items.

```
<uses-sdk android:minSdkVersion="10" />
```

FIGURE 5-10

FIGURE 5-11

How It Works

To display the options menu for your activity, you need to implement two methods in your activity: `onCreateOptionsMenu()` and `onOptionsItemSelected()`. The `onCreateOptionsMenu()` method is called when the MENU button is pressed. In this case, you call the `CreateMenu()` helper method to display the options menu. When a menu item is selected, the `onOptionsItemSelected()` method is called. In this case, you call the `MenuChoice()` method to display the menu item selected (and perform whatever action is appropriate).

Take note of the look and feel of the options menu in different versions of Android. Starting with Honeycomb, the options menu items do not have icons and display all menu items in a scrollable list. For versions of Android before Honeycomb, no more than five menu items are displayed; any additional menu items are part of a "More" menu item that represents the rest of the menu items.

Context Menu

The previous section showed how the options menu is displayed when the user presses the MENU button. Besides the options menu, you can also display a context menu. A context menu is usually associated with a view on an activity, and it is displayed when the user taps and holds an item. For example, if the user taps on a `Button` view and holds it for a few seconds, a context menu can be displayed.

If you want to associate a context menu with a view on an activity, you need to call the `setOnCreateContextMenuListener()` method of that particular view. The following Try It Out shows how you can associate a context menu with a Button view.

TRY IT OUT   Displaying a Context Menu

codefile Menus.zip available for download at Wrox.com

1.   Using the same project from the previous example, add the following statements to the `main.xml` file:

```xml
<?xml version="1.0" encoding="utf-8"?>
<LinearLayout xmlns:android="http://schemas.android.com/apk/res/android"
    android:layout_width="fill_parent"
    android:layout_height="fill_parent"
    android:orientation="vertical" >

    <TextView
        android:layout_width="fill_parent"
        android:layout_height="wrap_content"
        android:text="@string/hello" />

    <Button
        android:id="@+id/button1"
        android:layout_width="match_parent"
        android:layout_height="wrap_content"
        android:text="Click and hold on it" />

</LinearLayout>
```

2.   Add the following statements in bold to the `MenusActivity.java` file:

```java
package net.learn2develop.Menus;

import android.app.Activity;
import android.os.Bundle;
import android.view.ContextMenu;
import android.view.ContextMenu.ContextMenuInfo;
import android.view.Menu;
import android.view.MenuItem;
import android.view.View;
import android.widget.Button;
```

```java
import android.widget.Toast;

public class MenusActivity extends Activity {
    /** Called when the activity is first created. */
    @Override
    public void onCreate(Bundle savedInstanceState) {
        super.onCreate(savedInstanceState);
        setContentView(R.layout.main);

        Button btn = (Button) findViewById(R.id.button1);
        btn.setOnCreateContextMenuListener(this);
    }

    @Override
    public void onCreateContextMenu(ContextMenu menu, View view,
    ContextMenuInfo menuInfo)
    {
        super.onCreateContextMenu(menu, view, menuInfo);
        CreateMenu(menu);
    }

    @Override
    public boolean onCreateOptionsMenu(Menu menu) {
        //...
    }

    @Override
    public boolean onOptionsItemSelected(MenuItem item)
    {
        return MenuChoice(item);
    }

    private void CreateMenu(Menu menu)
    {
        //...
    }

    private boolean MenuChoice(MenuItem item)
    {
        //...
    }
}
```

NOTE *If you changed the minimum SDK attribute of the* `AndroidManifest.xml` *file to a value of 10 earlier, be sure to change it back to 14 before you debug your application in the next step.*

3.   Press F11 to debug the application on the Android emulator. Figure 5-12 shows the context menu that is displayed when you click and hold the `Button` view.

How It Works

In the preceding example, you call the `setOnCreateContextMenuListener()` method of the `Button` view to associate it with a context menu.

When the user taps and holds the `Button` view, the `onCreateContextMenu()` method is called. In this method, you call the `CreateMenu()` method to display the context menu. Similarly, when an item inside the context menu is selected, the `onContextItemSelected()` method is called, where you call the `MenuChoice()` method to display a message to the user.

Notice that the shortcut keys for the menu items do not work. To enable the shortcuts keys, you need to call the `setQuertyMode()` method of the `Menu` object, like this:

FIGURE 5-12

```
private void CreateMenu(Menu menu)
{
    menu.setQwertyMode(true);
    MenuItem mnu1 = menu.add(0, 0, 0, "Item 1");
    {
        mnu1.setAlphabeticShortcut('a');
        mnu1.setIcon(R.drawable.ic_launcher);
    }
    //...
}
```

SOME ADDITIONAL VIEWS

Besides the standard views that you have seen up to this point, the Android SDK provides some additional views that make your applications much more interesting. In this section, you will learn more about the following views: `AnalogClock`, `DigitalClock`, and `WebView`.

AnalogClock and DigitalClock Views

The `AnalogClock` view displays an analog clock with two hands — one for minutes and one for hours. Its counterpart, the `DigitalClock` view, displays the time digitally. Both views display the system time only, and do not allow you to display a particular time (such as the current time in another time zone). Hence, if you want to display the time for a particular region, you have to build your own custom views.

NOTE *Creating your own custom views in Android is beyond the scope of this book. However, if you are interested in this area, take a look at Google's Android documentation on this topic at* `http://developer.android.com/guide/ topics/ui/custom-components.html.`

Using the `AnalogClock` and `DigitalClock` views are straightforward; simply declare them in your XML file (such as `main.xml`), like this:

```xml
<?xml version="1.0" encoding="utf-8"?>
<LinearLayout
    xmlns:android="http://schemas.android.com/apk/res/android"
    android:layout_width="fill_parent"
    android:layout_height="fill_parent"
    android:orientation="vertical" >

<AnalogClock
    android:layout_width="wrap_content"
    android:layout_height="wrap_content" />

<DigitalClock
    android:layout_width="wrap_content"
    android:layout_height="wrap_content" />

</LinearLayout>
```

Figure 5-13 shows the `AnalogClock` and `DigitalClock` views in action.

WebView

The `WebView` enables you to embed a web browser in your activity. This is very useful if your application needs to embed some web content, such as maps from some other providers, and so on. The following Try It Out shows how you can programmatically load the content of a web page and display it in your activity.

FIGURE 5-13

TRY IT OUT   Using the WebView View

codefile WebView.zip available for download at Wrox.com

1.   Using Eclipse, create a new Android project and name it **WebView**.

2.   Add the following statements to the `main.xml` file:

```xml
<?xml version="1.0" encoding="utf-8"?>
<LinearLayout xmlns:android="http://schemas.android.com/apk/res/android"
    android:layout_width="fill_parent"
```

```
        android:layout_height="fill_parent"
        android:orientation="vertical" >

<WebView android:id="@+id/webview1"
        android:layout_width="wrap_content"
        android:layout_height="wrap_content" />

</LinearLayout>
```

3.   In the `WebViewActivity.java` file, add the following statements in bold:

```java
package net.learn2develop.WebView;

import android.app.Activity;
import android.os.Bundle;
import android.webkit.WebSettings;
import android.webkit.WebView;

public class WebViewActivity extends Activity {
    /** Called when the activity is first created. */
    @Override
    public void onCreate(Bundle savedInstanceState) {
        super.onCreate(savedInstanceState);
        setContentView(R.layout.main);

        WebView wv = (WebView) findViewById(R.id.webview1);

        WebSettings webSettings = wv.getSettings();
        webSettings.setBuiltInZoomControls(true);
        wv.loadUrl(
            "http://chart.apis.google.com/chart" +
            "?chs=300x225" +
            "&cht=v" +
            "&chco=FF6342,ADDE63,63C6DE" +
            "&chd=t:100,80,60,30,30,30,10" +
            "&chdl=A|B|C");
    }
}
```

4.   In the `AndroidManifest.xml` file, add the following permission:

```xml
<?xml version="1.0" encoding="utf-8"?>
<manifest xmlns:android="http://schemas.android.com/apk/res/android"
    package="net.learn2develop.WebView"
    android:versionCode="1"
    android:versionName="1.0" >

    <uses-sdk android:minSdkVersion="14" />
    <uses-permission android:name="android.permission.INTERNET"/>

    <application
        android:icon="@drawable/ic_launcher"
        android:label="@string/app_name" >
        <activity
```

```
            android:label="@string/app_name"
            android:name=".WebViewActivity" >
            <intent-filter >
                <action android:name="android.intent.action.MAIN" />

                <category android:name="android.intent.category.LAUNCHER" />
            </intent-filter>
        </activity>
    </application>

</manifest>
```

5. Press F11 to debug the application on the Android emulator. Figure 5-14 shows the content of the WebView.

How It Works

To use the WebView to load a web page, you use the loadUrl() method and pass it a URL, like this:

```
wv.loadUrl(
    "http://chart.apis.google.com/chart" +
    "?chs=300x225" +
    "&cht=v" +
    "&chco=FF6342,ADDE63,63C6DE" +
    "&chd=t:100,80,60,30,30,30,10" +
    "&chdl=A|B|C");
```

FIGURE 5-14

To display the built-in zoom controls, you need to first get the WebSettings property from the WebView and then call its setBuiltInZoomControls() method:

```
WebSettings webSettings = wv.getSettings();
webSettings.setBuiltInZoomControls(true);
```

Figure 5-15 shows the built-in zoom controls that appear when you use the mouse to click and drag the content of the WebView on the Android emulator.

 NOTE *While most Android devices support multi-touch screens, the built-in zoom controls are useful for zooming your web content when testing your application on the Android emulator.*

Sometimes when you load a page that redirects you (for example, loading www.wrox.com redirects you to www.wrox.com/wileyCDA), WebView will cause your application to launch the device's Browser application to load the desired page. In Figure 5-16, note the URL bar at the top of the screen.

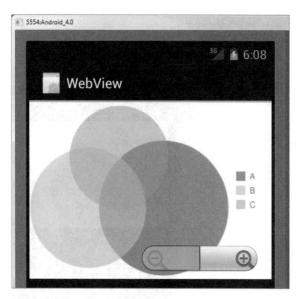

FIGURE 5-15

FIGURE 5-16

To prevent this from happening, you need to implement the `WebViewClient` class and override the `shouldOverrideUrlLoading()` method, as shown in the following example:

```java
package net.learn2develop.WebView;

import android.app.Activity;
import android.os.Bundle;
import android.webkit.WebSettings;
import android.webkit.WebView;
import android.webkit.WebViewClient;

public class WebViewActivity extends Activity {
    /** Called when the activity is first created. */
    @Override
    public void onCreate(Bundle savedInstanceState) {
        super.onCreate(savedInstanceState);
        setContentView(R.layout.main);

        WebView wv = (WebView) findViewById(R.id.webview1);

        WebSettings webSettings = wv.getSettings();
        webSettings.setBuiltInZoomControls(true);
        wv.setWebViewClient(new Callback());
        wv.loadUrl("http://www.wrox.com");
```

```
        }

    private class Callback extends WebViewClient {
        @Override
        public boolean shouldOverrideUrlLoading(
        WebView view, String url) {
            return(false);
        }
    }

}
```

Figure 5-17 shows the Wrox.com home page now loading correctly in the `WebView`.

FIGURE 5-17

You can also dynamically formulate an HTML string and load it into the `WebView`, using the `loadDataWithBaseURL()` method:

```
WebView wv = (WebView) findViewById(R.id.webview1);
final String mimeType = "text/html";
final String encoding = "UTF-8";
String html = "<H1>A simple HTML page</H1><body>" +
    "<p>The quick brown fox jumps over the lazy dog</p>" +
    "</body>";
wv.loadDataWithBaseURL("", html, mimeType, encoding, "");
```

Figure 5-18 shows the content displayed by the `WebView`.

FIGURE 5-18

Alternatively, if you have an HTML file located in the `assets` folder of the project (see Figure 5-19), you can load it into the `WebView` using the `loadUrl()` method:

```
WebView wv = (WebView) findViewById(R.id.webview1);
wv.loadUrl("file:///android_asset/Index.html");
```

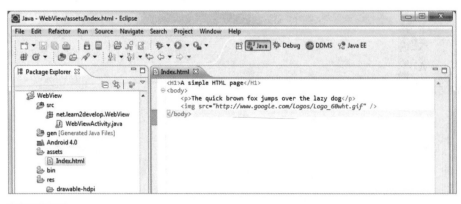

FIGURE 5-19

Figure 5-20 shows the content of the `WebView`.

FIGURE 5-20

SUMMARY

In this chapter, you have taken a look at the various views that enable you to display images: Gallery, ImageView, ImageSwitcher, and GridView. In addition, you learned about the difference between options menus and context menus, and how to display them in your application. Finally, you learned about the AnalogClock and DigitalClock views, which display the current time graphically, as well as the WebView, which displays the content of a web page.

EXERCISES

1. What is the purpose of the ImageSwitcher?

2. Name the two methods you need to override when implementing an options menu in your activity.

3. Name the two methods you need to override when implementing a context menu in your activity.

4. How do you prevent the WebView from invoking the device's web browser when a redirection occurs in the WebView?

Answers to the exercises can be found in Appendix C.

▶ **WHAT YOU LEARNED IN THIS CHAPTER**

TOPIC	KEY CONCEPTS
Using the Gallery view	Displays a series of images in a horizontal scrolling list
Gallery	```<Gallery` ` android:id="@+id/gallery1"` ` android:layout_width="fill_parent"` ` android:layout_height="wrap_content" />```
ImageView	```<ImageView` ` android:id="@+id/image1"` ` android:layout_width="320px"` ` android:layout_height="250px"` ` android:scaleType="fitXY" />```
Using the ImageSwitcher view	Performs animation when switching between images
ImageSwitcher	```<ImageSwitcher` ` android:id="@+id/switcher1"` ` android:layout_width="fill_parent"` ` android:layout_height="fill_parent"` ` android:layout_alignParentLeft="true"` ` android:layout_alignParentRight="true"` ` android:layout_alignParentBottom="true" />```
Using the GridView	Shows items in a two-dimensional scrolling grid
GridView	```<GridView` ` android:id="@+id/gridview"` ` android:layout_width="fill_parent"` ` android:layout_height="fill_parent"` ` android:numColumns="auto_fit"` ` android:verticalSpacing="10dp"` ` android:horizontalSpacing="10dp"` ` android:columnWidth="90dp"` ` android:stretchMode="columnWidth"` ` android:gravity="center" />```
AnalogClock	```<AnalogClock` ` android:layout_width="wrap_content"` ` android:layout_height="wrap_content" />```
DigitalClock	```<DigitalClock` ` android:layout_width="wrap_content"` ` android:layout_height="wrap_content" />```
WebView	```<WebView android:id="@+id/webview1"` ` android:layout_width="wrap_content"` ` android:layout_height="wrap_content" />```

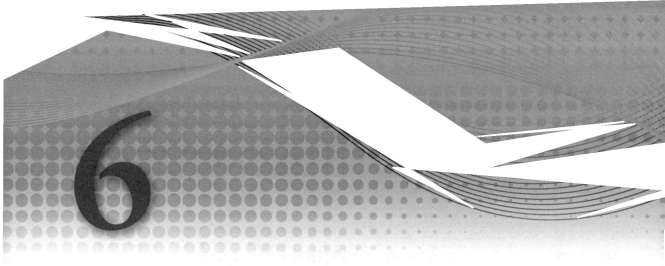

Data Persistence

WHAT YOU WILL LEARN IN THIS CHAPTER

➤ How to save simple data using the SharedPreferences object

➤ Enabling users to modify preferences using a PreferenceActivity class

➤ How to write and read files in internal and external storage

➤ Creating and using a SQLite database

In this chapter, you will learn how to persist data in your Android applications. Persisting data is an important topic in application development, as users typically expect to reuse data in the future. For Android, there are primarily three basic ways of persisting data:

➤ A lightweight mechanism known as *shared preferences* to save small chunks of data

➤ Traditional file systems

➤ A relational database management system through the support of SQLite databases

The techniques discussed in this chapter enable applications to create and access their own private data. In the next chapter you'll learn how you can share data across applications.

SAVING AND LOADING USER PREFERENCES

Android provides the SharedPreferences object to help you save simple application data. For example, your application may have an option that enables users to specify the font size of the text displayed in your application. In this case, your application needs to remember the size set by the user so that the next time he or she uses the application again, it can set the size appropriately. In order to do so, you have several options. You can save the data to a file, but you have to perform some file management routines, such as writing the data to the file, indicating how many characters to read from it, and so on. Also, if you have several pieces of information to save, such as text size, font name, preferred background color, and so on, then the task of writing to a file becomes more onerous.

An alternative to writing to a text file is to use a database, but saving simple data to a database is overkill, both from a developer's point of view and in terms of the application's run-time performance.

Using the `SharedPreferences` object, however, you save the data you want through the use of name/value pairs — specify a name for the data you want to save, and then both it and its value will be saved automatically to an XML file for you.

Accessing Preferences Using an Activity

In the following Try It Out, you learn how to use the `SharedPreferences` object to store application data. You will also learn how the stored application data can be modified directly by the user through a special type of activity provided by the Android OS.

TRY IT OUT Saving Data Using the SharedPreferences Object

codefile SharedPreferences.zip available for download at Wrox.com

1. Using Eclipse, create an Android project and name it **UsingPreferences**.

2. Create a new subfolder in the res folder and name it **xml**. In this newly created folder, add a file and name it **myapppreferences.xml** (see Figure 6-1).

3. Populate the `myapppreferences.xml` file as follows:

```xml
<?xml version="1.0" encoding="utf-8"?>
<PreferenceScreen
    xmlns:android="http://schemas.android.com/apk/res/android">
    <PreferenceCategory android:title="Category 1">
        <CheckBoxPreference
            android:title="Checkbox"
            android:defaultValue="false"
            android:summary="True or False"
            android:key="checkboxPref" />
    </PreferenceCategory>
    <PreferenceCategory android:title="Category 2">
        <EditTextPreference
            android:summary="Enter a string"
            android:defaultValue="[Enter a string here]"
            android:title="Edit Text"
            android:key="editTextPref" />
        <RingtonePreference
            android:summary="Select a ringtone"
            android:title="Ringtones"
            android:key="ringtonePref" />
        <PreferenceScreen
            android:title="Second Preference Screen"
```

FIGURE 6-1

```
                    android:summary=
                        "Click here to go to the second Preference Screen"
                    android:key="secondPrefScreenPref" >
                    <EditTextPreference
                        android:summary="Enter a string"
                        android:title="Edit Text (second Screen)"
                        android:key="secondEditTextPref" />
                </PreferenceScreen>
            </PreferenceCategory>
        </PreferenceScreen>
```

4. Under the package name, add a new Class file and name it **AppPreferenceActivity**.

5. Populate the AppPreferenceActivity.java file as follows:

```java
package net.learn2develop.UsingPreferences;

import android.os.Bundle;
import android.preference.PreferenceActivity;

public class AppPreferenceActivity extends PreferenceActivity {
    @Override
    public void onCreate(Bundle savedInstanceState) {
        super.onCreate(savedInstanceState);
        //---load the preferences from an XML file---
        addPreferencesFromResource(R.xml.myapppreferences);
    }
}
```

6. In the AndroidManifest.xml file, add the new entry for the AppPreferenceActivity class:

```xml
<?xml version="1.0" encoding="utf-8"?>
<manifest xmlns:android="http://schemas.android.com/apk/res/android"
    package="net.learn2develop.UsingPreferences"
    android:versionCode="1"
    android:versionName="1.0" >

    <uses-sdk android:minSdkVersion="14" />

    <application
        android:icon="@drawable/ic_launcher"
        android:label="@string/app_name" >
        <activity
            android:label="@string/app_name"
            android:name=".UsingPreferencesActivity" >
            <intent-filter >
                <action android:name="android.intent.action.MAIN" />

                <category android:name="android.intent.category.LAUNCHER" />
            </intent-filter>
        </activity>
        <activity android:name=".AppPreferenceActivity"
                android:label="@string/app_name">
            <intent-filter>
```

```
                <action
                    android:name="net.learn2develop.AppPreferenceActivity" />
                <category android:name="android.intent.category.DEFAULT" />
            </intent-filter>
        </activity>
    </application>

</manifest>
```

7. In the `main.xml` file, add the following code in bold (replacing the existing `TextView`):

```xml
<?xml version="1.0" encoding="utf-8"?>
<LinearLayout xmlns:android="http://schemas.android.com/apk/res/android"
    android:layout_width="fill_parent"
    android:layout_height="fill_parent"
    android:orientation="vertical" >

<Button
    android:id="@+id/btnPreferences"
    android:text="Load Preferences Screen"
    android:layout_width="fill_parent"
    android:layout_height="wrap_content"
    android:onClick="onClickLoad"/>

<Button
    android:id="@+id/btnDisplayValues"
    android:text="Display Preferences Values"
    android:layout_width="fill_parent"
    android:layout_height="wrap_content"
    android:onClick="onClickDisplay"/>

<EditText
    android:id="@+id/txtString"
    android:layout_width="fill_parent"
    android:layout_height="wrap_content" />

<Button
    android:id="@+id/btnModifyValues"
    android:text="Modify Preferences Values"
    android:layout_width="fill_parent"
    android:layout_height="wrap_content"
    android:onClick="onClickModify"/>

</LinearLayout>
```

8. Add the following lines in bold to the `UsingPreferencesActivity.java` file:

```java
package net.learn2develop.UsingPreferences;

import android.app.Activity;
import android.content.Intent;
import android.os.Bundle;
import android.view.View;

public class UsingPreferencesActivity extends Activity {
```

```
/** Called when the activity is first created. */
@Override
public void onCreate(Bundle savedInstanceState) {
    super.onCreate(savedInstanceState);
    setContentView(R.layout.main);
}

public void onClickLoad(View view) {
    Intent i = new Intent("net.learn2develop.AppPreferenceActivity");
    startActivity(i);
}
}
```

9. Press F11 to debug the application on the Android emulator. Click the Load Preferences Screen button to see the preferences screen, as shown in Figure 6-2.

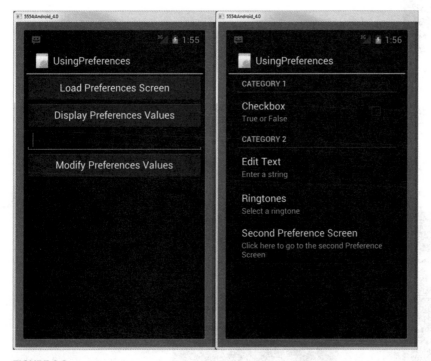

FIGURE 6-2

10. Clicking the Checkbox item toggles the checkbox's value between checked and unchecked. Note the two categories: Category 1 and Category 2. Click the Edit Text item and enter some values as shown in Figure 6-3. Click OK to dismiss the dialog.

FIGURE 6-3

11. Click the Ringtones item to select either the default ringtone or silent mode (see Figure 6-4). If you test the application on a real Android device, you can select from a more comprehensive list of ringtones.

12. Clicking the Second Preference Screen item will navigate to the next screen (see Figure 6-5).

FIGURE 6-4   FIGURE 6-5

13. To go back to the previous screen, click the Back button. To dismiss the preferences screen, you also click the Back button.

14. Once you have modified the value of at least one of the preferences, a file is created in the `/data/data/net.learn2develop.UsingPreferences/shared_prefs` folder of the Android emulator. To verify this, switch to the DDMS perspective in Eclipse and look at the File Explorer tab (see Figure 6-6); you will see an XML file named `net.learn2develop.UsingPreferences_preferences.xml`.

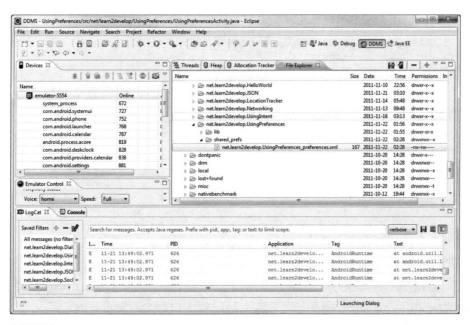

FIGURE 6-6

15. If you extract this file and examine its content, you will see something like the following:

```xml
<?xml version='1.0' encoding='utf-8' standalone='yes' ?>
<map>
<string name="editTextPref">[Enter a string here]</string>
<string name="ringtonePref"></string>
</map>
```

How It Works

You first created an XML file named `myapppreferences.xml` to store the types of preferences you want to save for your application:

```xml
<?xml version="1.0" encoding="utf-8"?>
<PreferenceScreen
    xmlns:android="http://schemas.android.com/apk/res/android">
    <PreferenceCategory android:title="Category 1">
```

```xml
        <CheckBoxPreference
            android:title="Checkbox"
            android:defaultValue="false"
            android:summary="True or False"
            android:key="checkboxPref" />
    </PreferenceCategory>
    <PreferenceCategory android:title="Category 2">
        <EditTextPreference
            android:summary="Enter a string"
            android:defaultValue="[Enter a string here]"
            android:title="Edit Text"
            android:key="editTextPref" />
        <RingtonePreference
            android:summary="Select a ringtone"
            android:title="Ringtones"
            android:key="ringtonePref" />
        <PreferenceScreen
            android:title="Second Preference Screen"
            android:summary=
                "Click here to go to the second Preference Screen"
            android:key="secondPrefScreenPref" >
            <EditTextPreference
                android:summary="Enter a string"
                android:title="Edit Text (second Screen)"
                android:key="secondEditTextPref" />
        </PreferenceScreen>
    </PreferenceCategory>
</PreferenceScreen>
```

In the preceding snippet, you created the following:

➤ Two preference categories for grouping different types of preferences

➤ Two checkbox preferences with keys named checkboxPref and secondEditTextPref

➤ A ringtone preference with a key named ringtonePref

➤ A preference screen to contain additional preferences

The android:key attribute specifies the key that you can programmatically reference in your code to set or retrieve the value of that particular preference.

To get the OS to display all these preferences for users to edit, you create an activity that extends the PreferenceActivity base class, and then call the addPreferencesFromResource() method to load the XML file containing the preferences:

```java
public class AppPreferenceActivity extends PreferenceActivity {
    @Override
    public void onCreate(Bundle savedInstanceState) {
        super.onCreate(savedInstanceState);
        //---load the preferences from an XML file---
        addPreferencesFromResource(R.xml.myapppreferences);
    }
}
```

The `PreferenceActivity` class is a specialized type of activity that displays a hierarchy of preferences to the user.

To display the activity for the preferences, you invoke it using an `Intent` object:

```
Intent i = new Intent("net.learn2develop.AppPreferenceActivity");
startActivity(i);
```

All the changes made to the preferences are automatically persisted to an XML file in the `shared_prefs` folder of the application.

Programmatically Retrieving and Modifying the Preferences Values

In the previous section, you saw how the `PreferenceActivity` class both enables developers to easily create preferences and enables users to modify them during runtime. To make use of these preferences in your application, you use the `SharedPreferences` class. The following Try It Out shows you how.

TRY IT OUT Retrieving and Modifying Preferences

1. Using the same project created in the previous section, add the following lines in bold to the `UsingPreferencesActivity.java` file:

```
package net.learn2develop.UsingPreferences;

import android.app.Activity;
import android.content.Intent;
import android.content.SharedPreferences;
import android.os.Bundle;
import android.view.View;
import android.widget.EditText;
import android.widget.Toast;

public class UsingPreferencesActivity extends Activity {
    /** Called when the activity is first created. */
    @Override
    public void onCreate(Bundle savedInstanceState) {
        super.onCreate(savedInstanceState);
        setContentView(R.layout.main);
    }

    public void onClickLoad(View view) {
        Intent i = new Intent("net.learn2develop.AppPreferenceActivity");
        startActivity(i);
    }

    public void onClickDisplay(View view) {
```

```
        SharedPreferences appPrefs =
                getSharedPreferences("net.learn2develop.UsingPreferences_preferences",
                        MODE_PRIVATE);
        DisplayText(appPrefs.getString("editTextPref", ""));
    }

    public void onClickModify(View view) {
        SharedPreferences appPrefs =
                getSharedPreferences("net.learn2develop.UsingPreferences_preferences",
                        MODE_PRIVATE);
        SharedPreferences.Editor prefsEditor = appPrefs.edit();
        prefsEditor.putString("editTextPref",
                ((EditText) findViewById(R.id.txtString)).getText().toString());
        prefsEditor.commit();
    }

    private void DisplayText(String str) {
        Toast.makeText(getBaseContext(), str, Toast.LENGTH_LONG).show();
    }
}
```

2. Press F11 to rerun the application on the Android emulator again. This time, clicking the Display Preferences Values button will display the value shown in Figure 6-7.

3. Enter a string in the EditText view and click the Modify Preferences Values button (see Figure 6-8).

FIGURE 6-7

FIGURE 6-8

4. Now click the Display Preferences Values button again. Note that the new value is saved.

How It Works

In the `onClickDisplay()` method, you first used the `getSharedPreferences()` method to obtain an instance of the `SharedPreferences` class. You do so by specifying the name of the XML file (in this case it is "`net.learn2develop.UsingPreferences_preferences`," using the format: `<PackageName>_preferences`). To retrieve a string preference, you used the `getString()` method, passing it the key to the preference that you want to retrieve:

```
public void onClickDisplay(View view) {
    SharedPreferences appPrefs =
            getSharedPreferences("net.learn2develop.UsingPreferences_preferences",
                MODE_PRIVATE);
    DisplayText(appPrefs.getString("editTextPref", ""));
}
```

The `MODE_PRIVATE` constant indicates that the preference file can only be opened by the application that created it.

In the `onClickModify()` method, you created a `SharedPreferences.Editor` object through the `edit()` method of the `SharedPreferences` object. To change the value of a string preference, use the `putString()` method. To save the changes to the preferences file, use the `commit()` method:

```
public void onClickModify(View view) {
    SharedPreferences appPrefs =
            getSharedPreferences("net.learn2develop.UsingPreferences_preferences",
                MODE_PRIVATE);
    SharedPreferences.Editor prefsEditor = appPrefs.edit();
    prefsEditor.putString("editTextPref",
            ((EditText) findViewById(R.id.txtString)).getText().toString());
    prefsEditor.commit();
}
```

Changing the Default Name of the Preferences File

Notice that by default the name of the preferences file saved on the device is `net.learn2develop.UsingPreferences_preferences.xml`, with the package name used as the prefix. However, sometimes it is useful to give the preferences file a specific name. In this case, you can do the following.

Add the following code in bold to the `AppPreferenceActivity.java` file:

```
package net.learn2develop.UsingPreferences;

import android.os.Bundle;
import android.preference.PreferenceActivity;
```

```
import android.preference.PreferenceManager;

public class AppPreferenceActivity extends PreferenceActivity {
    @Override
    public void onCreate(Bundle savedInstanceState) {
        super.onCreate(savedInstanceState);

        PreferenceManager prefMgr = getPreferenceManager();
        prefMgr.setSharedPreferencesName("appPreferences");

        //---load the preferences from an XML file---
        addPreferencesFromResource(R.xml.myapppreferences);
    }
}
```

Here, you make use of the `PreferenceManager` class to set the shared preferences file name to
appPreferences.xml.

Modify the `UsingPreferencesActivity.java` file as follows:

```
public void onClickDisplay(View view) {
    /*
    SharedPreferences appPrefs =
            getSharedPreferences("net.learn2develop.UsingPreferences_preferences",
                    MODE_PRIVATE);
    */
    SharedPreferences appPrefs =
            getSharedPreferences("appPreferences", MODE_PRIVATE);

    DisplayText(appPrefs.getString("editTextPref", ""));
}

public void onClickModify(View view) {
    /*
    SharedPreferences appPrefs =
            getSharedPreferences("net.learn2develop.UsingPreferences_preferences",
                    MODE_PRIVATE);
    */
    SharedPreferences appPrefs =
            getSharedPreferences("appPreferences", MODE_PRIVATE);

    SharedPreferences.Editor prefsEditor = appPrefs.edit();
    prefsEditor.putString("editTextPref",
            ((EditText) findViewById(R.id.txtString)).getText().toString());
    prefsEditor.commit();
}
```

When you rerun the application and make changes to the preferences, you will notice that the
appPreferences.xml file is now created (see Figure 6-9).

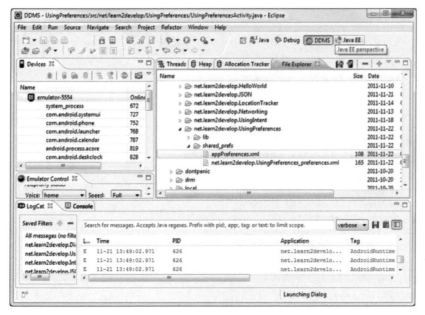

FIGURE 6-9

PERSISTING DATA TO FILES

The `SharedPreferences` object enables you to store data that is best stored as name/value pairs — for example, user ID, birth date, gender, driving license number, and so on. However, sometimes you might prefer to use the traditional file system to store your data. For example, you might want to store the text of poems you want to display in your applications. In Android, you can use the classes in the `java.io` package to do so.

Saving to Internal Storage

The first way to save files in your Android application is to write to the device's internal storage. The following Try It Out demonstrates how to save a string entered by the user to the device's internal storage.

TRY IT OUT Saving Data to Internal Storage

codefile Files.zip available for download at Wrox.com

1. Using Eclipse, create an Android project and name it **Files**.

2. In the `main.xml` file, add the following statements in bold:

```
<?xml version="1.0" encoding="utf-8"?>
<LinearLayout xmlns:android="http://schemas.android.com/apk/res/android"
    android:layout_width="fill_parent"
    android:layout_height="fill_parent"
```

```
        android:orientation="vertical" >

    <TextView
        android:layout_width="fill_parent"
        android:layout_height="wrap_content"
        android:text="Please enter some text" />

    <EditText
        android:id="@+id/txtText1"
        android:layout_width="fill_parent"
        android:layout_height="wrap_content" />

    <Button
        android:id="@+id/btnSave"
        android:text="Save"
        android:layout_width="fill_parent"
        android:layout_height="wrap_content"
        android:onClick="onClickSave" />

    <Button
        android:id="@+id/btnLoad"
        android:text="Load"
        android:layout_width="fill_parent"
        android:layout_height="wrap_content"
        android:onClick="onClickLoad" />

    </LinearLayout>
```

3. In the `FilesActivity.java` file, add the following statements in bold:

```
package net.learn2develop.Files;

import java.io.FileInputStream;
import java.io.FileOutputStream;
import java.io.IOException;
import java.io.InputStreamReader;
import java.io.OutputStreamWriter;

import android.app.Activity;
import android.os.Bundle;
import android.view.View;
import android.widget.EditText;
import android.widget.Toast;

public class FilesActivity extends Activity {
    EditText textBox;
    static final int READ_BLOCK_SIZE = 100;

    /** Called when the activity is first created. */
    @Override
    public void onCreate(Bundle savedInstanceState) {
        super.onCreate(savedInstanceState);
        setContentView(R.layout.main);

        textBox = (EditText) findViewById(R.id.txtText1);
    }

    public void onClickSave(View view) {
```

```
        String str = textBox.getText().toString();
        try
        {
            FileOutputStream fOut =
                    openFileOutput("textfile.txt",
                            MODE_WORLD_READABLE);
            OutputStreamWriter osw = new
                    OutputStreamWriter(fOut);

            //---write the string to the file---
            osw.write(str);
            osw.flush();
            osw.close();

            //---display file saved message---
            Toast.makeText(getBaseContext(),
                    "File saved successfully!",
                    Toast.LENGTH_SHORT).show();

            //---clears the EditText---
            textBox.setText("");
        }
        catch (IOException ioe)
        {
            ioe.printStackTrace();
        }

    }

    public void onClickLoad(View view) {
        try
        {
            FileInputStream fIn =
                    openFileInput("textfile.txt");
            InputStreamReader isr = new
                    InputStreamReader(fIn);

            char[] inputBuffer = new char[READ_BLOCK_SIZE];
            String s = "";

            int charRead;
            while ((charRead = isr.read(inputBuffer))>0)
            {
                //---convert the chars to a String---
                String readString =
                        String.copyValueOf(inputBuffer, 0,
                                charRead);
                s += readString;

                inputBuffer = new char[READ_BLOCK_SIZE];
            }
            //---set the EditText to the text that has been
            // read---
            textBox.setText(s);

            Toast.makeText(getBaseContext(),
                    "File loaded successfully!",
                    Toast.LENGTH_SHORT).show();
```

```
        }
        catch (IOException ioe) {
            ioe.printStackTrace();
        }

    }

}
```

4. Press F11 to debug the application on the Android emulator.

5. Type some text into the EditText view (see Figure 6-10) and then click the Save button.

6. If the file is saved successfully, you will see the Toast class displaying the "File saved successfully!" message. The text in the EditText view should disappear.

7. Click the Load button and you should see the string appearing in the EditText view again. This confirms that the text is saved correctly.

FIGURE 6-10

How It Works

To save text into a file, you use the FileOutputStream class. The openFileOutput() method opens a named file for writing, with the mode specified. In this example, you used the MODE_WORLD_READABLE constant to indicate that the file is readable by all other applications:

```
FileOutputStream fOut =
        openFileOutput("textfile.txt",
            MODE_WORLD_READABLE);
```

Apart from the MODE_WORLD_READABLE constant, you can select from the following: MODE_PRIVATE (the file can only be accessed by the application that created it), MODE_APPEND (for appending to an existing file), and MODE_WORLD_WRITEABLE (all other applications have write access to the file).

To convert a character stream into a byte stream, you use an instance of the OutputStreamWriter class, by passing it an instance of the FileOutputStream object:

```
OutputStreamWriter osw = new
        OutputStreamWriter(fOut);
```

You then use its write() method to write the string to the file. To ensure that all the bytes are written to the file, use the flush() method. Finally, use the close() method to close the file:

```
//---write the string to the file---
osw.write(str);
osw.flush();
osw.close();
```

To read the content of a file, you use the FileInputStream class, together with the InputStreamReader class:

```
FileInputStream fIn =
        openFileInput("textfile.txt");
```

```
InputStreamReader isr = new
        InputStreamReader(fIn);
```

Because you do not know the size of the file to read, the content is read in blocks of 100 characters into a buffer (character array). The characters read are then copied into a `String` object:

```
char[] inputBuffer = new char[READ_BLOCK_SIZE];
String s = "";

int charRead;
while ((charRead = isr.read(inputBuffer))>0)
{
    //---convert the chars to a String---
    String readString =
            String.copyValueOf(inputBuffer, 0,
                    charRead);
    s += readString;

    inputBuffer = new char[READ_BLOCK_SIZE];
}
```

The `read()` method of the `InputStreamReader` object checks the number of characters read and returns -1 if the end of the file is reached.

When testing this application on the Android emulator, you can use the DDMS perspective to verify that the application did indeed save the file into the application's files directory (see Figure 6-11; the entire path is `/data/data/net.learn2develop.Files/files`)

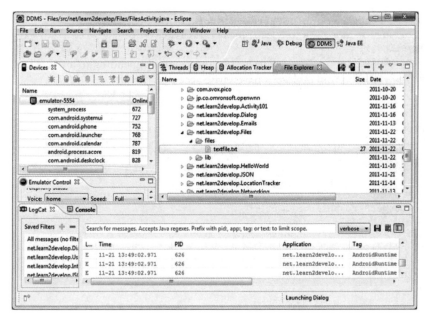

FIGURE 6-11

Saving to External Storage (SD Card)

The previous section showed how you can save your files to the internal storage of your Android device. Sometimes, it would be useful to save them to external storage (such as an SD card) because of its larger capacity, as well as the capability to share the files easily with other users (by removing the SD card and passing it to somebody else).

Using the project created in the previous section as the example, to save the text entered by the user in the SD card, modify the onClick() method of the Save button as shown in bold here:

```java
import java.io.File;
import java.io.FileInputStream;
import java.io.FileOutputStream;
import java.io.IOException;
import java.io.InputStreamReader;
import java.io.OutputStreamWriter;

import android.app.Activity;
import android.os.Bundle;
import android.os.Environment;
import android.view.View;
import android.widget.EditText;
import android.widget.Toast;

    public void onClickSave(View view) {
        String str = textBox.getText().toString();
        try
        {
            //---SD Card Storage---
            File sdCard = Environment.getExternalStorageDirectory();
            File directory = new File (sdCard.getAbsolutePath() +
                "/MyFiles");
            directory.mkdirs();
            File file = new File(directory, "textfile.txt");
            FileOutputStream fOut = new FileOutputStream(file);

            /*
            FileOutputStream fOut =
                    openFileOutput("textfile.txt",
                        MODE_WORLD_READABLE);
            */

            OutputStreamWriter osw = new
                    OutputStreamWriter(fOut);

            //---write the string to the file---
            osw.write(str);
            osw.flush();
            osw.close();

            //---display file saved message---
```

```
            Toast.makeText(getBaseContext(),
                    "File saved successfully!",
                    Toast.LENGTH_SHORT).show();

            //---clears the EditText---
            textBox.setText("");
        }
        catch (IOException ioe)
        {
            ioe.printStackTrace();
        }


    }
```

The preceding code uses the getExternalStorageDirectory() method to return the full path to the external storage. Typically, it should return the "/sdcard" path for a real device, and "/mnt/sdcard" for an Android emulator. However, you should never try to hardcode the path to the SD card, as manufacturers may choose to assign a different path name to the SD card. Hence, be sure to use the getExternalStorageDirectory() method to return the full path to the SD card.

You then create a directory called MyFiles in the SD card. Finally, you save the file into this directory.

To load the file from the external storage, modify the onClickLoad() method for the Load button:

```
public void onClickLoad(View view) {
    try
    {
        //---SD Storage---
        File sdCard = Environment.getExternalStorageDirectory();
        File directory = new File (sdCard.getAbsolutePath() +
            "/MyFiles");
        File file = new File(directory, "textfile.txt");
        FileInputStream fIn = new FileInputStream(file);
        InputStreamReader isr = new InputStreamReader(fIn);

        /*
        FileInputStream fIn =
                openFileInput("textfile.txt");
        InputStreamReader isr = new
                InputStreamReader(fIn);
        */

        char[] inputBuffer = new char[READ_BLOCK_SIZE];
        String s = "";

        int charRead;
        while ((charRead = isr.read(inputBuffer))>0)
        {
            //---convert the chars to a String---
            String readString =
```

```
                                String.copyValueOf(inputBuffer, 0,
                                        charRead);
                    s += readString;

                    inputBuffer = new char[READ_BLOCK_SIZE];
                }
                //---set the EditText to the text that has been
                // read---
                textBox.setText(s);

                Toast.makeText(getBaseContext(),
                        "File loaded successfully!",
                        Toast.LENGTH_SHORT).show();
            }
            catch (IOException ioe) {
                ioe.printStackTrace();
            }


        }
```

Note that in order to write to the external storage, you need to add the WRITE_EXTERNAL_STORAGE permission in your AndroidManifest.xml file:

```xml
<?xml version="1.0" encoding="utf-8"?>
<manifest xmlns:android="http://schemas.android.com/apk/res/android"
    package="net.learn2develop.Files"
    android:versionCode="1"
    android:versionName="1.0" >

    <uses-sdk android:minSdkVersion="14" />
    <uses-permission android:name="android.permission.WRITE_EXTERNAL_STORAGE" />

    <application
        android:icon="@drawable/ic_launcher"
        android:label="@string/app_name" >
        <activity
            android:label="@string/app_name"
            android:name=".FilesActivity" >
            <intent-filter >
                <action android:name="android.intent.action.MAIN" />

                <category android:name="android.intent.category.LAUNCHER" />
            </intent-filter>
        </activity>
    </application>

</manifest>
```

If you run the preceding modified code, you will see the text file created in the /mnt/sdcard/ MyFiles/ folder (see Figure 6-12).

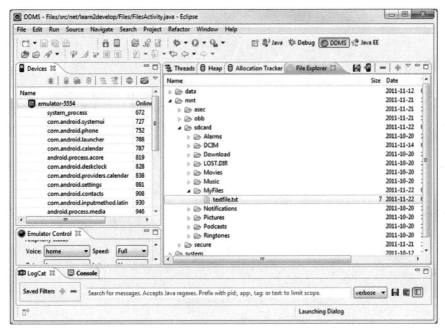

FIGURE 6-12

Choosing the Best Storage Option

The previous sections described three main ways to save data in your Android applications: the `SharedPreferences` object, internal storage, and external storage. Which one should you use in your applications? Here are some guidelines:

➤ If you have data that can be represented using name/value pairs, then use the `SharedPreferences` object. For example, if you want to store user preference data such as user name, background color, date of birth, or last login date, then the `SharedPreferences` object is the ideal way to store this data. Moreover, you don't really have to do much to store data this way; just use the `SharedPreferences` object to store and retrieve it.

➤ If you need to store ad-hoc data, then using the internal storage is a good option. For example, your application (such as an RSS reader) may need to download images from the web for display. In this scenario, saving the images to internal storage is a good solution. You may also need to persist data created by the user, such as when you have a note-taking application that enables users to take notes and save them for later use. In both of these scenarios, using the internal storage is a good choice.

➤ There are times when you need to share your application data with other users. For example, you may create an Android application that logs the coordinates of the locations that a user has been to, and you want to share all this data with other users. In this scenario, you can store your files on the SD card of the device so that users can easily transfer the data to other devices (and computers) for use later.

Using Static Resources

Besides creating and using files dynamically during runtime, it is also possible to add files to your package during design time so that you can use it during runtime. For example, you may want to bundle some help files with your package so that you can display some help messages when users need them. In this case, you can add the files to your package's res/raw folder (you need to create this folder yourself). Figure 6-13 shows the res/raw folder containing a file named textfile.txt.

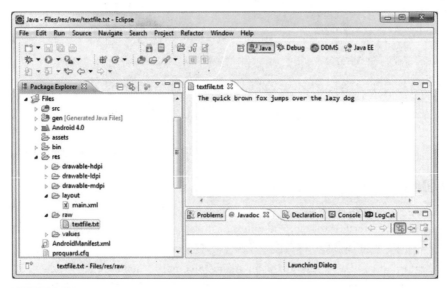

FIGURE 6-13

To make use of the file in code, use the getResources() method (of the Activity class) to return a Resources object, and then use its openRawResource() method to open the file contained in the res/raw folder:

```
import java.io.BufferedReader;
import java.io.InputStream;

public class FilesActivity extends Activity {
    EditText textBox;
    static final int READ_BLOCK_SIZE = 100;

    /** Called when the activity is first created. */
    @Override
```

```
public void onCreate(Bundle savedInstanceState) {
    super.onCreate(savedInstanceState);
    setContentView(R.layout.main);

    textBox = (EditText) findViewById(R.id.txtText1);

    InputStream is = this.getResources().openRawResource(R.raw.textfile);
    BufferedReader br = new BufferedReader(new InputStreamReader(is));
    String str = null;
    try {
        while ((str = br.readLine()) != null) {
            Toast.makeText(getBaseContext(),
                str, Toast.LENGTH_SHORT).show();
        }
        is.close();
        br.close();
    } catch (IOException e) {
        e.printStackTrace();
    }
}
```

The resource ID of the resource stored in the res/raw folder is named after its filename without its extension. For example, if the text file is textfile.txt, then its resource ID is R.raw.textfile.

CREATING AND USING DATABASES

So far, all the techniques you have seen are useful for saving simple sets of data. For saving relational data, using a database is much more efficient. For example, if you want to store the test results of all the students in a school, it is much more efficient to use a database to represent them because you can use database querying to retrieve the results of specific students. Moreover, using databases enables you to enforce data integrity by specifying the relationships between different sets of data.

Android uses the SQLite database system. The database that you create for an application is only accessible to itself; other applications will not be able to access it.

In this section, you will learn how to programmatically create a SQLite database in your Android application. For Android, the SQLite database that you create programmatically in an application is always stored in the /data/data/<package_name>/databases folder.

Creating the DBAdapter Helper Class

A good practice for dealing with databases is to create a helper class to encapsulate all the complexities of accessing the data so that it is transparent to the calling code.
Hence, for this section, you will create a helper class called DBAdapter that creates, opens, closes, and uses a SQLite database.

In this example, you are going to create a database named MyDB containing one table named contacts. This table will have three columns: _id, name, and email (see Figure 6-14).

_id	name	email

FIGURE 6-14

TRY IT OUT Creating the Database Helper Class

codefile Databases.zip available for download at Wrox.com

1. Using Eclipse, create an Android project and name it **Databases**.

2. Add a new Java Class file to the package and name it **DBAdapter** (see Figure 6-15).

3. Add the following statements in bold to the DBAdapter.java file:

FIGURE 6-15

```java
package net.learn2develop.Databases;

import android.content.ContentValues;
import android.content.Context;
import android.database.Cursor;
import android.database.SQLException;
import android.database.sqlite.SQLiteDatabase;
import android.database.sqlite.SQLiteOpenHelper;
import android.util.Log;

public class DBAdapter {
    static final String KEY_ROWID = "_id";
    static final String KEY_NAME = "name";
    static final String KEY_EMAIL = "email";
    static final String TAG = "DBAdapter";

    static final String DATABASE_NAME = "MyDB";
    static final String DATABASE_TABLE = "contacts";
    static final int DATABASE_VERSION = 1;

    static final String DATABASE_CREATE =
        "create table contacts (_id integer primary key autoincrement, "
        + "name text not null, email text not null);";

    final Context context;

    DatabaseHelper DBHelper;
    SQLiteDatabase db;

    public DBAdapter(Context ctx)
    {
        this.context = ctx;
        DBHelper = new DatabaseHelper(context);
    }

    private static class DatabaseHelper extends SQLiteOpenHelper
    {
        DatabaseHelper(Context context)
        {
            super(context, DATABASE_NAME, null, DATABASE_VERSION);
        }

        @Override
        public void onCreate(SQLiteDatabase db)
```

```
    {
        try {
            db.execSQL(DATABASE_CREATE);
        } catch (SQLException e) {
            e.printStackTrace();
        }
    }

    @Override
    public void onUpgrade(SQLiteDatabase db, int oldVersion, int newVersion)
    {
        Log.w(TAG, "Upgrading database from version " + oldVersion + " to "
                + newVersion + ", which will destroy all old data");
        db.execSQL("DROP TABLE IF EXISTS contacts");
        onCreate(db);
    }
}

//---opens the database---
public DBAdapter open() throws SQLException
{
    db = DBHelper.getWritableDatabase();
    return this;
}

//---closes the database---
public void close()
{
    DBHelper.close();
}

//---insert a contact into the database---
public long insertContact(String name, String email)
{
    ContentValues initialValues = new ContentValues();
    initialValues.put(KEY_NAME, name);
    initialValues.put(KEY_EMAIL, email);
    return db.insert(DATABASE_TABLE, null, initialValues);
}

//---deletes a particular contact---
public boolean deleteContact(long rowId)
{
    return db.delete(DATABASE_TABLE, KEY_ROWID + "=" + rowId, null) > 0;
}

//---retrieves all the contacts---
public Cursor getAllContacts()
{
    return db.query(DATABASE_TABLE, new String[] {KEY_ROWID, KEY_NAME,
            KEY_EMAIL}, null, null, null, null, null);
}

//---retrieves a particular contact---
public Cursor getContact(long rowId) throws SQLException
{
```

```
        Cursor mCursor =
                db.query(true, DATABASE_TABLE, new String[] {KEY_ROWID,
                KEY_NAME, KEY_EMAIL}, KEY_ROWID + "=" + rowId, null,
                null, null, null, null);
        if (mCursor != null) {
            mCursor.moveToFirst();
        }
        return mCursor;
    }


    //---updates a contact---
    public boolean updateContact(long rowId, String name, String email)
    {
        ContentValues args = new ContentValues();
        args.put(KEY_NAME, name);
        args.put(KEY_EMAIL, email);
        return db.update(DATABASE_TABLE, args, KEY_ROWID + "=" + rowId, null) > 0;
    }
}
```

How It Works

You first defined several constants to contain the various fields for the table that you are going to create in your database:

```
static final String KEY_ROWID = "_id";
static final String KEY_NAME = "name";
static final String KEY_EMAIL = "email";
static final String TAG = "DBAdapter";

static final String DATABASE_NAME = "MyDB";
static final String DATABASE_TABLE = "contacts";
static final int DATABASE_VERSION = 1;

static final String DATABASE_CREATE =
    "create table contacts (_id integer primary key autoincrement, "
    + "name text not null, email text not null);";
```

In particular, the DATABASE_CREATE constant contains the SQL statement for creating the contacts table within the MyDB database.

Within the DBAdapter class, you also added a private class that extended the SQLiteOpenHelper class, which is a helper class in Android to manage database creation and version management. In particular, you overrode the onCreate() and onUpgrade() methods:

```
private static class DatabaseHelper extends SQLiteOpenHelper
{
    DatabaseHelper(Context context)
    {
        super(context, DATABASE_NAME, null, DATABASE_VERSION);
    }

    @Override
    public void onCreate(SQLiteDatabase db)
```

```
    {
        try {
            db.execSQL(DATABASE_CREATE);
        } catch (SQLException e) {
            e.printStackTrace();
        }
    }

    @Override
    public void onUpgrade(SQLiteDatabase db, int oldVersion, int newVersion)
    {
        Log.w(TAG, "Upgrading database from version " + oldVersion + " to "
                + newVersion + ", which will destroy all old data");
        db.execSQL("DROP TABLE IF EXISTS contacts");
        onCreate(db);
    }
}
```

The onCreate() method creates a new database if the required database is not present. The onUpgrade() method is called when the database needs to be upgraded. This is achieved by checking the value defined in the DATABASE_VERSION constant. For this implementation of the onUpgrade() method, you simply drop the table and create it again.

You can then define the various methods for opening and closing the database, as well as the methods for adding/editing/deleting rows in the table:

```
//---opens the database---
public DBAdapter open() throws SQLException
{
    db = DBHelper.getWritableDatabase();
    return this;
}

//---closes the database---
public void close()
{
    DBHelper.close();
}

//---insert a contact into the database---
public long insertContact(String name, String email)
{
    ContentValues initialValues = new ContentValues();
    initialValues.put(KEY_NAME, name);
    initialValues.put(KEY_EMAIL, email);
    return db.insert(DATABASE_TABLE, null, initialValues);
}

//---deletes a particular contact---
public boolean deleteContact(long rowId)
{
    return db.delete(DATABASE_TABLE, KEY_ROWID + "=" + rowId, null) > 0;
}

//---retrieves all the contacts---
```

```
public Cursor getAllContacts()
{
    return db.query(DATABASE_TABLE, new String[] {KEY_ROWID, KEY_NAME,
            KEY_EMAIL}, null, null, null, null, null);
}

//---retrieves a particular contact---
public Cursor getContact(long rowId) throws SQLException
{
    Cursor mCursor =
            db.query(true, DATABASE_TABLE, new String[] {KEY_ROWID,
            KEY_NAME, KEY_EMAIL}, KEY_ROWID + "=" + rowId, null,
            null, null, null, null);
    if (mCursor != null) {
        mCursor.moveToFirst();
    }
    return mCursor;
}

//---updates a contact---
public boolean updateContact(long rowId, String name, String email)
{
    ContentValues args = new ContentValues();
    args.put(KEY_NAME, name);
    args.put(KEY_EMAIL, email);
    return db.update(DATABASE_TABLE, args, KEY_ROWID + "=" + rowId, null) > 0;
}
```

Notice that Android uses the Cursor class as a return value for queries. Think of the Cursor as a pointer to the result set from a database query. Using Cursor enables Android to more efficiently manage rows and columns as needed.

You use a ContentValues object to store name/value pairs. Its put() method enables you to insert keys with values of different data types.

To create a database in your application using the DBAdapter class, you create an instance of the DBAdapter class:

```
public DBAdapter(Context ctx)
{
    this.context = ctx;
    DBHelper = new DatabaseHelper(context);
}
```

The constructor of the DBAdapter class will then create an instance of the DatabaseHelper class to create a new database:

```
DatabaseHelper(Context context)
{
    super(context, DATABASE_NAME, null, DATABASE_VERSION);
}
```

Using the Database Programmatically

With the DBAdapter helper class created, you are now ready to use the database. In the following sections, you will learn how to perform the regular CRUD (create, read, update and delete) operations commonly associated with databases.

Adding Contacts

The following Try It Out demonstrates how you can add a contact to the table.

TRY IT OUT   Adding Contacts to a Table

codefile Databases.zip available for download at Wrox.com

1. Using the same project created earlier, add the following statements in bold to the DatabasesActivity.java file:

```
package net.learn2develop.Databases;

import android.app.Activity;
import android.os.Bundle;

public class DatabasesActivity extends Activity {
    /** Called when the activity is first created. */
    @Override
    public void onCreate(Bundle savedInstanceState) {
        super.onCreate(savedInstanceState);
        setContentView(R.layout.main);

        DBAdapter db = new DBAdapter(this);

        //---add a contact---
        db.open();
        long id = db.insertContact("Wei-Meng Lee", "weimenglee@learn2develop.net");
        id = db.insertContact("Mary Jackson", "mary@jackson.com");
        db.close();
    }
}
```

2. Press F11 to debug the application on the Android emulator.

How It Works

In this example, you first created an instance of the DBAdapter class:

```
DBAdapter db = new DBAdapter(this);
```

The insertContact() method returns the ID of the inserted row. If an error occurs during the operation, it returns -1.

If you examine the file system of the Android device/emulator using DDMS, you can see that the MyDB database is created under the databases folder (see Figure 6-16).

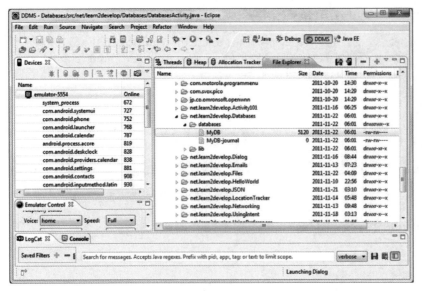

FIGURE 6-16

Retrieving All the Contacts

To retrieve all the contacts in the `contacts` table, use the `getAllContacts()` method of the `DBAdapter` class, as the following Try It Out shows.

TRY IT OUY   **Retrieving All Contacts from a Table**

codefile Databases.zip available for download at Wrox.com

1. Using the same project created earlier, add the following statements in bold to the `DatabasesActivity.java` file:

```
package net.learn2develop.Databases;

import android.app.Activity;
import android.database.Cursor;
import android.os.Bundle;
import android.widget.Toast;

public class DatabasesActivity extends Activity {
    /** Called when the activity is first created. */
    @Override
    public void onCreate(Bundle savedInstanceState) {
        super.onCreate(savedInstanceState);
        setContentView(R.layout.main);

        DBAdapter db = new DBAdapter(this);

        /*
        //---add a contact---
```

```
        db.open();
        ...
        db.close();
        */

        //---get all contacts---
        db.open();
        Cursor c = db.getAllContacts();
        if (c.moveToFirst())
        {
            do {
                DisplayContact(c);
            } while (c.moveToNext());
        }
        db.close();
    }

    public void DisplayContact(Cursor c)
    {
        Toast.makeText(this,
                "id: " + c.getString(0) + "\n" +
                "Name: " + c.getString(1) + "\n" +
                "Email:  " + c.getString(2),
                Toast.LENGTH_LONG).show();
    }
}
```

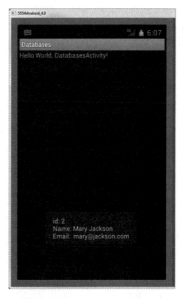

FIGURE 6-17

2. Press F11 to debug the application on the Android emulator. Figure 6-17 shows the Toast class displaying the contacts retrieved from the database.

How It Works

The getAllContacts() method of the DBAdapter class retrieves all the contacts stored in the database. The result is returned as a Cursor object. To display all the contacts, you first need to call the moveToFirst() method of the Cursor object. If it succeeds (which means at least one row is available), then you display the details of the contact using the DisplayContact() method. To move to the next contact, call the moveToNext() method of the Cursor object.

Retrieving a Single Contact

To retrieve a single contact using its ID, call the getContact() method of the DBAdapter class, as the following Try It Out shows.

TRY IT OUT Retrieving a Contact from a Table

codefile Databases.zip available for download at Wrox.com

1. Using the same project created earlier, add the following statements in bold to the DatabasesActivity.java file:

```
@Override
public void onCreate(Bundle savedInstanceState) {
    super.onCreate(savedInstanceState);
```

```
    setContentView(R.layout.main);

    DBAdapter db = new DBAdapter(this);

    /*
    //---add a contact---
    ...
    //--get all contacts---
    ...
    db.close();
    */

    //---get a contact---
    db.open();
    Cursor c = db.getContact(2);
    if (c.moveToFirst())
        DisplayContact(c);
    else
        Toast.makeText(this, "No contact found", Toast.LENGTH_LONG).show();
    db.close();
}
```

2. Press F11 to debug the application on the Android emulator. The details of the second contact will be displayed using the `Toast` class.

How It Works

The `getContact()` method of the `DBAdapter` class retrieves a single contact using its ID. You passed in the ID of the contact; in this case, you passed in an ID of 2 to indicate that you want to retrieve the second contact:

```
    Cursor c = db.getContact(2);
```

The result is returned as a `Cursor` object. If a row is returned, you display the details of the contact using the `DisplayContact()` method; otherwise, you display a message using the `Toast` class.

Updating a Contact

To update a particular contact, call the `updateContact()` method in the `DBAdapter` class by passing the ID of the contact you want to update, as the following Try It Out shows.

TRY IT OUT   Updating a Contact in a Table

codefile Databases.zip available for download at Wrox.com

1. Using the same project created earlier, add the following statements in bold to the `DatabasesActivity.java` file:

```
    @Override
    public void onCreate(Bundle savedInstanceState) {
```

```
        super.onCreate(savedInstanceState);
        setContentView(R.layout.main);

        DBAdapter db = new DBAdapter(this);

        /*
        //---add a contact---
        ...
        //--get all contacts---
        ...
        //---get a contact---
        ...
        db.close();
        */

        //---update contact---
        db.open();
        if (db.updateContact(1, "Wei-Meng Lee", "weimenglee@gmail.com"))
            Toast.makeText(this, "Update successful.", Toast.LENGTH_LONG).show();
        else
            Toast.makeText(this, "Update failed.", Toast.LENGTH_LONG).show();
        db.close();
    }
```

2. Press F11 to debug the application on the Android emulator. A message will be displayed if the update is successful.

How It Works

The updateContact() method in the DBAdapter class updates a contact's details by using the ID of the contact you want to update. It returns a Boolean value, indicating whether the update was successful.

Deleting a Contact

To delete a contact, use the deleteContact() method in the DBAdapter class by passing the ID of the contact you want to update, as the following Try It Out shows.

TRY IT OUT Deleting a Contact from a Table

codefile Databases.zip available for download at Wrox.com

1. Using the same project created earlier, add the following statements in bold to the DatabasesActivity.java file:

```
@Override
public void onCreate(Bundle savedInstanceState) {
    super.onCreate(savedInstanceState);
```

```
    setContentView(R.layout.main);

    DBAdapter db = new DBAdapter(this);

    /*
    //---add a contact---
    ...
    //--get all contacts---
    ...
    //---get a contact---
    ...
    //---update contact---
    ...
    db.close();
    */

    //---delete a contact---
    db.open();
    if (db.deleteContact(1))
        Toast.makeText(this, "Delete successful.", Toast.LENGTH_LONG).show();
    else
        Toast.makeText(this, "Delete failed.", Toast.LENGTH_LONG).show();
    db.close();
}
```

2. Press F11 to debug the application on the Android emulator. A message is displayed if the deletion was successful.

How It Works

The deleteContact() method in the DBAdapter class deletes a contact using the ID of the contact you want to delete. It returns a Boolean value, indicating whether the deletion was successful.

Upgrading the Database

Sometimes, after creating and using the database, you may need to add additional tables, change the schema of the database, or add columns to your tables. In this case, you need to migrate your existing data from the old database to a newer one.

To upgrade the database, change the DATABASE_VERSION constant to a value higher than the previous one. For example, if its previous value was 1, change it to 2:

```
public class DBAdapter {
    static final String KEY_ROWID = "_id";
    static final String KEY_NAME = "name";
    static final String KEY_EMAIL = "email";
    static final String TAG = "DBAdapter";

    static final String DATABASE_NAME = "MyDB";
    static final String DATABASE_TABLE = "contacts";
    static final int DATABASE_VERSION = 2;
```

NOTE *Before you run this example, be sure to comment out the block of delete statements described in the previous section. If not, the deletion will fail as the table in the database will be dropped (deleted).*

When you run the application one more time, you will see the following message in the LogCat window of Eclipse:

```
DBAdapter(8705): Upgrading database from version 1 to 2, which
will destroy all old data
```

In this example, for simplicity you simply drop the existing table and create a new one. In real life, you usually back up your existing table and then copy it over to the new table.

Pre-Creating the Database

In real-life applications, sometimes it would be more efficient to pre-create the database at design time rather than runtime. For example, you want to create an application to log the coordinates of all the places that you have been to. In this case, it is much easier to pre-create the database during the design time and simply use it during runtime.

To pre-create a SQLite database, you can use many of the free tools available on the Internet. One such tool is the SQLite Database Browser, which is available free for different platforms (http://sourceforge.net/projects/sqlitebrowser/).

Once you have installed the SQLite Database Browser, you can create a database visually. Figure 6-18 shows that I have created a `contacts` table with the fields indicated.

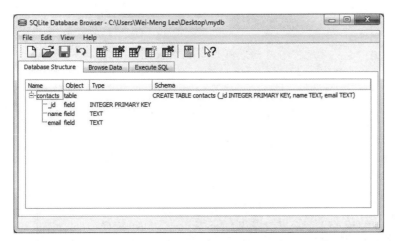

FIGURE 6-18

Populating the table with rows is also straightforward. Figure 6-19 shows how you can fill the table with data using the Browse Data tab.

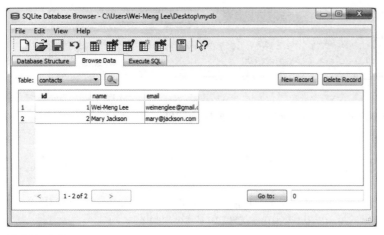

FIGURE 6-19

With the database created at design time, the next thing you should do is bundle it together with your application so that you can use it in your application. The following Try It Out shows you how.

TRY IT OUT   Bundling a Database

1.   Using the same project created earlier, drag and drop the SQLite database file that you have created in the previous section into the `assets` folder in your Android project in Eclipse (see Figure 6-20).

FIGURE 6-20

NOTE *Note that a filename for files added to the assets folder must be in lowercase letters. As such, a filename such as* `MyDB` *is invalid, whereas* `mydb` *is fine.*

2. Add the following statements in bold to the DatabasesActivity.java file:

```java
package net.learn2develop.Databases;

import java.io.File;
import java.io.FileNotFoundException;
import java.io.FileOutputStream;
import java.io.IOException;
import java.io.InputStream;
import java.io.OutputStream;

import android.app.Activity;
import android.database.Cursor;
import android.os.Bundle;
import android.widget.Toast;

public class DatabasesActivity extends Activity {
    /** Called when the activity is first created. */
    @Override
    public void onCreate(Bundle savedInstanceState) {
        super.onCreate(savedInstanceState);
        setContentView(R.layout.main);

        DBAdapter db = new DBAdapter(this);
        try {
            String destPath = "/data/data/" + getPackageName() +
                "/databases";
            File f = new File(destPath);
            if (!f.exists()) {
                f.mkdirs();
                f.createNewFile();

                //---copy the db from the assets folder into
                // the databases folder---
                CopyDB(getBaseContext().getAssets().open("mydb"),
                    new FileOutputStream(destPath + "/MyDB"));
            }
        } catch (FileNotFoundException e) {
            e.printStackTrace();
        } catch (IOException e) {
            e.printStackTrace();
        }

        //---get all contacts---
        db.open();
        Cursor c = db.getAllContacts();
        if (c.moveToFirst())
        {
            do {
                DisplayContact(c);
            } while (c.moveToNext());
        }
        db.close();
```

```
    }

    public void CopyDB(InputStream inputStream,
    OutputStream outputStream) throws IOException {
        //---copy 1K bytes at a time---
        byte[] buffer = new byte[1024];
        int length;
        while ((length = inputStream.read(buffer)) > 0) {
            outputStream.write(buffer, 0, length);
        }
        inputStream.close();
        outputStream.close();
    }

    public void DisplayContact(Cursor c)
    {
        Toast.makeText(this,
                "id: " + c.getString(0) + "\n" +
                "Name: " + c.getString(1) + "\n" +
                "Email:  " + c.getString(2),
                Toast.LENGTH_LONG).show();
    }
}
```

3. Press F11 to debug the application on the Android emulator. When the application runs, it will copy the mydb database file into the /data/data/net.learn2develop.Databases/databases/ folder with the name MyDB.

How It Works

You first defined the CopyDB() method to copy the database file from one location to another:

```
    public void CopyDB(InputStream inputStream,
    OutputStream outputStream) throws IOException {
        //---copy 1K bytes at a time---
        byte[] buffer = new byte[1024];
        int length;
        while ((length = inputStream.read(buffer)) > 0) {
            outputStream.write(buffer, 0, length);
        }
        inputStream.close();
        outputStream.close();
    }
```

Note that in this case you used the InputStream object to read from the source file, and then wrote it to the destination file using the OutputStream object.

When the activity is created, you copy the database file located in the assets folder into the /data/data/net.learn2develop.Databases/databases/ folder on the Android device (or emulator):

```
    try {
        String destPath = "/data/data/" + getPackageName() +
            "/databases";
        File f = new File(destPath);
```

```
        if (!f.exists()) {
            f.mkdirs();
            f.createNewFile();

            //---copy the db from the assets folder into
            // the databases folder---
            CopyDB(getBaseContext().getAssets().open("mydb"),
                new FileOutputStream(destPath + "/MyDB"));
        }
    } catch (FileNotFoundException e) {
        e.printStackTrace();
    } catch (IOException e) {
        e.printStackTrace();
    }
```

You copy the database file only if it does not exist in the destination folder. If you don't perform this check, every time the activity is created you will overwrite the database file with the one in the assets folder. This may not be desirable, as your application may make changes to the database file during runtime, and this will overwrite all the changes you have made so far.

To ensure that the database file is indeed copied, be sure to delete the database file in your emulator (if it already existed) prior to testing the application. You can delete the database using DDMS (see Figure 6-21).

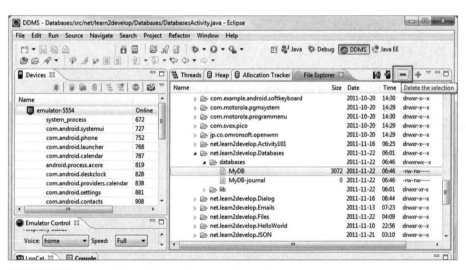

FIGURE 6-21

SUMMARY

In this chapter, you learned the different ways to save persistent data to your Android device. For simple unstructured data, using the SharedPreferences object is the ideal solution. If you need to store bulk data, then consider using the traditional file system. Finally, for structured data, it is more efficient to store it in a relational database management system. For this, Android provides the SQLite database, which you can access easily using the APIs exposed.

Note that for the SharedPreferences object and the SQLite database, the data is accessible only by the application that creates it. In other words, it is not shareable. If you need to share data among different applications, you need to create a *content provider*. Content providers are discussed in more detail in the next chapter.

EXERCISES

1. How do you display the preferences of your application using an activity?

2. Name the method that enables you to obtain the path of the external storage of an Android device.

3. What is the permission you need to declare when writing files to external storage?

Answers to the exercises can be found in Appendix C.

▶ WHAT YOU LEARNED IN THIS CHAPTER

TOPIC	KEY CONCEPTS
Saving simple user data	Use the `SharedPreferences` object.
Sharing data among activities in the same application	Use the `getSharedPreferences()` method.
Saving to a file	Use the `FileOutputStream` and `OutputStreamReader` classes.
Reading from a file	Use the `FileInputStream` and `InputStreamReader` classes.
Saving to external storage	Use the `getExternalStorageDirectory()` method to return the path to the external storage.
Accessing files in the `res/raw` folder	Use the `openRawResource()` method in the `Resources` object (obtained via the `getResources()` method).
Creating a database helper class	Extend the `SQLiteOpenHelper` class.

Content Providers

WHAT YOU WILL LEARN IN THIS CHAPTER

➤ What are content providers?

➤ How to use a content provider in Android

➤ How to create and use your own content provider

In the previous chapter, you learned about the various ways to persist data — using shared preferences, files, as well as SQLite databases. While using the database approach is the recommended way to save structured and complex data, sharing data is a challenge because the database is accessible to only the package that created it.

In this chapter, you will learn Android's way of sharing data through the use of *content providers*. You will learn how to use the built-in content providers, as well as implement your own content providers to share data across packages.

SHARING DATA IN ANDROID

In Android, using a content provider is the recommended way to share data across packages. Think of a content provider as a data store. How it stores its data is not relevant to the application using it; what is important is how packages can access the data stored in it using a consistent programming interface. A content provider behaves very much like a database — you can query it, edit its content, as well as add or delete content. However, unlike a database, a content provider can use different ways to store its data. The data can be stored in a database, in files, or even over a network.

Android ships with many useful content providers, including the following:

➤ **Browser** — Stores data such as browser bookmarks, browser history, and so on

➤ **CallLog** — Stores data such as missed calls, call details, and so on

➤ **Contacts** — Stores contact details

➤ **MediaStore** — Stores media files such as audio, video, and images

➤ **Settings** — Stores the device's settings and preferences

Besides the many built-in content providers, you can also create your own content providers.

To query a content provider, you specify the query string in the form of a URI, with an optional specifier for a particular row. The format of the query URI is as follows:

```
<standard_prefix>://<authority>/<data_path>/<id>
```

The various parts of the URI are as follows:

➤ The *standard prefix* for content providers is always `content://`.

➤ The *authority* specifies the name of the content provider. An example would be `contacts` for the built-in Contacts content provider. For third-party content providers, this could be the fully qualified name, such as `com.wrox.provider` or `net.learn2develop.provider`.

➤ The *data path* specifies the kind of data requested. For example, if you are getting all the contacts from the Contacts content provider, then the data path would be `people`, and the URI would look like this: `content://contacts/people`.

➤ The *id* specifies the specific record requested. For example, if you are looking for contact number 2 in the Contacts content provider, the URI would look like this: `content://contacts/people/2`.

Table 7-1 shows some examples of query strings.

TABLE 7-1: Example Query Strings

QUERY STRING	DESCRIPTION
`content://media/internal/images`	Returns a list of all the internal images on the device
`content://media/external/images`	Returns a list of all the images stored on the external storage (e.g., SD card) on the device
`content://call_log/calls`	Returns a list of all calls registered in the Call Log
`content://browser/bookmarks`	Returns a list of bookmarks stored in the browser

USING A CONTENT PROVIDER

The best way to understand content providers is to actually use one. The following Try It Out shows how you can use a content provider from within your Android application.

TRY IT OUT | Using the Contacts Content Provider

codefile Provider.zip available for download at Wrox.com

1. Using Eclipse, create a new Android project and name it **Provider**.

2. Add the following statements in bold to the `main.xml` file:

```xml
<?xml version="1.0" encoding="utf-8"?>
<LinearLayout xmlns:android="http://schemas.android.com/apk/res/android"
    android:layout_width="fill_parent"
    android:layout_height="fill_parent"
    android:orientation="vertical" >

<ListView
    android:id="@+id/android:list"
    android:layout_width="fill_parent"
    android:layout_height="wrap_content"
    android:layout_weight="1"
    android:stackFromBottom="false"
    android:transcriptMode="normal" />

<TextView
    android:id="@+id/contactName"
    android:textStyle="bold"
    android:layout_width="wrap_content"
    android:layout_height="wrap_content" />

<TextView
    android:id="@+id/contactID"
    android:layout_width="fill_parent"
    android:layout_height="wrap_content" />

</LinearLayout>
```

3. In the `ProviderActivity.java` class, code the following:

```java
package net.learn2develop.Provider;

import android.app.ListActivity;
import android.content.CursorLoader;
import android.database.Cursor;
import android.net.Uri;
import android.os.Bundle;
import android.provider.ContactsContract;
import android.widget.CursorAdapter;
import android.widget.SimpleCursorAdapter;

public class ProviderActivity extends ListActivity {
    /** Called when the activity is first created. */
    @Override
    public void onCreate(Bundle savedInstanceState) {
        super.onCreate(savedInstanceState);
```

```
        setContentView(R.layout.main);

        Uri allContacts = Uri.parse("content://contacts/people");

        Cursor c;
        if (android.os.Build.VERSION.SDK_INT <11) {
            //---before Honeycomb---
            c = managedQuery(allContacts, null, null, null, null);
        } else {
            //---Honeycomb and later---
            CursorLoader cursorLoader = new CursorLoader(
                    this,
                    allContacts,
                    null,
                    null,
                    null ,
                    null);
            c = cursorLoader.loadInBackground();
        }

        String[] columns = new String[] {
            ContactsContract.Contacts.DISPLAY_NAME,
            ContactsContract.Contacts._ID};

        int[] views = new int[] {R.id.contactName, R.id.contactID};

        SimpleCursorAdapter adapter;

        if (android.os.Build.VERSION.SDK_INT <11) {
            //---before Honeycomb---
            adapter = new SimpleCursorAdapter(
                    this, R.layout.main, c, columns, views);
        } else {
            //---Honeycomb and later---
            adapter = new SimpleCursorAdapter(
                    this, R.layout.main, c, columns, views,
                    CursorAdapter.FLAG_REGISTER_CONTENT_OBSERVER);
        }

        this.setListAdapter(adapter);    }
    }
```

4. Add the following statements in bold to the AndroidManifest.xml file:

```
<?xml version="1.0" encoding="utf-8"?>
<manifest xmlns:android="http://schemas.android.com/apk/res/android"
    package="net.learn2develop.Provider"
    android:versionCode="1"
    android:versionName="1.0" >

    <uses-sdk android:minSdkVersion="14" />
    <uses-permission android:name="android.permission.READ_CONTACTS"/>

    <application
```

```
            android:icon="@drawable/ic_launcher"
            android:label="@string/app_name" >
        <activity
            android:label="@string/app_name"
            android:name=".ProviderActivity" >
            <intent-filter >
                <action android:name="android.intent.action.MAIN" />

                <category android:name="android.intent.category.LAUNCHER" />
            </intent-filter>
        </activity>
    </application>

</manifest>
```

5. Launch an AVD and create a few contacts in the Android Emulator. To add a contact, go to the Phone application and click the Star icon at the top (see Figure 7-1). Click the MENU button on the emulator and click the New contact menu item. You will be warned about backing up your contacts. Click the Keep Local button and enter the name, phone number, and e-mail address of a few people.

6. Press F11 to debug the application on the Android emulator. Figure 7-2 shows the activity displaying the list of contacts you just created.

FIGURE 7-1

FIGURE 7-2

How It Works

In this example, you retrieved all the contacts stored in the Contacts application and displayed them in the `ListView`.

First, you specified the URI for accessing the Contacts application:

```
Uri allContacts = Uri.parse("content://contacts/people");
```

Next, observe that you have a conditional check to detect the version of the device on which the application is currently running:

```
Cursor c;
if (android.os.Build.VERSION.SDK_INT <11) {
    //---before Honeycomb---
    c = managedQuery(allContacts, null, null, null, null);
} else {
    //---Honeycomb and later---
    CursorLoader cursorLoader = new CursorLoader(
            this,
            allContacts,
            null,
            null,
            null ,
            null);
    c = cursorLoader.loadInBackground();
}
```

If the application is running on pre-Honeycomb devices (the value of the `android.os.Build.VERSION` `.SDK_INT` variable is lower than 11), you can use the `managedQuery()` method of the `Activity` class to retrieve a managed cursor. A *managed cursor* handles all the work of unloading itself when the application pauses and requerying itself when the application restarts. The statement

```
Cursor c = managedQuery(allContacts, null, null, null, null);
```

is equivalent to

```
Cursor c = getContentResolver().query(allContacts, null, null, null, null);
//---allows the activity to manage the Cursor's
// lifecyle based on the activity's lifecycle---
startManagingCursor(c);
```

The `getContentResolver()` method returns a `ContentResolver` object, which helps to resolve a content URI with the appropriate content provider.

However, beginning with Android API level 11 (Honeycomb and later), the `managedQuery()` method is deprecated (still available but not recommended for use). For Honeycomb or later devices, use the `CursorLoader` class:

```
CursorLoader cursorLoader = new CursorLoader(
        this,
        allContacts,
```

```
                    null,
                    null,
                    null ,
                    null);
         c = cursorLoader.loadInBackground();
```

The `CursorLoader` class (only available beginning with Android API level 11 and later) performs the cursor query on a background thread and hence does not block the application UI.

The `SimpleCursorAdapter` object maps a cursor to `TextViews` (or `ImageViews`) defined in your XML file (`main.xml`). It maps the data (as represented by `columns`) to views (as represented by `views`):

```
String[] columns = new String[] {
    ContactsContract.Contacts.DISPLAY_NAME,
    ContactsContract.Contacts._ID};

int[] views = new int[] {R.id.contactName, R.id.contactID};

SimpleCursorAdapter adapter;

if (android.os.Build.VERSION.SDK_INT <11) {
    //---before Honeycomb---
    adapter = new SimpleCursorAdapter(
            this, R.layout.main, c, columns, views);
} else {
    //---Honeycomb and later---
    adapter = new SimpleCursorAdapter(
            this, R.layout.main, c, columns, views,
            CursorAdapter.FLAG_REGISTER_CONTENT_OBSERVER);
}

this.setListAdapter(adapter);
```

Like the `managedQuery()` method, one of the constructors for the `SimpleCursorAdapter` class has been deprecated. For Honeycomb or later devices, you need to use the new constructor for the `SimpleCursorAdapter` class with one additional argument:

```
//---Honeycomb and later---
adapter = new SimpleCursorAdapter(
        this, R.layout.main, c, columns, views,
        CursorAdapter.FLAG_REGISTER_CONTENT_OBSERVER);
```

The flag registers the adapter to be informed when there is a change in the content provider.

Note that in order for your application to access the Contacts application, you need to have the READ_ CONTACTS permission in your `AndroidManifest.xml` file.

Predefined Query String Constants

Besides using the query URI, you can use a list of predefined query string constants in Android to specify the URI for the different data types. For example, besides using the query `content://contacts/people`, you can rewrite the statement

```
Uri allContacts = Uri.parse("content://contacts/people");
```

using one of the predefined constants in Android, as follows:

```
Uri allContacts = ContactsContract.Contacts.CONTENT_URI;
```

 NOTE *For Android 2.0 and later, to query the base Contacts records you need to use the* `ContactsContract.Contacts.CONTENT_URI` *URI.*

Some examples of predefined query string constants are as follows:

➤ `Browser.BOOKMARKS_URI`

➤ `Browser.SEARCHES_URI`

➤ `CallLog.CONTENT_URI`

➤ `MediaStore.Images.Media.INTERNAL_CONTENT_URI`

➤ `MediaStore.Images.Media.EXTERNAL_CONTENT_URI`

➤ `Settings.CONTENT_URI`

If you want to retrieve the first contact, specify the ID of that contact, like this:

```
Uri allContacts = Uri.parse("content://contacts/people/1");
```

Alternatively, use the predefined constant together with the `withAppendedId()` method of the `ContentUris` class:

```
import android.content.ContentUris;
...
        Uri allContacts = ContentUris.withAppendedId(
            ContactsContract.Contacts.CONTENT_URI, 1);
```

Besides binding to a `ListView`, you can also print out the results using the `Cursor` object, as shown here:

```
package net.learn2develop.Provider;

import android.app.ListActivity;
import android.content.CursorLoader;
import android.database.Cursor;
```

```java
import android.net.Uri;
import android.os.Bundle;
import android.provider.ContactsContract;
import android.widget.CursorAdapter;
import android.widget.SimpleCursorAdapter;
import android.util.Log;
public class ProviderActivity extends ListActivity  {
    /** Called when the activity is first created. */
    @Override
    public void onCreate(Bundle savedInstanceState) {
        super.onCreate(savedInstanceState);
        setContentView(R.layout.main);

        Uri allContacts = ContactsContract.Contacts.CONTENT_URI;
        ...
        ...
        if (android.os.Build.VERSION.SDK_INT <11) {
            //---before Honeycomb---
            adapter = new SimpleCursorAdapter(
                    this, R.layout.main, c, columns, views);
        } else {
            //---Honeycomb and later---
            adapter = new SimpleCursorAdapter(
                    this, R.layout.main, c, columns, views,
                    CursorAdapter.FLAG_REGISTER_CONTENT_OBSERVER);
        }

        this.setListAdapter(adapter);
        PrintContacts(c);
    }

    private void PrintContacts(Cursor c)
    {
        if (c.moveToFirst()) {
            do{
            String contactID = c.getString(c.getColumnIndex(
                    ContactsContract.Contacts._ID));
            String contactDisplayName =
                    c.getString(c.getColumnIndex(
                        ContactsContract.Contacts.DISPLAY_NAME));
                Log.v("Content Providers", contactID + ", " +
                    contactDisplayName);
            } while (c.moveToNext());
        }
    }
}
```

 NOTE If you don't know how to view the LogCat window, refer to Appendix A for a quick tour of the Eclipse IDE.

The `PrintContacts()` method will print out the following in the LogCat window:

```
12-13 08:32:50.471: V/Content Providers(12346): 1, Wei-Meng Lee
12-13 08:32:50.471: V/Content Providers(12346): 2, Linda Chen
12-13 08:32:50.471: V/Content Providers(12346): 3, Joanna Yip
```

It prints out the ID and name of each contact stored in the Contacts application. In this case, you access the `ContactsContract.Contacts._ID` field to obtain the ID of a contact, and `ContactsContract.Contacts.DISPLAY_NAME` for the name of a contact. If you want to display the phone number of a contact, you need to query the content provider again, as the information is stored in another table:

```java
private void PrintContacts(Cursor c)
{
    if (c.moveToFirst()) {
        do{
            String contactID = c.getString(c.getColumnIndex(
                    ContactsContract.Contacts._ID));
            String contactDisplayName =
                    c.getString(c.getColumnIndex(
                            ContactsContract.Contacts.DISPLAY_NAME));
            Log.v("Content Providers", contactID + ", " +
                    contactDisplayName);

            //---get phone number---
            int hasPhone =
                    c.getInt(c.getColumnIndex(
                            ContactsContract.Contacts.HAS_PHONE_NUMBER));
            if (hasPhone == 1) {
                Cursor phoneCursor =
                    getContentResolver().query(
                        ContactsContract.CommonDataKinds.Phone.CONTENT_URI, null,
                        ContactsContract.CommonDataKinds.Phone.CONTACT_ID + " = " +
                        contactID, null, null);
                while (phoneCursor.moveToNext()) {
                    Log.v("Content Providers",
                        phoneCursor.getString(
                            phoneCursor.getColumnIndex(
                                ContactsContract.CommonDataKinds.Phone.NUMBER)));
                }
                phoneCursor.close();
            }

        } while (c.moveToNext());
    }
}
```

> **NOTE** To access the phone number of a contact, you need to query against the URI stored in `ContactsContract.CommonDataKinds.Phone.CONTENT_URI`.

In the preceding code snippet, you first check whether a contact has a phone number using the ContactsContract.Contacts.HAS_PHONE_NUMBER field. If the contact has at least a phone number, you then query the content provider again based on the ID of the contact. Once the phone number(s) are retrieved, you then iterate through them and print out the numbers. You should see something like this:

```
12-13 08:59:31.881: V/Content Providers(13351): 1, Wei-Meng Lee
12-13 08:59:32.311: V/Content Providers(13351): +651234567
12-13 08:59:32.321: V/Content Providers(13351): 2, Linda Chen
12-13 08:59:32.511: V/Content Providers(13351): +1 876-543-21
12-13 08:59:32.545: V/Content Providers(13351): 3, Joanna Yip
12-13 08:59:32.641: V/Content Providers(13351): +239 846 5522
```

Projections

The second parameter of the managedQuery() method (third parameter for the CursorLoader class) controls how many columns are returned by the query; this parameter is known as the *projection*. Earlier, you specified null:

```
Cursor c;
if (android.os.Build.VERSION.SDK_INT <11) {
    //---before Honeycomb---
    c = managedQuery(allContacts, null, null, null, null);
} else {
    //---Honeycomb and later---
    CursorLoader cursorLoader = new CursorLoader(
            this,
            allContacts,
            null,
            null,
            null ,
            null);
    c = cursorLoader.loadInBackground();
}
```

You can specify the exact columns to return by creating an array containing the name of the column to return, like this:

```
String[] projection = new String[]
        {ContactsContract.Contacts._ID,
         ContactsContract.Contacts.DISPLAY_NAME,
         ContactsContract.Contacts.HAS_PHONE_NUMBER};

Cursor c;
if (android.os.Build.VERSION.SDK_INT <11) {
    //---before Honeycomb---
    c = managedQuery(allContacts, projection, null, null, null);
} else {
    //---Honeycomb and later---
    CursorLoader cursorLoader = new CursorLoader(
            this,
```

```
                    allContacts,
                    projection,
                    null,
                    null ,
                    null);
           c = cursorLoader.loadInBackground();
   }
```

In the above case, the _ID, DISPLAY_NAME, and HAS_PHONE_NUMBER fields will be retrieved.

Filtering

The third and fourth parameters of the managedQuery() method (fourth and fifth parameters for the CursorLoader class) enable you to specify a SQL WHERE clause to filter the result of the query. For example, the following statement retrieves only the people whose name ends with "Lee":

```
Cursor c;
if (android.os.Build.VERSION.SDK_INT <11) {
    //---before Honeycomb---
    c = managedQuery(allContacts, projection,
            ContactsContract.Contacts.DISPLAY_NAME + " LIKE '%Lee'", null, null);
} else {
    //---Honeycomb and later---
    CursorLoader cursorLoader = new CursorLoader(
            this,
            allContacts,
            projection,
            ContactsContract.Contacts.DISPLAY_NAME + " LIKE '%Lee'",
            null ,
            null);
    c = cursorLoader.loadInBackground();
}
```

Here, the third parameter (for the managedQuery() method, and the fourth parameter for the CursorLoader constructor) contains a SQL statement containing the name to search for ("Lee"). You can also put the search string into the next argument of the method/constructor, like this:

```
Cursor c;
if (android.os.Build.VERSION.SDK_INT <11) {
    //---before Honeycomb---
    c = managedQuery(allContacts, projection,
            ContactsContract.Contacts.DISPLAY_NAME + " LIKE ?",
            new String[] {"%Lee"}, null);
} else {
    //---Honeycomb and later---
    CursorLoader cursorLoader = new CursorLoader(
            this,
            allContacts,
            projection,
            ContactsContract.Contacts.DISPLAY_NAME + " LIKE ?",
```

```
                        new String[] {"%Lee"},
                    null);
        c = cursorLoader.loadInBackground();
    }
```

Sorting

The last parameter of the `managedQuery()` method (and constructor for the `CursorLoader` class) enables you to specify a SQL ORDER BY clause to sort the result of the query. For example, the following statement sorts the contact names in ascending order:

```
Cursor c;
if (android.os.Build.VERSION.SDK_INT <11) {
    //---before Honeycomb---
    c = managedQuery(allContacts, projection,
            ContactsContract.Contacts.DISPLAY_NAME + " LIKE ?",
            new String[] {"%Lee"},
            ContactsContract.Contacts.DISPLAY_NAME + " ASC");
} else {
    //---Honeycomb and later---
    CursorLoader cursorLoader = new CursorLoader(
            this,
            allContacts,
            projection,
            ContactsContract.Contacts.DISPLAY_NAME + " LIKE ?",
            new String[] {"%Lee"},
            ContactsContract.Contacts.DISPLAY_NAME + " ASC");
    c = cursorLoader.loadInBackground();
}
```

CREATING YOUR OWN CONTENT PROVIDERS

Creating your own content provider in Android is relatively simple. All you need to do is extend the abstract `ContentProvider` class and override the various methods defined within it.

In this section, you will learn how to create a simple content provider that stores a list of books. For ease of illustration, the content provider stores the books in a database table containing three fields, as shown in Figure 7-3.

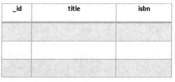

FIGURE 7-3

The following Try It Out shows you the steps.

TRY IT OUT   Creating Your Own Content Provider

codefile ContentProviders.zip available for download at Wrox.com

1.   Using Eclipse, create a new Android project and name it **ContentProviders**.

2.   In the `src` folder of the project, add a new Java class file and name it **BooksProvider**.

3. Populate the `BooksProvider.java` file as follows:

```java
package net.learn2develop.ContentProviders;

import android.content.ContentProvider;
import android.content.ContentUris;
import android.content.ContentValues;
import android.content.Context;
import android.content.UriMatcher;
import android.database.Cursor;
import android.database.SQLException;
import android.database.sqlite.SQLiteDatabase;
import android.database.sqlite.SQLiteOpenHelper;
import android.database.sqlite.SQLiteQueryBuilder;
import android.net.Uri;
import android.text.TextUtils;
import android.util.Log;

public class BooksProvider extends ContentProvider {
    static final String PROVIDER_NAME =
        "net.learn2develop.provider.Books";

    static final Uri CONTENT_URI =
        Uri.parse("content://"+ PROVIDER_NAME + "/books");

    static final String _ID = "_id";
    static final String TITLE = "title";
    static final String ISBN = "isbn";

    static final int BOOKS = 1;
    static final int BOOK_ID = 2;

    private static final UriMatcher uriMatcher;
    static{
        uriMatcher = new UriMatcher(UriMatcher.NO_MATCH);
        uriMatcher.addURI(PROVIDER_NAME, "books", BOOKS);
        uriMatcher.addURI(PROVIDER_NAME, "books/#", BOOK_ID);
    }

    //---for database use---
    SQLiteDatabase booksDB;
    static final String DATABASE_NAME = "Books";
    static final String DATABASE_TABLE = "titles";
    static final int DATABASE_VERSION = 1;
    static final String DATABASE_CREATE =
        "create table " + DATABASE_TABLE +
        " (_id integer primary key autoincrement, "
        + "title text not null, isbn text not null);";

    private static class DatabaseHelper extends SQLiteOpenHelper
    {
        DatabaseHelper(Context context) {
```

```java
        super(context, DATABASE_NAME, null, DATABASE_VERSION);
    }

    @Override
    public void onCreate(SQLiteDatabase db)
    {
        db.execSQL(DATABASE_CREATE);
    }

    @Override
    public void onUpgrade(SQLiteDatabase db, int oldVersion,
            int newVersion) {
        Log.w("Content provider database",
                "Upgrading database from version " +
                        oldVersion + " to " + newVersion +
                ", which will destroy all old data");
        db.execSQL("DROP TABLE IF EXISTS titles");
        onCreate(db);
    }
}

@Override
public int delete(Uri arg0, String arg1, String[] arg2) {
    // arg0 = uri
    // arg1 = selection
    // arg2 = selectionArgs
    int count=0;
    switch (uriMatcher.match(arg0)){
    case BOOKS:
        count = booksDB.delete(
                DATABASE_TABLE,
                arg1,
                arg2);
        break;
    case BOOK_ID:
        String id = arg0.getPathSegments().get(1);
        count = booksDB.delete(
                DATABASE_TABLE,
                _ID + " = " + id +
                (!TextUtils.isEmpty(arg1) ? " AND (" +
                        arg1 + ')' : ""),
                        arg2);
        break;
    default: throw new IllegalArgumentException("Unknown URI " + arg0);
    }
    getContext().getContentResolver().notifyChange(arg0, null);
    return count;
}

@Override
public String getType(Uri uri) {
    switch (uriMatcher.match(uri)){
    //---get all books---
    case BOOKS:
```

```
            return "vnd.android.cursor.dir/vnd.learn2develop.books ";

        //---get a particular book---
        case BOOK_ID:
            return "vnd.android.cursor.item/vnd.learn2develop.books ";

        default:
            throw new IllegalArgumentException("Unsupported URI: " + uri);
        }
    }

    @Override
    public Uri insert(Uri uri, ContentValues values) {
        //---add a new book---
        long rowID = booksDB.insert(
                DATABASE_TABLE,
                "",
                values);

        //---if added successfully---
        if (rowID>0)
        {
            Uri _uri = ContentUris.withAppendedId(CONTENT_URI, rowID);
            getContext().getContentResolver().notifyChange(_uri, null);
            return _uri;
        }
        throw new SQLException("Failed to insert row into " + uri);
    }

    @Override
    public boolean onCreate() {
        Context context = getContext();
        DatabaseHelper dbHelper = new DatabaseHelper(context);
        booksDB = dbHelper.getWritableDatabase();
        return (booksDB == null)? false:true;
    }

    @Override
    public Cursor query(Uri uri, String[] projection, String selection,
            String[] selectionArgs, String sortOrder) {
        SQLiteQueryBuilder sqlBuilder = new SQLiteQueryBuilder();
        sqlBuilder.setTables(DATABASE_TABLE);

        if (uriMatcher.match(uri) == BOOK_ID)
            //---if getting a particular book---
            sqlBuilder.appendWhere(
                    _ID + " = " + uri.getPathSegments().get(1));

        if (sortOrder==null || sortOrder=="")
            sortOrder = TITLE;

        Cursor c = sqlBuilder.query(
            booksDB,
            projection,
```

```
            selection,
            selectionArgs,
            null,
            null,
            sortOrder);

    //---register to watch a content URI for changes---
    c.setNotificationUri(getContext().getContentResolver(), uri);
    return c;
}

@Override
public int update(Uri uri, ContentValues values, String selection,
        String[] selectionArgs) {
    int count = 0;
    switch (uriMatcher.match(uri)){
    case BOOKS:
        count = booksDB.update(
                DATABASE_TABLE,
                values,
                selection,
                selectionArgs);
        break;
    case BOOK_ID:
        count = booksDB.update(
                DATABASE_TABLE,
                values,
                _ID + " = " + uri.getPathSegments().get(1) +
                (!TextUtils.isEmpty(selection) ? " AND (" +
                        selection + ')' : ""),
                        selectionArgs);
        break;
    default: throw new IllegalArgumentException("Unknown URI " + uri);
    }
    getContext().getContentResolver().notifyChange(uri, null);
    return count;
}
}
```

4. Add the following statements in bold to the AndroidManifest.xml file:

```
<?xml version="1.0" encoding="utf-8"?>
<manifest xmlns:android="http://schemas.android.com/apk/res/android"
    package="net.learn2develop.ContentProviders"
    android:versionCode="1"
    android:versionName="1.0" >

    <uses-sdk android:minSdkVersion="14" />

    <application
        android:icon="@drawable/ic_launcher"
        android:label="@string/app_name" >
        <activity
            android:label="@string/app_name"
            android:name=".ContentProvidersActivity" >
```

```
            <intent-filter >
                <action android:name="android.intent.action.MAIN" />

                <category android:name="android.intent.category.LAUNCHER" />
            </intent-filter>
        </activity>
        <provider android:name="BooksProvider"
            android:authorities="net.learn2develop.provider.Books">
        </provider>
    </application>

</manifest>
```

How It Works

In this example, you first created a class named `BooksProvider` that extends the `ContentProvider` base class. The various methods to override in this class are as follows:

➤ `getType()` — Returns the MIME type of the data at the given URI

➤ `onCreate()` — Called when the provider is started

➤ `query()` — Receives a request from a client. The result is returned as a `Cursor` object.

➤ `insert()` — Inserts a new record into the content provider

➤ `delete()` — Deletes an existing record from the content provider

➤ `update()` — Updates an existing record from the content provider

Within your content provider, you are free to choose how you want to store your data — a traditional file system, XML, a database, or even through web services. For this example, you used the SQLite database approach discussed in the previous chapter.

You then defined the following constants within the `BooksProvider` class:

```
static final String PROVIDER_NAME =
    "net.learn2develop.provider.Books";

static final Uri CONTENT_URI =
    Uri.parse("content://"+ PROVIDER_NAME + "/books");

static final String _ID = "_id";
static final String TITLE = "title";
static final String ISBN = "isbn";

static final int BOOKS = 1;
static final int BOOK_ID = 2;

private static final UriMatcher uriMatcher;
static{
    uriMatcher = new UriMatcher(UriMatcher.NO_MATCH);
    uriMatcher.addURI(PROVIDER_NAME, "books", BOOKS);
    uriMatcher.addURI(PROVIDER_NAME, "books/#", BOOK_ID);
}

//---for database use---
SQLiteDatabase booksDB;
```

```
static final String DATABASE_NAME = "Books";
static final String DATABASE_TABLE = "titles";
static final int DATABASE_VERSION = 1;
static final String DATABASE_CREATE =
    "create table " + DATABASE_TABLE +
    " (_id integer primary key autoincrement, "
    + "title text not null, isbn text not null);";
```

Observe in the preceding code that you used an UriMatcher object to parse the content URI that is passed to the content provider through a ContentResolver. For example, the following content URI represents a request for all books in the content provider:

content://net.learn2develop.provider.Books/books

The following represents a request for a particular book with _id 5:

content://net.learn2develop.provider.Books/books/5

Your content provider uses a SQLite database to store the books. Note that you used the SQLiteOpenHelper helper class to help manage your database:

```
private static class DatabaseHelper extends SQLiteOpenHelper
{
    DatabaseHelper(Context context) {
        super(context, DATABASE_NAME, null, DATABASE_VERSION);
    }

    @Override
    public void onCreate(SQLiteDatabase db)
    {
        db.execSQL(DATABASE_CREATE);
    }

    @Override
    public void onUpgrade(SQLiteDatabase db, int oldVersion,
            int newVersion) {
        Log.w("Content provider database",
                "Upgrading database from version " +
                        oldVersion + " to " + newVersion +
                ", which will destroy all old data");
        db.execSQL("DROP TABLE IF EXISTS titles");
        onCreate(db);
    }
}
```

Next, you override the getType() method to uniquely describe the data type for your content provider. Using the UriMatcher object, you returned vnd.android.cursor.item/vnd.learn2develop.books for a single book, and vnd.android.cursor.dir/vnd.learn2develop.books for multiple books:

```
@Override
public String getType(Uri uri) {
    switch (uriMatcher.match(uri)){
    //---get all books---
    case BOOKS:
```

```
            return "vnd.android.cursor.dir/vnd.learn2develop.books ";

        //---get a particular book---
        case BOOK_ID:
            return "vnd.android.cursor.item/vnd.learn2develop.books ";

        default:
            throw new IllegalArgumentException("Unsupported URI: " + uri);
        }
    }
```

Next, you overrode the onCreate() method to open a connection to the database when the content provider is started:

```
@Override
public boolean onCreate() {
    Context context = getContext();
    DatabaseHelper dbHelper = new DatabaseHelper(context);
    booksDB = dbHelper.getWritableDatabase();
    return (booksDB == null)? false:true;
}
```

You overrode the query() method to allow clients to query for books:

```
@Override
public Cursor query(Uri uri, String[] projection, String selection,
        String[] selectionArgs, String sortOrder) {
    SQLiteQueryBuilder sqlBuilder = new SQLiteQueryBuilder();
    sqlBuilder.setTables(DATABASE_TABLE);

    if (uriMatcher.match(uri) == BOOK_ID)
        //---if getting a particular book---
        sqlBuilder.appendWhere(
                _ID + " = " + uri.getPathSegments().get(1));

    if (sortOrder==null || sortOrder=="")
        sortOrder = TITLE;

    Cursor c = sqlBuilder.query(
        booksDB,
        projection,
        selection,
        selectionArgs,
        null,
        null,
        sortOrder);

    //---register to watch a content URI for changes---
    c.setNotificationUri(getContext().getContentResolver(), uri);
    return c;
}
```

By default, the result of the query is sorted using the title field. The resulting query is returned as a Cursor object.

To allow a new book to be inserted into the content provider, you override the insert() method:

```
@Override
public Uri insert(Uri uri, ContentValues values) {
    //---add a new book---
    long rowID = booksDB.insert(
            DATABASE_TABLE,
            "",
            values);

    //---if added successfully---
    if (rowID>0)
    {
        Uri _uri = ContentUris.withAppendedId(CONTENT_URI, rowID);
        getContext().getContentResolver().notifyChange(_uri, null);
        return _uri;
    }
    throw new SQLException("Failed to insert row into " + uri);
}
```

Once the record is inserted successfully, you call the notifyChange() method of the ContentResolver. This notifies registered observers that a row was updated.

To delete a book, you override the delete() method:

```
@Override
public int delete(Uri arg0, String arg1, String[] arg2) {
    // arg0 = uri
    // arg1 = selection
    // arg2 = selectionArgs
    int count=0;
    switch (uriMatcher.match(arg0)){
    case BOOKS:
        count = booksDB.delete(
                DATABASE_TABLE,
                arg1,
                arg2);
        break;
    case BOOK_ID:
        String id = arg0.getPathSegments().get(1);
        count = booksDB.delete(
                DATABASE_TABLE,
                _ID + " = " + id +
                (!TextUtils.isEmpty(arg1) ? " AND (" +
                        arg1 + ')' : ""),
                        arg2);
        break;
    default: throw new IllegalArgumentException("Unknown URI " + arg0);
    }
    getContext().getContentResolver().notifyChange(arg0, null);
    return count;
}
```

Likewise, call the `notifyChange()` method of the `ContentResolver` after the deletion. This will notify registered observers that a row was deleted.

Finally, to update a book, you override the `update()` method:

```
@Override
public int update(Uri uri, ContentValues values, String selection,
        String[] selectionArgs) {
    int count = 0;
    switch (uriMatcher.match(uri)){
    case BOOKS:
        count = booksDB.update(
                DATABASE_TABLE,
                values,
                selection,
                selectionArgs);
        break;
    case BOOK_ID:
        count = booksDB.update(
                DATABASE_TABLE,
                values,
                _ID + " = " + uri.getPathSegments().get(1) +
                (!TextUtils.isEmpty(selection) ? " AND (" +
                        selection + ')' : ""),
                        selectionArgs);
        break;
    default: throw new IllegalArgumentException("Unknown URI " + uri);
    }
    getContext().getContentResolver().notifyChange(uri, null);
    return count;
}
```

As with the `insert()` and `delete()` methods, you called the `notifyChange()` method of the `ContentResolver` after the update. This notifies registered observers that a row was updated.

Finally, to register your content provider with Android, modify the `AndroidManifest.xml` file by adding the `<provider>` element.

USING THE CONTENT PROVIDER

Now that you have built your new content provider, you can test it from within your Android application. The following Try It Out demonstrates how to do that.

TRY IT OUT Using the Newly Created Content Provider

1. Using the same project created in the previous section, add the following statements in bold to the `main.xml` file:

```
<?xml version="1.0" encoding="utf-8"?>
<LinearLayout xmlns:android="http://schemas.android.com/apk/res/android"
    android:layout_width="fill_parent"
```

```
    android:layout_height="fill_parent"
    android:orientation="vertical" >

<TextView
    android:layout_width="fill_parent"
    android:layout_height="wrap_content"
    android:text="ISBN" />

<EditText
    android:id="@+id/txtISBN"
    android:layout_height="wrap_content"
    android:layout_width="fill_parent" />

<TextView
    android:layout_width="fill_parent"
    android:layout_height="wrap_content"
    android:text="Title" />

<EditText
    android:id="@+id/txtTitle"
    android:layout_height="wrap_content"
    android:layout_width="fill_parent" />

<Button
    android:text="Add title"
    android:id="@+id/btnAdd"
    android:layout_width="fill_parent"
    android:layout_height="wrap_content"
    android:onClick="onClickAddTitle" />

<Button
    android:text="Retrieve titles"
    android:id="@+id/btnRetrieve"
    android:layout_width="fill_parent"
    android:layout_height="wrap_content"
    android:onClick="onClickRetrieveTitles" />

</LinearLayout>
```

2. In the ContentProvidersActivity.java file, add the following statements in bold:

```
package net.learn2develop.ContentProviders;

import android.app.Activity;
import android.content.ContentValues;
import android.content.CursorLoader;
import android.database.Cursor;
import android.net.Uri;
import android.os.Bundle;
import android.view.View;
import android.widget.EditText;
import android.widget.Toast;

public class ContentProvidersActivity extends Activity {
    /** Called when the activity is first created. */
```

```
@Override
public void onCreate(Bundle savedInstanceState) {
    super.onCreate(savedInstanceState);
    setContentView(R.layout.main);
}

public void onClickAddTitle(View view) {
    //---add a book---
    ContentValues values = new ContentValues();
    values.put(BooksProvider.TITLE, ((EditText)
            findViewById(R.id.txtTitle)).getText().toString());
    values.put(BooksProvider.ISBN, ((EditText)
            findViewById(R.id.txtISBN)).getText().toString());
    Uri uri = getContentResolver().insert(
            BooksProvider.CONTENT_URI, values);
    Toast.makeText(getBaseContext(),uri.toString(),
            Toast.LENGTH_LONG).show();
}

public void onClickRetrieveTitles(View view) {
    //---retrieve the titles---
    Uri allTitles = Uri.parse(
            "content://net.learn2develop.provider.Books/books");
    Cursor c;
    if (android.os.Build.VERSION.SDK_INT <11) {
        //---before Honeycomb---
        c = managedQuery(allTitles, null, null, null,
                "title desc");
    } else {
        //---Honeycomb and later---
        CursorLoader cursorLoader = new CursorLoader(
                this,
                allTitles, null, null, null,
                "title desc");
        c = cursorLoader.loadInBackground();
    }
    if (c.moveToFirst()) {
        do{
            Toast.makeText(this,
                c.getString(c.getColumnIndex(
                    BooksProvider._ID)) + ", " +
                c.getString(c.getColumnIndex(
                    BooksProvider.TITLE)) + ", " +
                c.getString(c.getColumnIndex(
                    BooksProvider.ISBN)),
                Toast.LENGTH_SHORT).show();
        } while (c.moveToNext());
    }
}

}
```

3. Press F11 to debug the application on the Android emulator.

4. Enter an ISBN and title for a book and click the Add title button. Figure 7-4 shows the Toast class displaying the URI of the book added to the content provider. To retrieve all the titles stored in the content provider, click the Retrieve titles button and observe the values displayed using the Toast class.

How It Works

First, you modified the activity so that users can enter a book's ISBN and title to add to the content provider that you have just created.

To add a book to the content provider, you create a new ContentValues object and then populate it with the various information about a book:

```
//---add a book---
ContentValues values = new ContentValues();
values.put(BooksProvider.TITLE, ((EditText)
        findViewById(R.id.txtTitle)).getText().toString());
values.put(BooksProvider.ISBN, ((EditText)
        findViewById(R.id.txtISBN)).getText().toString());
Uri uri = getContentResolver().insert(
        BooksProvider.CONTENT_URI, values);
```

FIGURE 7-4

Notice that because your content provider is in the same package, you can use the BooksProvider .TITLE and the BooksProvider.ISBN constants to refer to the "title" and "isbn" fields, respectively. If you were accessing this content provider from another package, then you would not be able to use these constants. In that case, you need to specify the field name directly, like this:

```
ContentValues values = new ContentValues();
values.put("title", ((EditText)
    findViewById(R.id.txtTitle)).getText().toString());
values.put("isbn", ((EditText)
    findViewById(R.id.txtISBN)).getText().toString());
Uri uri = getContentResolver().insert(
        Uri.parse(
            "content://net.learn2develop.provider.Books/books"),
            values);
```

Also note that for external packages, you need to refer to the content URI using the fully qualified content URI:

```
Uri.parse(
    "content://net.learn2develop.provider.Books/books"),
```

To retrieve all the titles in the content provider, you used the following code snippets:

```
//---retrieve the titles---
Uri allTitles = Uri.parse(
        "content://net.learn2develop.provider.Books/books");
Cursor c;
if (android.os.Build.VERSION.SDK_INT <11) {
    //---before Honeycomb---
    c = managedQuery(allTitles, null, null, null,
            "title desc");
} else {
    //---Honeycomb and later---
    CursorLoader cursorLoader = new CursorLoader(
            this,
            allTitles, null, null, null,
            "title desc");
    c = cursorLoader.loadInBackground();
}
if (c.moveToFirst()) {
    do{
        Toast.makeText(this,
            c.getString(c.getColumnIndex(
                BooksProvider._ID)) + ", " +
            c.getString(c.getColumnIndex(
                BooksProvider.TITLE)) + ", " +
            c.getString(c.getColumnIndex(
                BooksProvider.ISBN)),
            Toast.LENGTH_SHORT).show();
    } while (c.moveToNext());
}
```

The preceding query will return the result sorted in descending order based on the title field.

If you want to update a book's detail, call the update() method with the content URI, indicating the book's ID:

```
ContentValues editedValues = new ContentValues();
editedValues.put(BooksProvider.TITLE, "Android Tips and Tricks");
getContentResolver().update(
    Uri.parse(
        "content://net.learn2develop.provider.Books/books/2"),
        editedValues,
        null,
        null);
```

To delete a book, use the delete() method with the content URI, indicating the book's ID:

```
//---delete a title---
getContentResolver().delete(
        Uri.parse("content://net.learn2develop.provider.Books/books/2"),
        null, null);
```

To delete all books, simply omit the book's ID in your content URI:

```
//---delete all titles---
getContentResolver().delete(
        Uri.parse("content://net.learn2develop.provider.Books/books"),
        null, null);
```

SUMMARY

In this chapter, you learned what content providers are and how to use some of the built-in content providers in Android. In particular, you have seen how to use the Contacts content provider. Google's decision to provide content providers enables applications to share data through a standard set of programming interfaces. In addition to the built-in content providers, you can also create your own custom content provider to share data with other packages.

EXERCISES

1. Write the query to retrieve all contacts from the Contacts application that contain the word "jack."

2. Name the methods that you need to override in your own implementation of a content provider.

3. How do you register a content provider in your `AndroidManifest.xml` file?

Answers to the exercises can be found in Appendix C.

▶ **WHAT YOU LEARNED IN THIS CHAPTER**

TOPIC	KEY CONCEPTS
Retrieving a managed cursor	Use the `managedQuery()` method (for pre-Honeycomb devices) or use the `CursorLoader` class (for Honeycomb or later devices).
Two ways to specify a query for a content provider	Use either a query URI or a predefined query string constant.
Retrieving the value of a column in a content provider	Use the `getColumnIndex()` method.
Query URI for accessing a contact's name	`ContactsContract.Contacts.CONTENT_URI`
Query URI for accessing a contact's phone number	`ContactsContract.CommonDataKinds.Phone .CONTENT_URI`
Creating your own content provider	Create a class and extend the `ContentProvider` class.

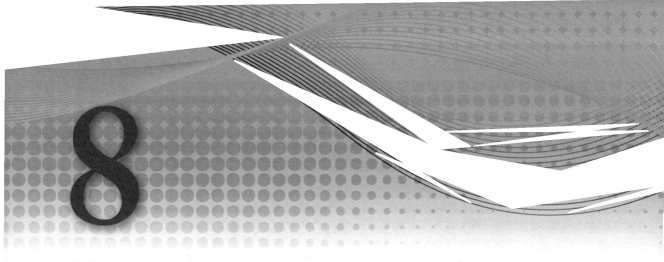

Messaging

WHAT YOU WILL LEARN IN THIS CHAPTER

- ➤ How to send SMS messages programmatically from within your application
- ➤ How to send SMS messages using the built-in Messaging application
- ➤ How to receive incoming SMS messages
- ➤ How to send e-mail messages from your application

Once your basic Android application is up and running, the next interesting thing you can add to it is the capability to communicate with the outside world. You may want your application to send an SMS message to another phone when an event happens (such as when a particular geographical location is reached), or you may wish to access a web service that provides certain services (such as currency exchange, weather, etc.).

In this chapter, you learn how to send and receive SMS messages programmatically from within your Android application. You will also learn how to invoke the Mail application from within your Android application to send e-mail messages to other users.

SMS MESSAGING

SMS messaging is one of the main *killer applications* on a mobile phone today — for some users as necessary as the phone itself. Any mobile phone you buy today should have at least SMS messaging capabilities, and nearly all users of any age know how to send and receive such messages. Android comes with a built-in SMS application that enables you to send and receive SMS messages. However, in some cases you might want to integrate SMS capabilities into your own Android application. For example, you might want to write an application that automatically sends an SMS message at regular time intervals. For example, this would be useful if you wanted to track the location of your kids — simply give them an Android device that sends out an SMS message containing its geographical location every 30 minutes. Now you know if they really went to the library after school! (Of course, such a capability also means you would have to pay the fees incurred from sending all those SMS messages...)

This section describes how you can programmatically send and receive SMS messages in your Android applications. The good news for Android developers is that you don't need a real device to test SMS messaging: The free Android emulator provides that capability.

Sending SMS Messages Programmatically

You will first learn how to send SMS messages programmatically from within your application. Using this approach, your application can automatically send an SMS message to a recipient without user intervention. The following Try It Out shows you how.

TRY IT OUT Sending SMS Messages

codefile SMS.zip available for download at Wrox.com

1. Using Eclipse, create a new Android project and name it **SMS**.

2. Replace the `TextView` with the following statements in bold in the `main.xml` file:

```xml
<?xml version="1.0" encoding="utf-8"?>
<LinearLayout xmlns:android="http://schemas.android.com/apk/res/android"
    android:layout_width="fill_parent"
    android:layout_height="fill_parent"
    android:orientation="vertical" >

<Button
    android:id="@+id/btnSendSMS"
    android:layout_width="fill_parent"
    android:layout_height="wrap_content"
    android:text="Send SMS"
    android:onClick="onClick" />

</LinearLayout>
```

3. In the `AndroidManifest.xml` file, add the following statements in bold:

```xml
<?xml version="1.0" encoding="utf-8"?>
<manifest xmlns:android="http://schemas.android.com/apk/res/android"
    package="net.learn2develop.SMS"
    android:versionCode="1"
    android:versionName="1.0" >

    <uses-sdk android:minSdkVersion="14" />
```

```xml
<uses-permission android:name="android.permission.SEND_SMS"/>

<application
    android:icon="@drawable/ic_launcher"
    android:label="@string/app_name" >
    <activity
        android:label="@string/app_name"
        android:name=".SMSActivity" >
        <intent-filter >
            <action android:name="android.intent.action.MAIN" />

            <category android:name="android.intent.category.LAUNCHER" />
        </intent-filter>
    </activity>
</application>

</manifest>
```

4. Add the following statements in bold to the `SMSActivity.java` file:

```java
package net.learn2develop.SMS;

import android.app.Activity;
import android.os.Bundle;

import android.telephony.SmsManager;
import android.view.View;

public class SMSActivity extends Activity {
    /** Called when the activity is first created. */
    @Override
    public void onCreate(Bundle savedInstanceState) {
        super.onCreate(savedInstanceState);
        setContentView(R.layout.main);
    }

    public void onClick(View v) {
        sendSMS("5556", "Hello my friends!");
    }

    //---sends an SMS message to another device---
    private void sendSMS(String phoneNumber, String message)
    {
        SmsManager sms = SmsManager.getDefault();
        sms.sendTextMessage(phoneNumber, null, message, null, null);
    }
}
```

5. Press F11 to debug the application on the Android emulator. Using the Android SDK and AVD Manager, launch another AVD.

6. On the first Android emulator (5554), click the Send SMS button to send an SMS message to the second emulator (5556). Figure 8-1 shows the SMS message received by the second emulator (note the notification bar at the top).

How It Works

Android uses a permissions-based policy whereby all the permissions needed by an application must be specified in the `AndroidManifest.xml` file. This ensures that when the application is installed, the user knows exactly which access permissions it requires.

Because sending SMS messages incurs additional costs on the user's end, indicating the SMS permissions in the `AndroidManifest` `.xml` file enables users to decide whether to allow the application to install or not.

To send an SMS message programmatically, you use the `SmsManager` class. Unlike other classes, you do not directly instantiate this class; instead, you call the `getDefault()` static method to obtain an `SmsManager` object. You then send the SMS message using the `sendTextMessage()` method:

FIGURE 8-1

```
//---sends an SMS message to another device---
private void sendSMS(String phoneNumber, String message)
{
    SmsManager sms = SmsManager.getDefault();
    sms.sendTextMessage(phoneNumber, null, message, null, null);
}
```

Following are the five arguments to the `sendTextMessage()` method:

➤ `destinationAddress` — Phone number of the recipient

➤ `scAddress` — Service center address; use `null` for default SMSC

➤ `text` — Content of the SMS message

➤ `sentIntent` — Pending intent to invoke when the message is sent (discussed in more detail in the next section)

➤ `deliveryIntent` — Pending intent to invoke when the message has been delivered (discussed in more detail in the next section)

> **NOTE** If you send an SMS message programmatically using the `SmsManager` class, the message sent will not appear in the built-in Messaging application of the sender.

Getting Feedback after Sending a Message

In the previous section, you learned how to programmatically send SMS messages using the SmsManager class; but how do you know that the message has been sent correctly? To do so, you can create two PendingIntent objects to monitor the status of the SMS message-sending process. These two PendingIntent objects are passed to the last two arguments of the sendTextMessage() method. The following code snippets show how you can monitor the status of the SMS message being sent:

```java
package net.learn2develop.SMS;

import android.app.Activity;
import android.app.PendingIntent;
import android.content.BroadcastReceiver;
import android.content.Context;
import android.content.Intent;
import android.content.IntentFilter;
import android.os.Bundle;

import android.telephony.SmsManager;
import android.view.View;
import android.widget.Toast;

public class SMSActivity extends Activity {
    String SENT = "SMS_SENT";
    String DELIVERED = "SMS_DELIVERED";
    PendingIntent sentPI, deliveredPI;
    BroadcastReceiver smsSentReceiver, smsDeliveredReceiver;

    /** Called when the activity is first created. */
    @Override
    public void onCreate(Bundle savedInstanceState) {
        super.onCreate(savedInstanceState);
        setContentView(R.layout.main);

        sentPI = PendingIntent.getBroadcast(this, 0,
                new Intent(SENT), 0);

        deliveredPI = PendingIntent.getBroadcast(this, 0,
                new Intent(DELIVERED), 0);
    }

    @Override
    public void onResume() {
        super.onResume();

        //---create the BroadcastReceiver when the SMS is sent---
        smsSentReceiver = new BroadcastReceiver(){
            @Override
            public void onReceive(Context arg0, Intent arg1) {
                switch (getResultCode())
```

```
                {
                case Activity.RESULT_OK:
                    Toast.makeText(getBaseContext(), "SMS sent",
                            Toast.LENGTH_SHORT).show();
                    break;
                case SmsManager.RESULT_ERROR_GENERIC_FAILURE:
                    Toast.makeText(getBaseContext(), "Generic failure",
                            Toast.LENGTH_SHORT).show();
                    break;
                case SmsManager.RESULT_ERROR_NO_SERVICE:
                    Toast.makeText(getBaseContext(), "No service",
                            Toast.LENGTH_SHORT).show();
                    break;
                case SmsManager.RESULT_ERROR_NULL_PDU:
                    Toast.makeText(getBaseContext(), "Null PDU",
                            Toast.LENGTH_SHORT).show();
                    break;
                case SmsManager.RESULT_ERROR_RADIO_OFF:
                    Toast.makeText(getBaseContext(), "Radio off",
                            Toast.LENGTH_SHORT).show();
                    break;
                }
            }
        };

        //---create the BroadcastReceiver when the SMS is delivered---
        smsDeliveredReceiver = new BroadcastReceiver(){
            @Override
            public void onReceive(Context arg0, Intent arg1) {
                switch (getResultCode())
                {
                case Activity.RESULT_OK:
                    Toast.makeText(getBaseContext(), "SMS delivered",
                            Toast.LENGTH_SHORT).show();
                    break;
                case Activity.RESULT_CANCELED:
                    Toast.makeText(getBaseContext(), "SMS not delivered",
                            Toast.LENGTH_SHORT).show();
                    break;
                }
            }
        };

        //---register the two BroadcastReceivers---
        registerReceiver(smsDeliveredReceiver, new IntentFilter(DELIVERED));
        registerReceiver(smsSentReceiver, new IntentFilter(SENT));
    }

    @Override
    public void onPause() {
        super.onPause();
        //---unregister the two BroadcastReceivers---
        unregisterReceiver(smsSentReceiver);
```

```
            unregisterReceiver(smsDeliveredReceiver);
    }

    public void onClick(View v) {
        sendSMS("5556", "Hello my friends!");
    }

    //---sends an SMS message to another device---
    private void sendSMS(String phoneNumber, String message)
    {
        SmsManager sms = SmsManager.getDefault();
        sms.sendTextMessage(phoneNumber, null, message, sentPI, deliveredPI);
    }
}
```

The preceding example created two PendingIntent objects in the onCreate() method:

```
sentPI = PendingIntent.getBroadcast(this, 0,
        new Intent(SENT), 0);

deliveredPI = PendingIntent.getBroadcast(this, 0,
        new Intent(DELIVERED), 0);
```

These two PendingIntent objects will be used to send broadcasts later when an SMS message has been sent ("SMS_SENT") and delivered ("SMS_DELIVERED").

In the onResume() method, you then created and registered two BroadcastReceivers. These two BroadcastReceivers listen for intents that match "SMS_SENT" and "SMS_DELIVERED" (which are fired by the SmsManager when the message has been sent and delivered, respectively):

```
//---register the two BroadcastReceivers---
registerReceiver(smsDeliveredReceiver, new IntentFilter(DELIVERED));
registerReceiver(smsSentReceiver, new IntentFilter(SENT));
```

Within each BroadcastReceiver you override the onReceive() method and get the current result code.

The two PendingIntent objects are passed into the last two arguments of the sendTextMessage() method:

```
SmsManager sms = SmsManager.getDefault();
sms.sendTextMessage(phoneNumber, null, message, sentPI, deliveredPI);
```

In this case, whether a message has been sent correctly or failed to be delivered, you will be notified of its status via the two PendingIntent objects.

Finally, in the onPause() method, you unregister the two BroadcastReceivers objects.

NOTE If you test the application on the Android emulator, only the sentPI PendingIntent object will be fired, but not the deliveredPI PendingIntent object. On a real device, both PendingIntent objects will fire.

Sending SMS Messages Using Intent

Using the `SmsManager` class, you can send SMS messages from within your application without the need to involve the built-in Messaging application. However, sometimes it would be easier if you could simply invoke the built-in Messaging application and let it do all the work of sending the message.

To activate the built-in Messaging application from within your application, you can use an `Intent` object together with the MIME type `"vnd.android-dir/mms-sms"`, as shown in the following code snippet:

```
Intent i = new
        Intent(android.content.Intent.ACTION_VIEW);
i.putExtra("address", "5556; 5558; 5560");

i.putExtra("sms_body", "Hello my friends!");
i.setType("vnd.android-dir/mms-sms");
startActivity(i);
```

This will invoke the Messaging application, as shown in Figure 8-2. Note that you can send your SMS to multiple recipients by simply separating each phone number with a semi-colon (in the `putExtra()` method). The numbers will be separated using commas in the Messaging application.

FIGURE 8-2

NOTE *If you use this method to invoke the Messaging application, there is no need to ask for the* SEND_SMS *permission in* AndroidManifest.xml *because your application is ultimately not the one sending the message.*

Receiving SMS Messages

Besides sending SMS messages from your Android applications, you can also receive incoming SMS messages from within your applications by using a BroadcastReceiver object. This is useful when you want your application to perform an action when a certain SMS message is received. For example, you might want to track the location of your phone in case it is lost or stolen. In this case, you can write an application that automatically listens for SMS messages containing some secret code. Once that message is received, you can then send an SMS message containing the location's coordinates back to the sender.

The following Try It Out shows how to programmatically listen for incoming SMS messages.

TRY IT OUT Receiving SMS Messages

1. Using the same project created in the previous section, add the following statements in bold to the AndroidManifest.xml file:

```xml
<?xml version="1.0" encoding="utf-8"?>
<manifest xmlns:android="http://schemas.android.com/apk/res/android"
    package="net.learn2develop.SMS"
    android:versionCode="1"
    android:versionName="1.0" >

    <uses-sdk android:minSdkVersion="10" />
    <uses-permission android:name="android.permission.SEND_SMS"/>
    <uses-permission android:name="android.permission.RECEIVE_SMS"/>

    <application
        android:icon="@drawable/ic_launcher"
        android:label="@string/app_name" >
        <activity
            android:label="@string/app_name"
            android:name=".SMSActivity" >
            <intent-filter >
                <action android:name="android.intent.action.MAIN" />
                <category android:name="android.intent.category.LAUNCHER" />
            </intent-filter>
        </activity>
        <receiver android:name=".SMSReceiver">
            <intent-filter>
                <action android:name=
                    "android.provider.Telephony.SMS_RECEIVED" />
            </intent-filter>
        </receiver>
    </application>

</manifest>
```

2. In the `src` folder of the project, add a new Class file to the package name and call it **SMSReceiver** (see Figure 8-3).

FIGURE 8-3

3. Code the `SMSReceiver.java` file as follows:

```
package net.learn2develop.SMS;

import android.content.BroadcastReceiver;
import android.content.Context;
import android.content.Intent;
import android.os.Bundle;
import android.telephony.SmsMessage;
import android.util.Log;
import android.widget.Toast;

public class SMSReceiver extends BroadcastReceiver
{
    @Override
    public void onReceive(Context context, Intent intent)
    {
        //---get the SMS message passed in---
        Bundle bundle = intent.getExtras();
        SmsMessage[] msgs = null;
        String str = "SMS from ";
        if (bundle != null)
```

```
        {
            //---retrieve the SMS message received---
            Object[] pdus = (Object[]) bundle.get("pdus");
            msgs = new SmsMessage[pdus.length];
            for (int i=0; i<msgs.length; i++){
                msgs[i] = SmsMessage.createFromPdu((byte[])pdus[i]);
                if (i==0) {
                    //---get the sender address/phone number---
                    str += msgs[i].getOriginatingAddress();
                    str += ": ";
                }
                //---get the message body---
                str += msgs[i].getMessageBody().toString();
            }
            //---display the new SMS message---
            Toast.makeText(context, str, Toast.LENGTH_SHORT).show();
            Log.d("SMSReceiver", str);
        }
    }
}
```

4. Press F11 to debug the application on the Android emulator.

5. Using the DDMS, send a message to the emulator. Your application should be able to receive the message and display it using the Toast class (see Figure 8-4).

FIGURE 8-4

How It Works

To listen for incoming SMS messages, you create a `BroadcastReceiver` class. The `BroadcastReceiver` class enables your application to receive intents sent by other applications using the `sendBroadcast()` method. Essentially, it enables your application to handle events raised by other applications. When an intent is received, the `onReceive()` method is called; hence, you need to override this.

When an incoming SMS message is received, the `onReceive()` method is fired. The SMS message is contained in the `Intent` object (`intent`; the second parameter in the `onReceive()` method) via a `Bundle` object. Note that each SMS message received will invoke the `onReceive()` method. If your device receives five SMS messages, then the `onReceive()` method will be called five times.

Each SMS message is stored in an `Object` array in the PDU format. If the SMS message is fewer than 160 characters, then the array will have one element. If an SMS message contains more than 160 characters, then the message will be split into multiple smaller messages and stored as multiple elements in the array.

To extract the content of each message, you use the static `createFromPdu()` method from the `SmsMessage` class. The phone number of the sender is obtained via the `getOriginatingAddress()` method; therefore, if you need to send an autoreply to the sender, this is the method to obtain the sender's phone number. To extract the body of the message, you use the `getMessageBody()` method.

One interesting characteristic of the `BroadcastReceiver` is that your application will continue to listen for incoming SMS messages even if it is not running; as long as the application is installed on the device, any incoming SMS messages will be received by the application.

Preventing the Messaging Application from Receiving a Message

In the previous section, you may have noticed that every time you send an SMS message to the emulator (or device), both your application and the built-in application receive it. This is because when an SMS message is received, all applications (including the Messaging application) on the Android device take turns handling the incoming message. Sometimes, however, this is not the behavior you want — for example, you might want your application to receive the message and prevent it from being sent to other applications. This is very useful, especially if you are building some kind of tracking application.

The solution is very simple. To prevent an incoming message from being handled by the built-in Messaging application, your application just needs to handle the message before the Messaging app has the chance to do so. To do this, add the `android:priority` attribute to the `<intent-filter>` element, like this:

```
<receiver android:name=".SMSReceiver">
    <intent-filter android:priority="100">
        <action android:name=
            "android.provider.Telephony.SMS_RECEIVED" />
    </intent-filter>
</receiver>
```

Set this attribute to a high number, such as 100. The higher the number, the earlier Android executes your application. When an incoming message is received, your application will execute first, and you can decide what to do with the message. To prevent other applications from seeing the message, simply call the `abortBroadcast()` method in your `BroadcastReceiver` class:

```
@Override
public void onReceive(Context context, Intent intent)
{
    //---get the SMS message passed in---
    Bundle bundle = intent.getExtras();
    SmsMessage[] msgs = null;
    String str = "SMS from ";
    if (bundle != null)
    {
        //---retrieve the SMS message received---
        Object[] pdus = (Object[]) bundle.get("pdus");
        msgs = new SmsMessage[pdus.length];
        for (int i=0; i<msgs.length; i++){
            msgs[i] = SmsMessage.createFromPdu((byte[])pdus[i]);
            if (i==0) {
                //---get the sender address/phone number---
                str += msgs[i].getOriginatingAddress();
                str += ": ";
            }
            //---get the message body---
            str += msgs[i].getMessageBody().toString();
        }

        //---display the new SMS message---
        Toast.makeText(context, str, Toast.LENGTH_SHORT).show();
        Log.d("SMSReceiver", str);

        //---stop the SMS message from being broadcasted---
        this.abortBroadcast();
    }
}
```

Once you do this, no other applications will be able to receive your SMS messages.

 NOTE *Be aware that after the preceding application is installed on your device, all incoming SMS messages will be intercepted by your application and will not appear in your Messaging application ever again.*

Updating an Activity from a BroadcastReceiver

The previous section demonstrated how you can use a `BroadcastReceiver` class to listen for incoming SMS messages and then use the `Toast` class to display the received SMS message. Often, you'll want to send the SMS message back to the main activity of your application. For example, you might wish to display the message in a `TextView`. The following Try It Out demonstrates how you can do this.

Creating a View-Based Application Project

1. Using the same project from the previous section, add the following lines in bold to the main.xml file:

```xml
<?xml version="1.0" encoding="utf-8"?>
<LinearLayout xmlns:android="http://schemas.android.com/apk/res/android"
    android:layout_width="fill_parent"
    android:layout_height="fill_parent"
    android:orientation="vertical" >

<Button
    android:id="@+id/btnSendSMS"
    android:layout_width="fill_parent"
    android:layout_height="wrap_content"
    android:text="Send SMS"
    android:onClick="onClick" />

<TextView
    android:id="@+id/textView1"
    android:layout_width="wrap_content"
    android:layout_height="wrap_content" />

</LinearLayout>
```

2. Add the following statements in bold to the SMSReceiver.java file:

```java
package net.learn2develop.SMS;

import android.content.BroadcastReceiver;
import android.content.Context;
import android.content.Intent;
import android.os.Bundle;
import android.telephony.SmsMessage;
import android.util.Log;
import android.widget.Toast;

public class SMSReceiver extends BroadcastReceiver
{
    @Override
    public void onReceive(Context context, Intent intent)
    {
        //---get the SMS message passed in---
        Bundle bundle = intent.getExtras();
        SmsMessage[] msgs = null;
        String str = "SMS from ";
        if (bundle != null)
        {
            //---retrieve the SMS message received---
            Object[] pdus = (Object[]) bundle.get("pdus");
                msgs = new SmsMessage[pdus.length];
            for (int i=0; i<msgs.length; i++){
                    msgs[i] = SmsMessage.createFromPdu((byte[])pdus[i]);
                if (i==0) {
```

```
                    //---get the sender address/phone number---
                    str += msgs[i].getOriginatingAddress();
                    str += ": ";
                }
                //---get the message body---
                str += msgs[i].getMessageBody().toString();
            }
            //---display the new SMS message---
            Toast.makeText(context, str, Toast.LENGTH_SHORT).show();
            Log.d("SMSReceiver", str);

            //---send a broadcast intent to update the SMS received in the activity---
            Intent broadcastIntent = new Intent();
            broadcastIntent.setAction("SMS_RECEIVED_ACTION");
            broadcastIntent.putExtra("sms", str);
            context.sendBroadcast(broadcastIntent);
        }
    }
}
```

3. Add the following statements in bold to the SMSActivity.java file:

```
package net.learn2develop.SMS;

import android.app.Activity;
import android.app.PendingIntent;
import android.content.BroadcastReceiver;
import android.content.Context;
import android.content.Intent;
import android.content.IntentFilter;
import android.os.Bundle;

import android.telephony.SmsManager;
import android.view.View;
import android.widget.TextView;
import android.widget.Toast;

public class SMSActivity extends Activity {
    String SENT = "SMS_SENT";
    String DELIVERED = "SMS_DELIVERED";
    PendingIntent sentPI, deliveredPI;
    BroadcastReceiver smsSentReceiver, smsDeliveredReceiver;
    IntentFilter intentFilter;

    private BroadcastReceiver intentReceiver = new BroadcastReceiver() {
        @Override
        public void onReceive(Context context, Intent intent) {
            //---display the SMS received in the TextView---
            TextView SMSes = (TextView) findViewById(R.id.textView1);
            SMSes.setText(intent.getExtras().getString("sms"));
        }
    };

    /** Called when the activity is first created. */
```

```java
@Override
public void onCreate(Bundle savedInstanceState) {
    super.onCreate(savedInstanceState);
    setContentView(R.layout.main);

    sentPI = PendingIntent.getBroadcast(this, 0,
            new Intent(SENT), 0);

    deliveredPI = PendingIntent.getBroadcast(this, 0,
            new Intent(DELIVERED), 0);

    //---intent to filter for SMS messages received---
    intentFilter = new IntentFilter();
    intentFilter.addAction("SMS_RECEIVED_ACTION");
}

@Override
public void onResume() {
    super.onResume();

    //---register the receiver---
    registerReceiver(intentReceiver, intentFilter);

    //---create the BroadcastReceiver when the SMS is sent---
    smsSentReceiver = new BroadcastReceiver(){
        @Override
        public void onReceive(Context arg0, Intent arg1) {
            switch (getResultCode())
            {
            case Activity.RESULT_OK:
                Toast.makeText(getBaseContext(), "SMS sent",
                        Toast.LENGTH_SHORT).show();
                break;
            case SmsManager.RESULT_ERROR_GENERIC_FAILURE:
                Toast.makeText(getBaseContext(), "Generic failure",
                        Toast.LENGTH_SHORT).show();
                break;
            case SmsManager.RESULT_ERROR_NO_SERVICE:
                Toast.makeText(getBaseContext(), "No service",
                        Toast.LENGTH_SHORT).show();
                break;
            case SmsManager.RESULT_ERROR_NULL_PDU:
                Toast.makeText(getBaseContext(), "Null PDU",
                        Toast.LENGTH_SHORT).show();
                break;
            case SmsManager.RESULT_ERROR_RADIO_OFF:
                Toast.makeText(getBaseContext(), "Radio off",
                        Toast.LENGTH_SHORT).show();
                break;
            }
        }
    };

    //---create the BroadcastReceiver when the SMS is delivered---
```

```java
        smsDeliveredReceiver = new BroadcastReceiver(){
            @Override
            public void onReceive(Context arg0, Intent arg1) {
                switch (getResultCode())
                {
                case Activity.RESULT_OK:
                    Toast.makeText(getBaseContext(), "SMS delivered",
                            Toast.LENGTH_SHORT).show();
                    break;
                case Activity.RESULT_CANCELED:
                    Toast.makeText(getBaseContext(), "SMS not delivered",
                            Toast.LENGTH_SHORT).show();
                    break;
                }
            }
        };

        //---register the two BroadcastReceivers---
        registerReceiver(smsDeliveredReceiver, new IntentFilter(DELIVERED));
        registerReceiver(smsSentReceiver, new IntentFilter(SENT));
    }

    @Override
    public void onPause() {
        super.onPause();

        //---unregister the receiver---
        unregisterReceiver(intentReceiver);

        //---unregister the two BroadcastReceivers---
        unregisterReceiver(smsSentReceiver);
        unregisterReceiver(smsDeliveredReceiver);
    }

    public void onClick(View v) {
        sendSMS("5556", "Hello my friends!");
    }

    public void onSMSIntentClick (View v) {
        Intent i = new
                Intent(android.content.Intent.ACTION_VIEW);
        i.putExtra("address", "5556; 5558; 5560");

        i.putExtra("sms_body", "Hello my friends!");
        i.setType("vnd.android-dir/mms-sms");
        startActivity(i);
    }

    //---sends an SMS message to another device---
    private void sendSMS(String phoneNumber, String message)
    {
        SmsManager sms = SmsManager.getDefault();
        sms.sendTextMessage(phoneNumber, null, message, sentPI, deliveredPI);
    }
}
```

4. Press F11 to debug the application on the Android emulator. Using the DDMS, send an SMS message to the emulator. Figure 8-5 shows the `Toast` class displaying the message received, and the `TextView` showing the message received.

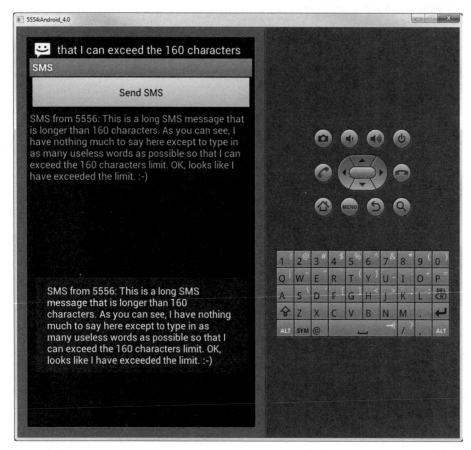

FIGURE 8-5

How It Works

You first added a `TextView` to your activity so that it can be used to display the received SMS message.

Next, you modified the `SMSReceiver` class so that when it receives an SMS message, it broadcasts another `Intent` object so that any applications listening for this intent can be notified (which you will implement in the activity next). The SMS received is also sent out via this intent:

```
//---send a broadcast intent to update the SMS received in the activity---
Intent broadcastIntent = new Intent();
broadcastIntent.setAction("SMS_RECEIVED_ACTION");
broadcastIntent.putExtra("sms", str);
context.sendBroadcast(broadcastIntent);
```

Next, in your activity you created a `BroadcastReceiver` object to listen for broadcast intents:

```java
private BroadcastReceiver intentReceiver = new BroadcastReceiver() {
    @Override
    public void onReceive(Context context, Intent intent) {
        //---display the SMS received in the TextView---
        TextView SMSes = (TextView) findViewById(R.id.textView1);
        SMSes.setText(intent.getExtras().getString("sms"));
    }
};
```

When a broadcast intent is received, you update the SMS message in the `TextView`.

You need to create an `IntentFilter` object so that you can listen for a particular intent. In this case, the intent is `"SMS_RECEIVED_ACTION"`:

```java
@Override
public void onCreate(Bundle savedInstanceState) {
    super.onCreate(savedInstanceState);
    setContentView(R.layout.main);

    sentPI = PendingIntent.getBroadcast(this, 0,
            new Intent(SENT), 0);

    deliveredPI = PendingIntent.getBroadcast(this, 0,
            new Intent(DELIVERED), 0);

    //---intent to filter for SMS messages received---
    intentFilter = new IntentFilter();
    intentFilter.addAction("SMS_RECEIVED_ACTION");
}
```

Finally, you register the `BroadcastReceiver` in the activity's `onResume()` event and unregister it in the `onPause()` event:

```java
@Override
protected void onResume() {
    //--register the receiver--
    registerReceiver(intentReceiver, intentFilter);
    super.onResume();
}

@Override
protected void onPause() {
    //--unregister the receiver--
    unregisterReceiver(intentReceiver);
    super.onPause();
}


@Override
public void onResume() {
    super.onResume();

    //---register the receiver---
```

```
        registerReceiver(intentReceiver, intentFilter);

        //---create the BroadcastReceiver when the SMS is sent---
        //...
    }

    @Override
    public void onPause() {
        super.onPause();

        //---unregister the receiver---
        unregisterReceiver(intentReceiver);

        //---unregister the two BroadcastReceivers---
        //...
    }
```

This means that the TextView will display the SMS message only when the message is received while the activity is visible on the screen. If the SMS message is received when the activity is not in the foreground, the TextView will not be updated.

Invoking an Activity from a BroadcastReceiver

The previous example shows how you can pass the SMS message received to be displayed in the activity. However, in many situations your activity may be in the background when the SMS message is received. In this case, it would be useful to be able to bring the activity to the foreground when a message is received. The following Try It Out shows you how.

TRY IT OUT   Invoking an Activity

1.   Using the same project used in the previous section, add the following lines in bold to the SMSActivity.java file:

```
    /** Called when the activity is first created. */
    @Override
    public void onCreate(Bundle savedInstanceState) {
        super.onCreate(savedInstanceState);
        setContentView(R.layout.main);

        sentPI = PendingIntent.getBroadcast(this, 0,
                new Intent(SENT), 0);

        deliveredPI = PendingIntent.getBroadcast(this, 0,
                new Intent(DELIVERED), 0);

        //---intent to filter for SMS messages received---
        intentFilter = new IntentFilter();
        intentFilter.addAction("SMS_RECEIVED_ACTION");

        //---register the receiver---
```

```java
        registerReceiver(intentReceiver, intentFilter);
}

@Override
public void onResume() {
    super.onResume();

    //---register the receiver---
    //registerReceiver(intentReceiver, intentFilter);

    //---create the BroadcastReceiver when the SMS is sent---
    smsSentReceiver = new BroadcastReceiver(){
        @Override
        public void onReceive(Context arg0, Intent arg1) {
            switch (getResultCode())
            {
            case Activity.RESULT_OK:
                Toast.makeText(getBaseContext(), "SMS sent",
                        Toast.LENGTH_SHORT).show();
                break;
            case SmsManager.RESULT_ERROR_GENERIC_FAILURE:
                Toast.makeText(getBaseContext(), "Generic failure",
                        Toast.LENGTH_SHORT).show();
                break;
            case SmsManager.RESULT_ERROR_NO_SERVICE:
                Toast.makeText(getBaseContext(), "No service",
                        Toast.LENGTH_SHORT).show();
                break;
            case SmsManager.RESULT_ERROR_NULL_PDU:
                Toast.makeText(getBaseContext(), "Null PDU",
                        Toast.LENGTH_SHORT).show();
                break;
            case SmsManager.RESULT_ERROR_RADIO_OFF:
                Toast.makeText(getBaseContext(), "Radio off",
                        Toast.LENGTH_SHORT).show();
                break;
            }
        }
    };

    //---create the BroadcastReceiver when the SMS is delivered---
    smsDeliveredReceiver = new BroadcastReceiver(){
        @Override
        public void onReceive(Context arg0, Intent arg1) {
            switch (getResultCode())
            {
            case Activity.RESULT_OK:
                Toast.makeText(getBaseContext(), "SMS delivered",
                        Toast.LENGTH_SHORT).show();
                break;
            case Activity.RESULT_CANCELED:
                Toast.makeText(getBaseContext(), "SMS not delivered",
                        Toast.LENGTH_SHORT).show();
                break;
```

```
                }
            }
        };

        //---register the two BroadcastReceivers---
        registerReceiver(smsDeliveredReceiver, new IntentFilter(DELIVERED));
        registerReceiver(smsSentReceiver, new IntentFilter(SENT));
    }

    @Override
    public void onPause() {
        super.onPause();

        //---unregister the receiver---
        //unregisterReceiver(intentReceiver);

        //---unregister the two BroadcastReceivers---
        unregisterReceiver(smsSentReceiver);
        unregisterReceiver(smsDeliveredReceiver);
    }

    @Override
    protected void onDestroy() {
        super.onDestroy();

        //---unregister the receiver---
        unregisterReceiver(intentReceiver);
    }
```

2. Add the following statements in bold to the SMSReceiver.java file:

```
    @Override
    public void onReceive(Context context, Intent intent)
    {
        //---get the SMS message passed in---
        Bundle bundle = intent.getExtras();
        SmsMessage[] msgs = null;
        String str = "SMS from ";
        if (bundle != null)
        {
            //---retrieve the SMS message received---
            Object[] pdus = (Object[]) bundle.get("pdus");
            msgs = new SmsMessage[pdus.length];
            for (int i=0; i<msgs.length; i++){
                msgs[i] = SmsMessage.createFromPdu((byte[])pdus[i]);
                if (i==0) {
                    //---get the sender address/phone number---
                    str += msgs[i].getOriginatingAddress();
                    str += ": ";
                }
                //---get the message body---
                str += msgs[i].getMessageBody().toString();
            }
            //---display the new SMS message---
```

```
Toast.makeText(context, str, Toast.LENGTH_SHORT).show();
Log.d("SMSReceiver", str);

//---launch the SMSActivity---
Intent mainActivityIntent = new Intent(context, SMSActivity.class);
mainActivityIntent.setFlags(Intent.FLAG_ACTIVITY_NEW_TASK);
context.startActivity(mainActivityIntent);

//---send a broadcast intent to update the SMS received in the activity---
Intent broadcastIntent = new Intent();
broadcastIntent.setAction("SMS_RECEIVED_ACTION");
broadcastIntent.putExtra("sms", str);
context.sendBroadcast(broadcastIntent);
    }
}
```

3. Modify the `AndroidManifest.xml` file as follows:

```
<activity
    android:label="@string/app_name"
    android:name=".SMSActivity"
    android:launchMode="singleTask" >
    <intent-filter >
        <action android:name="android.intent.action.MAIN" />
        <category android:name="android.intent.category.LAUNCHER" />
    </intent-filter>
</activity>
```

4. Press F11 to debug the application on the Android emulator. When the SMSActivity is shown, click the Home button to send the activity to the background.

5. Use the DDMS to send an SMS message to the emulator again. This time, note that the activity will be brought to the foreground, displaying the SMS message received.

How It Works

In the SMSActivity class, you first registered the BroadcastReceiver in the activity's onCreate() event, instead of the onResume() event; and instead of unregistering it in the onPause() event, you unregister it in the onDestroy() event. This ensures that even if the activity is in the background, it will still be able to listen for the broadcast intent.

Next, you modified the onReceive() event in the SMSReceiver class by using an intent to bring the activity to the foreground before broadcasting another intent:

```
//---launch the SMSActivity---
Intent mainActivityIntent = new Intent(context, SMSActivity.class);
mainActivityIntent.setFlags(Intent.FLAG_ACTIVITY_NEW_TASK);
context.startActivity(mainActivityIntent);

//---send a broadcast intent to update the SMS received in the activity---
Intent broadcastIntent = new Intent();
broadcastIntent.setAction("SMS_RECEIVED_ACTION");
broadcastIntent.putExtra("sms", str);
context.sendBroadcast(broadcastIntent);
```

The startActivity() method launches the activity and brings it to the foreground. Note that you needed to set the Intent.FLAG_ACTIVITY_NEW_TASK flag because calling startActivity() from outside of an activity context requires the FLAG_ACTIVITY_NEW_TASK flag.

You also needed to set the launchMode attribute of the <activity> element in the AndroidManifest .xml file to singleTask:

```
<activity
    android:label="@string/app_name"
    android:name=".SMSActivity"
    android:launchMode="singleTask" >
```

If you don't set this, multiple instances of the activity will be launched as your application receives SMS messages.

Note that in this example, when the activity is in the background (such as when you click the Home button to show the home screen), the activity is brought to the foreground and its TextView is updated with the SMS received. However, if the activity was killed (such as when you click the Back button to destroy it), the activity is launched again but the TextView is not updated.

Caveats and Warnings

While the capability to send and receive SMS messages makes Android a very compelling platform for developing sophisticated applications, this flexibility comes with a price. A seemingly innocent application may send SMS messages behind the scene without the user knowing, as demonstrated by a recent case of an SMS-based Trojan Android application (see http://forum.vodafone.co.nz/ topic/5719-android-sms-trojan-warning/). Claiming to be a media player, once installed, the application sends SMS messages to a premium-rate number, resulting in huge phone bills for the user.

While the user needs to explicitly give permissions (such as accessing the Internet, sending and receiving SMS messages, etc.) to your application, the request for permissions is shown only at installation time. If the user clicks the Install button, he or she is considered to have granted the application permission to send and receive SMS messages. This is dangerous, as after the application is installed it can send and receive SMS messages without ever prompting the user again.

In addition to this, the application can also "sniff" for incoming SMS messages. For example, based on the techniques you learned from the previous section, you can easily write an application that checks for certain keywords in the SMS message. When an SMS message contains the keyword you are looking for, you can then use the Location Manager (discussed in Chapter 9) to obtain your geographical location and then send the coordinates back to the sender of the SMS message. The sender could then easily track your location. All these tasks can be done easily without the user knowing it! That said, users should try to avoid installing Android applications that come from dubious sources, such as from unknown websites or strangers.

SENDING E-MAIL

Like SMS messaging, Android also supports e-mail. The Gmail/Email application on Android enables you to configure an e-mail account using POP3 or IMAP. Besides sending and receiving e-mails using the Gmail/Email application, you can also send e-mail messages programmatically from within your Android application. The following Try It Out shows you how.

TRY IT OUT Sending E-mail Programmatically

codefile Emails.zip available for download at Wrox.com

1. Using Eclipse, create a new Android project and name it **Emails**.

2. Add the following statements in bold to the `main.xml` file, replacing the `TextView`:

```xml
<?xml version="1.0" encoding="utf-8"?>
<LinearLayout xmlns:android="http://schemas.android.com/apk/res/android"
    android:layout_width="fill_parent"
    android:layout_height="fill_parent"
    android:orientation="vertical" >

<Button
    android:id="@+id/btnSendEmail"
    android:layout_width="fill_parent"
    android:layout_height="wrap_content"
    android:text="Send Email"
    android:onClick="onClick" />

</LinearLayout>
```

3. Add the following statements in bold to the `SMSActivity.java` file:

```java
package net.learn2develop.Emails;

import android.app.Activity;
import android.content.Intent;
import android.net.Uri;
import android.os.Bundle;
import android.view.View;

public class EmailsActivity extends Activity {
    /** Called when the activity is first created. */
    @Override
    public void onCreate(Bundle savedInstanceState) {
        super.onCreate(savedInstanceState);
        setContentView(R.layout.main);
    }

    public void onClick(View v) {
        //---replace the following email addresses with real ones---
        String[] to =
```

```
            {"someguy@example.com",
             "anotherguy@example.com"};
        String[] cc = {"busybody@example.com"};
        sendEmail(to, cc, "Hello", "Hello my friends!");
    }

    //---sends an SMS message to another device---
    private void sendEmail(String[] emailAddresses, String[] carbonCopies,
    String subject, String message)
    {
        Intent emailIntent = new Intent(Intent.ACTION_SEND);
        emailIntent.setData(Uri.parse("mailto:"));
        String[] to = emailAddresses;
        String[] cc = carbonCopies;
        emailIntent.putExtra(Intent.EXTRA_EMAIL, to);
        emailIntent.putExtra(Intent.EXTRA_CC, cc);
        emailIntent.putExtra(Intent.EXTRA_SUBJECT, subject);
        emailIntent.putExtra(Intent.EXTRA_TEXT, message);
        emailIntent.setType("message/rfc822");
        startActivity(Intent.createChooser(emailIntent, "Email"));
    }
}
```

4. Press F11 to test the application on the Android emulator/device (ensure that you have configured your e-mail before trying this example). Click the Send Email button and you should see the Email application launched in your emulator/device, as shown in Figure 8-6.

FIGURE 8-6

AN E-MAIL TIP FOR TESTING PURPOSES

If you are a gmail user, for testing purposes you can take advantage of the fact that you can append the plus sign (+) and any string to the user name of your account. You will continue to receive the e-mail as usual, but it can be used for filtering. For example, my Gmail account is weimenglee@gmail.com. When I am doing testing I will configure the recipient address as "weimenglee+android_book@gmail.com" and then I can easily filter out those messages for deletion later. In addition, I can also add periods to my Gmail address. For example, if you want to test sending an e-mail to a couple of people, you can send to weimeng.lee@gmail.com, wei.meng .lee@gmail.com, and wei.menglee@gmail.com; an e-mail to all these e-mail addresses will end up in my weimenglee@gmail.com account as a single message. This is very useful for testing!

Finally, take a look at http://smtp4dev.codeplex.com, which contains a dummy SMTP server that allows you to debug e-mail messages.

How It Works

In this example, you are launching the built-in Email application to send an e-mail message. To do so, you use an `Intent` object and set the various parameters using the `setData()`, `putExtra()`, and `setType()` methods:

```
Intent emailIntent = new Intent(Intent.ACTION_SEND);
emailIntent.setData(Uri.parse("mailto:"));
String[] to = emailAddresses;
String[] cc = carbonCopies;
emailIntent.putExtra(Intent.EXTRA_EMAIL, to);
emailIntent.putExtra(Intent.EXTRA_CC, cc);
emailIntent.putExtra(Intent.EXTRA_SUBJECT, subject);
emailIntent.putExtra(Intent.EXTRA_TEXT, message);
emailIntent.setType("message/rfc822");
startActivity(Intent.createChooser(emailIntent, "Email"));
```

SUMMARY

This chapter described the two key ways for your application to communicate with the outside world. You first learned how to send and receive SMS messages. Using SMS, you can build a wide variety of applications that rely on the service provided by your mobile operator. Chapter 9 shows you a good example of how to use SMS messaging to build a location tracker application.

You also learned how to send e-mail messages from within your Android application. You do that by invoking the built-in Email application through the use of an `Intent` object.

EXERCISES

1. Name the two ways in which you can send SMS messages in your Android application.

2. Name the permissions you need to declare in your `AndroidManifest.xml` file for sending and receiving SMS messages.

3. How do you notify an activity from a `BroadcastReceiver`?

Answers to the exercises can be found in Appendix C.

▶ **WHAT YOU LEARNED IN THIS CHAPTER**

TOPIC	KEY CONCEPTS
Programmatically sending SMS messages	Use the SmsManager class.
Getting feedback on messages sent	Use two **PendingIntent** objects in the sendTextMessage() method.
Sending SMS messages using Intent	Set the intent type to vnd.android-dir/mms-sms.
Receiving SMS messages	Implement a BroadcastReceiver and set it in the **AndroidManifest.xml** file.
Sending e-mail using Intent	Set the intent type to message/rfc822.

Location-Based Services

WHAT YOU WILL LEARN IN THIS CHAPTER

➤ Displaying Google Maps in your Android application

➤ Displaying zoom controls on the map

➤ Switching between the different map views

➤ Adding markers to maps

➤ How to get the address location touched on the map

➤ Performing geocoding and reverse geocoding

➤ Obtaining geographical data using GPS, Cell-ID, and Wi-Fi triangulation

➤ How to monitor for a location

➤ Building a Location Tracker application

You have all seen the explosive growth of mobile apps in recent years. One category of apps that is very popular is location-based services, commonly known as LBS. LBS apps track your location, and may offer additional services such as locating amenities nearby, as well as offer suggestions for route planning, and so on. Of course, one of the key ingredients in an LBS app is maps, which present a visual representation of your location.

In this chapter, you will learn how to make use of Google Maps in your Android application, and how to manipulate it programmatically. In addition, you will learn how to obtain your geographical location using the `LocationManager` class available in the Android SDK. This chapter ends with a project to build a Location Tracker application that you can install on an Android device and can use to track the location of friends and relatives using SMS messaging.

DISPLAYING MAPS

Google Maps is one of the many applications bundled with the Android platform. In addition to simply using the Maps application, you can also embed it into your own applications and make it do some very cool things. This section describes how to use Google Maps in your Android applications and programmatically perform the following:

➤ Change the views of Google Maps.

➤ Obtain the latitude and longitude of locations in Google Maps.

➤ Perform geocoding and reverse geocoding (translating an address to latitude and longitude and vice versa).

➤ Add markers to Google Maps.

Creating the Project

To get started, you need to first create an Android project so that you can display Google Maps in your activity.

TRY IT OUT Creating the Google APIs Project

codefile LBS.zip available for download at Wrox.com

1. Using Eclipse, create an Android project and name it **LBS**.

> **NOTE** *In order to use Google Maps in your Android application, you need to ensure that you check the Google APIs as your build target. Google Maps is not part of the standard Android SDK, so you need to find it in the Google APIs add-on.*

2. Once the project is created, note the additional JAR file (maps.jar) located under the Google APIs folder (see Figure 9-1).

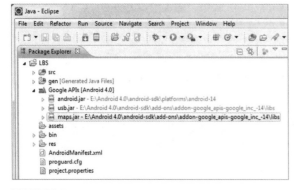

FIGURE 9-1

How It Works

This simple activity created an Android project that uses the Google APIs add-on. The Google APIs add-on, besides including the standard Android and USB libraries, also includes the Maps library, packaged within the `maps.jar` file.

Obtaining the Maps API Key

Beginning with the Android SDK release v1.0, you need to apply for a free Google Maps API key before you can integrate Google Maps into your Android application. When you apply for the key, you must also agree to Google's terms of use, so be sure to read them carefully.

To apply for a key, follow the series of steps outlined next.

 NOTE *Google provides detailed documentation about applying for a Maps API key at* `http://code.google.com/android/add-ons/google-apis/ mapkey.html`.

First, if you are testing the application on the Android emulator or an Android device directly connected to your development machine, locate the SDK debug certificate located in the default folder (`C:\Users\<username>\.android` for Windows 7 users). You can verify the existence of the debug certificate by going to Eclipse and selecting Window ⇨ Preferences. Expand the Android item and select Build (see Figure 9-2). On the right side of the window, you can see the debug certificate's location.

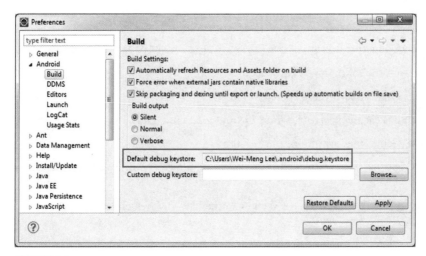

FIGURE 9-2

NOTE *For Windows XP users, the default Android folder is* `C:\Documents and Settings\<username>\Local Settings\Application Data\Android.`

The filename of the debug keystore is `debug.keystore`. This is the certificate that Eclipse uses to sign your application so that it may be run on the Android emulator or devices.

Using the debug keystore, you need to extract its MD5 fingerprint using the `Keytool.exe` application included with your JDK installation. This fingerprint is needed to apply for the free Google Maps key. You can usually find the `Keytool.exe` in the `C:\Program Files\Java\<JDK_version_number>\bin` folder.

Issue the following command (see also Figure 9-3) to extract the MD5 fingerprint:

```
keytool.exe -list -alias androiddebugkey -keystore
"C:\Users\<username>\.android\debug.keystore" -storepass android
-keypass android -v
```

```
C:\Program Files\Java\jre6\bin>keytool.exe -list -alias androiddebugkey -keystor
e "C:\Users\Wei-Meng Lee\.android\debug.keystore" -storepass android -keypass an
droid -v
Alias name: androiddebugkey
Creation date: Jul 4, 2011
Entry type: PrivateKeyEntry
Certificate chain length: 1
Certificate[1]:
Owner: CN=Android Debug, O=Android, C=US
Issuer: CN=Android Debug, O=Android, C=US
Serial number: 4e11b37d
Valid from: Mon Jul 04 20:35:09 SGT 2011 until: Tue Jul 03 20:35:09 SGT 2012
Certificate fingerprints:
         MD5:  5C:67:CE:30:82:C3:58:08:88:2D:CE:56:27:80:50:EB
         SHA1: D9:12:F3:5D:D3:4H:0D:10:06:85:H4:57:54:7E:89:C5:87:DF:62:5F
         Signature algorithm name: SHA1withRSA
         Version: 3

C:\Program Files\Java\jre6\bin>_
```

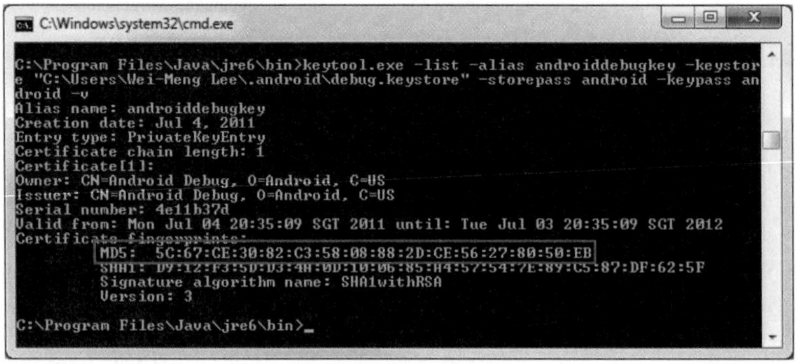

FIGURE 9-3

In this example, my MD5 fingerprint is `5C:67:CE:30:82:C3:58:08:88:2D:CE:56:27:80:50:EB.`

In the preceding command, the following arguments are used:

➤ `-list` — Shows details about the specified keystore

➤ `-alias` — The alias for the keystore, which is "`androiddebugkey`" for `debug.keystore`

➤ `-keystore` — Specifies the location of the keystore

➤ `-storepass` — Specifies the password for the keystore, which is "`android`" for `debug.keystore`

➤ `-keypass` — Specifies the password for the key in the keystore, which is "`android`" for `debug.keystore`

Copy the MD5 certificate fingerprint and navigate your web browser to: `http://code.google.com/android/maps-api-signup.html.` Follow the instructions on the page to complete the application and obtain the Google Maps key. When you are done, you should see something similar to what is shown in Figure 9-4.

FIGURE 9-4

 NOTE *Although you can use the MD5 fingerprint of the debug keystore to obtain the Maps API key for debugging your application on the Android emulator or devices, the key will not be valid if you try to deploy your Android application as an APK file. Once you are ready to deploy your application to the Android Market (or other methods of distribution), you need to reapply for a Maps API key using the certificate that will be used to sign your application. Chapter 12 discusses this topic in more detail.*

Displaying the Map

You are now ready to display Google Maps in your Android application. This involves two main tasks:

➤   Modify your `AndroidManifest.xml` file by adding both the `<uses-library>` element and the `INTERNET` permission.

➤   Add the `MapView` element to your UI.

The following Try It Out shows you how.

TRY IT OUT Displaying Google Maps

1. Using the project created in the previous section, replace the TextView with the following lines in bold in the main.xml file. (Be sure to replace the value of the android:apiKey attribute with the API key you obtained earlier):

```xml
<?xml version="1.0" encoding="utf-8"?>
<LinearLayout xmlns:android="http://schemas.android.com/apk/res/android"
    android:layout_width="fill_parent"
    android:layout_height="fill_parent"
    android:orientation="vertical" >

<com.google.android.maps.MapView
    android:id="@+id/mapView"
    android:layout_width="fill_parent"
    android:layout_height="fill_parent"
    android:enabled="true"
    android:clickable="true"
    android:apiKey="0AeGR0UwGH4pYmhcwaA9JF5mMEtrmwFe8RobTHA" />

</LinearLayout>
```

2. Add the following lines in bold to the AndroidManifest.xml file:

```xml
<?xml version="1.0" encoding="utf-8"?>
<manifest xmlns:android="http://schemas.android.com/apk/res/android"
    package="net.learn2develop.LBS"
    android:versionCode="1"
    android:versionName="1.0" >

    <uses-sdk android:minSdkVersion="14" />
    <uses-permission android:name="android.permission.INTERNET"/>

    <application
        android:icon="@drawable/ic_launcher"
        android:label="@string/app_name" >
        <uses-library android:name="com.google.android.maps" />
        <activity
            android:label="@string/app_name"
            android:name=".LBSActivity" >
            <intent-filter >
                <action android:name="android.intent.action.MAIN" />
                <category android:name="android.intent.category.LAUNCHER" />
            </intent-filter>
        </activity>
    </application>

</manifest>
```

3. Add the following statements in bold to the LBSActivity.java file. Note that LBSActivity should now extend the MapActivity base class.

```
package net.learn2develop.LBS;

import com.google.android.maps.MapActivity;
import android.os.Bundle;

public class LBSActivity extends MapActivity {
    /** Called when the activity is first created. */
    @Override
    public void onCreate(Bundle savedInstanceState) {
        super.onCreate(savedInstanceState);
        setContentView(R.layout.main);
    }

    @Override
    protected boolean isRouteDisplayed() {
        // TODO Auto-generated method stub
        return false;
    }
}
```

4. Press F11 to debug the application on the Android emulator. Figure 9-5 shows Google Maps displaying in the activity of the application.

FIGURE 9-5

How It Works

In order to display Google Maps in your application, you first needed the INTERNET permission in your manifest file. You then added the <com.google.android.maps.MapView> element to your UI file to embed the map within your activity. It is very important that your activity extends the MapActivity base class, which itself is an extension of the Activity class. For the MapActivity class, you need to implement one method: isRouteDisplayed(). This method is used for Google's accounting purposes, and you should return true for this method if you are displaying routing information on the map. For most simple cases, you can simply return false.

In order to test your application on the Android emulator, be sure to create an AVD with the Google Maps API chosen as the selected target.

CAN'T SEE THE MAP?

If instead of seeing Google Maps displayed you see an empty screen with grids, then most likely you are using the wrong API key in the main.xml file. It is also possible that you omitted the INTERNET permission in your AndroidManifest.xml file. Finally, ensure that you have Internet access on your emulator/devices.

If your program does not run (i.e., it crashes), then you probably forgot to add the following statement to the AndroidManifest.xml file:

```
<uses-library android:name="com.google.android.maps" />
```

Note its placement in the file; it should be located within the <Application> element.

Displaying the Zoom Control

The previous section showed how you can display Google Maps in your Android application. You can pan the map to any desired location and it will be updated on-the-fly. However, on the emulator there is no way to zoom in or out from a particular location (on a real Android device you can pinch the map to zoom it). Thus, in this section, you will learn how you can enable users to zoom in or out of the map using the built-in zoom controls.

TRY IT OUT   Displaying the Built-In Zoom Controls

1. Using the project created in the previous section, add the following statements in bold:

```
package net.learn2develop.LBS;

import com.google.android.maps.MapActivity;
import com.google.android.maps.MapView;

import android.os.Bundle;

public class LBSActivity extends MapActivity {
```

```
MapView mapView;
/** Called when the activity is first created. */
@Override
public void onCreate(Bundle savedInstanceState) {
    super.onCreate(savedInstanceState);
    setContentView(R.layout.main);

    mapView = (MapView) findViewById(R.id.mapView);
    mapView.setBuiltInZoomControls(true);
}

@Override
protected boolean isRouteDisplayed() {
    // TODO Auto-generated method stub
    return false;
}
}
```

2. Press F11 to debug the application on the Android emulator. Observe the built-in zoom controls that appear at the bottom of the map when you click and drag the map (see Figure 9-6). You can click the minus (–) icon to zoom out of the map, and the plus (+) icon to zoom into the map.

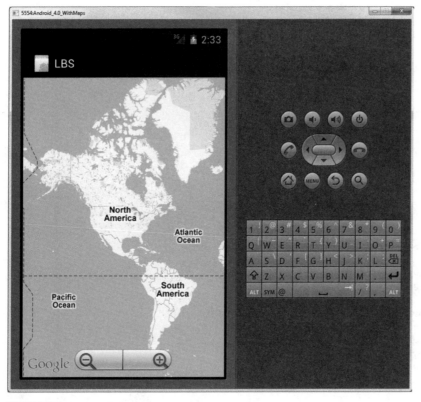

FIGURE 9-6

How It Works

To display the built-in zoom controls, you first get a reference to the MapView and then call the setBuiltInZoomControls() method:

```
mapView = (MapView) findViewById(R.id.mapView);
mapView.setBuiltInZoomControls(true);
```

Besides displaying the zoom controls, you can also programmatically zoom in or out of the map using the zoomIn() or zoomOut() method of the MapController class. The following Try It Out shows you how to achieve this.

TRY IT OUT Programmatically Zooming In or Out of the Map

1. Using the project created in the previous section, add the following statements in bold to the LBSActivity.java file:

```
package net.learn2develop.LBS;

import com.google.android.maps.MapActivity;
import com.google.android.maps.MapController;
import com.google.android.maps.MapView;

import android.os.Bundle;
import android.view.KeyEvent;

public class LBSActivity extends MapActivity {
    MapView mapView;
    /** Called when the activity is first created. */
    @Override
    public void onCreate(Bundle savedInstanceState) {
        super.onCreate(savedInstanceState);
        setContentView(R.layout.main);

        mapView = (MapView) findViewById(R.id.mapView);
        mapView.setBuiltInZoomControls(true);
    }

    public boolean onKeyDown(int keyCode, KeyEvent event)
    {
        MapController mc = mapView.getController();
        switch (keyCode)
        {
            case KeyEvent.KEYCODE_3:
                mc.zoomIn();
                break;
            case KeyEvent.KEYCODE_1:
                mc.zoomOut();
                break;
        }
```

```
        return super.onKeyDown(keyCode, event);
    }

    @Override
    protected boolean isRouteDisplayed() {
        // TODO Auto-generated method stub
        return false;
    }
}
```

2. Press F11 to debug the application on the Android emulator. You can now zoom into the map by clicking the numeric 3 key on the emulator. To zoom out of the map, click the numeric 1 key.

How It Works

To handle key presses on your activity, you handle the onKeyDown event:

```
public boolean onKeyDown(int keyCode, KeyEvent event)
{
    MapController mc = mapView.getController();
    switch (keyCode)
    {
        case KeyEvent.KEYCODE_3:
            mc.zoomIn();
            break;
        case KeyEvent.KEYCODE_1:
            mc.zoomOut();
            break;
    }
    return super.onKeyDown(keyCode, event);
}
```

To manage the panning and zooming of the map, you need to obtain an instance of the MapController class from the MapView object. The MapController class contains the zoomIn() and zoomOut() methods (plus some other methods to control the map) to enable users to zoom in or out of the map, respectively.

Note that if you deploy the application on a real Android device, you may not be able to test the zooming feature, as most Android devices today do not have a physical keyboard.

Changing Views

By default, Google Maps is displayed in *map view*, which is basically drawings of streets and places of interest. You can also set Google Maps to display in *satellite view* using the setSatellite() method of the MapView class:

```
@Override
public void onCreate(Bundle savedInstanceState) {
    super.onCreate(savedInstanceState);
```

```
        setContentView(R.layout.main);

        mapView = (MapView) findViewById(R.id.mapView);
        mapView.setBuiltInZoomControls(true);
        mapView.setSatellite(true);
    }
```

Figure 9-7 shows Google Maps displayed in satellite view.

FIGURE 9-7

If you want to display traffic conditions on the map, use the `setTraffic()` method:

```
    @Override
    public void onCreate(Bundle savedInstanceState) {
        super.onCreate(savedInstanceState);
        setContentView(R.layout.main);

        mapView = (MapView) findViewById(R.id.mapView);
        mapView.setBuiltInZoomControls(true);
        mapView.setSatellite(true);
        mapView.setTraffic(true);
    }
```

Figure 9-8 shows the map displaying the current traffic conditions (you have to zoom in to see the roads). The different colors reflect the varying traffic conditions. In general, green equates to smooth traffic of about 50 miles per hour, yellow equates to moderate traffic of about 25–50 miles per hour, and red equates to slow traffic about less than 25 miles per hour.

FIGURE 9-8

Note that the traffic information is available only in major cities in the United States, France, Britain, Australia, and Canada, with new cities and countries frequently added.

Navigating to a Specific Location

By default, Google Maps displays the map of the United States when it is first loaded. However, you can set Google Maps to display a particular location. To do so, you can use the `animateTo()` method of the `MapController` class.

The following Try It Out shows how you can programmatically animate Google Maps to a particular location.

TRY IT OUT   Navigating the Map to Display a Specific Location

1. Using the project created in the previous section, add the following statements in bold to the LBSActivity.java file:

```java
package net.learn2develop.LBS;

import com.google.android.maps.GeoPoint;
import com.google.android.maps.MapActivity;
import com.google.android.maps.MapController;
import com.google.android.maps.MapView;

import android.os.Bundle;
import android.view.KeyEvent;

public class LBSActivity extends MapActivity {
    MapView mapView;
    MapController mc;
    GeoPoint p;

    /** Called when the activity is first created. */
    @Override
    public void onCreate(Bundle savedInstanceState) {
        super.onCreate(savedInstanceState);
        setContentView(R.layout.main);

        mapView = (MapView) findViewById(R.id.mapView);
        mapView.setBuiltInZoomControls(true);
        mapView.setSatellite(true);
        mapView.setTraffic(true);

        mc = mapView.getController();
        String coordinates[] = {"1.352566007", "103.78921587"};
        double lat = Double.parseDouble(coordinates[0]);
        double lng = Double.parseDouble(coordinates[1]);

        p = new GeoPoint(
            (int) (lat * 1E6),
            (int) (lng * 1E6));

        mc.animateTo(p);
        mc.setZoom(13);
        mapView.invalidate();
    }

    public boolean onKeyDown(int keyCode, KeyEvent event)
    {
        //...
    }

    @Override
    protected boolean isRouteDisplayed() {
        //...
    }
}
```

2. Press F11 to debug the application on the Android emulator. When the map is loaded, observe that it now animates to a particular location in Singapore (see Figure 9-9).

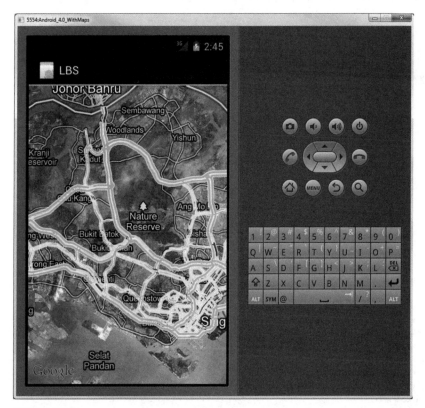

FIGURE 9-9

How It Works

In the preceding code, you first obtained a map controller from the MapView instance and assigned it to a MapController object (mc). You then used a GeoPoint object to represent a geographical location. Note that for this class, the latitude and longitude of a location are represented in micro degrees. This means that they are stored as integer values. For a latitude value of 40.747778, for example, you need to multiply it by 1e6 (which is one million) to obtain 40747778.

To navigate the map to a particular location, you can use the animateTo() method of the MapController class. The setZoom() method enables you to specify the zoom level at which the map is displayed (the bigger the number, the more details you see on the map). The invalidate() method forces the MapView to be redrawn.

Adding Markers

Adding markers to a map to indicate places of interest enables your users to easily locate the places they are looking for. The following Try It Out shows you how to add a marker to Google Maps.

TRY IT OUT   Adding Markers to the Map

1. Create a GIF image containing a pushpin (see Figure 9-10) and copy it into the `res/drawable-mdpi` folder of the existing project. For the best effect, make the background of the image transparent so that it does not block parts of the map when the image is added to the map.

2. Using the project created in the previous activity, add the following statements in bold to the `LBSActivity` `.java` file:

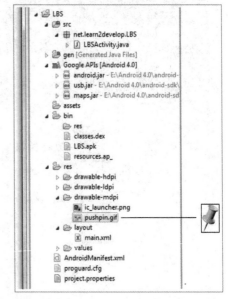

FIGURE 9-10

```java
package net.learn2develop.LBS;

import java.util.List;

import com.google.android.maps.GeoPoint;
import com.google.android.maps.MapActivity;
import com.google.android.maps.MapController;
import com.google.android.maps.MapView;
import com.google.android.maps.Overlay;

import android.graphics.Bitmap;
import android.graphics.BitmapFactory;
import android.graphics.Canvas;
import android.graphics.Point;
import android.os.Bundle;
import android.view.KeyEvent;

public class LBSActivity extends MapActivity {
    MapView mapView;
    MapController mc;
    GeoPoint p;

    private class MapOverlay extends com.google.android.maps.Overlay
    {
        @Override
        public boolean draw(Canvas canvas, MapView mapView,
        boolean shadow, long when)
        {
            super.draw(canvas, mapView, shadow);

            //---translate the GeoPoint to screen pixels---
            Point screenPts = new Point();
            mapView.getProjection().toPixels(p, screenPts);

            //---add the marker---
```

```java
            Bitmap bmp = BitmapFactory.decodeResource(
                getResources(), R.drawable.pushpin);
            canvas.drawBitmap(bmp, screenPts.x, screenPts.y-50, null);
            return true;
        }
    }

    /** Called when the activity is first created. */
    @Override
    public void onCreate(Bundle savedInstanceState) {
        super.onCreate(savedInstanceState);
        setContentView(R.layout.main);

        mapView = (MapView) findViewById(R.id.mapView);
        mapView.setBuiltInZoomControls(true);
        mapView.setSatellite(true);
        mapView.setTraffic(true);

        mc = mapView.getController();
        String coordinates[] = {"1.352566007", "103.78921587"};
        double lat = Double.parseDouble(coordinates[0]);
        double lng = Double.parseDouble(coordinates[1]);

        p = new GeoPoint(
            (int) (lat * 1E6),
            (int) (lng * 1E6));

        mc.animateTo(p);
        mc.setZoom(13);

        //---Add a location marker---
        MapOverlay mapOverlay = new MapOverlay();
        List<Overlay> listOfOverlays = mapView.getOverlays();
        listOfOverlays.clear();
        listOfOverlays.add(mapOverlay);

        mapView.invalidate();
    }

    public boolean onKeyDown(int keyCode, KeyEvent event)
    {
        //...
    }

    @Override
    protected boolean isRouteDisplayed() {
        //...
    }
}
```

3. Press F11 to debug the application on the Android emulator. Figure 9-11 shows the marker added to the map.

FIGURE 9-11

How It Works

To add a marker to the map, you first needed to define a class that extends the `Overlay` class:

```
private class MapOverlay extends com.google.android.maps.Overlay
{
    @Override
    public boolean draw(Canvas canvas, MapView mapView,
    boolean shadow, long when)
    {
        //...
    }
}
```

An overlay represents an individual item that you can draw on the map. You can add as many overlays as you want. In the `MapOverlay` class, you overrode the `draw()` method so that you could draw the pushpin image on the map. In particular, note that you needed to translate the geographical location (represented by a `GeoPoint` object, `p`) into screen coordinates:

```
//---translate the GeoPoint to screen pixels---
Point screenPts = new Point();
mapView.getProjection().toPixels(p, screenPts);
```

Because you want the pointed tip of the pushpin to indicate the position of the location, you need to deduct the height of the image (which is 50 pixels) from the *y* coordinate of the point (see Figure 9-12) and draw the image at that location:

```
//---add the marker---
Bitmap bmp = BitmapFactory.decodeResource(
    getResources(), R.drawable.pushpin);
canvas.drawBitmap(bmp, screenPts.x, screenPts.y-50, null);
```

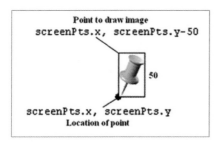

FIGURE 9-12

To add the marker, you created an instance of the `MapOverlay` class and added it to the list of overlays available on the `MapView` object:

```
//---Add a location marker---
MapOverlay mapOverlay = new MapOverlay();
List<Overlay> listOfOverlays = mapView.getOverlays();
listOfOverlays.clear();
listOfOverlays.add(mapOverlay);
```

Getting the Location That Was Touched

After using Google Maps for a while, you may want to know the latitude and longitude of a location corresponding to the position on the screen that was just touched. Knowing this information is very useful, as you can determine a location's address, a process known as *reverse geocoding* (you will learn how this is done in the next section).

If you have added an overlay to the map, you can override the `onTouchEvent()` method within the `MapOverlay` class. This method is fired every time the user touches the map. The method has two parameters: `MotionEvent` and `MapView`. Using the `MotionEvent` parameter, you can determine whether the user has lifted his or her finger from the screen using the `getAction()` method. In the following code snippet, if the user has touched and then lifted the finger, you display the latitude and longitude of the location touched:

```
package net.learn2develop.LBS;

import java.util.List;

import com.google.android.maps.GeoPoint;
```

```java
import com.google.android.maps.MapActivity;
import com.google.android.maps.MapController;
import com.google.android.maps.MapView;
import com.google.android.maps.Overlay;

import android.graphics.Bitmap;
import android.graphics.BitmapFactory;
import android.graphics.Canvas;
import android.graphics.Point;
import android.os.Bundle;
import android.view.KeyEvent;
import android.view.MotionEvent;
import android.widget.Toast;

public class LBSActivity extends MapActivity {
    MapView mapView;
    MapController mc;
    GeoPoint p;

    private class MapOverlay extends com.google.android.maps.Overlay
    {
        @Override
        public boolean draw(Canvas canvas, MapView mapView,
        boolean shadow, long when)
        {
            //...
        }

        @Override
        public boolean onTouchEvent(MotionEvent event, MapView mapView)
        {
            //---when user lifts his finger---
            if (event.getAction() == 1) {
                GeoPoint p = mapView.getProjection().fromPixels(
                    (int) event.getX(),
                    (int) event.getY());
                Toast.makeText(getBaseContext(),
                    "Location: "+
                    p.getLatitudeE6() / 1E6 + "," +
                    p.getLongitudeE6() /1E6 ,
                    Toast.LENGTH_SHORT).show();
            }
            return false;
        }
    }
    //...
}
```

The `getProjection()` method returns a projection for converting between screen-pixel coordinates and latitude/longitude coordinates. The `fromPixels()` method then converts the screen coordinates into a `GeoPoint` object.

Figure 9-13 shows the map displaying a set of coordinates when the user clicks a location on the map.

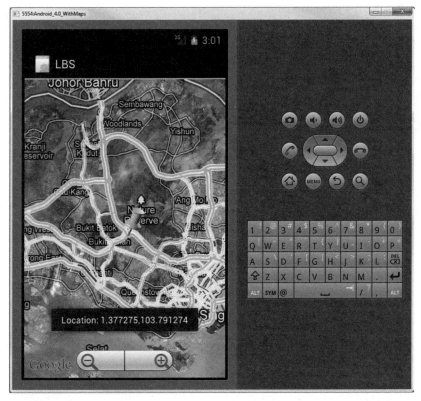

FIGURE 9-13

Geocoding and Reverse Geocoding

As mentioned in the preceding section, if you know the latitude and longitude of a location, you can find out its address using a process known as reverse geocoding. Google Maps in Android supports this via the `Geocoder` class. The following code snippet shows how you can retrieve the address of a location just touched using the `getFromLocation()` method:

```
package net.learn2develop.LBS;

import java.io.IOException;
import java.util.List;
import java.util.Locale;

import com.google.android.maps.GeoPoint;
import com.google.android.maps.MapActivity;
import com.google.android.maps.MapController;
import com.google.android.maps.MapView;
import com.google.android.maps.Overlay;

import android.graphics.Bitmap;
import android.graphics.BitmapFactory;
import android.graphics.Canvas;
```

```java
import android.graphics.Point;
import android.location.Address;
import android.location.Geocoder;
import android.os.Bundle;
import android.view.KeyEvent;
import android.view.MotionEvent;
import android.widget.Toast;

public class LBSActivity extends MapActivity {
    MapView mapView;
    MapController mc;
    GeoPoint p;

    private class MapOverlay extends com.google.android.maps.Overlay
    {
        @Override
        public boolean draw(Canvas canvas, MapView mapView,
        boolean shadow, long when)
        {
            //...
        }

        @Override
        public boolean onTouchEvent(MotionEvent event, MapView mapView)
        {
            //---when user lifts his finger---
            if (event.getAction() == 1) {
                GeoPoint p = mapView.getProjection().fromPixels(
                        (int) event.getX(),
                        (int) event.getY());

                /*
                    Toast.makeText(getBaseContext(),
                        "Location: "+
                        p.getLatitudeE6() / 1E6 + "," +
                        p.getLongitudeE6() /1E6 ,
                        Toast.LENGTH_SHORT).show();
                 */

                Geocoder geoCoder = new Geocoder(
                        getBaseContext(), Locale.getDefault());
                try {
                    List<Address> addresses = geoCoder.getFromLocation(
                            p.getLatitudeE6()  / 1E6,
                            p.getLongitudeE6() / 1E6, 1);

                    String add = "";
                    if (addresses.size() > 0)
                    {
                        for (int i=0; i<addresses.get(0).getMaxAddressLineIndex();
                                i++)
                            add += addresses.get(0).getAddressLine(i) + "\n";
                    }
                    Toast.makeText(getBaseContext(), add, Toast.LENGTH_SHORT).show();
```

```
                }
                catch (IOException e) {
                    e.printStackTrace();
                }
                return true;
            }
            return false;
        }
    }
    //...
}
```

The `Geocoder` object converts the latitude and longitude into an address using the `getFromLocation()` method. Once the address is obtained, you display it using the `Toast` class. Figure 9-14 shows the application displaying the address of a location that was touched on the map.

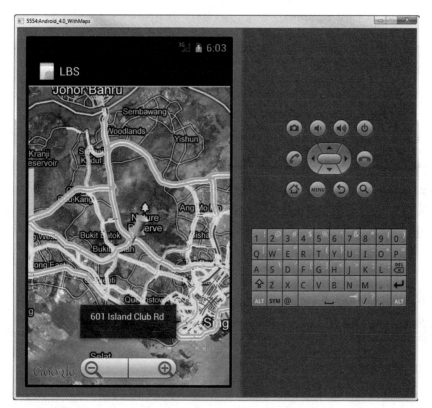

FIGURE 9-14

If you know the address of a location but want to know its latitude and longitude, you can do so via geocoding. Again, you can use the `Geocoder` class for this purpose. The following code shows how you can find the exact location of the Empire State Building by using the `getFromLocationName()` method:

```
@Override
public void onCreate(Bundle savedInstanceState) {
    super.onCreate(savedInstanceState);
    setContentView(R.layout.main);

    mapView = (MapView) findViewById(R.id.mapView);
    mapView.setBuiltInZoomControls(true);
    mapView.setSatellite(true);
    mapView.setTraffic(true);

    mc = mapView.getController();

    /*
    String coordinates[] = {"1.352566007", "103.78921587"};
    double lat = Double.parseDouble(coordinates[0]);
    double lng = Double.parseDouble(coordinates[1]);

    p = new GeoPoint(
        (int) (lat * 1E6),
        (int) (lng * 1E6));

    mc.animateTo(p);
    mc.setZoom(13);
    */

    //---geo-coding---
    Geocoder geoCoder = new Geocoder(this, Locale.getDefault());
    try {
        List<Address> addresses = geoCoder.getFromLocationName(
            "empire state building", 5);

        if (addresses.size() > 0) {
            p = new GeoPoint(
                    (int) (addresses.get(0).getLatitude() * 1E6),
                    (int) (addresses.get(0).getLongitude() * 1E6));
            mc.animateTo(p);
            mc.setZoom(20);
        }
    } catch (IOException e) {
        e.printStackTrace();
    }

    //---Add a location marker---
    MapOverlay mapOverlay = new MapOverlay();
    List<Overlay> listOfOverlays = mapView.getOverlays();
    listOfOverlays.clear();
    listOfOverlays.add(mapOverlay);

    mapView.invalidate();
}
```

Figure 9-15 shows the map navigating to the location of the Empire State Building.

FIGURE 9-15

GETTING LOCATION DATA

Nowadays, mobile devices are commonly equipped with GPS receivers. Because of the many satellites orbiting the earth, you can use a GPS receiver to find your location easily. However, GPS requires a clear sky to work and hence does not always work indoors or where satellites can't penetrate (such as a tunnel through a mountain).

Another effective way to locate your position is through *cell tower triangulation*. When a mobile phone is switched on, it is constantly in contact with base stations surrounding it. By knowing the identity of cell towers, it is possible to translate this information into a physical location through the use of various databases containing the cell towers' identities and their exact geographical locations. The advantage of cell tower triangulation is that it works indoors, without the need to obtain information from satellites. However, it is not as precise as GPS because its accuracy depends on overlapping signal coverage, which varies quite a bit. Cell tower triangulation works best in densely populated areas where the cell towers are closely located.

A third method of locating your position is to rely on Wi-Fi triangulation. Rather than connect to cell towers, the device connects to a Wi-Fi network and checks the service provider against databases to determine the location serviced by the provider. Of the three methods described here, Wi-Fi triangulation is the least accurate.

On the Android platform, the SDK provides the `LocationManager` class to help your device determine the user's physical location. The following Try It Out shows how this is done in code.

TRY IT OUT Navigating the Map to a Specific Location

1. Using the same project created in the previous section, add the following statements in bold to the `LBSActivity.java` file:

```java
package net.learn2develop.LBS;

import java.io.IOException;
import java.util.List;
import java.util.Locale;

import com.google.android.maps.GeoPoint;
import com.google.android.maps.MapActivity;
import com.google.android.maps.MapController;
import com.google.android.maps.MapView;
import com.google.android.maps.Overlay;

import android.content.Context;

import android.graphics.Bitmap;
import android.graphics.BitmapFactory;
import android.graphics.Canvas;
import android.graphics.Point;
import android.location.Address;
import android.location.Geocoder;

import android.location.Location;
import android.location.LocationListener;
import android.location.LocationManager;

import android.os.Bundle;
import android.view.KeyEvent;
import android.view.MotionEvent;
import android.widget.Toast;

public class LBSActivity extends MapActivity {
    MapView mapView;
    MapController mc;
    GeoPoint p;

    LocationManager lm;
    LocationListener locationListener;

    private class MapOverlay extends com.google.android.maps.Overlay
    {
        //...
    }

    /** Called when the activity is first created. */
    @Override
    public void onCreate(Bundle savedInstanceState) {
        super.onCreate(savedInstanceState);
        setContentView(R.layout.main);

        mapView = (MapView) findViewById(R.id.mapView);
```

```java
        mapView.setBuiltInZoomControls(true);
        mapView.setSatellite(true);
        mapView.setTraffic(true);

        mc = mapView.getController();

        /*
        String coordinates[] = {"1.352566007", "103.78921587"};
        double lat = Double.parseDouble(coordinates[0]);
        double lng = Double.parseDouble(coordinates[1]);

        p = new GeoPoint(
            (int) (lat * 1E6),
            (int) (lng * 1E6));

        mc.animateTo(p);
        mc.setZoom(13);
        */

        //---geo-coding---
        Geocoder geoCoder = new Geocoder(this, Locale.getDefault());
        try {
            //...
        }

        //---Add a location marker---
        MapOverlay mapOverlay = new MapOverlay();
        List<Overlay> listOfOverlays = mapView.getOverlays();
        listOfOverlays.clear();
        listOfOverlays.add(mapOverlay);

        mapView.invalidate();

        //---use the LocationManager class to obtain locations data---
        lm = (LocationManager)
            getSystemService(Context.LOCATION_SERVICE);

        locationListener = new MyLocationListener();
    }

    @Override
    public void onResume() {
        super.onResume();

        //---request for location updates---
        lm.requestLocationUpdates(
                LocationManager.GPS_PROVIDER,
                0,
                0,
                locationListener);
    }

    @Override
    public void onPause() {
        super.onPause();

        //---remove the location listener---
        lm.removeUpdates(locationListener);
```

```
    }

    private class MyLocationListener implements LocationListener
    {
        public void onLocationChanged(Location loc) {
            if (loc != null) {
                Toast.makeText(getBaseContext(),
                        "Location changed : Lat: " + loc.getLatitude() +
                        " Lng: " + loc.getLongitude(),
                        Toast.LENGTH_SHORT).show();

                p = new GeoPoint(
                        (int) (loc.getLatitude() * 1E6),
                        (int) (loc.getLongitude() * 1E6));

                mc.animateTo(p);
                mc.setZoom(18);
            }
        }

        public void onProviderDisabled(String provider) {
        }

        public void onProviderEnabled(String provider) {
        }

        public void onStatusChanged(String provider, int status,
            Bundle extras) {
        }
    }

    public boolean onKeyDown(int keyCode, KeyEvent event)
    {
        //...
    }

    @Override
    protected boolean isRouteDisplayed() {
        //...
    }
}
```

2. Add the following line in bold to the `AndroidManifest.xml` file:

```xml
<?xml version="1.0" encoding="utf-8"?>
<manifest xmlns:android="http://schemas.android.com/apk/res/android"
    package="net.learn2develop.LBS"
    android:versionCode="1"
    android:versionName="1.0" >

    <uses-sdk android:minSdkVersion="14" />
    <uses-permission android:name="android.permission.INTERNET"/>
    <uses-permission android:name="android.permission.ACCESS_FINE_LOCATION"/>

    <application
        android:icon="@drawable/ic_launcher"
        android:label="@string/app_name" >
```

```
<uses-library android:name="com.google.android.maps" />
<activity
    android:label="@string/app_name"
    android:name=".LBSActivity" >
    <intent-filter >
        <action android:name="android.intent.action.MAIN" />
        <category android:name="android.intent.category.LAUNCHER" />
    </intent-filter>
</activity>
</application>

</manifest>
```

3. Press F11 to debug the application on the Android emulator.

4. To simulate GPS data received by the Android emulator, you use the Location Controls tool (see Figure 9-16) located in the DDMS perspective of Eclipse.

5. Ensure that you have first selected the emulator in the Devices tab. Then, in the Emulator Control tab, locate the Location Controls tool and select the Manual tab. Enter a latitude and longitude and click the Send button.

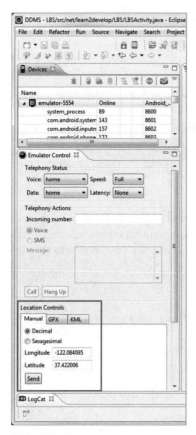

FIGURE 9-16

6. Observe that the map on the emulator now animates to another location (see Figure 9-17). This proves that the application has received the GPS data.

FIGURE 9-17

How It Works

In Android, location-based services are provided by the LocationManager class, located in the android .location package. Using the LocationManager class, your application can obtain periodic updates of the device's geographical locations, as well as fire an intent when it enters the proximity of a certain location.

In the LBSActivity.java file, you first obtained a reference to the LocationManager class using the getSystemService() method. You did this in the onCreate() method of the LBSActivity:

```
//---use the LocationManager class to obtain locations data---
lm = (LocationManager)
    getSystemService(Context.LOCATION_SERVICE);

locationListener = new MyLocationListener();
```

Next, you created an instance of the MyLocationListener class, which you defined next.

The `MyLocationListener` class implements the `LocationListener` abstract class. You need to override four methods in this implementation:

➤ `onLocationChanged(Location location)` — Called when the location has changed

➤ `onProviderDisabled(String provider)` — Called when the provider is disabled by the user

➤ `onProviderEnabled(String provider)` — Called when the provider is enabled by the user

➤ `onStatusChanged(String provider, int status, Bundle extras)` — Called when the provider status changes

In this example, you're more interested in what happens when a location changes, so you wrote some code in the `onLocationChanged()` method. Specifically, when a location changes, you display a small dialog on the screen showing the new location information: latitude and longitude. You show this dialog using the `Toast` class:

```
public void onLocationChanged(Location loc) {
    if (loc != null) {
        Toast.makeText(getBaseContext(),
                "Location changed : Lat: " + loc.getLatitude() +
                " Lng: " + loc.getLongitude(),
                Toast.LENGTH_SHORT).show();

        p = new GeoPoint(
                (int) (loc.getLatitude() * 1E6),
                (int) (loc.getLongitude() * 1E6));

        mc.animateTo(p);
        mc.setZoom(18);
    }
}
```

In the preceding method, you also navigate the map to the location that you have received.

To be notified whenever there is a change in location, you needed to register a request for location changes so that your program can be notified periodically. This is done via the `requestLocationUpdates()` method. You did this in the `onResume()` method of the activity:

```
@Override
public void onResume() {
    super.onResume();

    //---request for location updates---
    lm.requestLocationUpdates(
            LocationManager.GPS_PROVIDER,
            0,
            0,
            locationListener);
}
```

The `requestLocationUpdates()` method takes four arguments:

➤ provider — The name of the provider with which you register. In this case, you are using GPS to obtain your geographical location data.

➤ `minTime` — The minimum time interval for notifications, in milliseconds. 0 indicates that you want to be continually informed of location changes.

➤ `minDistance` — The minimum distance interval for notifications, in meters. 0 indicates that you want to be continually informed of location changes.

➤ `listener` — An object whose `onLocationChanged()` method will be called for each location update

Finally, in the `onPause()` method, you remove the listener when the activity is destroyed or goes into the background (so that the application no longer listens for changes in location, thereby saving the battery of the device). You did that using the `removeUpdates()` method:

```
@Override
public void onPause() {
    super.onPause();

    //---remove the location listener---
    lm.removeUpdates(locationListener);
}
```

If you want to use Cell-ID and Wi-Fi triangulation (important for indoor use) to obtain your location data, you can use the network provider, like this:

```
@Override
public void onResume() {
    super.onResume();

    //---request for location updates---
    lm.requestLocationUpdates(
            LocationManager.GPS_PROVIDER,
            0,
            0,
            locationListener);
}
```

To use the network provider, you need to add the `ACCESS_COARSE_LOCATION` permission to the `AndroidManifest.xml` file:

```
<?xml version="1.0" encoding="utf-8"?>
<manifest xmlns:android="http://schemas.android.com/apk/res/android"
    package="net.learn2develop.LBS"
    android:versionCode="1"
    android:versionName="1.0" >

    <uses-sdk android:minSdkVersion="14" />
    <uses-permission android:name="android.permission.INTERNET"/>
    <uses-permission android:name="android.permission.ACCESS_FINE_LOCATION"/>
    <uses-permission android:name="android.permission.ACCESS_COARSE_LOCATION"/>

    <application
        android:icon="@drawable/ic_launcher"
        android:label="@string/app_name" >
        <uses-library android:name="com.google.android.maps" />
        <activity
            android:label="@string/app_name"
```

```
            android:name=".LBSActivity" >
            <intent-filter >
                <action android:name="android.intent.action.MAIN" />

                <category android:name="android.intent.category.LAUNCHER" />
            </intent-filter>
        </activity>
    </application>

</manifest>
```

 NOTE *The network provider will not work on the Android emulator. If you test the preceding code on the emulator, it will result in an illegal argument exception. You need to test the code on a real device.*

You can combine both the GPS location provider with the network location provider within your application:

```
@Override
public void onResume() {
    super.onResume();

    //---request for location updates---
    lm.requestLocationUpdates(
            LocationManager.GPS_PROVIDER,
            0,
            0,
            locationListener);

    //---request for location updates---
    lm.requestLocationUpdates(
            LocationManager.NETWORK_PROVIDER,
            0,
            0,
            locationListener);
}
```

However, be aware that doing so will cause your application to receive two different sets of coordinates, as both the GPS provider and the NETWORK provider will try to get your location using their own methods (GPS versus Wi-Fi and Cell ID triangulation). Hence, it is important that you monitor the status of the two providers in your device and use the appropriate one. You can check the status of the two providers by implementing the following three methods (shown in bold) of the `MyLocationListener` class:

```
private class MyLocationListener implements LocationListener
{
    @Override
    public void onLocationChanged(Location loc) {
        if (loc != null) {
            Toast.makeText(getBaseContext(),
                    "Location changed : Lat: " + loc.getLatitude() +
                    " Lng: " + loc.getLongitude(),
```

```
                        Toast.LENGTH_SHORT).show();


            p = new GeoPoint(
                    (int) (loc.getLatitude() * 1E6),
                    (int) (loc.getLongitude() * 1E6));

            mc.animateTo(p);
            mc.setZoom(18);
        }
    }

    //---called when the provider is disabled---
    public void onProviderDisabled(String provider) {
        Toast.makeText(getBaseContext(),
                provider + " disabled",
                Toast.LENGTH_SHORT).show();
    }

    //---called when the provider is enabled---
    public void onProviderEnabled(String provider) {
        Toast.makeText(getBaseContext(),
                provider + " enabled",
                Toast.LENGTH_SHORT).show();
    }

    //---called when there is a change in the provider status---
    public void onStatusChanged(String provider, int status,
        Bundle extras) {
        String statusString = "";
        switch (status) {
            case android.location.LocationProvider.AVAILABLE:
                statusString = "available";
            case android.location.LocationProvider.OUT_OF_SERVICE:
                statusString = "out of service";
            case android.location.LocationProvider.TEMPORARILY_UNAVAILABLE:
                statusString = "temporarily unavailable";
        }

        Toast.makeText(getBaseContext(),
                provider + " " + statusString,
                Toast.LENGTH_SHORT).show();
    }
}
```

MONITORING A LOCATION

One very cool feature of the LocationManager class is its ability to monitor a specific location. This is achieved using the addProximityAlert() method.

The following code snippet shows how to monitor a particular location such that if the user is within a five-meter radius from that location, your application will fire an intent to launch the web browser:

```
import android.app.PendingIntent;
import android.content.Intent;
import android.net.Uri;

    //---use the LocationManager class to obtain locations data---
    lm = (LocationManager)
        getSystemService(Context.LOCATION_SERVICE);

    //---PendingIntent to launch activity if the user is within
    // some locations---
    PendingIntent pendingIntent = PendingIntent.getActivity(
        this, 0, new
        Intent(android.content.Intent.ACTION_VIEW,
          Uri.parse("http://www.amazon.com")), 0);

    lm.addProximityAlert(37.422006, -122.084095, 5, -1, pendingIntent);
```

The `addProximityAlert()` method takes five arguments: latitude, longitude, radius (in meters), expiration (duration for which the proximity alert is valid, after which it is deleted; -1 for no expiration), and the pending intent.

Note that if the Android device's screen goes to sleep, the proximity is also checked once every four minutes in order to preserve the battery life of the device.

PROJECT — BUILDING A LOCATION TRACKER

Now that you have seen how to build a location-based Android application, you can put that knowledge to good use by combining the techniques covered in this chapter with the techniques covered in Chapter 8, "Messaging," to build a cool working application. You will build a location tracker application that can be installed on a user's Android device. You can then send an SMS message containing a specific code to the user's device, and it will automatically return the location of the device through a return SMS message. This type of location tracker application could be used to keep track of your child or any elderly relative who lives alone (and it can be done without the person's knowledge).

WARNING *Before you roll out this application to your users, note that in some countries it is illegal to track the location of a person without his or her knowledge. If you install the location tracker application on a user's phone, that device will automatically return its location information to whomever sends it an SMS message beginning with the words "Where are you?" Therefore, if you want to use this project in real life, you must alert potential users about the application's functionality, so that they have the option to not reveal their location.*

TRY IT OUT   Invoking an Activity

1.   Using Eclipse, create a new Android project and name it **LocationTracker**.

2.   Add the following lines in bold to the `AndroidManifest.xml` file:

```xml
<?xml version="1.0" encoding="utf-8"?>
<manifest xmlns:android="http://schemas.android.com/apk/res/android"
      package="net.learn2develop.LocationTracker"
      android:versionCode="1"
      android:versionName="1.0">
   <uses-sdk android:minSdkVersion="14" />

   <uses-permission android:name="android.permission.RECEIVE_SMS" />
   <uses-permission android:name="android.permission.SEND_SMS" />
   <uses-permission android:name="android.permission.ACCESS_COARSE_LOCATION" />

   <application android:icon="@drawable/icon" android:label="@string/app_name">
      <activity android:name=".LocationTrackerActivity"
               android:label="@string/app_name">
         <intent-filter>
            <action android:name="android.intent.action.MAIN" />
            <category android:name="android.intent.category.LAUNCHER" />
         </intent-filter>
      </activity>

      <!-- put this here so that even if the app is not running,
      your app can be woken up when there is an incoming SMS message -->
      <receiver android:name=".SMSReceiver">
         <intent-filter android:priority="100">
            <action
               android:name="android.provider.Telephony.SMS_RECEIVED" />
         </intent-filter>
      </receiver>
   </application>
</manifest>
```

3.   Add a new Java class to the package name of the project and name it `SMSReceiver`. You should now have a Java file named `SMSReceiver.java` under the package name of your project (see Figure 9-18).

FIGURE 9-18

4.   Populate the `SMSReceiver.java` file with the following lines in bold:

```java
package net.learn2develop.LocationTracker;

import android.content.BroadcastReceiver;
import android.content.Context;
import android.content.Intent;
import android.location.Location;
import android.location.LocationListener;
import android.location.LocationManager;
import android.os.Bundle;
import android.telephony.SmsManager;
import android.telephony.SmsMessage;

public class SMSReceiver extends BroadcastReceiver
```

```java
{
    LocationManager lm;
    LocationListener locationListener;
    String senderTel;

    @Override
    public void onReceive(Context context, Intent intent)
    {
        //---get the SMS message that was received---
        Bundle bundle = intent.getExtras();
        SmsMessage[] msgs = null;
        String str="";
        if (bundle != null)
        {
            senderTel = "";
            //---retrieve the SMS message received---
            Object[] pdus = (Object[]) bundle.get("pdus");
            msgs = new SmsMessage[pdus.length];
            for (int i=0; i<msgs.length; i++){
                msgs[i] = SmsMessage.createFromPdu((byte[])pdus[i]);
                if (i==0) {
                    //---get the sender address/phone number---
                    senderTel = msgs[i].getOriginatingAddress();
                }
                //---get the message body---
                str += msgs[i].getMessageBody().toString();
            }

            if (str.startsWith("Where are you?")) {
                //---use the LocationManager class to obtain locations data---
                lm = (LocationManager)
                        context.getSystemService(Context.LOCATION_SERVICE);

                //---request location updates---
                locationListener = new MyLocationListener();
                lm.requestLocationUpdates(
                        LocationManager.NETWORK_PROVIDER,
                        60000,
                        1000,
                        locationListener);

                //---abort the broadcast; SMS messages won't be broadcasted---
                this.abortBroadcast();
            }
        }
    }

    private class MyLocationListener implements LocationListener
    {
        @
        public void onLocationChanged(Location loc) {
            if (loc != null) {
                //---send a SMS containing the current location---
                SmsManager sms = SmsManager.getDefault();
                sms.sendTextMessage(senderTel, null,
                        "http://maps.google.com/maps?q=" + loc.getLatitude() + "," +
```

```
                                    loc.getLongitude(), null, null);

                    //---stop listening for location changes---
                    lm.removeUpdates(locationListener);
                }
            }

            public void onProviderDisabled(String provider) {
            }

            public void onProviderEnabled(String provider) {
            }

            public void onStatusChanged(String provider, int status,
                    Bundle extras) {
            }
        }
    }
```

5. To test the application, first deploy it onto a real Android device. Then, use another phone (any type of mobile phone that can send SMS messages) to send an SMS message to it with the message "Where are you?"

6. After the SMS message has been sent, wait for the Android device to send back an SMS message. Figure 9-19 shows the reply from the Android device, containing its location (shown here using an iPhone).

7. Most smartphones recognize URL data in the SMS message; therefore, if you click the URL in the SMS message, you will see the location through Google Maps (see Figure 9-20).

FIGURE 9-19

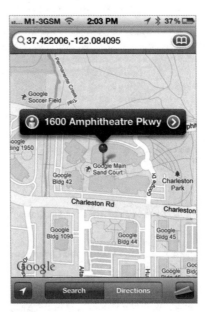

FIGURE 9-20

How It Works

This project combined the concepts that you learned in this chapter with the material about SMS messaging covered in Chapter 8 into one complete application. Once installed, the application will listen for incoming SMS messages that contain the text "Where are you?" It then intercepts these SMS messages, so the user won't be able to see the message in the Messaging application on the Android device.

When an SMS message is received, you first extract the phone number of the sender so that you can use it later to send a reply containing the location of the device:

```
//---retrieve the SMS message received---
senderTel = "";

//---retrieve the SMS message received---
Object[] pdus = (Object[]) bundle.get("pdus");
msgs = new SmsMessage[pdus.length];
for (int i=0; i<msgs.length; i++){
    msgs[i] = SmsMessage.createFromPdu((byte[])pdus[i]);
    if (i==0) {
        //---get the sender address/phone number---
        senderTel = msgs[i].getOriginatingAddress();
    }
    //---get the message body---
    str += msgs[i].getMessageBody().toString();
}
```

You then examine the content of the SMS message. If it starts with the sentence "Where are you?", you then request for location updates using the `LocationManager` class:

```
if (str.startsWith("Where are you?")) {
    //---use the LocationManager class to obtain locations data---
    lm = (LocationManager)
            context.getSystemService(Context.LOCATION_SERVICE);

    //---request location updates---
    locationListener = new MyLocationListener();
    lm.requestLocationUpdates(
            LocationManager.NETWORK_PROVIDER,
            60000,
            1000,
            locationListener);

    this.abortBroadcast();
}
```

Note that in this example, I have used the network provider to obtain my location because it does not require a line of sight to the sky (which is required by the GPS provider). However, using the network provider does require the device to have an Internet connection, so your application will not work if the device lacks one.

Once the location is obtained, you send a returning SMS message containing the location of the device, using a URL that points to Google Maps:

```
public void onLocationChanged(Location loc) {
    if (loc != null) {
```

```
                    //---send a SMS containing the current location---
                    SmsManager sms = SmsManager.getDefault();
                    sms.sendTextMessage(senderTel, null,
                            "http://maps.google.com/maps?q=" + loc.getLatitude() + "," +
                                    loc.getLongitude(), null, null);

                    //---stop listening for location changes---
                    lm.removeUpdates(locationListener);
            }
        }
```

Once the SMS message is sent, you immediately remove the location updates so that you do not listen for location changes anymore.

Note that I have used 60,000 ms and 1,000 meters for the `minTime` and `minDistance` arguments of the `requestLocationUpdates()` method, respectively. If you recall from the earlier part of this chapter, I used 0 for both arguments, because I wanted to be continually informed of location changes. However, in this project you should not do this, as it would cause the application to continuously send several SMS messages back to the sender at once. This is because by the time you stop listening for location updates, the Location Manager would have called the `onLocationChanged()` method several times, reporting the device's smallest changes in location and resulting in multiple SMS messages. In real testing, the number of SMS messages ranges from 10 to 60. Thus, you should set the `minTime` and `minDistance` arguments to a more reasonable value so that the Location Manager does not have a chance to fire the `onLocationChanged()` method repeatedly.

SUMMARY

This chapter took a whirlwind tour of the `MapView` object, which displays Google Maps in your Android application. You have learned the various ways in which the map can be manipulated, and you have also seen how you can obtain geographical location data using the various network providers: GPS, Cell-ID, or Wi-Fi triangulation. Finally, you learned to build a Location Tracker application that enables you to track a user's location using SMS messaging.

EXERCISES

1. If you have embedded the Google Maps API into your Android application but it does not show the map when the application is loaded, what could be the likely reasons?

2. What is the difference between geocoding and reverse geocoding?

3. Name the two location providers that you can use to obtain your location data.

4. What method is used for monitoring a location?

Answers to the exercises can be found in Appendix C.

▶ **WHAT YOU LEARNED IN THIS CHAPTER**

TOPIC	KEY CONCEPTS
Displaying the MapView	```<com.google.android.maps.MapView` ` android:id="@+id/mapView"` ` android:layout_width="fill_parent"` ` android:layout_height="fill_parent"` ` android:enabled="true"` ` android:clickable="true"` ` android:apiKey="YOUR_MAPS_API_KEY" />```
Referencing the Map library	`<uses-library android:name="com.google.android.maps" />`
Displaying the zoom controls	`mapView.setBuiltInZoomControls(true);`
Programmatically zooming in or out of the map	`mc.zoomIn();` `mc.zoomOut();`
Changing views	`mapView.setSatellite(true);` `mapView.setTraffic(true);`
Animating to a particular location	```mc = mapView.getController();` `String coordinates[] = {"1.352566007", "103.78921587"};` `double lat = Double.parseDouble(coordinates[0]);` `double lng = Double.parseDouble(coordinates[1]);` `p = new GeoPoint(` ` (int) (lat * 1E6),` ` (int) (lng * 1E6));` `mc.animateTo(p);```
Adding markers	Implement an `Overlay` class and override the `draw()` method
Getting the location of the map touched	```GeoPoint p = mapView.getProjection().fromPixels(` ` (int) event.getX(),` ` (int) event.getY());```
Geocoding and reverse geocoding	Use the `Geocoder` class

continues

(continued)

TOPIC	KEY CONCEPTS
| **Obtaining location data** | ```java
private LocationManager lm;

//...

    lm = (LocationManager)
        getSystemService(Context.LOCATION_SERVICE);

    locationListener = new MyLocationListener();

    lm.requestLocationUpdates(
            LocationManager.GPS_PROVIDER,
            0,
            0,
            locationListener);

//...

    private class MyLocationListener implements LocationListener
    {

        public void onLocationChanged(Location loc) {
            if (loc != null) {
            }
        }

        public void onProviderDisabled(String provider) {
        }

        public void onProviderEnabled(String provider) {
        }

        public void onStatusChanged(String provider, int status,
            Bundle extras) {
        }
    }
``` |
| **Monitoring a location** | ```java
lm.addProximityAlert(37.422006, -122.084095, 5, -1,
    pendingIntent);
``` |

Networking

WHAT YOU WILL LEARN IN THIS CHAPTER

➤ How to connect to the web using HTTP

➤ How to consume XML web services

➤ How to consume JSON web services

➤ How to connect to a Socket server

In Chapter 8, you learned about how your application can talk to the outside world through the use of SMS messaging and e-mails. Another way to communicate with the outside world is through the wireless network available on your Android device. Therefore, in this chapter you will learn how to use the HTTP protocol to talk to web servers so that you can download text and binary data. You will also learn how to parse XML files to extract the relevant parts of an XML document — a technique that is useful if you are accessing web services. Besides XML web services, this chapter also covers JSON (JavaScript Object Notation), which is a lightweight alternative to XML. You will make use of the classes available in the Android SDK to manipulate JSON content.

Finally, this chapter also demonstrates how to write an Android application to connect to servers using TCP sockets. Using sockets programming, you can write sophisticated, interesting networked applications.

CONSUMING WEB SERVICES USING HTTP

One common way to communicate with the outside world is through HTTP. HTTP is no stranger to most people; it is the protocol that drives much of the web's success. Using the HTTP protocol, you can perform a wide variety of tasks, such as downloading web pages from a web server, downloading binary data, and more.

The following Try It Out creates an Android project so you can use the HTTP protocol to connect to the web to download all sorts of content.

TRY IT OUT Creating the Base Project for HTTP Connection

codefile Networking.zip available for download at Wrox.com

1. Using Eclipse, create a new Android project and name it **Networking**.

2. Add the following statement in bold to the `AndroidManifest.xml` file:

```xml
<?xml version="1.0" encoding="utf-8"?>
<manifest xmlns:android="http://schemas.android.com/apk/res/android"
    package="net.learn2develop.Networking"
    android:versionCode="1"
    android:versionName="1.0" >

    <uses-sdk android:minSdkVersion="14" />
    <uses-permission android:name="android.permission.INTERNET"/>

    <application
        android:icon="@drawable/ic_launcher"
        android:label="@string/app_name" >
        <activity
            android:label="@string/app_name"
            android:name=".NetworkingActivity" >
            <intent-filter >
                <action android:name="android.intent.action.MAIN" />

                <category android:name="android.intent.category.LAUNCHER" />
            </intent-filter>
        </activity>
    </application>

</manifest>
```

3. Import the following packages in the `NetworkingActivity.java` file:

```java
package net.learn2develop.Networking;

import android.app.Activity;
import android.os.Bundle;
import java.io.IOException;
import java.io.InputStream;
import java.net.HttpURLConnection;
import java.net.URL;
import java.net.URLConnection;
import android.util.Log;
public class NetworkingActivity extends Activity {
    /** Called when the activity is first created. */
    @Override
    public void onCreate(Bundle savedInstanceState) {
        super.onCreate(savedInstanceState);
        setContentView(R.layout.main);
    }
}
```

4. Define the `OpenHttpConnection()` method in the `NetworkingActivity.java` file:

```java
public class NetworkingActivity extends Activity {
    private InputStream OpenHttpConnection(String urlString) throws IOException
    {
        InputStream in = null;
        int response = -1;

        URL url = new URL(urlString);
        URLConnection conn = url.openConnection();

        if (!(conn instanceof HttpURLConnection))
            throw new IOException("Not an HTTP connection");
        try{
            HttpURLConnection httpConn = (HttpURLConnection) conn;
            httpConn.setAllowUserInteraction(false);
            httpConn.setInstanceFollowRedirects(true);
            httpConn.setRequestMethod("GET");
            httpConn.connect();
            response = httpConn.getResponseCode();
            if (response == HttpURLConnection.HTTP_OK) {
                in = httpConn.getInputStream();
            }
        }
        catch (Exception ex)
        {
            Log.d("Networking", ex.getLocalizedMessage());
            throw new IOException("Error connecting");
        }
        return in;
    }

    /** Called when the activity is first created. */
    @Override
    public void onCreate(Bundle savedInstanceState) {
        super.onCreate(savedInstanceState);
        setContentView(R.layout.main);
    }
}
```

How It Works

Because you are using the HTTP protocol to connect to the web, your application needs the INTERNET permission; hence, the first thing you did was add the permission in the AndroidManifest.xml file.

You then defined the OpenHttpConnection() method, which takes a URL string and returns an InputStream object. Using an InputStream object, you can download the data by reading bytes from the stream object. In this method, you made use of the HttpURLConnection object to open an HTTP connection with a remote URL. You set all the various properties of the connection, such as the request method, and so on:

```java
HttpURLConnection httpConn = (HttpURLConnection) conn;
httpConn.setAllowUserInteraction(false);
httpConn.setInstanceFollowRedirects(true);
httpConn.setRequestMethod("GET");
```

After trying to establish a connection with the server, the HTTP response code is returned. If the connection is established (via the response code HTTP_OK), then you proceed to get an InputStream object from the connection:

```
httpConn.connect();
response = httpConn.getResponseCode();
if (response == HttpURLConnection.HTTP_OK) {
    in = httpConn.getInputStream();
}
```

Using the InputStream object, you can then start to download the data from the server.

Downloading Binary Data

A common task you need to perform is downloading binary data from the web. For example, you may want to download an image from a server so that you can display it in your application. The following Try It Out shows how this is done.

TRY IT OUT   Downloading Binary Data

1. Using the same project created earlier, replace the default TextView with the following statements in bold to the main.xml file:

```xml
<?xml version="1.0" encoding="utf-8"?>
<LinearLayout xmlns:android="http://schemas.android.com/apk/res/android"
    android:layout_width="fill_parent"
    android:layout_height="fill_parent"
    android:orientation="vertical" >

<ImageView
    android:id="@+id/img"
    android:layout_width="wrap_content"
    android:layout_height="wrap_content"
    android:layout_gravity="center" />

</LinearLayout>
```

2. Add the following statements in bold to the NetworkingActivity.java file:

```java
import android.widget.ImageView;
import android.graphics.Bitmap;
import android.graphics.BitmapFactory;
import android.os.AsyncTask;

public class NetworkingActivity extends Activity {
    ImageView img;

    private InputStream OpenHttpConnection(String urlString) throws IOException
```

```
    {
        InputStream in = null;
        int response = -1;

        URL url = new URL(urlString);
        URLConnection conn = url.openConnection();

        if (!(conn instanceof HttpURLConnection))
            throw new IOException("Not an HTTP connection");
        try{
            HttpURLConnection httpConn = (HttpURLConnection) conn;
            httpConn.setAllowUserInteraction(false);
            httpConn.setInstanceFollowRedirects(true);
            httpConn.setRequestMethod("GET");
            httpConn.connect();
            response = httpConn.getResponseCode();
            if (response == HttpURLConnection.HTTP_OK) {
                in = httpConn.getInputStream();
            }
        }
        catch (Exception ex)
        {
            Log.d("Networking", ex.getLocalizedMessage());
            throw new IOException("Error connecting");
        }
        return in;
    }

    private Bitmap DownloadImage(String URL)
    {
        Bitmap bitmap = null;
        InputStream in = null;
        try {
            in = OpenHttpConnection(URL);
            bitmap = BitmapFactory.decodeStream(in);
            in.close();
        } catch (IOException e1) {
            Log.d("NetworkingActivity", e1.getLocalizedMessage());
        }
        return bitmap;
    }

    private class DownloadImageTask extends AsyncTask<String, Void, Bitmap> {
        protected Bitmap doInBackground(String... urls) {
            return DownloadImage(urls[0]);
        }

        protected void onPostExecute(Bitmap result) {
            ImageView img = (ImageView) findViewById(R.id.img);
            img.setImageBitmap(result);
        }
    }

    /** Called when the activity is first created. */
```

```
    @Override
    public void onCreate(Bundle savedInstanceState) {
        super.onCreate(savedInstanceState);
        setContentView(R.layout.main);
        new DownloadImageTask().execute(
            "http://www.mayoff.com/5-01cablecarDCP01934.jpg");
    }
}
```

3. Press F11 to debug the application on the Android emulator. Figure 10-1 shows the image downloaded from the web and then displayed in the `ImageView`.

How It Works

The `DownloadImage()` method takes the URL of the image to download and then opens the connection to the server using the `OpenHttpConnection()` method that you have defined earlier. Using the `InputStream` object returned by the connection, the `decodeStream()` method from the `BitmapFactory` class is used to download and decode the data into a `Bitmap` object. The `DownloadImage()` method returns a `Bitmap` object.

To download an image and display it on the activity, you call the `DownloadImage()` method. However, starting with Android 3.0, synchronous operations can no longer be run directly from a UI thread. If you try to call the `DownloadImage()` method directly in your `onCreate()` method (as shown in the following code snippet), your application will crash when it is run on a device running Android 3.0 and later:

```
/** Called when the activity is first created. */
@Override
public void onCreate(Bundle savedInstanceState) {
    super.onCreate(savedInstanceState);
    setContentView(R.layout.main);
    //---download an image---
    //---code will not run in Android 3.0 and beyond---
    Bitmap bitmap =
        DownloadImage("http://www.mayoff.com/5-01cablecarDCP01934.jpg");
    img = (ImageView) findViewById(R.id.img);
    img.setImageBitmap(bitmap);
}
```

FIGURE 10-1

Because the `DownloadImage()` method is synchronous — that is, it will not return control until the image is downloaded — calling it directly will freeze the UI of your activity. This is not allowed in Android 3.0 and later; all synchronous code must be wrapped using an `AsyncTask` class. Using `AsyncTask` enables you to perform background tasks in a separate thread and then return the result in a UI thread. That way, you can perform background operations without needing to handle complex threading issues.

To call the `DownloadImage()` method asynchronously, you need to wrap the code in a subclass of the `AsyncTask` class, as shown here:

```
private class DownloadImageTask extends AsyncTask<String, Void, Bitmap> {
    protected Bitmap doInBackground(String... urls) {
        return DownloadImage(urls[0]);
    }
    protected void onPostExecute(Bitmap result) {
        ImageView img = (ImageView) findViewById(R.id.img);
        img.setImageBitmap(result);
    }
}
```

Basically, you defined a class (`DownloadImageTask`) that extends the `AsyncTask` class. In this case, there are two methods within the `DownloadImageTask` class: `doInBackground()` and `onPostExecute()`.

You put all the code that needs to be run asynchronously in the `doInBackground()` method. When the task is completed, the result is passed back via the `onPostExecute()` method. In this case, you use the `ImageView` to display the image downloaded.

RUNNING SYNCHRONOUS OPERATIONS IN A UI THREAD

To be specific, if you set the `android:minSdkVersion` attribute in your `AndroidManifest.xml` file to a value of 9 or less and then run your application on an Android 3.0 or later device, your synchronous code will still work in a UI thread (though not recommended). However, if the `android:minSdkVersion` attribute value is set to 10 or above, your synchronous code will not work in a UI thread.

 NOTE Chapter 11 discusses the `AsyncTask` class in more detail.

To call the `DownloadImageTask` class, create an instance of it and then call its `execute()` method, passing it the URL of the image to download:

```
@Override
public void onCreate(Bundle savedInstanceState) {
    super.onCreate(savedInstanceState);
    setContentView(R.layout.main);
    new DownloadImageTask().execute(
        "http://www.mayoff.com/5-01cablecarDCP01934.jpg");
}
```

If you want to download a series of images asynchronously, you can modify the `DownloadImageTask` class as follows:

```
...
import android.widget.Toast;
...
    private class DownloadImageTask extends AsyncTask
    <String, Bitmap, Long> {
        //---takes in a list of image URLs in String type---
        protected Long doInBackground(String... urls) {
            long imagesCount = 0;
            for (int i = 0; i < urls.length; i++) {
                //---download the image---
                Bitmap imageDownloaded = DownloadImage(urls[i]);
                if (imageDownloaded != null)   {
                    //---increment the image count---
                    imagesCount++;
                    try {
                        //---insert a delay of 3 seconds---
                        Thread.sleep(3000);
                    } catch (InterruptedException e) {
                        e.printStackTrace();
                    }
                    //---return the image downloaded---
                    publishProgress(imageDownloaded);
                }
            }
            //---return the total images downloaded count---
            return imagesCount;
        }

        //---display the image downloaded---
        protected void onProgressUpdate(Bitmap... bitmap) {
            img.setImageBitmap(bitmap[0]);
        }

        //---when all the images have been downloaded---
        protected void onPostExecute(Long imagesDownloaded) {
            Toast.makeText(getBaseContext(),
                "Total " + imagesDownloaded + " images downloaded" ,
                Toast.LENGTH_LONG).show();
        }
    }
```

Note that in this example, the `DownloadImageTask` class has one more method: `onProgressUpdate()`. Because the task to be performed inside an `AsyncTask` class can be lengthy, you call the `publishProgress()` method to update the progress of the operation. This will trigger the `onProgressUpdate()` method, which in this case displays the image to be downloaded. The `onProgressUpdate()` method is executed on the UI thread; hence it is thread-safe to update the `ImageView` with the bitmap downloaded from the server.

To download a series of images asynchronously in the background, create an instance of the `BackgroundTask` class and call its `execute()` method, like this:

```
@Override
public void onCreate(Bundle savedInstanceState) {
    super.onCreate(savedInstanceState);
    setContentView(R.layout.main);

    /* new DownloadImageTask().execute(
        "http://www.mayoff.com/5-01cablecarDCP01934.jpg");
    */

    img = (ImageView) findViewById(R.id.img);
    new DownloadImageTask().execute(
            "http://www.mayoff.com/5-01cablecarDCP01934.jpg",
            "http://www.hartiesinfo.net/greybox/Cable_Car_
                Hartbeespoort.jpg",
            "http://mcmanuslab.ucsf.edu/sites/default/files/
                imagepicker/m/mmcmanus/
                CaliforniaSanFranciscoPaintedLadiesHz.jpg",
            "http://www.fantom-xp.com/wallpapers/63/San_Francisco
                _-_Sunset.jpg",
            "http://travel.roro44.com/europe/france/
                Paris_France.jpg",
            "http://wwp.greenwichmeantime.com/time-zone/usa/nevada
                /las-vegas/hotel/the-strip/paris-las-vegas/paris-
                las-vegas-hotel.jpg",
            "http://designheaven.files.wordpress.com/2010/04/
                eiffel_tower_paris_france.jpg");
}
```

When you run the preceding code, the images are downloaded in the background and displayed at an interval of three seconds. When the last image has been downloaded, the `Toast` class displays the total number of images downloaded.

REFERRING TO LOCALHOST FROM YOUR EMULATOR

When working with the Android emulator, you may frequently need to access data hosted on the local web server using `localhost`. For example, your own web services are likely to be hosted on your local computer during development, and you'll want to test them on the same development machine you use to write your Android applications. In such cases, you should use the special IP address of 10.0.2.2 (not 127.0.0.1) to refer to the host computer's loopback interface. From the Android emulator's perspective, `localhost` (127.0.0.1) refers to its own loopback interface.

Downloading Text Content

Besides downloading binary data, you can also download plain-text content. For example, you might want to access a web service that returns a string of random quotes. The following Try It Out shows how you can download a string from a web service in your application.

TRY IT OUT Downloading Plain-Text Content

1. Using the same project created earlier, add the following statements in bold to the NetworkingActivity.java file:

```java
import java.io.InputStreamReader;

private String DownloadText(String URL)
{
    int BUFFER_SIZE = 2000;
    InputStream in = null;
    try {
        in = OpenHttpConnection(URL);
    } catch (IOException e) {
        Log.d("Networking", e.getLocalizedMessage());
        return "";
    }

    InputStreamReader isr = new InputStreamReader(in);
    int charRead;
    String str = "";
    char[] inputBuffer = new char[BUFFER_SIZE];
    try {
        while ((charRead = isr.read(inputBuffer))>0) {
            //---convert the chars to a String---
            String readString =
                String.copyValueOf(inputBuffer, 0, charRead);
            str += readString;
            inputBuffer = new char[BUFFER_SIZE];
        }
        in.close();
    } catch (IOException e) {
        Log.d("Networking", e.getLocalizedMessage());
        return "";
    }
    return str;
}

private class DownloadTextTask extends AsyncTask<String, Void, String> {
    protected String doInBackground(String... urls) {
        return DownloadText(urls[0]);
    }

    @Override
    protected void onPostExecute(String result) {
        Toast.makeText(getBaseContext(), result, Toast.LENGTH_LONG).show();
    }
```

```
    }

    /** Called when the activity is first created. */
    @Override
    public void onCreate(Bundle savedInstanceState) {
        super.onCreate(savedInstanceState);
        setContentView(R.layout.main);

        //---download text---
        new DownloadTextTask().execute(
            "http://iheartquotes.com/api/v1/random?max_characters=256&max_lines=10");
    }
```

2. Press F11 to debug the application on the Android emulator. Figure 10-2 shows the random quote downloaded and displayed using the Toast class.

How It Works

The DownloadText() method takes the URL of the text file to download and then returns the string of the text file downloaded. It basically opens an HTTP connection to the server and then uses an InputStreamReader object to read each character from the stream and save it in a String object. As shown in the previous section, you had to create a subclass of the AsyncTask class in order to call the DownloadText() method asynchronously.

FIGURE 10-2

Accessing Web Services Using the GET Method

So far, you have learned how to download images and text from the web. The previous section showed how to download some plain text from a server. Very often, you need to download XML files and parse the contents (a good example of this is consuming web services). Therefore, in this section you learn how to connect to a web service using the HTTP GET method. Once the web service returns a result in XML, you extract the relevant parts and display its content using the Toast class.

In this example, you use the web method from http://services.aonaware.com/DictService/ DictService.asmx?op=Define. This web method is from a dictionary web service that returns the definition of a given word.

The web method takes a request in the following format:

```
GET /DictService/DictService.asmx/Define?word=string HTTP/1.1
Host: services.aonaware.com
HTTP/1.1 200 OK
Content-Type: text/xml; charset=utf-8
Content-Length: length
```

It returns a response in the following format:

```
<?xml version="1.0" encoding="utf-8"?>
<WordDefinition xmlns="http://services.aonaware.com/webservices/">
  <Word>string</Word>
  <Definitions>
    <Definition>
      <Word>string</Word>
      <Dictionary>
        <Id>string</Id>
        <Name>string</Name>
      </Dictionary>
      <WordDefinition>string</WordDefinition>
    </Definition>
    <Definition>
      <Word>string</Word>
      <Dictionary>
        <Id>string</Id>
        <Name>string</Name>
      </Dictionary>
      <WordDefinition>string</WordDefinition>
    </Definition>
  </Definitions>
</WordDefinition>
```

Hence, to obtain the definition of a word, you need to establish an HTTP connection to the web method and then parse the XML result that is returned. The following Try It Out shows you how.

TRY IT OUT Consuming Web Services

1. Using the same project created earlier, add the following statements in bold to the
`NetworkingActivity.java` file:

```java
import javax.xml.parsers.DocumentBuilder;
import javax.xml.parsers.DocumentBuilderFactory;
import javax.xml.parsers.ParserConfigurationException;

import org.w3c.dom.Document;
import org.w3c.dom.Element;
import org.w3c.dom.Node;
import org.w3c.dom.NodeList;

    private String WordDefinition(String word) {
        InputStream in = null;
        String strDefinition = "";
        try {
            in = OpenHttpConnection(
"http://services.aonaware.com/DictService/DictService.asmx/Define?word=" + word);
            Document doc = null;
            DocumentBuilderFactory dbf =
                DocumentBuilderFactory.newInstance();
            DocumentBuilder db;
            try {
                db = dbf.newDocumentBuilder();
                doc = db.parse(in);
            } catch (ParserConfigurationException e) {
                // TODO Auto-generated catch block
                e.printStackTrace();
            } catch (Exception e) {
                // TODO Auto-generated catch block
                e.printStackTrace();
            }
            doc.getDocumentElement().normalize();

            //---retrieve all the <Definition> elements---
            NodeList definitionElements =
                doc.getElementsByTagName("Definition");

            //---iterate through each <Definition> elements---
            for (int i = 0; i < definitionElements.getLength(); i++) {
                Node itemNode = definitionElements.item(i);
                if (itemNode.getNodeType() == Node.ELEMENT_NODE)
                {
                    //---convert the Definition node into an Element---
                    Element definitionElement = (Element) itemNode;

                    //---get all the <WordDefinition> elements under
                    // the <Definition> element---
                    NodeList wordDefinitionElements =
                        (definitionElement).getElementsByTagName(
```

```
                              "WordDefinition");

                   strDefinition = "";
                   //---iterate through each <WordDefinition> elements---
                   for (int j = 0; j < wordDefinitionElements.getLength(); j++) {
                       //---convert a <WordDefinition> node into an Element---
                       Element wordDefinitionElement =
                           (Element) wordDefinitionElements.item(j);

                       //---get all the child nodes under the
                       // <WordDefinition> element---
                       NodeList textNodes =
                           ((Node) wordDefinitionElement).getChildNodes();

                       strDefinition +=
                           ((Node) textNodes.item(0)).getNodeValue() + ". \n";
                   }

               }
           }
       } catch (IOException e1) {
           Log.d("NetworkingActivity", e1.getLocalizedMessage());
       }
       //---return the definitions of the word---
       return strDefinition;
   }

   private class AccessWebServiceTask extends AsyncTask<String, Void, String> {
       protected String doInBackground(String... urls) {
           return WordDefinition(urls[0]);
       }

       protected void onPostExecute(String result) {
           Toast.makeText(getBaseContext(), result, Toast.LENGTH_LONG).show();
       }
   }

   /** Called when the activity is first created. */
   @Override
   public void onCreate(Bundle savedInstanceState) {
       super.onCreate(savedInstanceState);
       setContentView(R.layout.main);

       //---access a Web Service using GET---
       new AccessWebServiceTask().execute("apple");
   }
```

2. Press F11 to debug the application on the Android emulator. Figure 10-3 shows the result of the web service call being parsed and then displayed using the `Toast` class.

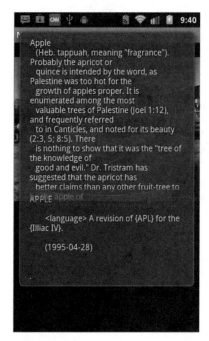

FIGURE 10-3

How It Works

The `WordDefinition()` method first opens an HTTP connection to the web service, passing in the word that you are interested in:

```
in = OpenHttpConnection(
   "http://services.aonaware.com/DictService/DictService.asmx/Define?word=" + word);
```

It then uses the `DocumentBuilderFactory` and `DocumentBuilder` objects to obtain a `Document` (DOM) object from an XML file (which is the XML result returned by the web service):

```
Document doc = null;
DocumentBuilderFactory dbf =
    DocumentBuilderFactory.newInstance();
DocumentBuilder db;
try {
    db = dbf.newDocumentBuilder();
    doc = db.parse(in);
} catch (ParserConfigurationException e) {
    // TODO Auto-generated catch block
    e.printStackTrace();
} catch (Exception e) {
    // TODO Auto-generated catch block
    e.printStackTrace();
}
doc.getDocumentElement().normalize();
```

Once the `Document` object is obtained, you find all the elements with the `<Definition>` tag:

```
//---retrieve all the <Definition> elements---
NodeList definitionElements =
    doc.getElementsByTagName("Definition");
```

Figure 10-4 shows the structure of the XML document returned by the web service.

```
▼ <WordDefinition xmlns:xsi="http://www.w3.org/2001/
  XMLSchema-instance" xmlns:xsd="http://www.w3.org/2001/
  XMLSchema" xmlns="http://services.aonaware.com/
  webservices/">
    <Word>apple</Word>
  ▼ <Definitions>
    ▼ <Definition>
        <Word>apple</Word>
      ▶ <Dictionary>…</Dictionary>
      ▶ <WordDefinition>…</WordDefinition>
      </Definition>
    ▼ <Definition>
        <Word>apple</Word>
      ▶ <Dictionary>…</Dictionary>
      ▶ <WordDefinition>…</WordDefinition>
      </Definition>
    ▶ <Definition>…</Definition>
    ▶ <Definition>…</Definition>
    ▶ <Definition>…</Definition>
    </Definitions>
  </WordDefinition>
```

FIGURE 10-4

Because the definition of a word is contained within the `<WordDefinition>` element, you then proceed to extract all the definitions:

```
//---iterate through each <Definition> elements---
for (int i = 0; i < definitionElements.getLength(); i++) {
    Node itemNode = definitionElements.item(i);
    if (itemNode.getNodeType() == Node.ELEMENT_NODE)
    {
        //---convert the Definition node into an Element---
        Element definitionElement = (Element) itemNode;

        //---get all the <WordDefinition> elements under
        // the <Definition> element---
        NodeList wordDefinitionElements =
            (definitionElement).getElementsByTagName(
            "WordDefinition");

        strDefinition = "";
        //---iterate through each <WordDefinition> elements---
        for (int j = 0; j < wordDefinitionElements.getLength(); j++) {
            //---convert a <WordDefinition> node into an Element---
            Element wordDefinitionElement =
                (Element) wordDefinitionElements.item(j);

            //---get all the child nodes under the
            // <WordDefinition> element---
            NodeList textNodes =
                ((Node) wordDefinitionElement).getChildNodes();

            strDefinition +=
```

```
                            ((Node) textNodes.item(0)).getNodeValue() + ". \n";
                }                              }
        }
```

The preceding code loops through all the `<Definition>` elements looking for a child element named `<WordDefinition>`. The text content of the `<WordDefinition>` element contains the definition of a word, and the definitions of a word are then concatenated and returned by the `WordDefinition()` method:

```
            //---return the definitions of the word---
            return strDefinition;
```

As usual, you need to create a subclass of the `AsyncTask` class to call the `WordDefinition()` method asynchronously:

```
        private class AccessWebServiceTask extends AsyncTask<String, Void, String> {
            protected String doInBackground(String... urls) {
                return WordDefinition(urls[0]);
            }

            protected void onPostExecute(String result) {
                Toast.makeText(getBaseContext(), result, Toast.LENGTH_LONG).show();
            }
        }
```

Finally, you access the web service asynchronously using the `execute()` method:

```
            //---access a Web Service using GET---
            new AccessWebServiceTask().execute("apple");
```

CONSUMING JSON SERVICES

In the previous section, you learned how to consume XML web services by using HTTP to connect to the web server and then obtain the results in XML. You also learned how to use DOM to parse the result of the XML document. However, manipulating XML documents is a computationally expensive operation for mobile devices, for the following reasons:

➤   XML documents are lengthy. They use tags to embed information, and the size of an XML document can get very big pretty quickly. A large XML document means that your device has to use more bandwidth to download it, which translates into higher cost.

➤   XML documents are more difficult to process. As shown earlier, you have to use DOM to traverse the tree in order to locate the information you want. In addition, DOM itself has to build the entire document in memory as a tree structure before you can traverse it. This is both memory and CPU intensive.

A much more efficient way to represent information exists in the form of JSON (JavaScript Object Notation). JSON is a lightweight data-interchange format that is easy for humans to read and write.

It is also easy for machines to parse and generate. The following lines of code show what a JSON message looks like:

```
[
    {
            "appeId":"1",
            "survId":"1",
            "location":"",
            "surveyDate":"2008-03 14",
            "surveyTime":"12:19:47",
            "inputUserId":"1",
            "inputTime":"2008-03-14 12:21:51",
            "modifyTime":"0000-00-00 00:00:00"
    },
    {
            "appeId":"2",
            "survId":"32",
            "location":"",
            "surveyDate":"2008-03-14",
            "surveyTime":"22:43:09",
            "inputUserId":"32",
            "inputTime":"2008-03-14 22:43:37",
            "modifyTime":"0000-00-00 00:00:00"
    },
    {
            "appeId":"3",
            "survId":"32",
            "location":"",
            "surveyDate":"2008-03-15",
            "surveyTime":"07:59:33",
            "inputUserId":"32",
            "inputTime":"2008-03-15 08:00:44",
            "modifyTime":"0000-00-00 00:00:00"
    },
    {
            "appeId":"4",
            "survId":"1",
            "location":"",
            "surveyDate":"2008-03-15",
            "surveyTime":"10:45:42",
            "inputUserId":"1",
            "inputTime":"2008-03-15 10:46:04",
            "modifyTime":"0000-00-00 00:00:00"
    },
    {
            "appeId":"5",
            "survId":"32",
            "location":"",
            "surveyDate":"2008-03-16",
            "surveyTime":"08:04:49",
            "inputUserId":"32",
            "inputTime":"2008-03-16 08:05:26",
            "modifyTime":"0000-00-00 00:00:00"
    },
```

```
{
    "appeId":"6",
    "survId":"32",
    "location":"",
    "surveyDate":"2008-03-20",
    "surveyTime":"20:19:01",
    "inputUserId":"32",
    "inputTime":"2008-03-20 20:19:32",
    "modifyTime":"0000-00-00 00:00:00"
}
]
```

The preceding block of lines represents a set of data taken for a survey. Note that the information is represented as a collection of key/value pairs; and each key/value pair is grouped into an ordered list of objects. Unlike XML, there are no lengthy tag names, only brackets and braces.

The following Try It Out demonstrates how to process JSON messages easily using the JSONArray and JSONObject classes available in the Android SDK.

TRY IT OUT   Consuming JSON Services

1. Using Eclipse, create a new Android project and name it **JSON**.

2. Add the following line in bold to the AndroidManifest.xml file:

```xml
<?xml version="1.0" encoding="utf-8"?>
<manifest xmlns:android="http://schemas.android.com/apk/res/android"
    package="net.learn2develop.JSON"
    android:versionCode="1"
    android:versionName="1.0" >

    <uses-sdk android:minSdkVersion="14" />
    <uses-permission android:name="android.permission.INTERNET"/>

    <application
        android:icon="@drawable/ic_launcher"
        android:label="@string/app_name" >
        <activity
            android:label="@string/app_name"
            android:name=".JSONActivity" >
            <intent-filter >
                <action android:name="android.intent.action.MAIN" />
                <category android:name="android.intent.category.LAUNCHER" />
            </intent-filter>
        </activity>
    </application>

</manifest>
```

3. Add the following lines of code in bold to the JSONActivity.java file:

```java
package net.learn2develop.JSON;

import java.io.BufferedReader;
import java.io.IOException;
```

```java
import java.io.InputStream;
import java.io.InputStreamReader;

import org.apache.http.HttpEntity;
import org.apache.http.HttpResponse;
import org.apache.http.StatusLine;
import org.apache.http.client.ClientProtocolException;
import org.apache.http.client.HttpClient;
import org.apache.http.client.methods.HttpGet;
import org.apache.http.impl.client.DefaultHttpClient;
import org.json.JSONArray;
import org.json.JSONObject;

import android.app.Activity;
import android.os.AsyncTask;
import android.os.Bundle;
import android.util.Log;
import android.widget.Toast;

public class JSONActivity extends Activity {

    public String readJSONFeed(String URL) {
        StringBuilder stringBuilder = new StringBuilder();
        HttpClient client = new DefaultHttpClient();
        HttpGet httpGet = new HttpGet(URL);
        try {
            HttpResponse response = client.execute(httpGet);
            StatusLine statusLine = response.getStatusLine();
            int statusCode = statusLine.getStatusCode();
            if (statusCode == 200) {
                HttpEntity entity = response.getEntity();
                InputStream content = entity.getContent();
                BufferedReader reader = new BufferedReader(
                        new InputStreamReader(content));
                String line;
                while ((line = reader.readLine()) != null) {
                    stringBuilder.append(line);
                }
            } else {
                Log.e("JSON", "Failed to download file");
            }
        } catch (ClientProtocolException e) {
            e.printStackTrace();
        } catch (IOException e) {
            e.printStackTrace();
        }
        return stringBuilder.toString();
    }

    private class ReadJSONFeedTask extends AsyncTask<String, Void, String> {
        protected String doInBackground(String... urls) {
            return readJSONFeed(urls[0]);
        }

        protected void onPostExecute(String result) {
            try {
```

```
                JSONArray jsonArray = new JSONArray(result);
                Log.i("JSON", "Number of surveys in feed: " +
                        jsonArray.length());

                //---print out the content of the json feed---
                for (int i = 0; i < jsonArray.length(); i++) {
                    JSONObject jsonObject = jsonArray.getJSONObject(i);
                    Toast.makeText(getBaseContext(), jsonObject.getString("appeId") +
                            " - " + jsonObject.getString("inputTime"),
                            Toast.LENGTH_SHORT).show();
                }
            } catch (Exception e) {
                e.printStackTrace();
            }
        }
    }

    /** Called when the activity is first created. */
    @Override
    public void onCreate(Bundle savedInstanceState) {
        super.onCreate(savedInstanceState);
        setContentView(R.layout.main);
        new ReadJSONFeedTask().execute(
            "http://extjs.org.cn/extjs/examples/grid/survey.html");
    }
}
```

4. Press F11 to debug the application on the Android emulator. You will see the Toast class appear a couple of times, displaying the information (see Figure 10-5).

FIGURE 10-5

How It Works

The first thing you did in this project was define the `readJSONFeed()` method:

```java
public String readJSONFeed(String URL) {
    StringBuilder stringBuilder = new StringBuilder();
    HttpClient client = new DefaultHttpClient();
    HttpGet httpGet = new HttpGet(URL);
    try {
        HttpResponse response = client.execute(httpGet);
        StatusLine statusLine = response.getStatusLine();
        int statusCode = statusLine.getStatusCode();
        if (statusCode == 200) {
            HttpEntity entity = response.getEntity();
            InputStream content = entity.getContent();
            BufferedReader reader = new BufferedReader(
                    new InputStreamReader(content));
            String line;
            while ((line = reader.readLine()) != null) {
                stringBuilder.append(line);
            }
        } else {
            Log.e("JSON", "Failed to download file");
        }
    } catch (ClientProtocolException e) {
        e.printStackTrace();
    } catch (IOException e) {
        e.printStackTrace();
    }
    return stringBuilder.toString();
}
```

This method simply connects to the specified URL and then reads the response from the web server. It returns a string as the result.

To call the `readJSONFeed()` method asynchronously, you created a subclass of the `AsyncTask` class:

```java
private class ReadJSONFeedTask extends AsyncTask<String, Void, String> {
    protected String doInBackground(String... urls) {
        return readJSONFeed(urls[0]);
    }

    protected void onPostExecute(String result) {
        try {
            JSONArray jsonArray = new JSONArray(result);
            Log.i("JSON", "Number of surveys in feed: " +
                    jsonArray.length());

            //---print out the content of the json feed---
            for (int i = 0; i < jsonArray.length(); i++) {
                JSONObject jsonObject = jsonArray.getJSONObject(i);
                Toast.makeText(getBaseContext(), jsonObject.getString("appeId") +
                        " - " + jsonObject.getString("inputTime"),
                        Toast.LENGTH_SHORT).show();
            }
        } catch (Exception e) {
```

```
                e.printStackTrace();
        }
    }
}
```

You called the readJSONFeed() method in the doInBackground() method, and the JSON string that you have fetched is passed in through the onPostExecute() method. The JSON string used in this example (and as illustrated earlier) is from http://extjs.org.cn/extjs/examples/grid/survey.html.

To obtain the list of objects in the JSON string, you used the JSONArray class, passing it the JSON feed as the constructor for the class:

```
JSONArray jsonArray = new JSONArray(result);
Log.i("JSON", "Number of surveys in feed: " +
        jsonArray.length());
```

The length() method returns the number of objects in the jsonArray object. With the list of objects stored in the jsonArray object, you iterated through it to obtain each object using the getJSONObject() method:

```
//---print out the content of the json feed---
for (int i = 0; i < jsonArray.length(); i++) {
    JSONObject jsonObject = jsonArray.getJSONObject(i);

    Toast.makeText(this, jsonObject.getString("appeId") +
            " - " + jsonObject.getString("inputTime"),
            Toast.LENGTH_SHORT).show();
}
```

The getJSONObject() method returns an object of type JSONObject. To obtain the value of the key/value pair stored inside the object, you used the getString() method (you can also use the getInt(), getLong(), and getBoolean() methods for other data types).

Finally, you accessed the JSON feed asynchronously using the execute() method:

```
new ReadJSONFeedTask().execute(
        "http://extjs.org.cn/extjs/examples/grid/survey.html");
```

This example showed how you can consume a JSON service and quickly parse its result. A much more interesting example is to use a real-life scenario: Twitter. The following changes make the application fetch my latest tweets from Twitter and then display the tweets in the Toast class (see Figure 10-6):

```
private class ReadJSONFeedTask extends AsyncTask<String, Void, String> {
    protected String doInBackground(String... urls) {
        return readJSONFeed(urls[0]);
    }

    protected void onPostExecute(String result) {
        try {
            JSONArray jsonArray = new JSONArray(result);
            Log.i("JSON", "Number of surveys in feed: " +
                    jsonArray.length());

            //---print out the content of the json feed---
```

```
            for (int i = 0; i < jsonArray.length(); i++) {
                JSONObject jsonObject = jsonArray.getJSONObject(i);
                /*
                 Toast.makeText(getBaseContext(), jsonObject.getString("appeId") +
                         " - " + jsonObject.getString("inputTime"),
                         Toast.LENGTH_SHORT).show();
                 */

                Toast.makeText(getBaseContext(), jsonObject.getString("text") +
                        " - " + jsonObject.getString("created_at"),
                        Toast.LENGTH_SHORT).show();
            }
        } catch (Exception e) {
            e.printStackTrace();
        }
    }
}

/** Called when the activity is first created. */
@Override
public void onCreate(Bundle savedInstanceState) {
    super.onCreate(savedInstanceState);
    setContentView(R.layout.main);
    /*
     new ReadJSONFeedTask().execute(
         "http://extjs.org.cn/extjs/examples/grid/survey.html");
     */
    new ReadJSONFeedTask().execute(
        "https://twitter.com/statuses/user_timeline/weimenglee.json");
}
```

FIGURE 10-6

SOCKETS PROGRAMMING

So far, you have seen the use of HTTP to consume XML and JSON web services. While most web services use HTTP for communication, they inherently suffer from one huge disadvantage: They are stateless. When you connect to a web service using HTTP, every connection is treated as a new connection — the web server does not maintain a persistent connection with the clients.

Consider a scenario in which your application connects to a web service that books cinema seats. When seats are booked on the server by a client, all the other clients are not aware of this until they connect to the web service again to obtain the new seat allocations. This constant polling by the clients incurs unnecessary bandwidth and makes your application inefficient. A much better solution is to have the server maintain individual connections to each client, and send a message to each one whenever seats are booked by another client.

If you want your application to maintain a persistent connection to the server and be notified by the server whenever changes occur, you need to use a programming technique known as *sockets programming*. Sockets programming is a technique through which you use to establish a connection between a client and a server. The following Try It Out demonstrates how you can build an Android chat client application that connects to a socket server. Multiple applications can connect to the server and chat at the same time.

TRY IT OUT Connecting to a Socket Server

1. Using Eclipse, create a new Android project and name it **Sockets**.

2. Add the following line in bold to the `AndroidManifest.xml` file:

```xml
<?xml version="1.0" encoding="utf-8"?>
<manifest xmlns:android="http://schemas.android.com/apk/res/android"
    package="net.learn2develop.Sockets"
    android:versionCode="1"
    android:versionName="1.0" >

    <uses-sdk android:minSdkVersion="14" />
    <uses-permission android:name="android.permission.INTERNET"/>

    <application
        android:icon="@drawable/ic_launcher"
        android:label="@string/app_name" >
        <activity
            android:label="@string/app_name"
            android:name=".SocketsActivity" >
            <intent-filter >
                <action android:name="android.intent.action.MAIN" />

                <category android:name="android.intent.category.LAUNCHER" />
            </intent-filter>
        </activity>
    </application>

</manifest>
```

3. Add the following lines in bold to the `main.xml` file, replacing the `TextView`:

```xml
<?xml version="1.0" encoding="utf-8"?>
<LinearLayout xmlns:android="http://schemas.android.com/apk/res/android"
    android:layout_width="fill_parent"
    android:layout_height="fill_parent"
    android:orientation="vertical" >

<EditText
    android:id="@+id/txtMessage"
    android:layout_width="fill_parent"
    android:layout_height="wrap_content" />

<Button
    android:layout_width="fill_parent"
    android:layout_height="wrap_content"
    android:text="Send Message"
    android:onClick="onClickSend"/>

<TextView
    android:id="@+id/txtMessagesReceived"
    android:layout_width="fill_parent"
    android:layout_height="200dp"
    android:scrollbars = "vertical" />

</LinearLayout>
```

4. Add a new Java Class file to the package and name it `CommsThread`. Populate the `CommsThread`
`.java` file as follows:

```java
package net.learn2develop.Sockets;

import java.io.IOException;
import java.io.InputStream;
import java.io.OutputStream;
import java.net.Socket;
import android.util.Log;

public class CommsThread extends Thread {
    private final Socket socket;
    private final InputStream inputStream;
    private final OutputStream outputStream;

    public CommsThread(Socket sock) {
        socket = sock;
        InputStream tmpIn = null;
        OutputStream tmpOut = null;
        try {
            //---creates the inputstream and outputstream objects
            // for reading and writing through the sockets---
            tmpIn = socket.getInputStream();
            tmpOut = socket.getOutputStream();
        } catch (IOException e) {
            Log.d("SocketChat", e.getLocalizedMessage());
        }
```

```java
            inputStream = tmpIn;
            outputStream = tmpOut;
        }

    public void run() {
        //---buffer store for the stream---
        byte[] buffer = new byte[1024];

        //---bytes returned from read()---
        int bytes;

        //---keep listening to the InputStream until an
        // exception occurs---
        while (true) {
            try {
                //---read from the inputStream---
                bytes = inputStream.read(buffer);

                //---update the main activity UI---
                SocketsActivity.UIupdater.obtainMessage(
                    0,bytes, -1, buffer).sendToTarget();
            } catch (IOException e) {
                break;
            }
        }
    }

    //---call this from the main activity to
    // send data to the remote device---
    public void write(byte[] bytes) {
        try {
            outputStream.write(bytes);
        } catch (IOException e) { }
    }

    //---call this from the main activity to
    // shutdown the connection---
    public void cancel() {
        try {
            socket.close();
        } catch (IOException e) { }
    }
}
```

5. In the SocketsActivity.java file, add the following lines in bold:

```java
package net.learn2develop.Sockets;

import java.io.IOException;
import java.net.InetAddress;
import java.net.Socket;
import java.net.UnknownHostException;

import android.app.Activity;
import android.os.AsyncTask;
```

```java
import android.os.Bundle;
import android.os.Handler;
import android.os.Message;
import android.view.View;
import android.widget.EditText;
import android.widget.TextView;

import android.util.Log;

public class SocketsActivity extends Activity {
    static final String NICKNAME = "Wei-Meng";
    InetAddress serverAddress;
    Socket socket;

    //---all the Views---
    static TextView txtMessagesReceived;
    EditText txtMessage;

    //---thread for communicating on the socket---
    CommsThread commsThread;

    //---used for updating the UI on the main activity---
    static Handler UIupdater = new Handler() {
        @Override
        public void handleMessage(Message msg) {
            int numOfBytesReceived = msg.arg1;
            byte[] buffer = (byte[]) msg.obj;

            //---convert the entire byte array to string---
            String strReceived = new String(buffer);

            //---extract only the actual string received---
            strReceived = strReceived.substring(
                    0, numOfBytesReceived);

            //---display the text received on the TextView---
            txtMessagesReceived.setText(
                    txtMessagesReceived.getText().toString() +
                    strReceived);
        }
    };

    private class CreateCommThreadTask extends AsyncTask
    <Void, Integer, Void> {
        @Override
        protected Void doInBackground(Void... params) {
            try {
                //---create a socket---
                serverAddress =
                    InetAddress.getByName("192.168.1.142");
                    //--remember to change the IP address above to match your own--
                socket = new Socket(serverAddress, 500);
                commsThread = new CommsThread(socket);
                commsThread.start();
                //---sign in for the user; sends the nick name---
                sendToServer(NICKNAME);
```

```java
            } catch (UnknownHostException e) {
                Log.d("Sockets", e.getLocalizedMessage());
            } catch (IOException e) {
                Log.d("Sockets", e.getLocalizedMessage());
            }
            return null;
        }
    }

    private class WriteToServerTask extends AsyncTask
    <byte[], Void, Void> {
        protected Void doInBackground(byte[]...data) {
            commsThread.write(data[0]);
            return null;
        }
    }

    private class CloseSocketTask extends AsyncTask
    <Void, Void, Void> {
        @Override
        protected Void doInBackground(Void... params) {
            try {
                socket.close();
            } catch (IOException e) {
                Log.d("Sockets", e.getLocalizedMessage());
            }
            return null;
        }
    }

    /** Called when the activity is first created. */
    @Override
    public void onCreate(Bundle savedInstanceState) {
        super.onCreate(savedInstanceState);
        setContentView(R.layout.main);

        //---get the views---
        txtMessage = (EditText) findViewById(R.id.txtMessage);
        txtMessagesReceived = (TextView)
                findViewById(R.id.txtMessagesReceived);
    }

    public void onClickSend(View view) {
        //---send the message to the server---
        sendToServer(txtMessage.getText().toString());
    }

    private void sendToServer(String message) {
        byte[] theByteArray =
                message.getBytes();
        new WriteToServerTask().execute(theByteArray);
    }

    @Override
    public void onResume() {
        super.onResume();
```

```
        new CreateCommThreadTask().execute();
    }

    @Override
    public void onPause() {
        super.onPause();
        new CloseSocketTask().execute();
    }
}
```

6. For testing, you will be using a socket server application that I have written (you can obtain this application through the source code download for this book at wrox.com). This application is a multi-user console application (for Windows) that simply listens at port 500 of the local computer and then broadcasts all the messages it receives to all the other clients connected to it. To run the server, open a Command window in Windows and type in the following command: **C:\>Server.exe** *Your_IP_Address*. For example, if your computer had an IP address of 192.168.1.142, then you would enter the following:

```
C:\>Server.exe 192.168.1.142
```

7. Before you deploy the application onto a real device, ensure that the device is connected to the same network as your computer running the server described in the previous step. In a common setup, your computer is connected to the wireless router (either wired or wirelessly) and your device is connected wirelessly to the same wireless router. Once this is done, press F11 to deploy the application onto the Android device.

8. Type a message and tap the Send Message button (see Figure 10-7).

FIGURE 10-7

9. You will be able to see the message received by the server, as shown in Figure 10-8.

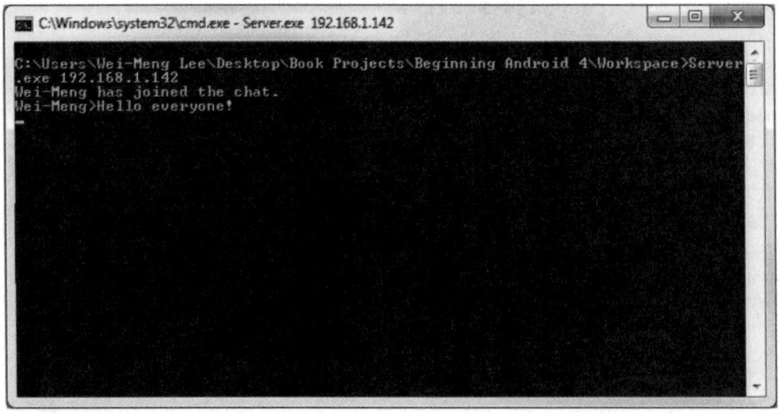

FIGURE 10-8

How It Works

To handle the intricacies of sockets communication, you created a separate class and called it the CommsThread (for communication thread). This class extends the Thread class so that all the sockets communication can be performed on a different thread, separate from the main UI thread:

```
public class CommsThread extends Thread {
}
```

Within this class, you declared three objects:

```
private final Socket socket;
private final InputStream inputStream;
private final OutputStream outputStream;
```

The first is a Socket object, which provides a client-side TCP socket. The InputStream object helps to read data from the socket connection. The OutputStream object helps to write data to the socket connection.

The constructor for the CommsThread class takes in a Socket instance and then tries to obtain an InputStream and OutputStream objects from the socket connection:

```
public CommsThread(Socket sock) {
    socket = sock;
    InputStream tmpIn = null;
    OutputStream tmpOut = null;
    try {
        //---creates the inputstream and outputstream objects
        // for reading and writing through the sockets---
        tmpIn = socket.getInputStream();
        tmpOut = socket.getOutputStream();
    } catch (IOException e) {
        Log.d("SocketChat", e.getLocalizedMessage());
    }
    inputStream = tmpIn;
    outputStream = tmpOut;
}
```

The run() method (which is called when you call the start() method of this thread) keeps listening for incoming data by reading perpetually using the InputStream object. When data is received, it updates the main activity's UI by passing it a message containing the data received:

```
public void run() {
    //---buffer store for the stream---
    byte[] buffer = new byte[1024];

    //---bytes returned from read()---
    int bytes;

    //---keep listening to the InputStream until an
    // exception occurs---
    while (true) {
```

```
        try {
            //---read from the inputStream---
            bytes = inputStream.read(buffer);

            //---update the main activity UI---
            SocketsActivity.UIupdater.obtainMessage(
                0,bytes, -1, buffer).sendToTarget();
        } catch (IOException e) {
            break;
        }
    }
}
```

The write() method helps to write data to the socket connection:

```
//---call this from the main activity to
// send data to the remote device---
public void write(byte[] bytes) {
    try {
        outputStream.write(bytes);
    } catch (IOException e) { }
}
```

Finally, the cancel() method closes the socket connection:

```
//---call this from the main activity to
// shutdown the connection---
public void cancel() {
    try {
        socket.close();
    } catch (IOException e) { }
}
```

In the SocketsActivity.java file, you created three subclasses that extended the AsyncTask class:

```
private class CreateCommThreadTask extends AsyncTask
<Void, Integer, Void> {
    @Override
    protected Void doInBackground(Void... params) {
        try {
            //---create a socket---
            serverAddress =
                InetAddress.getByName("192.168.1.142");
            socket = new Socket(serverAddress, 500);
            commsThread = new CommsThread(socket);
            commsThread.start();
            //---sign in for the user; sends the nick name---
            sendToServer(NICKNAME);
        } catch (UnknownHostException e) {
            Log.d("Sockets", e.getLocalizedMessage());
        } catch (IOException e) {
            Log.d("Sockets", e.getLocalizedMessage());
        }
        return null;
```

```
        }
    }

    private class WriteToServerTask extends AsyncTask
    <byte[], Void, Void> {
        protected Void doInBackground(byte[]...data) {
            commsThread.write(data[0]);
            return null;
        }
    }

    private class CloseSocketTask extends AsyncTask
    <Void, Void, Void> {
        @Override
        protected Void doInBackground(Void... params) {
            try {
                socket.close();
            } catch (IOException e) {
                Log.d("Sockets", e.getLocalizedMessage());
            }
            return null;
        }
    }
}
```

The `CreateCommThreadTask` class asynchronously creates a socket connection with the server. For the socket server, the first string sent by the client after the connection is established will be treated as the nickname for the client. Hence, after the socket connection is started, you immediately send a message to the server containing the nickname you want to use for your client:

```
//---sign in for the user; sends the nick name---
sendToServer(NICKNAME);
```

The `WriteToServerTask` class enables you to send data to the server asynchronously, while the `CloseSocketTask` class closes a socket connection.

The `sendToServer()` method takes in a `String` argument and converts it into a byte array. It then calls the `execute()` method of the `WriteToServerTask` class to send the data to the server asynchronously:

```
private void sendToServer(String message) {
    byte[] theByteArray =
            message.getBytes();
    new WriteToServerTask().execute(theByteArray);
}
```

Finally, when the activity is paused, you close the socket connection; and when it is resumed, you establish the connection again:

```
@Override
public void onPause() {
    super.onPause();
    new CloseSocketTask().execute();
}

@Override
```

```
public void onResume() {
    super.onResume();
    new CreateCommThreadTask().execute();
}
```

SUMMARY

In this chapter, you learned how your application can connect with the outside world through the use of the HTTP protocol. Using the HTTP protocol, you can download various types of data from web servers. One good application of this is to talk to web services, whereby you need to parse XML files. In addition to XML web services, you also saw how to consume JSON services, which are more lightweight than XML web services. Finally, you saw an alternative to HTTP: using sockets for communication. Sockets enable your application to remain connected to a server so that it can receive data as and when it becomes available. A very important lesson learned in this chapter is that all synchronous operations must be encapsulated using the AsyncTask class; otherwise, your application will not work on devices running Honeycomb or later.

EXERCISES

1. Name the permissions you need to declare in your AndroidManifest.xml file for an HTTP connection.

2. Name the classes used for dealing with JSON messages.

3. Name the class for performing background asynchronous tasks.

Answers to the exercises can be found in Appendix C.

▶ **WHAT YOU LEARNED IN THIS CHAPTER**

TOPIC	KEY CONCEPTS
Establishing an HTTP connection	Use the `HttpURLConnection` class.
Accessing XML web services	Use the `Document`, `DocumentBuilderFactory`, and `DocumentBuilder` classes to parse the XML result returned by the web service.
Dealing with JSON messages	Use the `JSONArray` and `JSONObject` classes.
Sockets programming	Use the `Socket` class to establish a TCP connection. Use the `InputStream` and `OutputStream` objects for receiving and sending data, respectively.
The three methods in an AsyncTask class	The three methods are `doInBackground()`, `onProgressUpdate()`, and `onPostExecute()`.

11

Developing Android Services

WHAT YOU WILL LEARN IN THIS CHAPTER

➤ How to create a service that runs in the background

➤ How to perform long-running tasks in a separate thread

➤ How to perform repeated tasks in a service

➤ How an activity and a service communicate

A service is an application in Android that runs in the background without needing to interact with the user. For example, while using an application, you may want to play some background music at the same time. In this case, the code that is playing the background music has no need to interact with the user, and hence it can be run as a service. Services are also ideal for situations in which there is no need to present a UI to the user. A good example of this scenario is an application that continually logs the geographical coordinates of the device. In this case, you can write a service to do that in the background. In this chapter, you will learn how to create your own services and use them to perform background tasks asynchronously.

CREATING YOUR OWN SERVICES

The best way to understand how a service works is by creating one. The following Try It Out shows you the steps to create a simple service. Subsequent sections add more functionality to this service. For now, you will learn how to start and stop a service.

Creating a Simple Service

codefile Services.zip available for download at Wrox.com

1. Using Eclipse, create a new Android project and name it **Services**.

2. Add a new Java Class file to the project and name it **MyService**. Populate the `MyService.java` file with the following code:

```java
package net.learn2develop.Services;

import android.app.Service;
import android.content.Intent;
import android.os.IBinder;
import android.widget.Toast;

public class MyService extends Service {

    @Override
    public IBinder onBind(Intent arg0) {
        return null;
    }

    @Override
    public int onStartCommand(Intent intent, int flags, int startId) {
        // We want this service to continue running until it is explicitly
        // stopped, so return sticky.
        Toast.makeText(this, "Service Started", Toast.LENGTH_LONG).show();
        return START_STICKY;
    }

    @Override
    public void onDestroy() {
        super.onDestroy();
        Toast.makeText(this, "Service Destroyed", Toast.LENGTH_LONG).show();
    }
}
```

3. In the `AndroidManifest.xml` file, add the following statement in bold:

```xml
<?xml version="1.0" encoding="utf-8"?>
<manifest xmlns:android="http://schemas.android.com/apk/res/android"
    package="net.learn2develop.Services"
    android:versionCode="1"
    android:versionName="1.0" >

    <uses-sdk android:minSdkVersion="14" />

    <application
        android:icon="@drawable/ic_launcher"
        android:label="@string/app_name" >
        <activity
```

```
            android:label="@string/app_name"
            android:name=".ServicesActivity" >
            <intent-filter >
                <action android:name="android.intent.action.MAIN" />

                <category android:name="android.intent.category.LAUNCHER" />
            </intent-filter>
        </activity>
        <service android:name=".MyService" />
    </application>

</manifest>
```

4. In the `main.xml` file, add the following statements in bold, replacing `TextView`:

```xml
<?xml version="1.0" encoding="utf-8"?>
<LinearLayout xmlns:android="http://schemas.android.com/apk/res/android"
    android:layout_width="fill_parent"
    android:layout_height="fill_parent"
    android:orientation="vertical" >

<Button android:id="@+id/btnStartService"
    android:layout_width="fill_parent"
    android:layout_height="wrap_content"
    android:text="Start Service"
    android:onClick="startService"/>

<Button android:id="@+id/btnStopService"
    android:layout_width="fill_parent"
    android:layout_height="wrap_content"
    android:text="Stop Service"
    android:onClick="stopService" />

</LinearLayout>
```

5. Add the following statements in bold to the `ServicesActivity.java` file:

```java
package net.learn2develop.Services;

import android.app.Activity;
import android.content.Intent;
import android.os.Bundle;
import android.view.View;

public class ServicesActivity extends Activity {
    /** Called when the activity is first created. */
    @Override
    public void onCreate(Bundle savedInstanceState) {
        super.onCreate(savedInstanceState);
        setContentView(R.layout.main);
    }

    public void startService(View view) {
```

```
            startService(new Intent(getBaseContext(), MyService.class));
    }

    public void stopService(View view) {
            stopService(new Intent(getBaseContext(),
    MyService.class));
    }

}
```

6. Press F11 to debug the application on the Android emulator.

7. Clicking the Start Service button will start the service (see Figure 11-1). To stop the service, click the Stop Service button.

How It Works

This example demonstrated the simplest service that you can create. The service itself is not doing anything useful, of course, but it serves to illustrate the creation process.

First, you defined a class that extends the Service base class. All services extend the Service class:

FIGURE 11-1

```
public class MyService extends Service {
}
```

Within the MyService class, you implemented three methods:

```
@Override
public IBinder onBind(Intent arg0) {  ...  }

@Override
public int onStartCommand(Intent intent, int flags, int startId) { ... }

@Override
public void onDestroy() { ... }
```

The onBind() method enables you to bind an activity to a service. This in turn enables an activity to directly access members and methods inside a service. For now, you simply return a null for this method. Later in this chapter you will learn more about binding.

The onStartCommand() method is called when you start the service explicitly using the startService() method (discussed shortly). This method signifies the start of the service, and you code it to do the things you need to do for your service. In this method, you returned the constant START_STICKY so that the service will continue to run until it is explicitly stopped.

The `onDestroy()` method is called when the service is stopped using the `stopService()` method. This is where you clean up the resources used by your service.

All services that you have created must be declared in the `AndroidManifest.xml` file, like this:

```
<service android:name=".MyService" />
```

If you want your service to be available to other applications, you can always add an intent filter with an action name, like this:

```
<service android:name=".MyService">
    <intent-filter>
        <action android:name="net.learn2develop.MyService" />
    </intent-filter>
</service>
```

To start a service, you use the `startService()` method, like this:

```
startService(new Intent(getBaseContext(), MyService.class));
```

If you are calling this service from an external application, then the call to the `startService()` method looks like this:

```
startService(new Intent("net.learn2develop.MyService"));
```

To stop a service, use the `stopService()` method:

```
stopService(new Intent(getBaseContext(), MyService.class));
```

Performing Long-Running Tasks in a Service

Because the service you created in the previous section does not do anything useful, in this section you will modify it so that it performs a task. In the following Try It Out, you will simulate the service of downloading a file from the Internet.

TRY IT OUT Making Your Service Useful

1. Using the Services project created in the first example, add the following statements in bold to the `ServicesActivity.java` file:

```
package net.learn2develop.Services;

import java.net.MalformedURLException;
import java.net.URL;

import android.app.Service;
```

```java
import android.content.Intent;
import android.os.IBinder;
import android.widget.Toast;

public class MyService extends Service {

    @Override
    public IBinder onBind(Intent arg0) {
        return null;
    }

    @Override
    public int onStartCommand(Intent intent, int flags, int startId) {
        // We want this service to continue running until it is explicitly
        // stopped, so return sticky.
        //Toast.makeText(this, "Service Started", Toast.LENGTH_LONG).show();

        try {
            int result = DownloadFile(new URL("http://www.amazon.com/somefile.pdf"));
            Toast.makeText(getBaseContext(),
                "Downloaded " + result + " bytes",
                Toast.LENGTH_LONG).show();
        } catch (MalformedURLException e) {
            // TODO Auto-generated catch block
            e.printStackTrace();
        }
        return START_STICKY;
    }

    private int DownloadFile(URL url) {
        try {
            //---simulate taking some time to download a file---
            Thread.sleep(5000);
        } catch (InterruptedException e) {
            e.printStackTrace();
        }
        //---return an arbitrary number representing
        // the size of the file downloaded---
        return 100;
    }

    @Override
    public void onDestroy() {
        super.onDestroy();
        Toast.makeText(this, "Service Destroyed", Toast.LENGTH_LONG).show();
    }
```

2. Press F11 to debug the application on the Android emulator.

3. Click the Start Service button to start the service to download the file. Note that the activity is frozen for a few seconds before the `Toast` class displays the "Downloaded 100 bytes" message (see Figure 11-2).

How It Works

In this example, your service calls the `DownloadFile()` method to simulate downloading a file from a given URL. This method returns the total number of bytes downloaded (which you have hardcoded as 100). To simulate the delays experienced by the service when downloading the file, you used the `Thread.Sleep()` method to pause the service for five seconds (5,000 milliseconds).

As you start the service, note that the activity is suspended for about five seconds, which is the time taken for the file to be downloaded from the Internet. During this time, the entire activity is not responsive, demonstrating a very important point: The service runs on the same thread as your activity. In this case, because the service is suspended for five seconds, so is the activity.

FIGURE 11-2

Hence, for a long-running service, it is important that you put all long-running code into a separate thread so that it does not tie up the application that calls it. The following Try It Out shows you how.

TRY IT OUT Performing Tasks in a Service Asynchronously

codefile Services.zip available for download at Wrox.com

1. Using the Services project created in the first example, add the following statements in bold to the `MyService.java` file:

```java
package net.learn2develop.Services;

import java.net.MalformedURLException;
import java.net.URL;

import android.app.Service;
import android.content.Intent;
import android.os.AsyncTask;
import android.os.IBinder;
import android.util.Log;
import android.widget.Toast;

public class MyService extends Service {

    @Override
    public IBinder onBind(Intent arg0) {
```

```java
            return null;
    }

    @Override
    public int onStartCommand(Intent intent, int flags, int startId) {
        // We want this service to continue running until it is explicitly
        // stopped, so return sticky.
        //Toast.makeText(this, "Service Started", Toast.LENGTH_LONG).show();

        try {
            new DoBackgroundTask().execute(
                    new URL("http://www.amazon.com/somefiles.pdf"),
                    new URL("http://www.wrox.com/somefiles.pdf"),
                    new URL("http://www.google.com/somefiles.pdf"),
                    new URL("http://www.learn2develop.net/somefiles.pdf"));

        } catch (MalformedURLException e) {
            // TODO Auto-generated catch block
            e.printStackTrace();
        }
        return START_STICKY;
    }

    private int DownloadFile(URL url) {
        try {
            //---simulate taking some time to download a file---
            Thread.sleep(5000);
        } catch (InterruptedException e) {
            e.printStackTrace();
        }
        //---return an arbitrary number representing
        // the size of the file downloaded---
        return 100;
    }

    private class DoBackgroundTask extends AsyncTask<URL, Integer, Long> {
        protected Long doInBackground(URL... urls) {
            int count = urls.length;
            long totalBytesDownloaded = 0;
            for (int i = 0; i < count; i++) {
                totalBytesDownloaded += DownloadFile(urls[i]);
                //---calculate percentage downloaded and
                // report its progress---
                publishProgress((int) (((i+1) / (float) count) * 100));
            }
            return totalBytesDownloaded;
        }

        protected void onProgressUpdate(Integer... progress) {
            Log.d("Downloading files",
                    String.valueOf(progress[0]) + "% downloaded");
            Toast.makeText(getBaseContext(),
                String.valueOf(progress[0]) + "% downloaded",
```

```
                    Toast.LENGTH_LONG).show();
        }

        protected void onPostExecute(Long result) {
            Toast.makeText(getBaseContext(),
                    "Downloaded " + result + " bytes",
                    Toast.LENGTH_LONG).show();
            stopSelf();
        }
    }

    @Override
    public void onDestroy() {
        super.onDestroy();
        Toast.makeText(this, "Service Destroyed", Toast.LENGTH_LONG).show();
    }
}
```

2. Press F11 to debug the application on the Android emulator.

3. Click the Start Service button. The `Toast` class will display a message indicating what percentage of the download is completed. You should see four of them: 25%, 50%, 75%, and 100%.

4. You can see output similar to the following in the LogCat window:

```
12-06 01:58:24.967: D/Downloading files(6020): 25% downloaded
12-06 01:58:30.019: D/Downloading files(6020): 50% downloaded
12-06 01:58:35.078: D/Downloading files(6020): 75% downloaded
12-06 01:58:40.096: D/Downloading files(6020): 100% downloaded
```

How It Works

This example illustrates one way in which you can execute a task asynchronously within your service. You do so by creating an inner class that extends the `AsyncTask` class. The `AsyncTask` class enables you to perform background execution without needing to manually handle threads and handlers.

The `DoBackgroundTask` class extends the `AsyncTask` class by specifying three generic types:

```
private class DoBackgroundTask extends AsyncTask<URL, Integer, Long> {
```

In this case, the three types specified are `URL`, `Integer` and `Long`. These three types specify the data type used by the following three methods that you implement in an `AsyncTask` class:

➤ `doInBackground()` — This method accepts an array of the first generic type specified earlier. In this case, the type is `URL`. This method is executed in the background thread and is where you put your long-running code. To report the progress of your task, you call the `publishProgress()` method, which invokes the next method, `onProgressUpdate()`, which you implement in an `AsyncTask` class. The return type of this method takes the third generic type specified earlier, which is `Long` in this case.

➤ onProgressUpdate() — This method is invoked in the UI thread and is called when you call the publishProgress() method. It accepts an array of the second generic type specified earlier. In this case, the type is Integer. Use this method to report the progress of the background task to the user.

➤ onPostExecute() — This method is invoked in the UI thread and is called when the doInBackground() method has finished execution. This method accepts an argument of the third generic type specified earlier, which in this case is a Long.

Figure 11-3 summarizes the types specified and their relationship to the three methods inside a subclass of the AsyncTask class.

```
private class DoBackgroundTask extends AsyncTask<URL, Integer, Long> {
    protected Long doInBackground(URL... urls) {
        int count = urls.length;
        long totalBytesDownloaded = 0;
        for (int i = 0; i < count; i++) {
            totalBytesDownloaded += DownloadFile(urls[i]);
            //---calculate percentage downloaded and
            // report its progress---
            publishProgress((int) (((i+1) / (float) count) * 100));
        }
        return totalBytesDownloaded;
    }

    protected void onProgressUpdate(Integer... progress) {
        Log.d("Downloading files",
                String.valueOf(progress[0]) + "% downloaded");
        Toast.makeText(getBaseContext(),
                String.valueOf(progress[0]) + "% downloaded",
                Toast.LENGTH_LONG).show();
    }

    protected void onPostExecute(Long result) {
        Toast.makeText(getBaseContext(),
                "Downloaded " + result + " bytes",
                Toast.LENGTH_LONG).show();
        stopSelf();
    }
}
```

FIGURE 11-3

To download multiple files in the background, you created an instance of the DoBackgroundTask class and then called its execute() method by passing in an array of URLs:

```
try {
    new DoBackgroundTask().execute(
            new URL("http://www.amazon.com/somefiles.pdf"),
            new URL("http://www.wrox.com/somefiles.pdf"),
            new URL("http://www.google.com/somefiles.pdf"),
            new URL("http://www.learn2develop.net/somefiles.pdf"));

} catch (MalformedURLException e) {
    // TODO Auto-generated catch block
    e.printStackTrace();
}
```

The preceding causes the service to download the files in the background, and reports the progress as a percentage of files downloaded. More important, the activity remains responsive while the files are downloaded in the background, on a separate thread.

Note that when the background thread has finished execution, you can manually call the stopSelf() method to stop the service:

```
protected void onPostExecute(Long result) {
    Toast.makeText(getBaseContext(),
            "Downloaded " + result + " bytes",
            Toast.LENGTH_LONG).show();
    stopSelf();
}
```

The stopSelf() method is the equivalent of calling the stopService() method to stop the service.

Performing Repeated Tasks in a Service

In addition to performing long-running tasks in a service, you might also perform some repeated tasks in a service. For example, you may write an alarm clock service that runs persistently in the background. In this case, your service may need to periodically execute some code to check whether a prescheduled time has been reached so that an alarm can be sounded. To execute a block of code to be executed at a regular time interval, you can use the Timer class within your service. The following Try It Out shows you how.

TRY IT OUT   Running Repeated Tasks Using the Timer Class

codefile Services.zip available for download at Wrox.com

1.   Using the Services project again, add the following statements in bold to the MyService.java file:

```java
package net.learn2develop.Services;

import java.net.MalformedURLException;
import java.net.URL;
import java.util.Timer;
import java.util.TimerTask;

import android.app.Service;
import android.content.Intent;
import android.os.AsyncTask;
import android.os.IBinder;
import android.util.Log;
import android.widget.Toast;

public class MyService extends Service {
    int counter = 0;
    static final int UPDATE_INTERVAL = 1000;
    private Timer timer = new Timer();

    @Override
    public IBinder onBind(Intent arg0) {
        return null;
    }

    @Override
    public int onStartCommand(Intent intent, int flags, int startId) {
        // We want this service to continue running until it is explicitly
        // stopped, so return sticky.
        //Toast.makeText(this, "Service Started", Toast.LENGTH_LONG).show();

        doSomethingRepeatedly();

        try {
            new DoBackgroundTask().execute(
                    new URL("http://www.amazon.com/somefiles.pdf"),
                    new URL("http://www.wrox.com/somefiles.pdf"),
                    new URL("http://www.google.com/somefiles.pdf"),
                    new URL("http://www.learn2develop.net/somefiles.pdf"));

        } catch (MalformedURLException e) {
```

```
            // TODO Auto-generated catch block
            e.printStackTrace();
        }
        return START_STICKY;
    }

    private void doSomethingRepeatedly() {
        timer.scheduleAtFixedRate(new TimerTask() {
            public void run() {
                Log.d("MyService", String.valueOf(++counter));
            }
        }, 0, UPDATE_INTERVAL);
    }

    private int DownloadFile(URL url) {
        try {
            //---simulate taking some time to download a file---
            Thread.sleep(5000);
        } catch (InterruptedException e) {
            e.printStackTrace();
        }
        //---return an arbitrary number representing
        // the size of the file downloaded---
        return 100;
    }

    private class DoBackgroundTask extends AsyncTask<URL, Integer, Long> {
        protected Long doInBackground(URL... urls) {
            int count = urls.length;
            long totalBytesDownloaded = 0;
            for (int i = 0; i < count; i++) {
                totalBytesDownloaded += DownloadFile(urls[i]);
                //---calculate percentage downloaded and
                // report its progress---
                publishProgress((int) (((i+1) / (float) count) * 100));
            }
            return totalBytesDownloaded;
        }

        protected void onProgressUpdate(Integer... progress) {
            Log.d("Downloading files",
                    String.valueOf(progress[0]) + "% downloaded");
            Toast.makeText(getBaseContext(),
                String.valueOf(progress[0]) + "% downloaded",
                Toast.LENGTH_LONG).show();
        }

        protected void onPostExecute(Long result) {
            Toast.makeText(getBaseContext(),
                    "Downloaded " + result + " bytes",
                    Toast.LENGTH_LONG).show();
            stopSelf();
        }
    }
}

@Override
```

```
public void onDestroy() {
    super.onDestroy();

    if (timer != null){
        timer.cancel();
    }

    Toast.makeText(this, "Service Destroyed", Toast.LENGTH_LONG).show();
    }
}
```

2. Press F11 to debug the application on the Android emulator.

3. Click the Start Service button.

4. Observe the output displayed in the LogCat window. It will be similar to the following:

```
12-06 02:37:54.118: D/MyService(7752): 1
12-06 02:37:55.109: D/MyService(7752): 2
12-06 02:37:56.120: D/MyService(7752): 3
12-06 02:37:57.111: D/MyService(7752): 4
12-06 02:37:58.125: D/MyService(7752): 5
12-06 02:37:59.137: D/MyService(7752): 6
```

How It Works

In this example, you created a Timer object and called its scheduleAtFixedRate() method inside the doSomethingRepeatedly() method that you have defined:

```
private void doSomethingRepeatedly() {
    timer.scheduleAtFixedRate( new TimerTask() {
        public void run() {
            Log.d("MyService", String.valueOf(++counter));
        }
    }, 0, UPDATE_INTERVAL);
}
```

You passed an instance of the TimerTask class to the scheduleAtFixedRate() method so that you can execute the block of code within the run() method repeatedly. The second parameter to the scheduleAtFixedRate() method specifies the amount of time, in milliseconds, before first execution. The third parameter specifies the amount of time, in milliseconds, between subsequent executions.

In the preceding example, you essentially print out the value of the counter every second (1,000 milliseconds). The service repeatedly prints the value of counter until the service is terminated:

```
@Override
public void onDestroy() {
    super.onDestroy();

    if (timer != null){
        timer.cancel();
    }

    Toast.makeText(this, "Service Destroyed", Toast.LENGTH_LONG).show();
    }
}
```

For the `scheduleAtFixedRate()` method, your code is executed at fixed time intervals, regardless of how long each task takes. For example, if the code within your `run()` method takes two seconds to complete, then your second task will start immediately after the first task has ended. Similarly, if your delay is set to three seconds and the task takes two seconds to complete, then the second task will wait for one second before starting.

Also, observe that you call the `doSomethingRepeatedly()` method directly in the `onStartCommand()` method, without needing to wrap it in a subclass of the `AsyncTask` class. This is because the `TimerTask` class itself implements the `Runnable` interface, which allows it to run on a separate thread.

Executing Asynchronous Tasks on Separate Threads Using IntentService

Earlier in this chapter, you learned how to start a service using the `startService()` method and stop a service using the `stopService()` method. You have also seen how you should execute long-running task on a separate thread — not the same thread as the calling activities. It is important to note that once your service has finished executing a task, it should be stopped as soon as possible so that it does not unnecessarily hold up valuable resources. That's why you use the `stopSelf()` method to stop the service when a task has been completed. Unfortunately, a lot of developers often forgot to terminate a service when it is done performing its task. To easily create a service that runs a task asynchronously and terminates itself when it is done, you can use the `IntentService` class.

The `IntentService` class is a base class for `Service` that handles asynchronous requests on demand. It is started just like a normal service; and it executes its task within a worker thread and terminates itself when the task is completed. The following Try It Out demonstrates how to use the `IntentService` class.

TRY IT OUT — Using the IntentService Class to Auto-Stop a Service

codefile Services.zip available for download at Wrox.com

1. Using the Services project created in the first example, add a new Class file named **MyIntentService.java**.

2. Populate the `MyIntentService.java` file as follows:

```java
package net.learn2develop.Services;

import java.net.MalformedURLException;
import java.net.URL;

import android.app.IntentService;
import android.content.Intent;
import android.util.Log;

public class MyIntentService extends IntentService {

    public MyIntentService() {
        super("MyIntentServiceName");
    }

    @Override
```

```java
    protected void onHandleIntent(Intent intent) {
        try {
            int result =
                DownloadFile(new URL("http://www.amazon.com/somefile.pdf"));
            Log.d("IntentService", "Downloaded " + result + " bytes");
        } catch (MalformedURLException e) {
            e.printStackTrace();
        }
    }

    private int DownloadFile(URL url) {
        try {
            //---simulate taking some time to download a file---
            Thread.sleep(5000);
        } catch (InterruptedException e) {
            e.printStackTrace();
        }
        return 100;
    }
}
```

3. Add the following statement in bold to the `AndroidManifest.xml` file:

```xml
<?xml version="1.0" encoding="utf-8"?>
<manifest xmlns:android="http://schemas.android.com/apk/res/android"
    package="net.learn2develop.Services"
    android:versionCode="1"
    android:versionName="1.0" >

    <uses-sdk android:minSdkVersion="14" />

    <application
        android:icon="@drawable/ic_launcher"
        android:label="@string/app_name" >
        <activity
            android:label="@string/app_name"
            android:name=".ServicesActivity" >
            <intent-filter >
                <action android:name="android.intent.action.MAIN" />

                <category android:name="android.intent.category.LAUNCHER" />
            </intent-filter>
        </activity>

        <service android:name=".MyService">
            <intent-filter>
                <action android:name="net.learn2develop.MyService" />
            </intent-filter>
        </service>
        <service android:name=".MyIntentService" />

    </application>

</manifest>
```

4. Add the following statement in bold to the `ServicesActivity.java` file:

```
public void startService(View view) {
    //startService(new Intent(getBaseContext(), MyService.class));
    //OR
    //startService(new Intent("net.learn2develop.MyService"));
    startService(new Intent(getBaseContext(), MyIntentService.class));
}
```

5. Press F11 to debug the application on the Android emulator.

6. Click the Start Service button. After about five seconds, you should see something similar to the following statement in the LogCat window:

```
12-06 13:35:32.181: D/IntentService(861): Downloaded 100 bytes
```

How It Works

First, you defined the `MyIntentService` class, which extends the `IntentService` class instead of the `Service` class:

```
public class MyIntentService extends IntentService {
}
```

You needed to implement a constructor for the class and call its superclass with the name of the intent service (setting it with a string):

```
public MyIntentService() {
    super("MyIntentServiceName");
}
```

You then implemented the `onHandleIntent()` method, which is executed on a worker thread:

```
@Override
protected void onHandleIntent(Intent intent) {
    try {
        int result =
            DownloadFile(new URL("http://www.amazon.com/somefile.pdf"));
        Log.d("IntentService", "Downloaded " + result + " bytes");
    } catch (MalformedURLException e) {
        e.printStackTrace();
    }
}
```

The `onHandleIntent()` method is where you place the code that needs to be executed on a separate thread, such as downloading a file from a server. When the code has finished executing, the thread is terminated and the service is stopped automatically.

ESTABLISHING COMMUNICATION BETWEEN A SERVICE AND AN ACTIVITY

Often a service simply executes in its own thread, independently of the activity that calls it. This doesn't pose any problem if you simply want the service to perform some tasks periodically and the activity does not need to be notified about the service's status. For example, you may have a service that periodically logs the geographical location of the device to a database. In this case, there is no need for your service to interact with any activities, because its main purpose is to save the coordinates into a database. However, suppose you want to monitor for a particular location. When the service logs an address that is near the location you are monitoring, it might need to communicate that information to the activity. If so, you need to devise a way for the service to interact with the activity.

The following Try It Out demonstrates how a service can communicate with an activity using a `BroadcastReceiver`.

TRY IT OUT Invoking an Activity from a Service

codefile Services.zip available for download at Wrox.com

1. Using the Services project created earlier, add the following statements in bold to the `MyIntentService.java` file:

```java
package net.learn2develop.Services;

import java.net.MalformedURLException;
import java.net.URL;

import android.app.IntentService;
import android.content.Intent;
import android.util.Log;

public class MyIntentService extends IntentService {

    public MyIntentService() {
        super("MyIntentServiceName");
    }

    @Override
    protected void onHandleIntent(Intent intent) {
        try {
            int result =
                DownloadFile(new URL("http://www.amazon.com/somefile.pdf"));
            Log.d("IntentService", "Downloaded " + result + " bytes");

            //---send a broadcast to inform the activity
            // that the file has been downloaded---
            Intent broadcastIntent = new Intent();
            broadcastIntent.setAction("FILE_DOWNLOADED_ACTION");
            getBaseContext().sendBroadcast(broadcastIntent);

        } catch (MalformedURLException e) {
            e.printStackTrace();
        }
```

```
    }

    private int DownloadFile(URL url) {
        try {
            //---simulate taking some time to download a file---
            Thread.sleep(5000);
        } catch (InterruptedException e) {
            // TODO Auto-generated catch block
            e.printStackTrace();
        }
        return 100;
    }
}
```

2. Add the following statements in bold to the ServicesActivity.java file:

```
package net.learn2develop.Services;

import android.app.Activity;
import android.content.BroadcastReceiver;
import android.content.Context;
import android.content.Intent;
import android.content.IntentFilter;
import android.os.Bundle;
import android.view.View;
import android.widget.Toast;

public class ServicesActivity extends Activity {
    IntentFilter intentFilter;

    /** Called when the activity is first created. */
    @Override
    public void onCreate(Bundle savedInstanceState) {
        super.onCreate(savedInstanceState);
        setContentView(R.layout.main);
    }

    @Override
    public void onResume() {
        super.onResume();

        //---intent to filter for file downloaded intent---
        intentFilter = new IntentFilter();
        intentFilter.addAction("FILE_DOWNLOADED_ACTION");

        //---register the receiver---
        registerReceiver(intentReceiver, intentFilter);
    }

    @Override
    public void onPause() {
        super.onPause();

        //---unregister the receiver---
```

```
                    unregisterReceiver(intentReceiver);
            }

            public void startService(View view) {
                //startService(new Intent(getBaseContext(), MyService.class));
                //OR
                //startService(new Intent("net.learn2develop.MyService"));
                startService(new Intent(getBaseContext(), MyIntentService.class));
            }

            public void stopService(View view) {
                stopService(new Intent(getBaseContext(), MyService.class));
            }

            private BroadcastReceiver intentReceiver = new BroadcastReceiver() {
                @Override
                public void onReceive(Context context, Intent intent) {
                    Toast.makeText(getBaseContext(), "File downloaded!",
                            Toast.LENGTH_LONG).show();
                }
            };

        }
```

3. Press F11 to debug the application on the Android emulator.

4. Click the Start Service button. After about five seconds, the Toast class will display a message indicating that the file has been downloaded (see Figure 11-4).

FIGURE 11-4

How It Works

To notify an activity when a service has finished its execution, you broadcast an intent using the
`sendBroadcast()` method:

```
@Override
protected void onHandleIntent(Intent intent) {
    try {
        int result =
            DownloadFile(new URL("http://www.amazon.com/somefile.pdf"));
        Log.d("IntentService", "Downloaded " + result + " bytes");

        //---send a broadcast to inform the activity
        // that the file has been downloaded---
        Intent broadcastIntent = new Intent();
        broadcastIntent.setAction("FILE_DOWNLOADED_ACTION");
        getBaseContext().sendBroadcast(broadcastIntent);

    } catch (MalformedURLException e) {
        e.printStackTrace();
    }
}
```

The action of this intent that you are broadcasting is set to `"FILE_DOWNLOADED_ACTION"`, which means
any activity that is listening for this intent will be invoked. Hence, in your `ServicesActivity.java`
file, you listen for this intent using the `registerReceiver()` method from the `IntentFilter` class:

```
@Override
public void onResume() {
    super.onResume();

    //---intent to filter for file downloaded intent---
    intentFilter = new IntentFilter();
    intentFilter.addAction("FILE_DOWNLOADED_ACTION");

    //---register the receiver---
    registerReceiver(intentReceiver, intentFilter);
}
```

When the intent is received, it invokes an instance of the `BroadcastReceiver` class that you have defined:

```
private BroadcastReceiver intentReceiver = new BroadcastReceiver() {
    @Override
    public void onReceive(Context context, Intent intent) {
        Toast.makeText(getBaseContext(), "File downloaded!",
                Toast.LENGTH_LONG).show();
    }
};
```

NOTE *Chapter 8 discusses the* BroadcastReceiver *class in more detail.*

In this case, you displayed the message "File downloaded!" Of course, if you need to pass some data from the service to the activity, you can make use of the Intent object. The next section discusses this.

BINDING ACTIVITIES TO SERVICES

So far, you have seen how services are created and how they are called and terminated when they are done with their task. All the services that you have seen are simple — either they start with a counter and increment at regular intervals or they download a fixed set of files from the Internet. However, real-world services are usually much more sophisticated, requiring the passing of data so that they can do the job correctly for you.

Using the service demonstrated earlier that downloads a set of files, suppose you now want to let the calling activity determine what files to download, instead of hardcoding them in the service. Here is what you need to do.

First, in the calling activity, you create an Intent object, specifying the service name:

```
public void startService(View view) {
    Intent intent = new Intent(getBaseContext(), MyService.class);
}
```

You then create an array of URL objects and assign it to the Intent object through its putExtra() method. Finally, you start the service using the Intent object:

```
public void startService(View view) {
    Intent intent = new Intent(getBaseContext(), MyService.class);
    try {
        URL[] urls = new URL[] {
                new URL("http://www.amazon.com/somefiles.pdf"),
                new URL("http://www.wrox.com/somefiles.pdf"),
                new URL("http://www.google.com/somefiles.pdf"),
                new URL("http://www.learn2develop.net/somefiles.pdf")};
        intent.putExtra("URLs", urls);
    } catch (MalformedURLException e) {
        e.printStackTrace();
    }
    startService(intent);
}
```

Note that the URL array is assigned to the Intent object as an Object array.

On the service's end, you need to extract the data passed in through the Intent object in the onStartCommand() method:

```
@Override
public int onStartCommand(Intent intent, int flags, int startId) {
    // We want this service to continue running until it is explicitly
    // stopped, so return sticky.
    Toast.makeText(this, "Service Started", Toast.LENGTH_LONG).show();
    Object[] objUrls = (Object[]) intent.getExtras().get("URLs");
    URL[] urls = new URL[objUrls.length];
    for (int i=0; i<objUrls.length-1; i++) {
        urls[i] = (URL) objUrls[i];
    }
    new DoBackgroundTask().execute(urls);
    return START_STICKY;
}
```

The preceding first extracts the data using the getExtras() method to return a Bundle object. It then uses the get() method to extract out the URL array as an Object array. Because in Java you cannot directly cast an array from one type to another, you have to create a loop and cast each member of the array individually. Finally, you execute the background task by passing the URL array into the execute() method.

This is one way in which your activity can pass values to the service. As you can see, if you have relatively complex data to pass to the service, you have to do some additional work to ensure that the data is passed correctly. A better way to pass data is to bind the activity directly to the service so that the activity can call any public members and methods on the service directly. The following Try It Out shows you how to bind an activity to a service.

TRY IT OUT   Accessing Members of a Property Directly through Binding

codefile Services.zip available for download at Wrox.com

1. Using the Services project created earlier, add the following statements in bold to the MyService .java file (note that you are modifying the existing onStartCommand()):

```
import android.os.Binder;

import android.os.IBinder;

public class MyService extends Service {
    int counter = 0;
    URL[] urls;
    static final int UPDATE_INTERVAL = 1000;
    private Timer timer = new Timer();
    private final IBinder binder = new MyBinder();

    public class MyBinder extends Binder {
        MyService getService() {
            return MyService.this;
        }
    }

    @Override
    public IBinder onBind(Intent arg0) {
```

```
            return binder;
    }

    @Override
    public int onStartCommand(Intent intent, int flags, int startId) {
        // We want this service to continue running until it is explicitly
        // stopped, so return sticky.
        Toast.makeText(this, "Service Started", Toast.LENGTH_LONG).show();
        new DoBackgroundTask().execute(urls);
        return START_STICKY;
    }


    private void doSomethingRepeatedly() { … }

    private int DownloadFile(URL url) { ... }

    private class DoBackgroundTask extends AsyncTask<URL, Integer, Long> { ... }

    @Override
    public void onDestroy() { ... }
}
```

2. In the ServicesActivity.java file, add the following statements in bold (note the change to the existing startService() method):

```
import android.content.ComponentName;
import android.os.IBinder;
import android.content.ServiceConnection;
import java.net.MalformedURLException;
import java.net.URL;

public class ServicesActivity extends Activity {
    IntentFilter intentFilter;

    MyService serviceBinder;
    Intent i;

    private ServiceConnection connection = new ServiceConnection() {
        public void onServiceConnected(
            ComponentName className, IBinder service) {
            //---called when the connection is made---
            serviceBinder = ((MyService.MyBinder)service).getService();
            try {
                URL[] urls = new URL[] {
                    new URL("http://www.amazon.com/somefiles.pdf"),
                    new URL("http://www.wrox.com/somefiles.pdf"),
                    new URL("http://www.google.com/somefiles.pdf"),
                    new URL("http://www.learn2develop.net/somefiles.pdf")};
                    //---assign the URLs to the service through the
                    // serviceBinder object---
                    serviceBinder.urls = urls;
            } catch (MalformedURLException e) {
                e.printStackTrace();
            }
```

```
                    startService(i);
        }
        public void onServiceDisconnected(ComponentName className) {
            //---called when the service disconnects---
            serviceBinder = null;
        }
    };

    public void startService(View view) {
        i = new Intent(ServicesActivity.this, MyService.class);
        bindService(i, connection, Context.BIND_AUTO_CREATE);
    }

    @Override
    public void onCreate(Bundle savedInstanceState) { ... }

    @Override
    public void onResume() { ... }

    @Override
    public void onPause() { ... }

    public void stopService(View view) { ... }

    private BroadcastReceiver intentReceiver = new BroadcastReceiver() {
        ...
    };

}
```

3. Press F11 to debug the application. Clicking the Start Service button will start the service as normal.

How It Works

To bind activities to a service, you must first declare an inner class in your service that extends the `Binder` class:

```
public class MyBinder extends Binder {
    MyService getService() {
        return MyService.this;
    }
}
```

Within this class you implemented the `getService()` method, which returns an instance of the service. You then created an instance of the `MyBinder` class:

```
private final IBinder binder = new MyBinder();
```

You also modified the `onBind()` method to return the `MyBinder` instance:

```
@Override
public IBinder onBind(Intent arg0) {
    return binder;
}
```

In the onStartCommand() method, you then called the execute() method using the urls array, which you declared as a public member in your service:

```
public class MyService extends Service {
    int counter = 0;
    URL[] urls;
...
...
    @Override
    public int onStartCommand(Intent intent, int flags, int startId) {
        // We want this service to continue running until it is explicitly
        // stopped, so return sticky.
        Toast.makeText(this, "Service Started", Toast.LENGTH_LONG).show();
        new DoBackgroundTask().execute(urls);
        return START_STICKY;
    }
}
```

This URL array can be set directly from your activity, which you did next.

In the ServicesActivity.java file, you first declared an instance of your service and an Intent object:

```
MyService serviceBinder;
Intent i;
```

The serviceBinder object will be used as a reference to the service, which you accessed directly.

You then created an instance of the ServiceConnection class so that you could monitor the state of the service:

```
private ServiceConnection connection = new ServiceConnection() {
    public void onServiceConnected(
        ComponentName className, IBinder service) {
        //---called when the connection is made---
        serviceBinder = ((MyService.MyBinder)service).getService();
        try {
            URL[] urls = new URL[] {
                new URL("http://www.amazon.com/somefiles.pdf"),
                new URL("http://www.wrox.com/somefiles.pdf"),
                new URL("http://www.google.com/somefiles.pdf"),
                new URL("http://www.learn2develop.net/somefiles.pdf")};
                //---assign the URLs to the service through the
                // serviceBinder object---
                serviceBinder.urls = urls;
            } catch (MalformedURLException e) {
                e.printStackTrace();
            }
            startService(i);
        }
    public void onServiceDisconnected(ComponentName className) {
        //---called when the service disconnects---
        serviceBinder = null;
    }
};
```

You need to implement two methods: `onServiceConnected()` and `onServiceDisconnected()`. The `onServiceConnected()` method is called when the activity is connected to the service; the `onServiceDisconnected()` method is called when the service is disconnected from the activity.

In the `onServiceConnected()` method, when the activity is connected to the service, you obtained an instance of the service by using the `getService()` method of the `service` argument and then assigning it to the `serviceBinder` object. The `serviceBinder` object is a reference to the service, and all the members and methods in the service can be accessed through this object. Here, you created a URL array and then directly assigned it to the public member in the service:

```
URL[] urls = new URL[] {
    new URL("http://www.amazon.com/somefiles.pdf"),
    new URL("http://www.wrox.com/somefiles.pdf"),
    new URL("http://www.google.com/somefiles.pdf"),
    new URL("http://www.learn2develop.net/somefiles.pdf")};
    //---assign the URLs to the service through the
    // serviceBinder object---
    serviceBinder.urls = urls;
```

You then started the service using an `Intent` object:

```
startService(i);
```

Before you can start the service, you have to bind the activity to the service. This you did in the `startService()` method of the Start Service button:

```
public void startService(View view) {
    i = new Intent(ServicesActivity.this, MyService.class);
    bindService(i, connection, Context.BIND_AUTO_CREATE);
}
```

The `bindService()` method enables your activity to be connected to the service. It takes three arguments: an `Intent` object, a `ServiceConnection` object, and a flag to indicate how the service should be bound.

UNDERSTANDING THREADING

So far, you have seen how services are created and why it is important to ensure that your long-running tasks are properly handled, especially when updating the UI thread. Earlier in this chapter (as well as in Chapter 10), you also saw how to use the `AsyncTask` class for executing long-running code in the background. This section briefly summarizes the various ways to handle long-running tasks correctly using a variety of methods available.

For this discussion, assume that you have an Android project named **Threading**. The `main.xml` file contains a Button and TextView:

```
<?xml version="1.0" encoding="utf-8"?>
<LinearLayout xmlns:android="http://schemas.android.com/apk/res/android"
    android:layout_width="fill_parent"
```

```xml
        android:layout_height="fill_parent"
        android:orientation="vertical" >

    <TextView
        android:layout_width="fill_parent"
        android:layout_height="wrap_content"
        android:text="@string/hello" />

    <Button
        android:id="@+id/btnStartCounter"
        android:layout_width="match_parent"
        android:layout_height="wrap_content"
        android:text="Start"
        android:onClick="startCounter" />

    <TextView
        android:id="@+id/textView1"
        android:layout_width="match_parent"
        android:layout_height="wrap_content"
        android:text="TextView" />

</LinearLayout>
```

Suppose you want to display a counter on the activity, from 0 to 1,000. In your ThreadingActivity class, you have the following code:

```java
package net.learn2develop.Threading;

import android.app.Activity;
import android.os.Bundle;
import android.util.Log;
import android.view.View;
import android.widget.TextView;

public class ThreadingActivity extends Activity {
    TextView txtView1;

    /** Called when the activity is first created. */
    @Override
    public void onCreate(Bundle savedInstanceState) {
        super.onCreate(savedInstanceState);
        setContentView(R.layout.main);

        txtView1 = (TextView) findViewById(R.id.textView1);
    }

    public void startCounter(View view) {
        for (int i=0; i<=1000; i++) {
            txtView1.setText(String.valueOf(i));
            try {
                Thread.sleep(1000);
            } catch (InterruptedException e) {
```

```
                            Log.d("Threading", e.getLocalizedMessage());
                    }
              }
          }
      }
```

When you run the application and click the Start button, the application is briefly frozen, and after a while you may see the message shown in Figure 11-5.

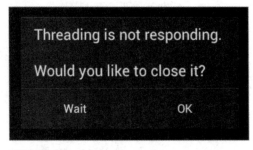

The UI freezes because the application is continuously trying to display the value of the counter at the same time it is pausing for one second

FIGURE 11-5

after it has been displayed. This ties up the UI, which is waiting for the display of the numbers to be completed. The result is a nonresponsive application that will frustrate your users.

To solve this problem, one option is to wrap the part of the code that contains the loop using a `Thread` and `Runnable` class, like this:

```
public void startCounter(View view) {
    new Thread(new Runnable() {
        public void run() {
            for (int i=0; i<=1000; i++) {
                txtView1.setText(String.valueOf(i));
                try {
                    Thread.sleep(1000);
                } catch (InterruptedException e) {
                    Log.d("Threading", e.getLocalizedMessage());
                }
            }
        }
    }).start();
}
```

In the preceding code, you first create a class that implements the `Runnable` interface. Within this class, you put your long-running code within the `run()` method. The `Runnable` block is then started using the `Thread` class.

 NOTE *A* Runnable *is a block of code that can be executed by a thread.*

However, the preceding application will not work, and it will crash if you try to run it. This code that is placed inside the `Runnable` block is on a separate thread, and in the preceding example you are trying to update the UI from another thread, which is not a safe thing to do because Android UIs are not thread-safe. To resolve this, you need to use the `post()` method of a `View` to create another `Runnable` block to be added to the message queue. In short, the new `Runnable` block created will be executed in the UI thread, so it would now be safe to execute your application:

```java
public void startCounter(View view) {
    new Thread(new Runnable() {
        @Override
        public void run() {
            for (int i=0; i<=1000; i++) {
                final int valueOfi = i;

                //---update UI---
                txtView1.post(new Runnable() {
                    public void run() {
                        //---UI thread for updating---
                        txtView1.setText(String.valueOf(valueOfi));
                    }
                });

                //---insert a delay
                try {
                    Thread.sleep(1000);
                } catch (InterruptedException e) {
                    Log.d("Threading", e.getLocalizedMessage());
                }
            }
        }
    }).start();
}
```

This application will now work correctly, but it is complicated and makes your code difficult to maintain.

A second option to update the UI from another thread is to use the `Handler` class. A `Handler` enables you to send and process messages, similar to using the `post()` method of a `View`. The following code snippets shows a `Handler` class called `UIupdater` that updates the UI using the message that it receives:

 NOTE *For the following code to work, you need to import the* `android.os` *`.Handler` package as well as add the* `static` *modifier to* `txtView1`.

```java
//---used for updating the UI on the main activity---
static Handler UIupdater = new Handler() {
    @Override
    public void handleMessage(Message msg) {
        byte[] buffer = (byte[]) msg.obj;

        //---convert the entire byte array to string---
        String strReceived = new String(buffer);

        //---display the text received on the TextView---
        txtView1.setText(strReceived);
```

```
                Log.d("Threading", "running");
        }
    };

    public void startCounter(View view) {
        new Thread(new Runnable() {
            @Override
            public void run() {
                for (int i=0; i<=1000; i++) {
                    //---update the main activity UI---
                    ThreadingActivity.UIupdater.obtainMessage(
                        0,  String.valueOf(i).getBytes() ).sendToTarget();
                    //---insert a delay
                    try {
                        Thread.sleep(1000);
                    } catch (InterruptedException e) {
                        Log.d("Threading", e.getLocalizedMessage());
                    }
                }
            }
        }).start();
    }

}
```

A detailed discussion of the Handler class is beyond the scope of this book. For more details, check out the documentation at http://developer.android.com/reference/android/os/Handler.html.

So far, the two methods just described enable you to update the UI from a separate thread. In Android, you could use the simpler AsyncTask class to do this. Using the AsyncTask, you could rewrite the preceding code as follows:

```
    private class DoCountingTask extends AsyncTask<Void, Integer, Void> {
        protected Void doInBackground(Void... params) {
            for (int i = 0; i < 1000; i++) {
                //---report its progress---
                publishProgress(i);
                try {
                    Thread.sleep(1000);
                } catch (InterruptedException e) {
                    Log.d("Threading", e.getLocalizedMessage());
                }
            }
            return null;
        }

        protected void onProgressUpdate(Integer... progress) {
            txtView1.setText(progress[0].toString());
            Log.d("Threading", "updating...");
        }
    }

    public void startCounter(View view) {
        new DoCountingTask().execute();
    }
```

The preceding code will update the UI safely from another thread. What about stopping the task? If you run the preceding application and then click the Start button, the counter will start to display from zero. However, if you press the back button on the emulator/device, the task continues to run even though the activity has been destroyed. You can verify this through the LogCat window. If you want to stop the task, use the following code snippets:

```java
public class ThreadingActivity extends Activity {
    static TextView txtView1;

    DoCountingTask task;

    /** Called when the activity is first created. */
    @Override
    public void onCreate(Bundle savedInstanceState) {
        super.onCreate(savedInstanceState);
        setContentView(R.layout.main);

        txtView1 = (TextView) findViewById(R.id.textView1);
    }

    public void startCounter(View view) {
        task = (DoCountingTask) new DoCountingTask().execute();
    }

    public void stopCounter(View view) {
        task.cancel(true);
    }

    private class DoCountingTask extends AsyncTask<Void, Integer, Void> {
        protected Void doInBackground(Void... params) {
            for (int i = 0; i < 1000; i++) {
                //---report its progress---
                publishProgress(i);
                try {
                    Thread.sleep(1000);
                } catch (InterruptedException e) {
                    Log.d("Threading", e.getLocalizedMessage());
                }
                if (isCancelled()) break;
            }
            return null;
        }

        protected void onProgressUpdate(Integer... progress) {
            txtView1.setText(progress[0].toString());
            Log.d("Threading", "updating...");
        }
    }

    @Override
    protected void onPause() {
        super.onPause();
        stopCounter(txtView1);
    }
}
```

To stop the `AsyncTask` subclass, you need to get an instance of it first. To stop the task, call its `cancel()` method. Within the task, you call the `isCancelled()` method to check whether the task should be terminated.

SUMMARY

In this chapter, you learned how to create a service in your Android project to execute long-running tasks. You have seen the many approaches you can use to ensure that the background task is executed in an asynchronous fashion, without tying up the main calling activity. You have also learned how an activity can pass data into a service, and how you can alternatively bind to an activity so that it can access a service more directly.

EXERCISES

1. Why is it important to put long-running code in a service on a separate thread?

2. What is the purpose of the `IntentService` class?

3. Name the three methods you need to implement in an `AsyncTask` class.

4. How can a service notify an activity of an event happening?

5. For threading, what is the recommended method to ensure that your code runs without tying up the UI of your application?

Answers to the exercises can be found in Appendix C.

▶ WHAT YOU LEARNED IN THIS CHAPTER

TOPIC	KEY CONCEPTS
Creating a service	Create a class and extend the `Service` class.
Implementing the methods in a service	Implement the following methods: `onBind()`, `onStartCommand()`, and `onDestroy()`.
Starting a service	Use the `startService()` method.
Stopping a service	Use the `stopService()` method.
Performing long-running tasks	Use the `AsyncTask` class and implement three methods: `doInBackground()`, `onProgressUpdate()`, and `onPostExecute()`.
Performing repeated tasks	Use the `Timer` class and call its `scheduleAtFixedRate()` method.
Executing tasks on a separate thread and auto-stopping a service	Use the `IntentService` class.
Enabling communication between an activity and a service	Use the `Intent` object to pass data into the service. For a service, broadcast an `Intent` to notify an activity.
Binding an activity to a service	Use the `Binder` class in your service and implement the `ServiceConnection` class in your calling activity.
Updating the UI from a `Runnable` block	Use the `post()` method of a view to update the UI. Alternatively, you can also use a `Handler` class. The recommended way is to use the `AsyncTask` class.

12

Publishing Android Applications

WHAT YOU WILL LEARN IN THIS CHAPTER

➤ How to prepare your application for deployment

➤ Exporting your application as an APK file and signing it with a new certificate

➤ How to distribute your Android application

➤ Publishing your application on the Android Market

So far you have seen quite a lot of interesting things you can do with your Android device. However, in order to get your application running on users' devices, you need a way to deploy it and distribute it. In this chapter, you will learn how to prepare your Android applications for deployment and get them onto your customer's devices. In addition, you will learn how to publish your applications on the Android Market, where you can sell them and make some money!

PREPARING FOR PUBLISHING

Google has made it relatively easy to publish your Android application so that it can be quickly distributed to end users. The steps to publishing your Android application generally involve the following:

1. Export your application as an APK (Android Package) file.

2. Generate your own self-signed certificate and digitally sign your application with it.

3. Deploy the signed application.

4. Use the Android Market for hosting and selling your application.

In the following sections, you will learn how to prepare your application for signing, and then learn about the various ways to deploy your applications.

This chapter uses the LBS project created in Chapter 9 to demonstrate how to deploy an Android application.

Versioning Your Application

Beginning with version 1.0 of the Android SDK, the AndroidManifest.xml file of every Android application includes the android:versionCode and android:versionName attributes:

```xml
<?xml version="1.0" encoding="utf-8"?>
<manifest xmlns:android="http://schemas.android.com/apk/res/android"
    package="net.learn2develop.LBS"
    android:versionCode="1"
    android:versionName="1.0" >

    <uses-sdk android:minSdkVersion="14" />
    <uses-permission android:name="android.permission.INTERNET"/>
    <uses-permission android:name="android.permission.ACCESS_FINE_LOCATION"/>
    <uses-permission android:name="android.permission.ACCESS_COARSE_LOCATION"/>

    <application
        android:icon="@drawable/ic_launcher"
        android:label="@string/app_name" >
        <uses-library android:name="com.google.android.maps" />
        <activity
            android:label="@string/app_name"
            android:name=".LBSActivity" >
            <intent-filter >
                <action android:name="android.intent.action.MAIN" />

                <category android:name="android.intent.category.LAUNCHER" />
            </intent-filter>
        </activity>
    </application>

</manifest>
```

The android:versionCode attribute represents the version number of your application. For every revision you make to the application, you should increment this value by 1 so that you can programmatically differentiate the newest version from the previous one. This value is never used by the Android system, but it is useful for developers as a means to obtain an application's version number. However, the android:versionCode attribute is used by Android Market to determine whether a newer version of your application is available.

You can programmatically retrieve the value of the android:versionCode attribute by using the getPackageInfo() method from the PackageManager class, like this:

```java
import android.content.pm.PackageInfo;
import android.content.pm.PackageManager;
```

```
import android.content.pm.PackageManager.NameNotFoundException;

private void checkVersion() {
    PackageManager pm = getPackageManager();
    try {
        //---get the package info---
        PackageInfo pi =
            pm.getPackageInfo("net.learn2develop.LBS", 0);
        //---display the versioncode---
        Toast.makeText(getBaseContext(),
            "VersionCode: " +Integer.toString(pi.versionCode),
            Toast.LENGTH_SHORT).show();
    } catch (NameNotFoundException e) {
        // TODO Auto-generated catch block
        e.printStackTrace();
    }
}
```

The android:versionName attribute contains versioning information that is visible to users. It should contain values in the format *<major>.<minor>.<point>*. If your application undergoes a major upgrade, you should increase the *<major>* by 1. For small incremental updates, you can increase either the *<minor>* or *<point>* by 1. For example, a new application may have a version name of "1.0.0." For a small incremental update, you might change it to "1.1.0" or "1.0.1." For the next major update, you might change it to "2.0.0."

If you are planning to publish your application on the Android Market (www.android.com/market/), the AndroidManifest.xml file must have the following attributes:

➤   android:versionCode (within the <manifest> element)

➤   android:versionName (within the <manifest> element)

➤   android:icon (within the <application> element)

➤   android:label (within the <application> element)

The android:label attribute specifies the name of your application. This name is displayed in the Settings ⇨ Apps section of your Android device. For the LBS project, give the application the name "Where Am I":

```
<?xml version="1.0" encoding="utf-8"?>
<manifest xmlns:android="http://schemas.android.com/apk/res/android"
    package="net.learn2develop.LBS"
    android:versionCode="1"
    android:versionName="1.0" >

    <uses-sdk android:minSdkVersion="14" />
    <uses-permission android:name="android.permission.INTERNET"/>
    <uses-permission android:name="android.permission.ACCESS_FINE_LOCATION"/>
    <uses-permission android:name="android.permission.ACCESS_COARSE_LOCATION"/>

    <application
        android:icon="@drawable/ic_launcher"
        android:label="Where Am I" >
```

```
            <uses-library android:name="com.google.android.maps" />
            <activity
                android:label="@string/app_name"
                android:name=".LBSActivity" >
                <intent-filter >
                    <action android:name="android.intent.action.MAIN" />

                    <category android:name="android.intent.category.LAUNCHER" />
                </intent-filter>
            </activity>
        </application>

    </manifest>
```

In addition, if your application needs a minimum version of the Android OS to run, you can specify it in the AndroidManifest.xml file using the <uses-sdk> element:

```
    <?xml version="1.0" encoding="utf-8"?>
    <manifest xmlns:android="http://schemas.android.com/apk/res/android"
        package="net.learn2develop.LBS"
        android:versionCode="1"
        android:versionName="1.0" >

        <uses-sdk android:minSdkVersion="13" />
        <uses-permission android:name="android.permission.INTERNET"/>
        <uses-permission android:name="android.permission.ACCESS_FINE_LOCATION"/>
        <uses-permission android:name="android.permission.ACCESS_COARSE_LOCATION"/>

        <application
            android:icon="@drawable/ic_launcher"
            android:label="Where Am I" >
            <uses-library android:name="com.google.android.maps" />
            <activity
                android:label="@string/app_name"
                android:name=".LBSActivity" >
                <intent-filter >
                    <action android:name="android.intent.action.MAIN" />

                    <category android:name="android.intent.category.LAUNCHER" />
                </intent-filter>
            </activity>
        </application>

    </manifest>
```

In the preceding example, the application requires a minimum of SDK version 13, which is Android 3.2.1. In general, you should set this version number to the lowest one that your application can support. This ensures that a wider range of users will be able to run your application.

Digitally Signing Your Android Applications

All Android applications must be digitally signed before they are allowed to be deployed onto a device (or emulator). Unlike some mobile platforms, you need not purchase digital certificates from a certificate authority (CA) to sign your applications. Instead, you can generate your own self-signed certificate and use it to sign your Android applications.

When you use Eclipse to develop your Android application and then press F11 to deploy it to an emulator, Eclipse automatically signs it for you. You can verify this by going to Windows ⇨ Preferences in Eclipse, expanding the Android item, and selecting Build (see Figure 12-1). Eclipse uses a default debug keystore (appropriately named "debug.keystore") to sign your application. A keystore is commonly known as a *digital certificate*.

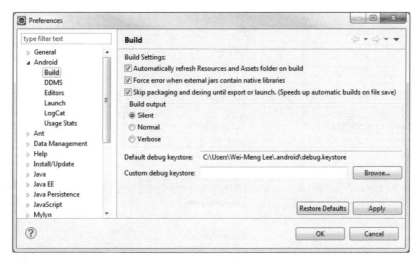

FIGURE 12-1

If you are publishing an Android application, you must sign it with your own certificate. Applications signed with the debug certificate cannot be published. Although you can manually generate your own certificates using the keytool.exe utility provided by the Java SDK, Eclipse makes it easy for you by including a wizard that walks you through the steps to generate a certificate. It will also sign your application with the generated certificate (which you can sign manually using the jarsigner.exe tool from the Java SDK).

The following Try It Out demonstrates how to use Eclipse to export an Android application and sign it with a newly generated certificate.

TRY IT OUT   Exporting and Signing an Android Application

For this Try It Out, you will use the LBS project created in Chapter 9.

1.   Select the LBS project in Eclipse and then select File ⇨ Export. . . .

2.   In the Export dialog, expand the Android item and select Export Android Application (see Figure 12-2). Click Next.

3.   The LBS project should now be displayed (see Figure 12-3). Click Next.

FIGURE 12-2

FIGURE 12-3

4. Select the "Create new keystore" option to create a new certificate (keystore) for signing your application (see Figure 12-4). Enter a path to save your new keystore and then enter a password to protect the keystore. For this example, enter **keystorepassword** as the password. Click Next.

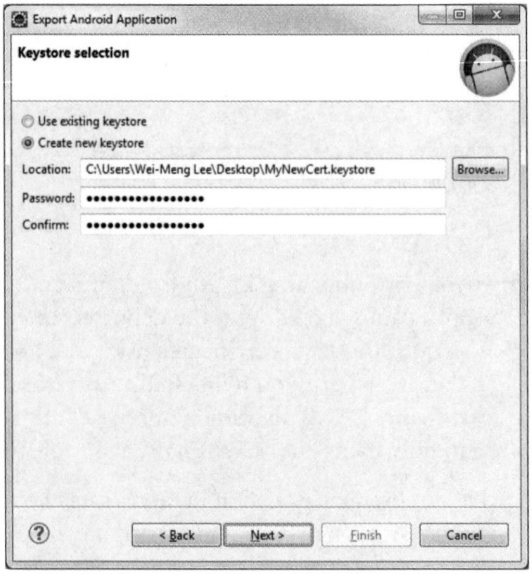

5. Provide an alias for the private key (name it **DistributionKeyStoreAlias;** see Figure 12-5) and enter a password to protect the private key. For this example, enter **keypassword** as the password. You also need to enter a validity period for the key. According to Google, your application must be signed with a cryptographic private key whose validity period ends after 22 October 2033. Hence, enter a number that is greater than 2033 minus the current year. Finally, enter your name in the field labeled First and Last Name. Click Next.

FIGURE 12-4

6. Enter a path to store the destination APK file (see Figure 12-6). Click Finish. The APK file will now be generated.

FIGURE 12-5

FIGURE 12-6

7. Recall from Chapter 9 that the LBS application requires the use of the Google Maps API key, which you applied by using your debug.keystore's MD5 fingerprint. This means that the Google Maps API key is essentially tied to the debug.keystore used to sign your application. Because you are now generating your new keystore to sign your application for deployment, you need to apply for the Google Maps API key again, using the new keystore's MD5 fingerprint. To do so, go to the command prompt and enter the following command (the location of your keytool.exe utility might differ slightly; see Figure 12-7):

```
C:\Program Files\Java\jre6\bin>keytool.exe -list -v -alias DistributionKeyStoreAlias
-keystore "C:\Users\Wei-Meng Lee\Desktop\MyNewCert.keystore"
-storepass keystorepassword -keypass keypassword -v
```

FIGURE 12-7

8.   Using the MD5 fingerprint obtained from the previous step, go to `http://code.google.com/` `android/add-ons/google-apis/maps-api-signup.html` and sign up for a new Maps API key.

9.   Enter the new Maps API key in the `main.xml` file:

```xml
<?xml version="1.0" encoding="utf-8"?>
<LinearLayout xmlns:android="http://schemas.android.com/apk/res/android"
    android:layout_width="fill_parent"
    android:layout_height="fill_parent"
    android:orientation="vertical" >

<com.google.android.maps.MapView
    android:id="@+id/mapView"
    android:layout_width="fill_parent"
    android:layout_height="fill_parent"
    android:enabled="true"
    android:clickable="true"
    android:apiKey="your_key_here" />

</LinearLayout>
```

10.   With the new Maps API key entered in the `main.xml` file, you now need to export the application once more and resign it. Repeat steps 2 through 4. When you are asked to select a keystore, select the "Use existing keystore" option (see Figure 12-8) and enter the password you used earlier to protect your keystore (in this case, **keystorepassword**). Click Next.

11.   Select the "Use existing key" option (see Figure 12-9) and enter the password you set earlier to secure the private key (enter **keypassword**). Click Next.

FIGURE 12-8

FIGURE 12-9

12. Click Finish (see Figure 12-10) to generate the APK file again.

That's it! The APK is now generated and contains the new Map API key that is tied to the new keystore.

How It Works

Eclipse provides the Export Android Application option, which helps you to both export your Android application as an APK file and generate a new keystore to sign the APK file. For applications that use the Maps API key, note that the Maps API key must be associated with the new keystore that you use to sign your APK file.

FIGURE 12-10

DEPLOYING APK FILES

After you have signed your APK files, you need a way to get them onto your users' devices. The following sections describe the various ways to deploy your APK files. Three methods are covered:

➤ Deploying manually using the `adb.exe` tool

➤ Hosting the application on a web server

➤ Publishing through the Android Market

Besides these methods, you can install your applications on users' devices using e-mail, an SD card, and so on. As long as you can transfer the APK file onto the user's device, the application can be installed.

Using the adb.exe Tool

Once your Android application is signed, you can deploy it to emulators and devices using the `adb.exe` (Android Debug Bridge) tool (located in the `platform-tools` folder of the Android SDK).

Using the command prompt in Windows, navigate to the `<Android_SDK>\platform-tools` folder. To install the application to an emulator/device (assuming the emulator is currently up and running or a device is currently connected), issue the following command:

```
adb install "C:\Users\Wei-Meng Lee\Desktop\LBS.apk"
```

EXPLORING THE ADB.EXE TOOL

The `adb.exe` tool is a very versatile tool that enables you to control Android devices (and emulators) connected to your computer.

By default, when you use the `adb` command, it assumes that currently there is only one connected device/emulator. If more than one device is connected, the `adb` command returns an error message:

```
error: more than one device and emulator
```

You can view the devices currently connected to your computer by using the `devices` option with `adb`, like this:

```
D:\Android 4.0\android-sdk-windows\platform-tools>adb devices
List of devices attached
HT07YPY09335    device
emulator-5554   device
emulator-5556   device
```

As the preceding example shows, this returns the list of devices currently attached. To issue a command for a particular device, you need to indicate the device using the `-s` option, like this:

```
adb -s emulator-5556 install LBS.apk
```

If you try to install an APK file onto a device that already has the APK file, it will display the following error message:

```
Failure [INSTALL_FAILED_ALREADY_EXISTS]
```

If the LBS application is still on your device or emulator from earlier, you can delete it via Settings ⇨ Apps ⇨ LBS ⇨ Uninstall.

Sometimes the ADB will fail (when too many ADVs are opened at the same time; you will notice that you can no longer deploy applications from Eclipse onto your real devices or emulators). In this case, you need to kill the server and then restart it:

```
adb kill-server
adb start-server
```

When you inspect the launcher on the Android device/emulator, you will be able to see the LBS icon (on the top of Figure 12-11). If you select Settings ➪ Apps on your Android device/emulator, you will see the Where Am I application (on the bottom of Figure 12-11).

Besides using the adb.exe tool to install applications, you can also use it to remove an installed application. To do so, use the uninstall option to remove an application from its installed folder:

```
adb uninstall net.learn2develop.LBS
```

Another way to deploy an application is to use the DDMS tool in Eclipse (see Figure 12-12). With an emulator (or device) selected, use the File Explorer in DDMS to go to the /data/app folder and use the "Push a file onto the device" button to copy the APK file onto the device.

FIGURE 12-11

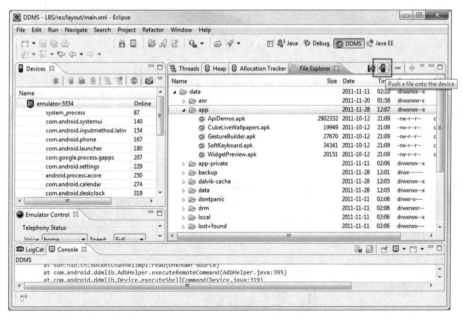

FIGURE 12-12

Using a Web Server

If you wish to host your application on your own, you can use a web server to do that. This is ideal if you have your own web hosting services and want to provide the application free of charge to your users (or you can restrict access to certain groups of people).

> **NOTE** *Even if you restrict your application to a certain group of people, there is nothing to stop users from redistributing your application to other users after they have downloaded your APK file.*

To demonstrate this, I use the Internet Information Server (IIS) on my Windows 7 computer. Copy the signed `LBS.apk` file to `c:\inetpub\wwwroot\`. In addition, create a new HTML file named `index.html` with the following content:

```
<html>
<title>Where Am I application</title>
<body>
Download the Where Am I application <a href="LBS.apk">here</a>
</body>
</html>
```

> **NOTE** *If you are unsure how to set up IIS on your Windows 7 computer, check out the following link:* `http://technet.microsoft.com/en-us/library/cc725762.aspx`.

On your web server, you may need to register a new MIME type for the APK file. The MIME type for the `.apk` extension is `application/vnd.android.package-archive`.

> **NOTE** *If you are unsure how to set up the MIME type on IIS, check out the following link:*
>
> `http://technet.microsoft.com/en-us/library/cc725608(WS.10).aspx`.

> **NOTE** *To install APK files over the Web, you need an SD card installed on your emulator or device. This is because the downloaded APK files are saved to the* `download` *folder created on the SD card. For testing this using the emulator, ensure that your SD card has at least a size of 128MB. There are reports of developers having problems installing their apps with an SD card size smaller than 128MB.*

By default, for online installation of Android applications, the Android emulator or device only allows applications to be installed from the Android Market (www.android.com/market). Hence, for installation over a web server, you need to configure your Android emulator/device to accept applications from non-Market sources.

In the Settings application, click the Security item and scroll to the bottom of the screen. Check the "Unknown sources" item (see Figure 12-13). You will be prompted with a warning message. Click OK. Checking this item will allow the emulator/device to install applications from other non-Market sources (such as from a web server).

To install the LBS.apk application from the IIS web server running on your computer, launch the Browser application on the Android emulator/device and navigate to the URL pointing to the APK file. To refer to the computer running the emulator, you should use the computer's IP address. Figure 12-14 shows the index.html file loaded on the web browser. Clicking the "here" link will download the APK file onto your device. Click the status bar at the top of the screen to reveal the download's status.

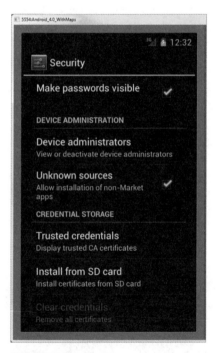

FIGURE 12-13

FIGURE 12-14

To install the downloaded application, simply tap on it. It will show the permission(s) required by the application. Click the Install button to proceed with the installation. When the application is installed, you can launch it by clicking the Open button.

Besides using a web server, you can also e-mail your application to users as an attachment; when the users receive the e-mail, they can download the attachment and install the application directly onto their device.

Publishing on the Android Market

So far, you have learned how to package your Android application and distribute it in various ways — via web server, the `adb.exe` file, e-mail, and SD card.

However, these methods do not provide a way for users to discover your applications easily. A better way is to host your application on the Android Market, a Google-hosted service that makes it very easy for users to discover and download (i.e., purchase) applications for their Android devices. Users simply need to launch the Market application on their Android device in order to discover a wide range of applications that they can install on their devices.

In this section, you will learn how to publish your Android application on the Android Market. You will walk through each of the steps involved, including the various items you need in order to prepare your application for submission to the Android Market.

Creating a Developer Profile

The first step toward publishing on the Android Market is to create a developer profile at `http://market.android.com/publish/Home`. For this, you need a Google account (such as your Gmail account). Once you have logged in to the Android Market, you first create your developer profile (see Figure 12-15). Click Continue after entering the required information.

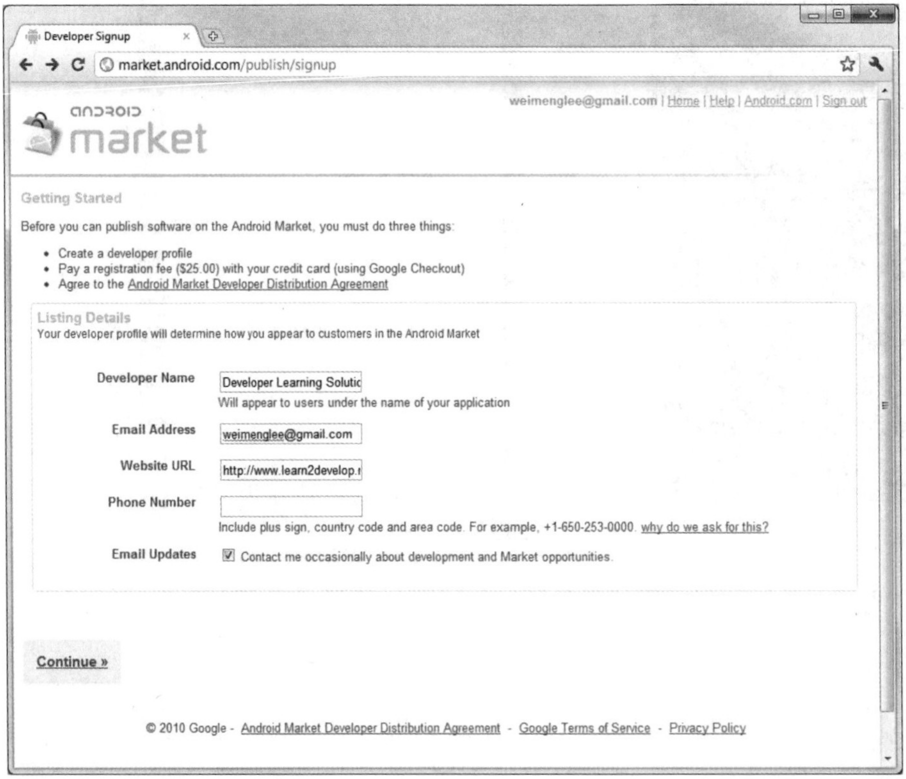

FIGURE 12-15

For publishing on the Android Market, you need to pay a one-time registration fee, currently U.S. $25. Click the Google Checkout button to be redirected to a page where you can pay the registration fee. After paying, click the Continue link.

Next, you need to agree to the Android Market Developer Distribution Agreement. Check the "I agree" checkbox and then click the "I agree. Continue" link.

Submitting Your Apps

After you have set up your profile, you are ready to submit your application to the Android Market. If you intend to charge for your application, click the Setup Merchant Account link located at the bottom of the screen. Here you enter additional information such as bank account and tax ID.

For free applications, click the Upload Application link, shown in Figure 12-16.

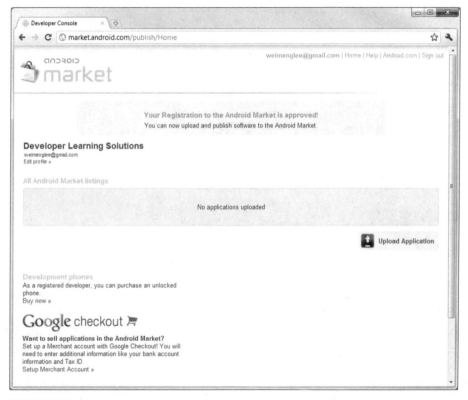

FIGURE 12-16

You will be asked to supply some information about your application. Figure 12-17 shows the first set of details you need to provide. Among the information needed, the following are compulsory:

➤ The application must be in APK format

➤ You need to provide at least two screenshots. You can use the DDMS perspective in Eclipse to capture screenshots of your application running on the emulator or real device.

➤ You need to provide a high-resolution application icon. This size of this image must be 512 × 512 pixels.

The other information details are optional, and you can always supply them later.

FIGURE 12-17

Figure 12-18 shows the LBS.apk file uploaded to the Android Market site. In particular, note that based on the APK file that you have uploaded, users are warned about any specific permissions required, and your application's features are used to filter search results. For example, because my application requires GPS access, it will not appear in the search result list if a user searches for my application on a device that does not have a GPS receiver.

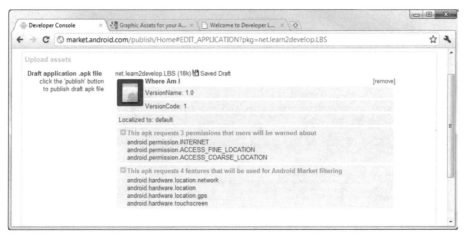

FIGURE 12-18

The next set of information you need to supply, shown in Figure 12-19, includes the title of your application, its description, as well as details about recent changes (useful for application updates). You can also select the application type and the category in which it will appear in the Android Market.

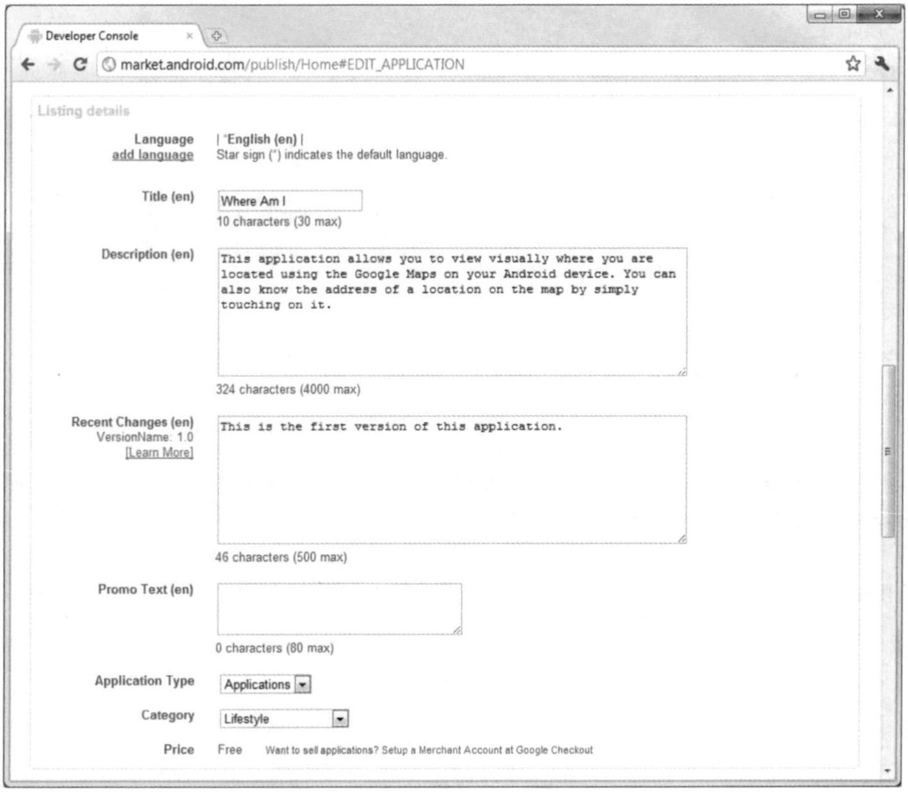

FIGURE 12-19

In the last dialog, you indicate whether your application employs copy protection, and specify a content rating. You also supply your website URL and your contact information (see Figure 12-20). When you have given your consent to the two guidelines and agreements, click Publish to publish your application on the Android Market.

FIGURE 12-20

That's it. Your application is now available on the Android Market. You will be able to monitor any comments submitted about your application (see Figure 12-21), as well as bug reports and total number of downloads.

Good luck! All you need to do now is wait for the good news; and hopefully you can laugh your way to the bank soon!

FIGURE 12-21

SUMMARY

In this chapter, you have learned how you can export your Android application as an APK file and then digitally sign it with a keystore you create yourself. You also learned about the various ways you can distribute your application, and the advantages of each method. Finally, you walked through the steps required to publish on the Android Market, which enables you to sell your application and reach out to a wider audience. It is hoped that this exposure enables you to sell a lot of copies and thereby make some decent money.

EXERCISES

1. How do you specify the minimum version of Android required by your application?

2. How do you generate a self-signed certificate for signing your Android application?

3. How do you configure your Android device to accept applications from non-Market sources?

Answers to the exercises can be found in Appendix C.

▶ WHAT YOU LEARNED IN THIS CHAPTER

TOPIC	KEY CONCEPTS

Checklist for publishing your apps	To publish an application on the Android Market, an application must have the following four attributes in the `AndroidManifest.xml` file:
	
	`android:versionCode`
	`android:versionName`
	`android:icon`
	`android:label`

Signing applications	All applications to be distributed must be signed with a self-signed certificate. The debug keystore is not valid for distribution.
Exporting an application and signing it	Use the Export feature of Eclipse to export the application as an APK file and then sign it with a self-signed certificate.
Deploying APK files	You can deploy using various means, including web server, e-mail, `adb.exe`, and DDMS.
Publishing your application on the Android Market	To sell and host your apps on the Android Market, you can apply with a one-time fee of U.S. $25.

A

Using Eclipse for Android Development

Although Google supports the development of Android applications using IDEs such as IntelliJ, or basic editors like Emacs, Google's recommendation is to use the Eclipse IDE together with the Android Development Tools (ADT) plug-in. Doing so makes developing Android applications much easier and more productive. This appendix describes some of the neat features available in Eclipse that can greatly improve your development work.

 WARNING *If you have not downloaded Eclipse yet, please start with Chapter 1, where you will learn how to obtain Eclipse and configure it to work with the Android SDK. This appendix assumes that you have already set up your Eclipse environment for Android development.*

GETTING AROUND IN ECLIPSE

Eclipse is a highly extensible multi-language software development environment that supports application development of all sorts. Using Eclipse, you can write and test your applications using a wide variety of languages, such as Java, C, C++, PHP, Ruby, and more. Because of its extensibility, new users of Eclipse often feel overwhelmed by the IDE. Hence, the following sections aim to make you more at home with Eclipse when you develop your Android applications.

Workspaces

Eclipse adopts the concept of a *workspace*. A workspace is a folder that you have chosen to store all your projects.

When you first start Eclipse, you are prompted to select a workspace (see Figure A-1).

FIGURE A-1

When Eclipse has finished loading the projects located in your workspace, several panes are displayed in the IDE (see Figure A-2).

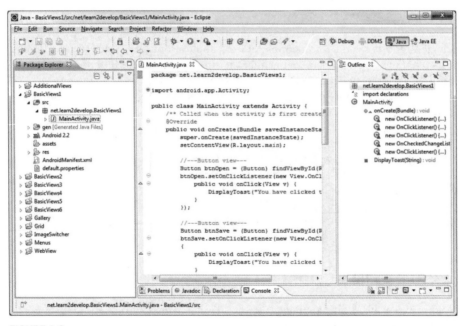

FIGURE A-2

The following sections highlight some of the more important panes that you need to know about when developing Android applications.

Package Explorer

The Package Explorer, shown in Figure A-3, lists all the projects currently in your workspace. To edit a particular item in your project, you can double-click on it and the file will be displayed in the respective editor.

You can also right-click on each item displayed in the Package Explorer to display context-sensitive menu(s) related to the selected item. For example, if you wish to add a new .java file to the project, you can right-click on the package name in the Package Explorer and then select New ⇨ Class (see Figure A-4).

FIGURE A-3

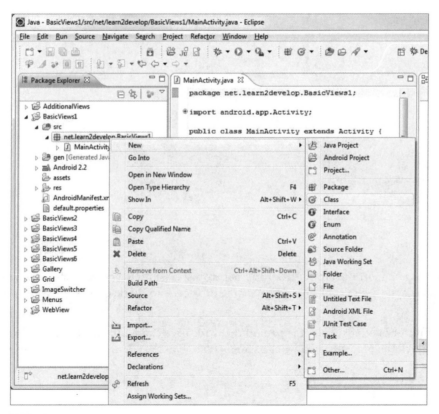

FIGURE A-4

Using Projects from Other Workspaces

There may be times when you have several workspaces created to store different projects. If you need to access the project in another workspace, there are generally two ways to go about doing so. First, you can switch to the desired workspace by selecting File ⇨ Switch Workspace (see Figure A-5). Specify the new workspace to work on and then restart Eclipse.

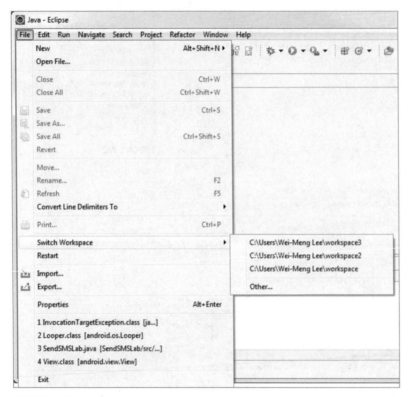

FIGURE A-5

The second method is to import the project from another workspace into the current one. To do so, select File ⇨ Import... and then select General ⇨ Existing Projects into Workspace (see Figure A-6). Click Next.

In the Select root directory textbox, enter the path of the workspace containing the project(s) you want to import and tick the project(s) you want to import (see Figure A-7). To import the selected project(s), click Finish.

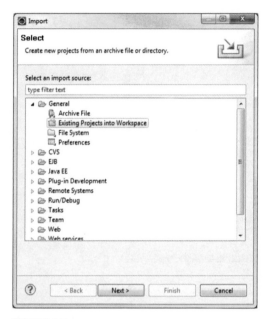

FIGURE A-6

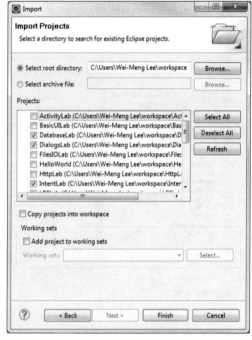

FIGURE A-7

Note that even when you import a project from another workspace into the current workspace, the physical location of the imported project remains unchanged. That is, it will still be located in its original directory. To add a copy of the project to the current workspace, check the "Copy projects into workspace" option.

Using Editors within Eclipse

Depending on the type of items you have double-clicked in the Package Explorer, Eclipse will open the appropriate editor for you to edit the file. For example, if you double-click on a .java file, the text editor for editing the source file will be opened (see Figure A-8).

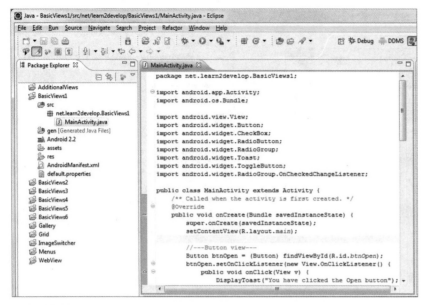

FIGURE A-8

If you double-click on the `ic_launcher.png` file in the `res/drawable-mdpi` folder, the Windows Photo Viewer application will be invoked to display the image (see Figure A-9).

FIGURE A-9

If you double-click on the `main.xml` file in the `res/layout` folder, Eclipse will display the UI editor, where you can graphically view and build the layout of your UI (see Figure A-10).

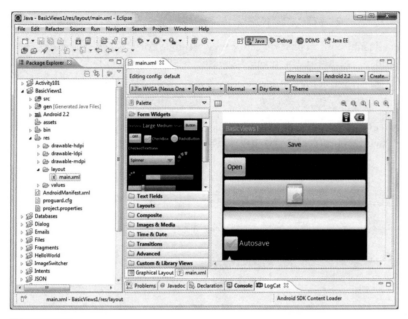

FIGURE A-10

To edit the UI manually using XML, you can switch to XML view by clicking on the main.xml tab located at the bottom of the editor (see Figure A-11).

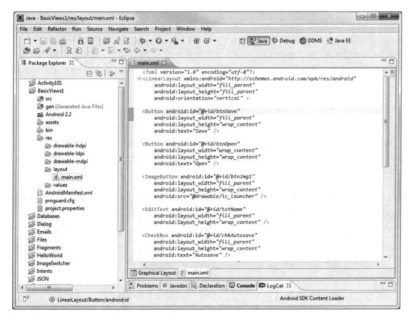

FIGURE A-11

Understanding Eclipse Perspectives

In Eclipse, a *perspective* is a visual container for a set of views and editors. When you edit your Android/Java project in Eclipse, you are in the Java perspective (see Figure A-12).

The Java EE perspective is used for developing enterprise Java applications, and it includes other modules that are relevant to it.

You can switch to other perspectives by clicking the perspective name. If the perspective name is not shown, you can click the Open Perspective button and add a new perspective (see Figure A-13).

FIGURE A-12

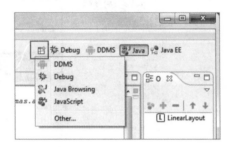

FIGURE A-13

The DDMS perspective contains tools for communicating with Android emulators and devices. This is covered in more detail in Appendix B. The Debug perspective contains panes used for debugging your Android applications. You will learn more about that later in this appendix.

Automatically Importing Packages

The various classes in the Android library are organized into packages. As such, when you use a particular class from a package, you need to import the appropriate packages, like this:

```
import android.app.Activity;
import android.os.Bundle;
```

Because the number of classes in the Android Library is very large, remembering the correct namespace for each class is not an easy task. Fortunately, Eclipse can help you find the correct namespace, which enables you to import it with just a click.

Figure A-14 shows that I have declared an object of type `Button`. Because I did not import the correct package for the `Button` class, Eclipse signals an error beneath the statement. When you move the mouse over the `Button` class, Eclipse displays a list of suggested fixes. In this case, I need to import the `android.widget.Button` package. Clicking the "Import 'Button' (android.widget)" link will add the import statement to the top of the file.

FIGURE A-14

Alternatively, you can use the following key combination: Ctrl+Shift+o. This key combination will cause Eclipse to automatically import all the namespaces required by your class.

Using the Code Completion Feature

Another very useful feature of Eclipse is its support for code completion. Code completion displays a context-sensitive list of relevant classes, objects, methods, and property names as you type in the code editor. For example, Figure A-15 shows code-completion in action. As I type the word "`fin`," I can activate the code-completion feature by pressing Ctrl+space. This brings up a list of names that begin with "`fin`."

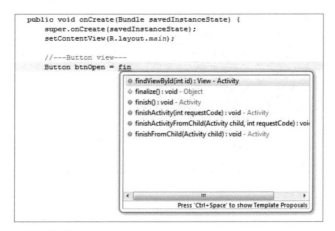

FIGURE A-15

To select the required name, simply double-click on it or use your cursor to highlight it and then press the Enter key.

Code completion also works when you type a period (.) after an object/class name. Figure A-16 shows an example.

Refactoring

Refactoring is a very useful feature that most modern IDEs support. Eclipse supports a whole slew of refactoring features that make application development efficient.

In Eclipse, when you position the cursor at a particular object/variable, the editor will highlight all occurrences of the selected object in the current source (see Figure A-17).

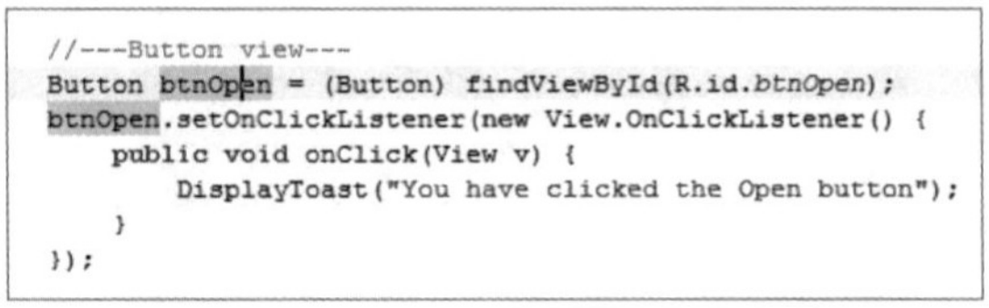

This feature is very helpful for identifying where a particular object is used in your code. To change the name of an object, simply right-click on it and select Refactor ➪ Rename. . . (see Figure A-18).

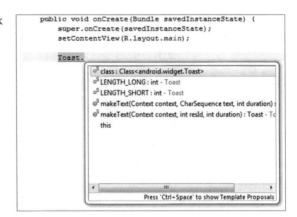

FIGURE A-16

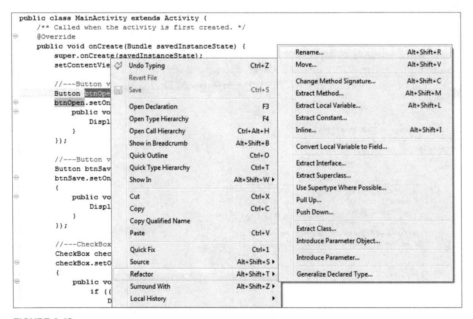

FIGURE A-17

FIGURE A-18

After entering a new name for the object, all occurrences of the object will be changed automatically (see Figure A-19). Note that in order for refactoring to work correctly, your code must not have any syntax errors and must be able to be compiled correctly by the compiler.

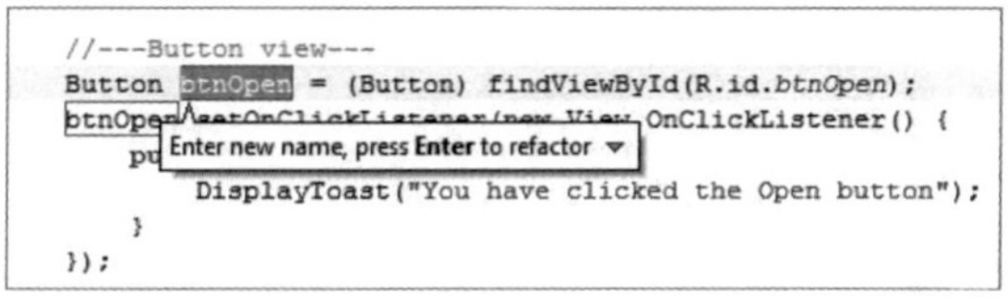

```
//---Button view---
Button btnOpen = (Button) findViewById(R.id.btnOpen);
btnOpen.setOnClickListener(new View.OnClickListener() {
    pu Enter new name, press Enter to refactor ▼
            DisplayToast("You have clicked the Open button");
    }
});
```

FIGURE A-19

Another area where refactoring is very useful is for extracting string constants from your UI files. As I mentioned earlier in Chapter 1, all the string constants that you use in your user interface should preferably be stored in the `strings.xml` file so that it is easy to perform localization later. However, it is very common during development to take the shortcut of entering the string constant directly. For example, you may set the `android:text` attribute of a `Button` view using a string constant:

```
<Button android:id="@+id/btnSave"
    android:layout_width="fill_parent"
    android:layout_height="wrap_content"
    android:text="Save" />
```

Using the refactoring feature in Eclipse, you could select the string constant and then select the Refactor ➪ Android ➪ Extract Android String... (see Figure A-20).

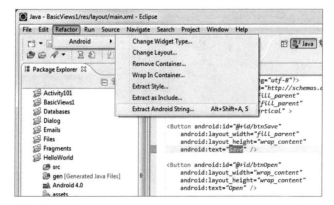

FIGURE A-20

You are then prompted to specify a name for this string constant (see Figure A-21). Click OK when you are done.

FIGURE A-21

After doing so, the value of the `android:text` attribute is now replaced with `@string/save`:

```xml
<Button android:id="@+id/btnSave"
    android:layout_width="fill_parent"
    android:layout_height="wrap_content"
    android:text="@string/save" />
```

If you examine the `strings.xml` file, it will now contain a new entry named `save`:

```xml
<?xml version="1.0" encoding="utf-8"?>
<resources>
    <string name="hello">Hello World, BasicViews1Activity!</string>
    <string name="app_name">BasicViews1</string>
    <string name="save">Save</string>

</resources>
```

A detailed discussion of refactoring is beyond the scope of this book. For more information on refactoring in Eclipse, refer to `www.ibm.com/developerworks/library/os-ecref/`.

DEBUGGING YOUR APPLICATION

Eclipse supports debugging your application on both Android emulators as well as real Android devices. When you press F11 in Eclipse, Eclipse first determines whether an Android emulator instance is already running or a real device is connected. If at least one emulator (or device) is running, Eclipse will deploy the application onto the running emulator or the connected device. If no emulator is running and no device is connected, Eclipse automatically launches an instance of the Android emulator and deploys the application onto it.

If you have more than one emulator or device connected, Eclipse will prompt you to select the target emulator/device on which to deploy the application (see Figure A-22). Select the target device you want to use and click OK. Devices that do not have the minimum OS version required by your application will be marked with an X.

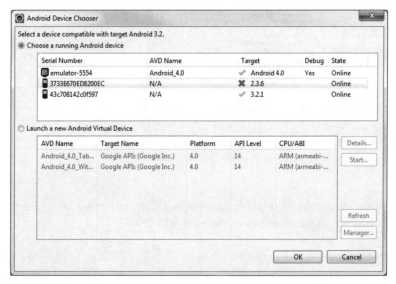

FIGURE A-22

If you want to launch a new emulator instance to test the application, select Window ⇨ Android SDK and AVD Manager to launch the AVD Manager.

Setting Breakpoints

Setting breakpoints is a good way to temporarily pause the execution of the application and then examine the content of variables and objects.

To set a breakpoint, double-click on the leftmost column in the code editor. Figure A-23 shows a breakpoint set on a particular statement.

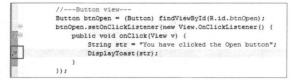

FIGURE A-23

When the application is running and the first breakpoint is reached, Eclipse will display a Confirm Perspective Switch dialog. Basically, it wants to switch to the Debug perspective. To prevent this window from appearing again, check the "Remember my decision" checkbox at the bottom and click Yes. Eclipse will highlight the breakpoint (see Figure A-24).

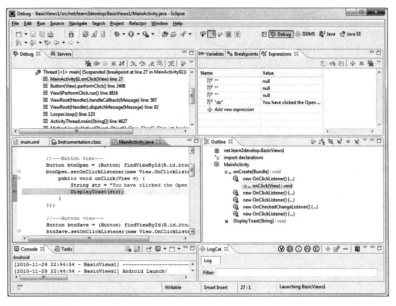

FIGURE A-24

At this point, you can right-click on any selected object/variable and view its content using the various options (e.g., Watch, Inspect, Display) shown in Figure A-25.

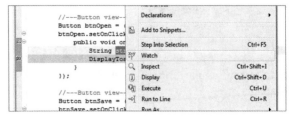

FIGURE A-25

Figure A-26 shows the Inspect option displaying the content of the `str` variable.

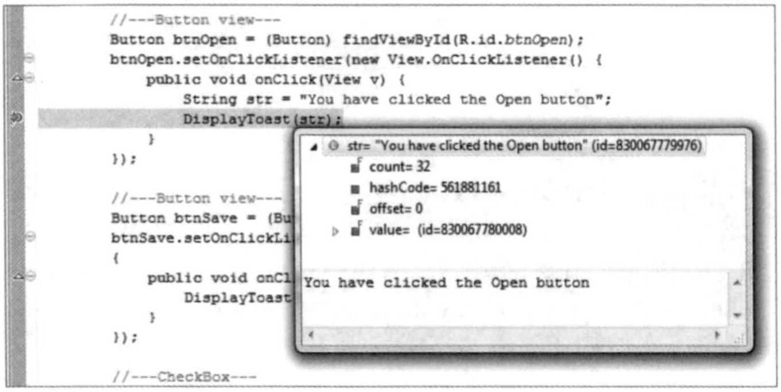

FIGURE A-26

You have several options at this point to continue the execution:

➤ **Step Into** — Press F5 to step into the next method call/statement.

➤ **Step Over** — Press F6 to step over the next method call without entering it.

➤ **Step Return** — Press F7 to return from a method that has been stepped into.

➤ **Resume Execution** — Press F8 to resume the execution.

Dealing with Exceptions

As you develop in Android, you will encounter numerous run-time exceptions that prevent your program from continuing. Examples of run-time exceptions include the following:

➤ Null reference exception (accessing an object that is null)

➤ Failure to specify the permissions required by your application

➤ Arithmetic operation exceptions

Figure A-27 shows the current state of an application when an exception occurred. In this example, I am trying to send an SMS message from my application and it crashes when the message is about to be sent.

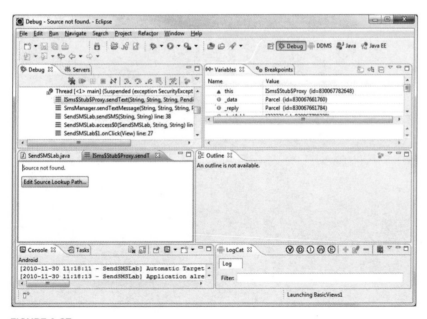

FIGURE A-27

The various windows do not really identify the cause of the exception. To find out more, press F6 in Eclipse so that it can step over the current statement. The Variables window, shown in Figure A-28, indicates the cause of the exception. In this case, the SEND_SMS permission is missing.

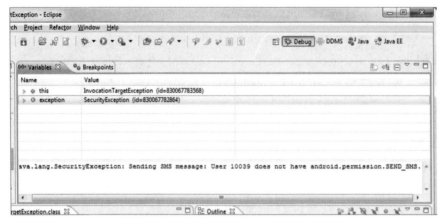

FIGURE A-28

To remedy this, all you need to do is add the following permission statement in the
AndroidManifest.xml file:

```
<uses-permission android:name="android.permission.SEND_SMS"/>
```

Using the Android Emulator

The Android emulator ships with the Android SDK and is an invaluable tool to help test your application without requiring you to purchase a real device. While you should thoroughly test your applications on real devices before you deploy them, the emulator mimics most of the capabilities of real devices. It is a very handy tool that you should make use of during the development stage of your project. This appendix provides some common tips and tricks for mastering the Android emulator.

USES OF THE ANDROID EMULATOR

As discussed in Chapter 1, you can use the Android emulator to emulate the different Android configurations by creating Android Virtual Devices (AVDs).

If you want to emulate a real device, first create an AVD with the same screen resolution and abstracted LCD density as that of your real device (see the section "Emulating Devices with Different Screen Sizes" in this appendix for how to do this). You then launch the Android emulator by directly starting the AVD you have created in the AVD Manager window (see Figure B-1). Simply select the AVD and click the Start button. If you want the emulator to display using the same screen size as a real device, check the "Scale display to real size" option and set the "Screen Size (in)" option to the size of your real device. Enter the dpi of your current monitor (if you don't know it, click the ? button and select your monitor size and resolution). The Android emulator will then display a screen size that is close to your real device. This useful option enables you to preview what your application will look like on different actual screen sizes.

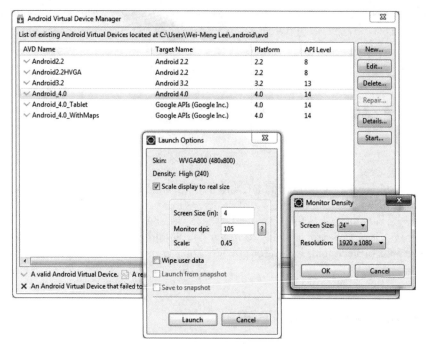

FIGURE B-1

 NOTE *For best performance of the Android emulator, set the screen size to the smallest size that you can allow. Doing so will make the emulator run faster.*

Alternatively, when you run an Android project in Eclipse, the Android emulator is automatically invoked to test your application. You can customize the Android emulator for each of your Android projects in Eclipse. To do so, simply select Run ⇨ Run Configurations. Select the project name listed under Android Application on the left (see Figure B-2), and on the right you will see the Target tab. You can choose your preferred AVD to use for testing your application, as well as emulate different scenarios such as network speed and network latency.

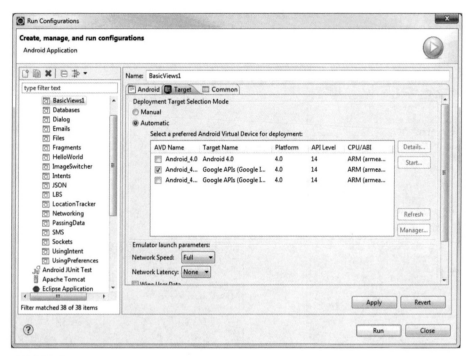

FIGURE B-2

CREATING SNAPSHOTS

In the latest version of the AVD Manager, you now have the option to save an emulator's state to a snapshot file. Saving an emulator's state to a snapshot file enables the emulator to be started quickly the next time you try to launch it, effectively bypassing the lengthy boot-up time. This is especially useful for the Android 3.0 (and later) emulator, which can take up to five minutes to boot up.

To use the snapshot feature, simply check the Snapshot Enabled checkbox when you create a new AVD (see Figure B-3).

When you launch the AVD from the Start . . . button, check the "Launch from snapshot" and "Save to snapshot" checkboxes (see Figure B-4). The first time you launch the emulator, it will boot up normally. When you close the emulator, it will then save the state to a snapshot file. The next time you launch the emulator, it will appear almost instantly, restoring its state from the snapshot file.

FIGURE B-3   **FIGURE B-4**

SD CARD EMULATION

When you create a new AVD, you can emulate the existence of an SD card (see Figure B-5). Simply enter the size of the SD card that you want to emulate (in the figure, it is 200MB).

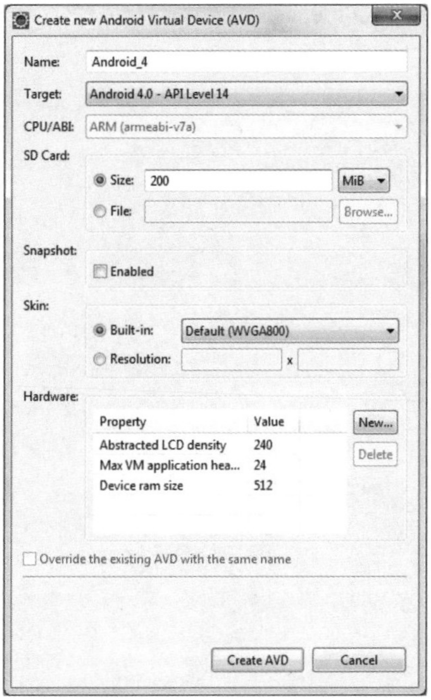

FIGURE B-5

Alternatively, you can simulate the presence of an SD card in the Android emulator by creating a disk image first and then attaching it to the AVD. The mksdcard.exe utility (located in the tools folder of the Android SDK) enables you to create an ISO disk image. The following command creates an ISO image that is 2GB in size (see also Figure B-6):

```
mksdcard 2048M sdcard.iso
```

FIGURE B-6

Once the image is created, you can specify the location of the ISO file, as shown in Figure B-7.

FIGURE B-7

EMULATING DEVICES WITH DIFFERENT SCREEN SIZES

Besides emulating an SD card, you can also emulate devices with different screen sizes. Figure B-8 indicates that the AVD is emulating the HVGA skin, which has a resolution of 320 × 480 pixels. Note that the Abstracted LCD density is 160, which means that this screen has a pixel density of 160 pixels per inch.

For each target that you select, a list of skins is available. The following screen resolutions are supported by Android:

- ➤ **HVGA** — 320 × 480
- ➤ **QVGA** — 240 × 320
- ➤ **WQVGA400** — 240 × 400
- ➤ **WQVGA432** — 240 × 432
- ➤ **WVGA800** — 480 × 800
- ➤ **WVGA854** — 480 × 854

In addition to using the built-in screen resolution, you can also specify your own custom resolution. For example, you can emulate the Samsung Galaxy Tab 10.1 by creating an AVD with the specifications shown in Figure B-9.

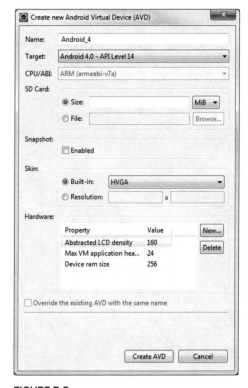

FIGURE B-8

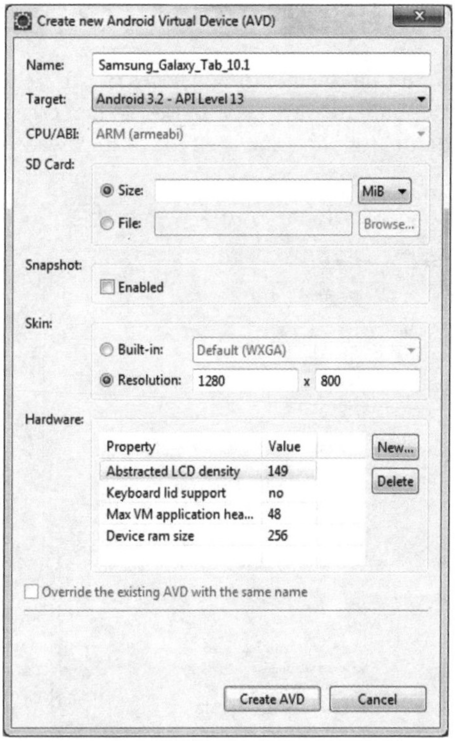

FIGURE B-9

When the AVD is started, you will see the Android emulator emulating a Honeycomb tablet (see Figure B-10).

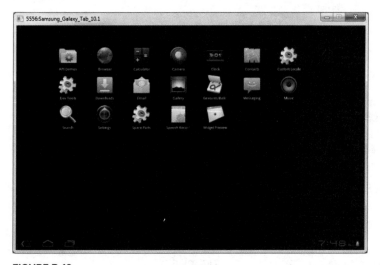

FIGURE B-10

EMULATING PHYSICAL CAPABILITIES

In addition to emulating devices of different screen sizes, you also have the option to emulate different hardware capabilities. When creating a new AVD, clicking the New . . . button will display a dialog for choosing the type of hardware you want to emulate (see Figure B-11).

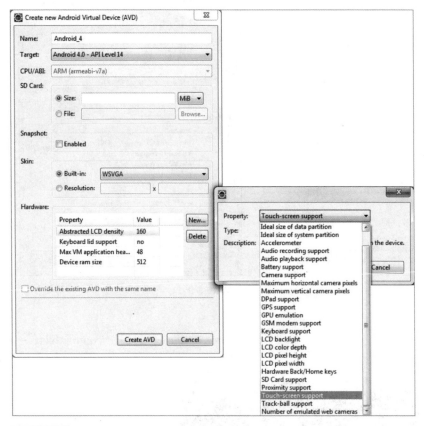

FIGURE B-11

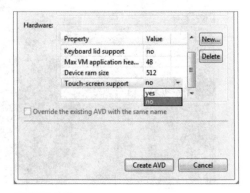

For example, if you want to emulate an Android device with no touch screen, select the "Touch-screen support" property and click OK. Back in the AVD dialog, change the value of the property from yes to no (see Figure B-12).

This will create an AVD with no touch-screen support (i.e., users won't be able to use their mouse to click on the screen).

You can also simulate location data using the Android emulator. Chapter 9 discusses this in more detail.

FIGURE B-12

KEYBOARD SHORTCUTS

The Android emulator supports several keyboard shortcuts that enable you to mimic the behavior of a real handset. The following list describes some of the shortcuts that you can use with the emulator:

➤ **Esc** — Back

➤ **Home** — Main screen

➤ **F2** — Toggles context-sensitive menu

➤ **F3** — Call Log

➤ **F4** — Hang up/end call button

➤ **F7** — Power button

➤ **F5** — Search

➤ **F6** — Toggle trackball mode

➤ **F8** — Toggles data network (3G)

➤ **Ctrl+F5** — Ringer volume up

➤ **Ctrl+F6** — Ringer volume down

➤ **Ctrl+F11/Ctrl+F12** — Toggle orientation

For example, by pressing Ctrl+F11, you can change the orientation of the emulator to portrait mode (see Figure B-13).

FIGURE B-13

One useful tip to make your development more productive is to keep your Android emulator running during development — avoid closing and restarting it. Because the emulator takes time to boot up, it is much better to leave it running when you are debugging your applications.

SENDING SMS MESSAGES TO THE EMULATOR

You can emulate sending SMS messages to the Android emulator using either the Dalvik Debug Monitor Service (DDMS) tool (available in Eclipse) or the Telnet client.

 NOTE The Telnet client is not installed by default in Windows 7. To install it, type the following at the Windows command prompt: `pkgmgr /iu:"TelnetClient"`.

Take a look at how this is done in Telnet. First, ensure that the Android emulator is running. In order to telnet to the emulator, you need to know the port number of the emulator. You can obtain this by looking at the title bar of the Android emulator window. It normally starts with 5554, with each subsequent emulator having a port number incremented by two, such as 5556, 5558, and so on. Assuming that you currently have one Android emulator running, you can telnet to it using the following command (replace 5554 with the actual number of your emulator):

```
C:\telnet localhost 5554
```

To send an SMS message to the emulator, use the following command:

```
sms send +1234567 Hello my friend!
```

The syntax of the `sms send` command is as follows:

```
sms send <phone_number> <message>
```

FIGURE B-14

Figure B-14 shows the emulator receiving the sent SMS message.

Besides using Telnet for sending SMS messages, you can also use the DDMS perspective in Eclipse. If the DDMS perspective is not visible within Eclipse, you can display it by clicking the Open Perspective button (highlighted in Figure B-15) and selecting Other.

Select the DDMS perspective (see Figure B-16) and click OK.

FIGURE B-15

Once the DDMS perspective is displayed, you will see the Devices tab (see Figure B-17), which shows the list of emulators currently running. Select the emulator instance to which you want to send the SMS message, and under the Emulator Control tab you will see the Telephony Actions section. In the Incoming number field, enter an arbitrary phone number and check the SMS radio button. Enter a message and click the Send button.

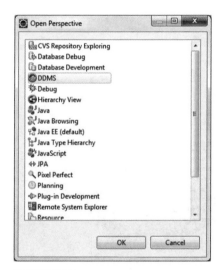

FIGURE B-16

FIGURE B-17

The selected emulator will now receive the incoming SMS message.

If you have multiple AVDs running at the same time, you can send SMS messages between each AVD by using the port number of the emulator as the phone number. For example, if you have an emulator running on port number 5554 and another on 5556, their phone numbers will be 5554 and 5556, respectively.

MAKING PHONE CALLS

In addition to sending SMS messages to the emulator, you can also use the Telnet client to make a phone call to the emulator. To do so, simply use the following commands.

To telnet to the emulator, use this command (replace 5554 with the actual number of your emulator):

```
C:\telnet localhost 5554
```

To make a phone call to the emulator, use this command:

```
gsm call +1234567
```

The syntax of the `gsm send` command is as follows:

```
gsm call <phone_number>
```

Figure B-18 shows the emulator receiving an incoming call.

As with sending SMS messages, you can also use the DDMS perspective to make a phone call to the emulator. Figure B-19 shows how to make a phone call using the Telephony Actions section.

FIGURE B-18

FIGURE B-19

You can also make phone calls between AVDs by using their port numbers as phone numbers.

TRANSFERRING FILES INTO AND OUT OF THE EMULATOR

Occasionally, you may need to transfer files into or out of the emulator. The easiest way is to use the DDMS perspective. From the DDMS perspective, select the emulator (or device if you have a real Android device connected to your computer) and click the File Explorer tab to examine its file systems (see Figure B-20).

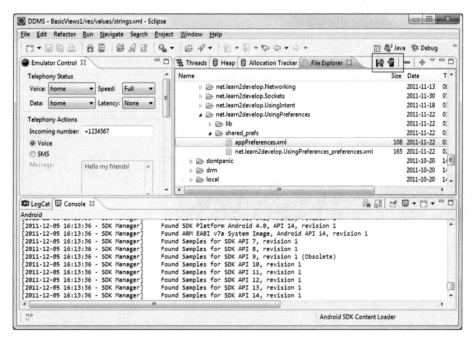

FIGURE B-20

NOTE When using the `adb.exe` utility to pull or push files from or into the emulator, ensure that only one AVD is running.

The two buttons highlighted in Figure B-20 enable you to either pull a file from the emulator or push a file into the emulator.

Alternatively, you can also use the `adb.exe` utility that is shipped with the Android SDK to push or pull files to and from the emulator. This utility is located in the `<Android_SDK_Folder>\`
`platform-tools\` folder.

To copy a file from the connected emulator/device onto the computer, use the following command:

```
adb.exe pull <source path on emulator>
```

Figure B-21 shows how you can extract an XML file from the emulator and save it onto your computer.

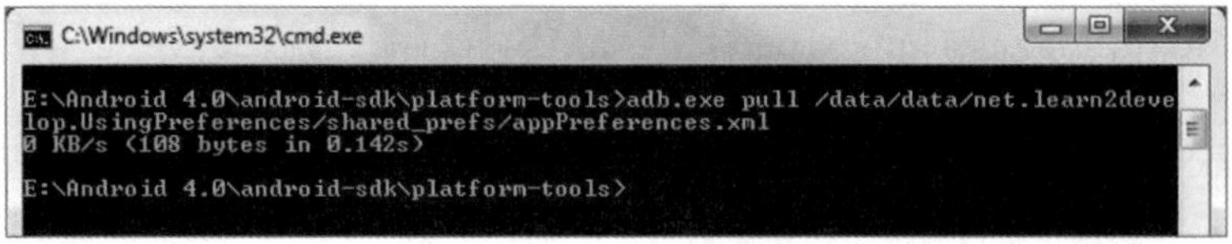

FIGURE B-21

To copy a file into the connected emulator/device, use the following command:

```
adb.exe push <filename> <destination path on emulator>
```

The command in Figure B-22 copies the NOTICE.txt file located in the current directory and saves it onto the emulator's /data/data/net.learn2develop.UsingPreferences/shared_prefs folder.

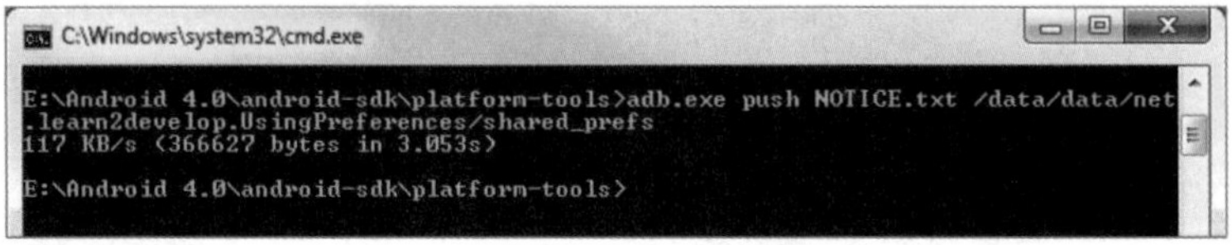

FIGURE B-22

If you need to modify the permissions of the files in the emulator, you can use the adb.exe utility together with the shell option, like this:

```
adb.exe shell
```

Figure B-23 shows how you can change the permissions of the NOTICE.txt file by using the chmod command.

Using the adb.exe utility, you can issue Unix commands against your Android emulator.

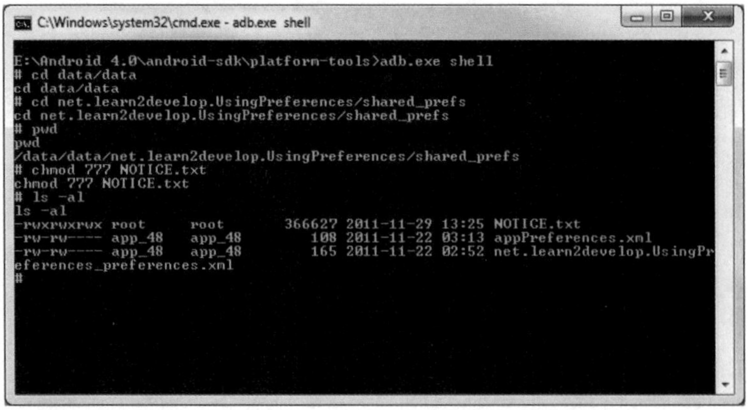

FIGURE B-23

RESETTING THE EMULATOR

There are times where you want to install your application onto a fresh AVD. For example, you may have installed other applications earlier that might interfere with your current application (a good example is an SMS-intercepting application that might intercept SMS messages meant for your application). In this case, you can either uninstall each application from the Settings application, or (a much easier way) you can wipe out the image for the emulator so as to restore it to its original state.

All applications and files that you have deployed to the Android emulator are stored in a file named `userdata-qemu.img` located in the `C:\Users\<username>\.android\avd\<avd_name>.avd` folder. For example, I have an AVD named AndroidTabletWithMaps; hence, the `userdata-qemu.img` file is located in the `C:\Users\Wei-Meng Lee\.android\avd\AndroidTabletWithMaps.avd` folder.

If you want to restore the emulator to its original state (i.e., reset it), simply delete the `userdata-qemu.img` file. All the previously installed applications on this AVD will now be gone.

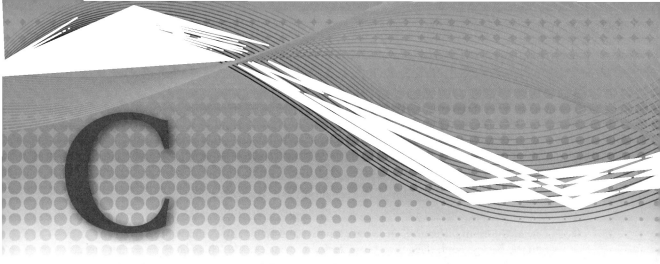

Answers to Exercises

This appendix includes the answers to the end of chapter exercises.

CHAPTER 1 ANSWERS

1. An AVD is an Android Virtual Device. It represents an Android emulator, which emulates a particular configuration of an actual Android device.

2. The `android:versionCode` attribute is used to programmatically check whether an application can be upgraded. It should contain a running number (an updated application is set to a higher number than the older version). The `android:versionName` attribute is used mainly for displaying to the user. It is a string, such as `"1.0.1"`.

3. The `strings.xml` file is used to store all string constants in your application. This enables you to easily localize your application by simply replacing the strings and then recompiling your application.

CHAPTER 2 ANSWERS

1. The Android OS will display a dialog from which users can choose which activity they want to use.

2. Use the following code:

```
Intent i = new
    Intent(android.content.Intent.ACTION_VIEW,
      Uri.parse("http://www.amazon.com"));
startActivity(i);
```

3. In an intent filter, you can specify the following: action, data, type, and category.

4. The Toast class is used to display alerts to the user; it disappears after a few seconds. The NotificationManager class is used to display notifications on the device's status bar. The alert displayed by the NotificationManager class is persistent and can only be dismissed by the user when selected.

5. You can either use the <fragment> element in the XML file, or use the FragmentManager and FragmentTransaction classes to dynamically add/remove fragments from an activity.

6. One of the main differences between activities and fragments is that when an activity goes into the background, the activity is placed in the back stack. This allows an activity to be resumed when the user presses the Back button. Conversely, fragments are not automatically placed in the back stack when they go into the background.

CHAPTER 3 ANSWERS

1. The dp unit is density independent and 1dp is equivalent to one pixel on a 160 dpi screen. The px unit corresponds to an actual pixel on screen. You should always use the dp unit because it enables your activity to scale properly when run on devices of varying screen size.

2. With the advent of devices with different screen sizes, using the AbsoluteLayout makes it difficult for your application to have a consistent look and feel across devices.

3. The onPause() event is fired whenever an activity is killed or sent to the background. The onSaveInstanceState() event is like the onPause() event, except that it is not always called, such as when the user presses the back button to kill the activity.

4. The three events are onPause(), onSaveInstanceState(), and onRetainNonConfigurationInstance(). You generally use the onPause() method to preserve the activity's state because the method is always called when the activity is about to be destroyed. However, for screen orientation changes, it is easier to use the onSaveInstanceState() method to save the state of the activity (such as the data entered by the user) using a Bundle object. The onRetainNonConfigurationInstance() method is useful for momentarily saving data (such as images or files downloaded from a web service) which might be too large to fit into a Bundle object.

5. Adding action items to the Action Bar is similar to creating menu items for an options menu — simply handle the onCreateOptionsMenu() and onOptionsItemSelected() events.

CHAPTER 4 ANSWERS

1. You should check the isChecked() method of each RadioButton to determine whether it has been checked.

2. You can use the getResources() method.

3. The code snippet to obtain the current date is as follows:

```
//---get the current date---
Calendar today = Calendar.getInstance();
yr = today.get(Calendar.YEAR);
month = today.get(Calendar.MONTH);
day = today.get(Calendar.DAY_OF_MONTH);
showDialog(DATE_DIALOG_ID);
```

4. The three specialized fragments are `ListFragment`, `DialogFragment`, and `PreferenceFragment`. The `ListFragment` is useful for displaying a list of items, such as an RSS listing of news items. The `DialogFragment` allows you to display a dialog window modally and is useful to get a response from the user before allowing him to continue with your application. The `PreferenceFragment` displays a window containing your application's preferences and allows the user to edit them directly in your application.

CHAPTER 5 ANSWERS

1. The `ImageSwitcher` enables images to be displayed with animation. You can animate the image when it is being displayed, as well as when it is being replaced by another image.

2. The two methods are `onCreateOptionsMenu()` and `onOptionsItemSelected()`.

3. The two methods are `onCreateContextMenu()` and `onContextItemSelected()`.

4. To prevent launching the device's web browser, you need to implement the `WebViewClient` class and override the `shouldOverrideUrlLoading()` method.

CHAPTER 6 ANSWERS

1. You can do so using the `PreferenceActivity` class.

2. The method name is `getExternalStorageDirectory()`.

3. The permission is `WRITE_EXTERNAL_STORAGE`.

CHAPTER 7 ANSWERS

1. The code is as follows:

```
Cursor c;
if (android.os.Build.VERSION.SDK_INT <11) {
    //---before Honeycomb---
    c = managedQuery(allContacts, projection,
            ContactsContract.Contacts.DISPLAY_NAME + " LIKE ?",
            new String[] {"%jack"},
            ContactsContract.Contacts.DISPLAY_NAME + " ASC");
} else {
    //---Honeycomb and later---
```

```
CursorLoader cursorLoader = new CursorLoader(
        this,
        allContacts,
        projection,
        ContactsContract.Contacts.DISPLAY_NAME + " LIKE ?",
        new String[] {"%jack"},
        ContactsContract.Contacts.DISPLAY_NAME + " ASC");
c = cursorLoader.loadInBackground();
}
```

2. The methods are `getType()`, `onCreate()`, `query()`, `insert()`, `delete()`, and `update()`.

3. The code is as follows:

```
<provider android:name="BooksProvider"
        android:authorities="net.learn2develop.provider.Books" />
```

CHAPTER 8 ANSWERS

1. You can either programmatically send an SMS message from within your Android application or invoke the built-in Messaging application to send it on your application's behalf.

2. The two permissions are `SEND_SMS` and `RECEIVE_SMS`.

3. The Broadcast receiver should fire a new intent to be received by the activity. The activity should implement another `BroadcastReceiver` to listen for this new intent.

CHAPTER 9 ANSWERS

1. The likely reasons are as follows:

- ➤ No Internet connection

- ➤ Incorrect placement of the `<uses-library>` element in the `AndroidManifest.xml` file

- ➤ Missing `INTERNET` permission in the `AndroidManifest.xml` file

2. Geocoding is the act of converting an address into its coordinates (latitude and longitude). Reverse geocoding converts a pair of location coordinates into an address.

3. The two providers are as follows:

- ➤ `LocationManager.GPS_PROVIDER`

- ➤ `LocationManager.NETWORK_PROVIDER`

4. The method is `addProximityAlert()`.

CHAPTER 10 ANSWERS

1. The permission is INTERNET.

2. The classes are JSONArray and JSONObject.

3. The class is AsyncTask.

CHAPTER 11 ANSWERS

1. A separate thread should be used because a service runs on the same process as the calling activity. If a service is long-running, you need to run it on a separate thread so that it does not block the activity.

2. The IntentService class is similar to the Service class, except that it runs the tasks in a separate thread and automatically stops the service when the task has finished execution.

3. The three methods are doInBackground(), onProgressUpdate(), and onPostExecute().

4. The service can broadcast an intent, and the activity can register an intent using an IntentFilter class.

5. The recommended method is to create a class that subclasses the AsyncTask class. This will ensure that the UI is updated in a thread-safe manner.

CHAPTER 12 ANSWERS

1. You specify the minimum Android version required using the minSdkVersion attribute in the AndroidManifest.xml file.

2. To generate a certificate, you can either use the keytool.exe utility from the Java SDK or use Eclipse's Export feature.

3. Go to the Settings application and select the Security item. Check the "Unknown sources" item.

INDEX

C